UI

THE DIMENSIONS OF
DREAMS

THE DIMENSIONS OF
DREAMS

---

*The nature, function,
and interpretation of dreams*

Ole Vedfelt

Translated by
KENNETH TINDALL

FROMM INTERNATIONAL
NEW YORK

First U.S. Edition, 1999
Originally published in Denmark by Gyldendal
Translation based on Fifth Edition

LIBRARY OF CONGRESS CATALOGING-IN-PUBLICATION DATA

Vedfelt, Ole.
    [Drommenes dimensioner. English]
    Dimensions of dreams / Ole Vedfelt. — 1st Fromm International ed.
        p.   cm.
    Includes bibliographical references and index.
    ISBN 0-88064-230-0 (hardcover)
    1. Dreams.   2. Dream interpretation.   I. Title.
    BF1091.V4313   1998
    154.6'3—dc21   98-34683
                                                          CIP

10 9 8 7 6 5 4 3 2 1

Manufactured in the United States of America

Contents

15. Multidimensional dream interpretation

Everyone dreams. All cultures ascribe meaning to dreams. Dreams have given rise to the most profound theories about the human psyche. But what do dreams mean? How can we work with them? Where can we get knowledge and help in understanding them?

The twentieth century has produced many valuable theories about dreams. Dreams have been investigated by Freudians, Jungians, and existentialists. They have been examined statistically and in laboratories. Also explored: their connection to the body, as well as to parapsychology, meditation, birth experiences, consciousness-expanding techniques, and psychotic states, both in groups and within society at large. So today there exists considerable knowledge about dreams—insight into their nature, familiarity with their functions—and a number of models by which to interpret them.

Meanwhile, the various movements in dream therapy are limited in their knowledge of each other, both in the literature and in practical application. And so a book is needed that encompasses the many theories and methods in a general presentation.

My professional background for writing *The Dimensions of Dreams* includes ten years of analysis and supervision by graduate analysts of the C. G. Jung Institute in Zurich, with emphasis on dream interpretation. Later I learned to integrate painting therapy and gestalt therapy with dreamwork. I've been systematically trained in psychodrama, body psychotherapy, and meditation, and I've undergone psychedelic sessions. My teachers have been both men and women. Whenver possible, the insights gained have been integrated into my own therapeutic practice.

An additional ten years' experience with dreams was accumulated in the study of nearly fifteen thousand dreams from two hundred subjects. At the start they were long-term individual series, but increasingly the work involved groups of various configurations, often together with gestalt, group, and psychodrama therapists. With the conclusion of this revised edition, nine more years of therapeutical experience have been gained.

In my own analysis the dreams were usually interpreted from a Freudian or Jungian frame of reference. Then, as my therapeutic universe expanded, unsuspected themes were revealed. A few were entirely new and appeared to be stimulated by the therapeutic process. When leafing through my dream files, however, I could see that other themes had been present earlier but had gone unrecognized year after year. What had previously been regarded as true or definitive interpretations referred, as far as I could see, only to one or a few aspects of the dream, seen from a particular level of consciousness determined by the setting and by the assumptions of the therapist.

In attending professional gatherings it became clear to me that the different movements in dream therapy thrive in mutual ignorance; that there exists a groundless confidence that "our method is the rightest and profoundest." This could have been dismissed as a subjective impression if I hadn't found it abundantly corroborated by the literature. The Freudians gave little acknowledgement to the investigations of the Jungians. Jung fumed at Freud but often did not properly understand him. The existentialist Medard Boss spent enormous amounts of energy on worthless controversy. Perls thought his therapy was the only "truly adequate" therapy. And so forth.

Nonetheless, the dream interpreters of the different schools all made valuable contributions to their clients' self-understanding. They elaborated material, techniques, and theories I was able to fruitfully transpose to my own practice. At the same time, I have seen how the many skilled dream interpreters I know are more flexible in practice than their theories allow; this applies equally to the great dream theorists whom the book enumerates.

What interests me is first of all how the working methods of the different schools can supplement each other. My endeavor has been to arrive at a creative syntheses of the material at hand, and to find whether the diverse viewpoints fall into a pattern that can provide a fuller picture of the potentialities of dreams than what has been seen so far. As it turns out, the existing mass of knowledge concerning dreams can be divided into fourteen subject areas corresponding to the book's first fourteen chapters, and all the material can be incorporated in a Multidimensional Dream Theory put forth in chapter 15.

I have regarded it as important to account for the efforts of the pioneer dream investigators on their own premises, as concretely and as lucidly as possible. Equally important is to show how they can be combined in a fruitful way. This is done in chapter after chapter using the dream material and the knowledge of the different schools to shed light upon one other. It is thus step by step demonstrated that any dream contains a lot of information that can be used in different ways, depending on the dreamer's and the interpreter's needs and skills. Further, to get another perspective on the various theories there is at the end of each chapter an evaluation of empirical basis and philosophical background.

In chapter 1 the view of dreams of Freud and his followers is explained. The Freudians maintain that dreams arise from primitive and infantile drives that are disguised by the psyche's defense mechanisms. With a knowledge of the Freudians' findings and theories we can use dreams to examine and process repressed childhood conflicts. Freudian association technique and the significance of "the day's residues" are described. We learn about defense mechanisms in dreams, about the way in which we "transfer" our inner conflicts to others, particularly therapists, and about our ability to integrate psychic insights.

In the same chapter we also see demonstrated the practical usefulness of Freudian models for sexual and social individuation. We are given important knowledge about how the dream interpreter should relate to his material. Within the Freudian school we find a fruitful methodological variation and development in the understanding of dreams. At the end of the first chapter I use the method of letting the different views mutually mirror each other in order to deepen our understanding of the dream phenomenon.

Chapter 2 deals with Jung and his followers' conception of dreams. Jung didn't think that dreams concealed anything; on the contrary, he saw them as sources of revelation of age-old wisdom. He was less interested in what went wrong in childhood than in what dreams can tell about our potential.

We examine Jung's nuanced set of interpretation rules, which add much to Freud's views. The significance of the particularly important archetypal dreams and of the adult individuation process in dreams is considered. We have a look at the relationships of dreams to alchemical symbols, to the death process, to vocation experiences, to problem solving and creativity, and to individual destiny. A life seen through dreams is described.

The neo-Jungian schools have produced alternatives to Freud's individual psychology, and the connection of dreams to gender-role development is described. I discuss some of the fundamental rules for comparing and combining different theories. It is shown where the methods can work together and where the strength in one theory can be used to rule out weaknesses in another. This is done on a practical as well as on a philosophical level.

In spite of their differences, Freud and Jung were in agreement that dreams originate in the unconscious. In chapter 3 a third movement in dream analysis explains that the origin of dreams is in waking life, and that the function of dreams is to solve problems. The movement's most important spokesmen are Alfred Adler, Erich Fromm, Montague Ullman, and in particular Calvin Hall, who discovered a method for making statistical analyses of masses of dream material. Hall thereby demonstrates the connection between dream and waking lifestyle. He could diagnose personalities on the basis of dream series without knowledge of the individuals or their associations. Through Hall we obtain important guidelines as to what dreams typically mean to all of us—women, men, children—and to the meaning of dreams that span the course of a life.

It is shown how insights can be added to the Freudian and Jungian methods; on the other hand, knowledge from the first two schools can be used to enrich and correct the results of the third rather pragmatic direction.

A fourth direction in dream interpretation has its main representative in the existential psychoanalyst Medard Boss, who proposed a more phenomenological method intended to let dreams appear as they are instead of being reduced by arbitrary theorizing. In chapter 4 we see examples of Boss's dream interpretation, and of a considerate, therapeutic method of communicating the insights gained. The phenomenological method can be combined with what we have already presented. But it is also shown that an antitheoretical attitude such as the phenomenological can lead to hidden interpretations and to an impoverishment of the knowledge that has been developed through the other methods of dream interpretation.

In light of the newer experiential therapies, it becomes obvious that interpretations of and associations to dreams do not always have an impact powerful enough to produce emotional change. Described in chapter 5 is dreamwork in gestalt therapy and psychodrama. These techniques form a useful supplement to the four main schools of dream interpretation, but they cannot stand alone.

Modern laboratory investigations of sleep and dreaming are described in chapter 6. The conceptual apparatus here has for the most part evolved from psychoanalysis, but the array of experiments and observations helps us to better understand the theories concerning the nature and function of dreams, and gives rise to a number of complementary theories.

Chapter 7 deals with dream and the body. We learn about dreams in connection with organic diseases and physical symptoms, with body shape, kinesthetic sense, body language, and touching. In addition, we examine dreams from clients in various body therapies. The new insights are integrated with what has already been put forth.

Parapsychological phenomena have interested many dream investigators. Chapter 8 discusses Freud's telepathy hypothesis, Jung's synchronicity concept, and Montague Ullman's laboratory experiments with telepathy in dreams. We are given historical and present-day examples of precognition and telepathy in dreams. Psychotherapeutic modes of relation to parapsychological phenomena in dreams are described. This adds to the understanding of the complexity of our nightly experiences.

Chapter 9 considers esoteric dream understanding. The connection between dreams, meditation, and chakras is investigated, and an account is given of lucid dreams, which occupy a special place in dream life. These new approaches contribute to our understanding of the dream's multilayered nature.

In chapter 10 the topic is dreams with birth symbolism and how they are regarded by different movements in psychoanalysis and experiential therapy.

Chapter 11 takes up the connection between consciousness-expanding techniques and dreams, with an emphasis on Stanislav Grof's LSD therapy. Examples are given of the connection between dreams and LSD experiences. A comparison is made with the rest of the material, making it still more clear that the dream is a condensed package of information.

Chapter 12 treats another extreme area of experience: the connection between dream and psychosis. Many examples are given of dreams in psychotic states, and different working methods of dream therapy are described. This special area also sheds light on the fundamentals of dreaming.

In chapter 13 we learn about the conception of dreams in different societies and historical periods. Similiarities and differences in the dream content of cultural groups, as well as under extreme social conditions, give us new information about some general aspects of dreaming.

Alternative movements and methods are discussed in chapter 14, with an emphasis on group work and dream and painting therapy.

Chapter 15 is a consideration of the sum total of the existing knowledge, and it advances the hypothesis of the multidimensional nature and function of dreams. Throughout the book it has been systematically shown how different methods of interpretation can be applied to the same dream. In this concluding chapter it is shown that the psychic material in dreams can be processed meaningfully going from more theoretical and methodological angles of approach than a normally focused product of waking consciousness. How it is possible for the psyche to keep house with such complex patterns of creativity is explained from the viewpoint of information theory. Finally, the philosophical consequences of this hypothesis are considered and are found to reinforce the many efforts to find a suitable new paradigm for science, art, and everyday life.

The Dimensions of Dreams is written with a view to both the general reader and the professional psychotherapist and researcher. The book can be read as one organic whole where all the parts have their place and contribute to a more complete understanding of the world of dreams, and it can be understood as an undogmatic introduction to the existing body of knowledge on dreams.

The Dimensions of Dreams is intended for everyone who uses dreams in connection with therapy and personality development. It provides both a comprehensive and a comparative account of the many dream therapy methods, and an evaluation of the advantages and disadvantages of different modes of working and their possible syntheses. It should appeal to the investigator who wants an exposition of the different methods' theoretical premises, their empirical foundation, and their philosophy. The book is moreover a dream handbook and a guide to in-depth studies.

Finally, it is my hope that the multidimensional theory and method will find application in other disciplines that concern themselves with the processing of phenomena of the conscious and the unconscious—whether art, literature, or mythology.

I want to express my gratitude to the Danish Research Council for the Humanities for having subsidied the translation from Danish to American. I would also like to thank clients who willingly placed material at my disposal. My wife, Lene Vedfelt, has inspired me during the book's genesis. And a special word of thanks is extended to Ulla Olsen. Without her tremendous help in translating and typing, *The Dimensions of Dreams* would not have been possible.

THE DIMENSIONS OF
DREAMS

1. FREUD AND THE NEO-FREUDIANS

FREUD'S UNVEILING OF THE MYSTERY OF DREAMS

By the mid-1890s, Sigmund Freud, the founder of psychoanalysis, had already been working for a number of years with psychic disturbances like hysteria and compulsion neuroses. Inspired by his mentor, Josef Breuer, he made the discovery that if during an analysis you could trace the neurotic symptoms back to the elements in the patient's mental processes which had caused them, then you could "unravel" the neurotic idea and thereby rid the patient of it. The analysis of a neurotic idea and its removal is one and the same thing, Freud claimed. Later, however, he had to acknowledge that interpretation in itself is not enough.

In these psychoanalytical researches Freud told his patients to report all of the associations and thoughts that came into their heads in connection with the problem being treated. They now began relating their dreams, and Freud saw that a dream can be built into a complex of notions leading from the abnormal idea back to recollections from childhood. This led him to treat the dream itself as a symptom, and to transpose the analytical method he had used on the neurotic symptoms to dreams.

Like all psychotherapists who are any good, Freud tried out this method on himself, and on July 24, 1895, he felt that through the analysis of his own dreams he had "unveiled the mystery of dreams." Five years later there appeared his monumental work *Die Traumdeutung* (The interpretation of dreams), in which he presents an entirely new and complete method of dream analysis; it is also where some of his most important psychological concepts come to expression. Freud himself and those familiar with his psychology regarded the book as being his most important work. Even though Freud constantly revised his concepts, *The Interpretation of Dreams* is the chief contribution to his theory of dreams.

THE UNCONSCIOUS IN FREUD

It is not by chance that as the epigraph for *The Interpretation of Dreams* Freud used the following line from Virgil: "If I cannot bend the Higher Powers, I will move the Infernal Regions." The psychic regions Freud penetrated he experienced as mainly negative. The unconscious was to him "the dark, inaccessible part of our personality," "a chaos, a cauldron full of seething excitations." Its content is for the most part of an infantile sexual character, and its mode of thinking resembles an insane person's hallucinations. The inner world is confused with the outer; boundaries of space and time are canceled; and mental conceptions merge so that one can symbolize another.

In opposition to this unconstructive and uncreative chaos stands the consciousness, the part of the personality we know, which thinks logically and rationally, distinguishes between inner and outer reality, and can be modified upon influence from the outer world.

Between the conscious and the unconscious there exists a psychic system that Freud calls the *preconscious*. The preconscious is like a screen that filters and disguises any contents from the dangerous unconscious before they are admitted to the conscious. In a psychic model Freud finalized twenty-three years after *The Interpretation of Dreams*, the most important psychic instances are the *ego*, the *superego*, and the *id*, with the id corresponding to the unconscious.

THE NATURE AND FUNCTION OF DREAMS IN FREUD

Like all later dream theorists of significance, Freud maintained that dreams perform a simple although important psychological function: to benefit to the dreamer. The content of a dream is in no way meaningless or happenstance. On the contrary, dreams reflect complex mental activities that observe their own laws. In Freud's view these are closely bound up with conscious thought processes.

Freud's simplest definition of dreams is that they are wish fulfillments. He describes them as substitutes for unresolved events in childhood, predominantly repressed sexuality. He believed that dreams begin in a form that is as rational as waking thoughts, but that they are disguised because the conscious can not accept them. The original dream is called the *latent dream*, and the disguised dream—the one you remember when you wake up—is called the *manifest dream*.

Even though the energy and motivation for dreams is provided by repressed infantile sexual wishes, what was significant for Freud is that the dreams do not portray the unconscious but on the contrary are thoughts that might have been conscious had the preconscious not protected the dreamer from knowing the truth about him- or herself.

Essentially dreams are a compromise between the unconscious and the conscious. On the one hand they allow the repressed drives of the unconscious to be satisfied through fantasy; on the other hand they protect the conscious mind from thoughts so shocking that the dreamer would be awakened. The dream thus has two functions: to fulfill wishes and to preserve sleep.

THE FREE-ASSOCIATION METHOD

Freud's method for getting at the meaning of a dream is to break down its separate elements, and for each element the patient is to tell what occurs to him. This requires a certain preparation. He must relax sitting or lying down; he must sharpen his attentiveness and receptiveness toward what is taking place inside him; and he must not sort out the thoughts that turn up. Especially important is to keep the critical intellect from rejecting the "freely surfacing" thoughts and thus checking the new openness for the otherwise inaccessible parts of the psyche. This is called *free association*.

Freud gives the following example in *The Interpretation of Dreams*: When he was between eleven and thirteen years old, a man had dreamed repeatedly and with severe anxiety that a man with a hatchet was pursuing him; he tried to run away but seemed to be paralyzed and could not move from the spot. First the dreamer thought of an uncle who was once attacked by a suspicious-looking individual; he may also have heard of a similar episode at the time of the dream. He further related that at about that same time he had injured himself chopping wood with a hatchet. He then thought of his brother, toward whom he could be so violent that their mother had said, "I'm afraid he'll be the death of him one day." While his associations were revolving around the violence theme, suddenly a recollection from his ninth year turned up. He had heard sounds of panting and other noises that seemed to him uncanny coming from his parents' bedroom. He had often noticed blood in his mother's bed and concluded from this that there had been violence and struggling between his parents.

The dream's separate elements had been traced back to their source, and Freud could assemble them into an interpretation. From his clients he had learned that children who witness adult sexual intercourse find it alarming and feel anxiety. This anxiety is a sexual excitation that children are unable to cope with, Freud thought, and which they reject because their parents are involved in it.

DREAM CENSORSHIP

The function that keeps the unconscious wishes under control in the sleeping state Freud calls *dream censorship*. It was not made an independent entity in his models of the psyche but was regarded as a part of the repressing forces.

To introduce the concept, Freud chose a dream of his own. *My friend R. was my uncle. I had a great feeling of affection for him.* From this Freud associated that he only had one uncle, namely Uncle Josef, and that his father not without reason called Uncle (Josef) a simpleton. The manifest dream is saying that Freud is very fond of R., but the underlying implication in the latent dream is that by making him his uncle he is reproving him for being a simpleton. It's like in a country, Freud says, where the people are in revolt against an unpopular official but the autocrat chooses that moment to bestow a high distinction on the official. The form of censorship in this case is the defense mechanism Freud later called a *reaction formation*, in which one defends oneself against negative feelings by feeling the opposite.

THE DREAM SOURCES

To avoid misunderstanding I should point out that by *dream sources* it is not meant the dream's motivational energy source, which according to Freud is unsatisfied bodily needs, but rather the source of the *material*, the components of the dream: the dream images, the persons, and the dramatic situations. These come from three sources: bodily (somatic) sources; the day's residues; and infantile material.

Bodily (somatic) sources: It has always been a popular assumption that the content of dreams is inspired by physical factors like the dreamer's body position, poor digestion, fever, pain, and other physical influences like noise, light, cold, and heat. Freud found that such stimuli only seldom provoke dreams without being connected with psychically significant sources (see "External stimuli and dreams," chapter 6).

The day's residues: By "the day's residues" Freud means emotion- and energy-laden thought processes from the preceding day that recur in a dream. He thought these could be found in any dream. He divided the day's residues into two groups: "indifferent" impressions that recur in the manifest dream, and "freshly experienced" significant events that precisely on account of their importance are disguised and can be retrieved only through a painstaking analysis and unmasking.

In *The Interpretation of Dreams*, Freud tells about a woman who dreams she came too late to the market and can get nothing from the butcher. The indifferent day's residue is that the previous day the woman had actually gone to the market too late and got nothing. Freud points out that the phrase "the meat shop is open" can be used about a man who has forgotten to button his fly, and that the apparently indifferent event acquired an anything but innocent meaning in the dream. Meanwhile, to trigger the dream, impressions are needed that are not indifferent but, on the contrary, psychologically significant. In connection with the dream about the butcher shop, Freud contents himself with suggesting that the *significant* impression was of a sexual nature. But as it was unacceptable for the dreamer to have certain sexual feelings and thoughts, they recurred in the dream in disguised form.

Ninety years after the publication of *The Interpretation of Dreams*, the import of the day's residues is still misjudged by most people who do not have special knowledge of dreams. If a person dreams that the light went out in the basement, the objection might be heard that it is merely because there was a power failure the day before. But it doesn't explain why thousands of other citizens didn't dream the same night about the light going out in the basement. All dream theorists since Freud are in agreement with him on that point: in one way or another the day's residues in our dreams are always intertwined with something psychologically significant.

The infantile as dream source: In *The Interpretation of Dreams*, Freud gives a number of examples of long since forgotten childhood scenes that are relived in dreams and whose authenticity could subsequently be corroborated.

A man who decided to visit his native town after a twenty-year absence dreamed the night prior to departure that he found himself in a village he didn't know, and on the street there he met a gentleman unknown to him whom he spoke with. When he arrived at the native town it turned out that the village from the dream was located nearby, and that the "unknown" man was a friend of his deceased father. Another man dreamed that his former tutor was in bed with the nursemaid he had had until his eleventh year. This was corroborated by his older brother. The lovers got the brother intoxicated on beer when they wanted to be together, but the dreamer they did not regard as a hindrance. He was only three years old at the time.

Far more often, however, Freud found that childhood experiences are disguised and can be detected only upon close analysis. It could be as in the hatchet dream, where associations led to a sexual scene with the father and mother. Or it could be as with a woman who dreamed that she fainted on the street and so recalled the epileptic seizures of a janitor's son in childhood.

Freud had at his disposal a large collection of dreams that could be traced to recall experiences from the first three years of life. Often a complicated job of unraveling preceded the materializing recollection. There is scarcely a dream investigator today who disagrees with Freud that we possess a vast file of recollections in the unconscious which reaches back to events very early in childhood. Even the childishness in us, understood as infantile impulses, supplies copious material for dreams.

DREAMWORK

Freud defines *dreamwork*—not to be confused as the analytical work with dreams—as the psychic process that transforms the original latent dream-thoughts into the finished manifest dream. Its four operational modes are called condensation, displacement, plastic representation, and secondary revision. Condensation and displacement are the most important.

By *condensation* Freud means that the individual dream elements are points of intersection for many dream-thoughts simultaneously; the dream elements are "overdetermined." For example, when Freud dreamed about a botanical book in which there was a pressed specimen of a plant, he could find a wealth of connections to the incidents, thoughts, and feelings of the previous day. He had met a certain Professor Gärtner, whose wife he found "blooming." He had seen a book on the genus *Cyclamen*, which he thought was his wife's favorite flower, and so forth and so on. These thought connections, which he had an astonishing talent for finding and which fill several pages in *The Interpretation of Dreams*, were all psychologically significant and bound up with the dream's meaning.

Displacement occurs when the emotional energy of a specific dream-thought is transferred to another dream element. In the dream just mentioned in which the butcher shop was closed, the dangerous, emotionally intense sexual content was displaced to a harmless everyday scene.

The two latter and less important mechanisms aim to give the dream a dramatic intelligible form and a smooth facade.

THE TECHNIQUE OF DREAM INTERPRETATION

"The lay world has from the earliest times concerned itself with 'interpreting' dreams, and in its attempts to do so it has made use of two essentially different methods," Freud writes.

The first he calls the *symbolic method* (later in these pages *symbolic* will be used with a different meaning). This technique considers the dream content as a whole, and sees a parallel between the dream and an external event that will occur sometime in the future. For example, in the biblical Joseph's interpretation of Pharaoh's dream, seven fat cows followed by seven lean ones that consume the first seven is symbolic of the prediction for seven years' famine in Egypt, in which all the surplus created by seven abundant years would be consumed. Freud didn't set much store by such interpretations.

The second technique he calls the *decoding method*, since it treats dreams as a kind of cryptography in which each sign can be translated into another sign having a known meaning, in accordance with a fixed key. "Suppose, for instance, that I have dreamed of a letter and also of a funeral. If I consult a 'dream book' I find that 'letter' must be translated by 'trouble' and 'funeral' by 'betrothal.' It then remains for me to link together the key words which I have deciphered in this way and, once more, to transpose the result into the future tense."

Freud considered his own technique to be closest to the decoding method. The dream is divided into separate elements and a meaning for each one is arrived at—to be sure, without the aid of a dream book but by means of free association. He also believed that dreams have an unambiguous meaning and that this meaning can be found through interpretation.

DREAMS ARE REGRESSIVE

Freud's stroke of genius was that he put the dream's meaning in the individual, saw it as expression of internal patterns. Contrary to the traditional folk method, he did not focus his interpretation on the future but traced it back to childhood. To be sure, other and later techniques reinstate both the external and the prospective interpretation, but Freud could rightly claim to be the first to base an interpretation on the inner psychic and the regressive aspects of the dream.

This mode of interpretation is closely bound up with Freud's entire view of the psyche and the dream. In its essence the dream is a returning to earlier forms of experience, a regression.

The regression has three forms: a *topographical regression*, meaning that the psyche is considered to be a map with a conscious above and an unconscious below, and that thoughts pass from the conscious down into the unconscious; a *temporal regression*, which leads back to experiences in childhood; and a *formal regression*, whose effect is that the dream's idiom is more primitive than that of the waking conscious. Ultimately, all three forms of regression occur together, which is to say that the deeper you delve into the unconscious, the further back in childhood you go and the more primitive and unrealistic the language of dreams becomes.

FREUD AND THE PROSPECTIVE IN DREAMS

Freud admitted that attempts at problem solving were discernible in dreams, and he was cognizant of the idea first put forth by his colleague Alfred Adler that the dream can think prospectively. But Freud didn't regard this as having to do with any creative activity in the unconscious. He found it indisputable that even very complex and difficult intellectual performance is possible outside of the conscious, and that one can wake up with the solution to a knotty problem one could not have solved in the waking state. His explanation for these phenomena—in line with the theory—was that the preconscious solves the problem, perhaps already in the waking state, and afterward the solution is revealed in the dream. He thought though that such solutions were uncommon.

DREAM AFFECTS AND THE CONTRAST PRINCIPLE

Both Freud and other early dream investigators were surprised that "in dreams the ideational content is not accompanied by the affective consequences that we should regard as inevitable in waking thought." In one of Freud's own dreams, a man (whom Freud regards as a fill-in for himself) drops dead without Freud becoming the least horrified. On the other hand, elsewhere in the dream Freud is horrified at something that in the waking state would cause gladness. Or to paraphrase Freud: The affects in the dream can be detached from here and placed over there.

While in some instances Freud saw inhibitions or repressions of the emotions in dreams, at other times there was the question of their complete reversal. For example, this dream of Freud's:

> *A hill, on which there was something like an open-air closet: a very long seat with a large hole at the end of it. Its back edge was thickly covered with small heaps of faeces of all sizes and degrees of freshness. There were bushes behind the seat. I micturated on the seat; a long stream of urine washed everything clean; the lumps of faeces came away easily and fell into the opening. It was as though at the end there was still some left.*

Freud marveled that he had felt no disgust at this dream. But on closer analysis he found that paradoxically it covered over quite different feelings. To clear away manure made him think immediately of Hercules himself, who cleaned out the stables of the mythological king Augeas. The day before the dream, Freud had lectured on the connection between hysteria and perversions, and he had felt disgust at his own "grubbing about in human dirt." But a student had flattered him by saying that he had "cleansed the Augean stables of errors and prejudices." The dream took place where his children were staying at the time, and he had just "discovered the infantile aetiology of the neuroses and had thus saved my own children from falling ill." The bench (which in reality, however, did not have a privy hole) had been given to him by a devoted female client, which reminded him that his patients were attached to him, and so on. And so he found *in back* of the dream nothing but positive notions.

Dream interpretations of this sort contributed to Freud's assuming that it was at times necessary to utilize a *contrast principle*, which is to say that each element in the dream could represent both its opposite and itself.

Another dream in which the feelings did not match the content came from an older gentleman:

> *I was lying in bed when a gentleman who was unknown to me entered the room. I tried to turn on the light but was unable to. Thereupon my wife got out of bed to help me, but she could not. As she felt awkward in front of the gentleman, being en négligé, she gave up and went back to bed. All of this was so funny that I couldn't help roaring with laughter.*

The man was awakened from sleep by his wife because he was laughing uproariously. But in Freud's analytical regard the dream appeared less jolly. The dreamer suffered from arteriosclerosis and the day before had thought of death. The gentleman who came inside could be construed as death, "the great unknown," and it was "the light of life" the dreamer was unable to turn on. The ungovernable laughter in reality represented the place where he weeps at the thought that he must die.

Wish fulfillment and its absence

The idea that all dreams are wish fulfillments has by most later dream theorists been countered with the fact that there are plenty of dreams that are distressing and unpleasant—something one would not wish for. But Freud himself disputed a number of apparent exceptions to the theory of wish fulfillment, both in *The Interpretation of Dreams* and in later writings. He describes four types of dreams: counter-wish dreams, punishment dreams, anxiety dreams, and dreams in the traumatic neuroses. It was not much trouble for Freud to fit counter-wish dreams and punishment dreams into his theoretical system.

A male acquaintance, who was described by Freud as an intelligent jurist, dreamed: *I came up to my house with a lady on my arm. A closed carriage was standing in front of it and a man came up to me, showed me his credentials as a police officer, and requested me to follow him. I asked him to allow me a little time to put my affairs in order.* The jurist had expected the police to charge him with infanticide.

On analysis Freud worked out that his acquaintance had spent the previous night with a woman. On that occasion he had practiced coitus interruptus to avoid making her pregnant. The morning prior to the dream he had also had intercourse with the woman. A few days previously Freud and the jurist had discussed that it was still common to equate birth control with infanticide. Finally, the jurist suffered moral qualms because once he had occasioned an induced abortion.

The dream has the appearance of an aversion dream. But behind the anxiety caused by a charge of infanticide, Freud saw a deeper motive: the wish that the woman should not become pregnant. According to Freud, in this case it was a matter of finding the counter-wish dream's true wish motif. In other cases Freud saw unpleasant dreams as manifesting a masochistic tendency in the dreamer.

Punishment dreams are dreams in which the dreamer is subjected to maltreatment, either physical or emotional. An example is a poet who previously had been a tailor. He kept dreaming he was back in the tailor's workshop, where he felt chagrin at having to waste time and being scolded by the boss. Freud thought that in these instances the dreamer in reality wished to be punished for his overt or repressed desires. The masochistic wish originated not from the unconscious but from censored preconscious forces in the psyche.

Anxiety dreams, which are so charged with anxiety that they wake the sleeper, are apparently a serious contradiction of the theory that dreams preserve sleep and are wish-fulfilling. Here Freud thought that at first the censorship fails the unconscious wish but then comes through by simply breaking off the dream with an awakening.

Freud found an exception to the principle of wish fulfillment in one type of dream, namely *dreams in the traumatic neuroses*. Freud's attention was drawn to these particularly during the First World War, when they appeared in great numbers. The dream life of the traumatic neuroses again and again takes the sufferer back to the calamitous situation, whereupon he wakes up with renewed terror.

As Freud conceived it, man has a natural *anxiety preparedness* that safeguards him from being taken unawares by terror-inducing experiences. But in situations of war and disaster the influence can be so violent that the measure's "protective shield against stimuli" is penetrated. By actualizing the calamity in the dream, the organism attempts too late and unrealistically to generate an anxiety preparedness.

This attempt at mastering aversional experiences by repeating them again and again Freud also found in children's play. It led him to the assumption that beyond the pleasure principle there exists a deeper drive, a self-destructive death principle driven by the compulsion to repeat. The supposition of this principle denotes a turning point in Freud's theory formation, and he changed his original definition "the dream is a wish fulfillment" to "the dream is an attempt at a wish fulfillment."

SYMBOLS AND WORDPLAY IN DREAMS

In addition to the use of free association to get from the manifest (censored) dream to the latent (uncensored) dream, Freud uses the reading of symbols.

To Freud, symbols have fixed meanings, and in the dream they are nearly exclusively sexual. Weapons, implements, and tools stand for the male genitals, while hollow objects and things that get worked up are the female genitals. Climbing up a ladder or stairs can symbolize the sexual act with its ascending scale of pleasure. Falling and flying produced sensations as in the sexual act. Violets are reminiscent of the word *violate*, meaning rape, and so on. As so many symbols were fixed, it was possible under certain conditions to interpret the dream without asking the dreamer himself. But this demanded "great virtuosity" and was generally not recommended.

Freud thus acknowledged the existence of universal symbols, and it is interesting that he considered the language of symbols as inherited unconscious knowledge from the individual's—and the species's—evolutionary history, "as if a parlormaid had a perfect knowledge of Sanskrit without knowing it." In the use of symbol translations, Freud approximated the old-fashioned cipher technique, but he made it clear that reading symbols took second place to free association.

An absorbing aspect of dream interpretation that Freud had a great flair for was wordplay referring to figures of speech. We have already seen how the expression "the butcher shop is open" put Freud on the track of a dream's sexual meaning. In other examples, *a wretched hotel, the moisture runs down the walls and the beds are damp* becomes "superfluous," and *his uncle is kissing him in the automobile* is equated with "autoerotism." That a dreamer *pulls a woman out from someplace in back of the bed* means that he prefers her (the play on *hervorziehen* [to draw forth] and *vorziehen* [prefer]). *Der alte Blasel* (Old Blasel, an actor) was thought to allude to a bladder ailment (*Blasenleiden*), and a girl in a white blouse alluded to a certain Fräulein Weiss.

THE NEO-FREUDIANS

The Interpretation of Dreams remained relatively unchallenged within the Freudian tradition for close to half a century. But as the themes of Freudian analysis became defined, it was increasingly possible to arrive at the same diagnoses and solutions to problems without the aid of dreams. While dream interpretation was regarded by Freud as "the royal road to the unconscious," it appears to have had less significance to his successors, who at times regarded it nearly as a detour to the unconscious. After all, the technique of free association was laborious and could be used as a direct evasive action by patients having a knowledge of the theory. But from the forties onward, Freud's followers again began to further develop the dream theory.

While Freud's psychology was first and foremost a theory of the unconscious, the neo-Freudians became increasingly interested in the ego and its defense mechanisms. Some have compared dreams to the creative process, and whereas Freud concerned himself nearly exclusively with the latent dream, one began seeing the manifest dream (that is, the dream as it is immediately recalled) as a meaningful statement in itself.

The therapist/client relationship, with its transference and countertransference of irrational feelings, has attracted growing interest. Meanwhile, Freud's models of the psyche have undergone changes that have been significant to the understanding of dream content.

DREAMS AND DEFENSE MECHANISMS

In Freud's psychology the ego is a frail entity that is constantly threatened by unconscious drives, a punishing superego, and dangers from without. To ward off these perils the psyche in early childhood builds up a set of various typical *defense mechanisms* during the different development stages. This theory was furthered by the neo-Freudians. Freud's daughter Anna Freud described nine common defense mechanisms, and later theorists have given prominence to a few more, mostly primitive mechanisms that in adults are seen especially in pathological narcissists.

Defense mechanisms can encompass all the techniques of mastering, channeling, and using forces that would otherwise lead to neuroses. But in therapy they are usually understood as blockages that narrow a person's experience potential and contact surface. Defense mechanisms are related to the ego, but in the course of development they have declined and become preconscious automatisms that can't immediately be integrated into consciousness. Therefore the younger a child is, the more directly impulses from the unconscious manifest themselves in dreams. The Freudian textbook writer Charles Brenner mentions as an example a two-year-old child who in connection with the mother's giving birth to yet another child relates the following dream: "See baby go away." The dream is understood as an undisguised wish to get rid of the new competitor for the parents' love. In an older individual the hostile feelings would presumably be represented in a more camouflaged form.

With the elaboration of the defense mechanism concept, it became obvious that the disguising of the original unconscious content in dreams does not take place according to a fixed formula but varies for each dreamer, based on the intensity of the unconscious impulses and the efficacy of the defense mechanisms. For example, Brenner imagines a woman whose latent dream content originates in a so-called oedipal desire for a sexual relationship with the father. This could be represented by a recalled image of the woman and her father that corresponds to the *oedipal stage* (three to five years old), in which they have a fight with an accompanying feeling of sexual arousal in the girl. In the manifest dream it becomes fighting with father but with her sexual feelings omitted. If this is too close to the original fantasy, the father can be replaced with another person, such as her own son. If this is still too close to the original image, the fight can be replaced with the dreamer dancing with her son, or, still more distant, with a strange woman dancing with her son, and so forth.

The potential for disguises is unlimited. The manifest dream result depends on a balance of strength between the unconscious content (the id contents) and the defense mechanisms—in other words, on a compromise. The defense can also be effected through content, which originally is coherent in the latent dream and appears broken up and spread out in the manifest dream. For instance, the father can be present in one part of the dream while the woman fights with a different man later. Another common compromise phenomenon is that the dream appears diffuse.

Defense mechanisms in dreams can include *projection*—for instance, when the woman in the above example shifts her own sexual wish onto a strange woman—displacement of emotional intensity from one content to another, isolation of feelings that can't be contained in the same object (as when the feminine figures in a man's dream are split up into harlots and madonnas), reversal or denial of feelings, etc.

As an example of reversal of feeling, psychoanalyst Bela Mittelmann mentions the following dream from a fifty-year-old housewife with phobias (exaggerated anxiety in particular situations) and strong sexual inhibitions: *My husband and I are looking at a five-year-old girl who is getting married. We are laughing heartily.* That the woman was five years old in the dream is due to the mother having punished her at that age for masturbating, and the laughter could be regarded as an attempt at relieving the anxiety. (Note the previous example of the man who couldn't turn on the light of life and woke up laughing.) Other reversals of feelings include anxiety that becomes aggressiveness, hatred turning to "love," etc.

As an example of denial of anxiety by means of a fantasy of "high aesthetic quality," Mittelmann mentions a dream from "an attractive and intelligent twenty-eight-year-old unmarried woman" who had broken seven engagements. One night following intercourse she has a dream. *She is in the sea, rising and falling with large threatening waves. The waves finally assume the shape of a beautiful orchid and become calm. Her anxiety subsides.* (Another possible interpretation of this dream is suggested in "Phenomenology compared with other methods," chapter 4.)

Resistance can also be evidenced if a dream is forgotten on awakening. This was systematically investigated by R. M. Whitman, a neo-Freudian who found that dreams having an unacceptably aggressive content especially were forgotten. Resistance is often unconscious and can occur without the dreamer himself having understood the frightening element in the dream.

Dream theorist Emil Gutheil has provided the following dream example from a male homosexual patient: *I was a woman. I was kneeling alongside a bed. Another woman was lying in it. A red scar was visible on her abdomen between her vagina and her navel. I seemed to want to fondle this red scar. . . . I woke up thinking this was an unimportant dream; forgot all about it.* Gutheil comments: "Whenever a patient makes such a deprecatory remark about a dream, we take it for granted that the dream contains a very important detail."

The cesareanlike scar in the dream was connected with the dreamer's mother when he was a child. She often said, "When you were born you ripped me open." The patient had always thought that the mother held him responsible for this "cruel act," and that she didn't like him for that reason.

THE DREAMER'S ABILITY TO INTEGRATE

An area where the neo-Freudians have modified Freud's work is in the psychology of creativity. Freud thought that artistic creativity was wish fulfillment, but one of his successors, Ernest Kris, has described the creative process as "regression in service of the ego." By this is meant that the creative person can think and experience in a primitive and infantile manner, but that this is in no way pathological; on the contrary it is a criterion of psychic health, provided the ego can use the regression for its own purposes. A number of other Freudian psychoanalysts have transferred this viewpoint to the dream state, which is then regarded as a regression with a certain degree of control and selection of unconscious material.

This theory has important consequences for dream interpretation. It means that you can't, on the basis of the regression's depth in a dream, draw conclusions about the dreamer's psychic health if you don't at the same time take into consideration the ego's ability to integrate the dream contents. Not all dreamers can integrate like amounts, and conversely a dreamer's ability to integrate dream interpretations can be used as a measurement of ego strength.

Bela Mittelmann has described five degrees of integration ability:

1. The dream is clear; the patient accepts the interpretation and supplies relevant associations.
2. The dreamer accepts the interpretation only after some effort.
3. The dreamer supplies relevant associations but is emotionally indifferent toward the dream.
4. There are numerous lengthy dreams, but the associations are not coherent and the dream can't be placed in connection with daily life.
5. The interpretation of a dream makes the dreamer even more anxious and unsure of himself.

As an example of high integration ability, Mittelmann uses two dreams from the above fifty-year-old housewife with phobias.

1. She is four or five years old and is about to make sexual advances to an idiot, a girl, in the lavatory, when the door opens and she stops with anxiety, shame, and guilt.
2. Her mother is away from the house and she feels happy and free.

In connection with the dream, the patient reported that her mother had severely shamed her for masturbating when she was five years old. She couldn't stop; she developed nightmares and the fear of being alone in the house, and she clung to the mother. There was an idiot living in the house then, but she recognized that the idiot in the dream represented herself. She suffered from "affective stupidity," which resulted in difficulty in her schoolwork.

The dream was interpreted as an attempt to deny responsibility for her sexual activity as well as for her hostility toward her mother. This, together with the constantly anticipated disapproval and condemnation by the mother, increased her fear of abandonment. The patient readily accepted the interpretation and supplied relevant associations.

A lower integration ability is exemplified by a forty-two-year-old homosexual's dream. According to Mittelmann, the dreamer presents all of the significant emotional experiences but lacks contact with the dream. *He sees a curving staircase down which a Negro man is running toward him and then disappears. . . . He looks at the stairs in a manner which can make them appear as vertical or horizontal. This gives him the feeling of being in complete control of the situation.* The dreamer was for the first time in his life developing both a sexual and an affectionate relationship. During the dream analysis he recalled that the Negro's movement was characteristic of his friend's. He experienced no anxiety in the dream, but the Negro appeared afraid. Mittelmann saw the dream as expressing the dreamer's attempt by magic omnipotence to master his fear of the prospective relationship, an anxiety which he in fact did not feel.

Around the 1940s there occurred a shift of clientele in psychoanalytic therapy, with an increase in so-called narcissistic neuroses cases. Narcissistic disorders originate earlier in the child's development, and the narcissistic ego calls upon more primitive defense mechanisms than do the psychosexual conflicts Freud worked with most often.

The disorder of narcissism is serious when it involves pathological narcissism or "borderline states." The American psychoanalyst Masud Khan has pointed out that such clients often *misuse* dreams and their interpretations, because even the ego functions that are to integrate the dream have been distorted. The dreams are then used to create a magical and all-powerful fantasy world and to flee from contact with their surroundings. Among Khan's clients were many who, while being able to understand the dreams and associate from them, "froze" with anxiety. I myself have encountered clients with such anxiety about what the dreams could tell that the only thing which interested them was "Is it good or bad?" In my experience, in such cases it is a waste of effort to work with the dream before you have worked with the anxiety.

DREAM AND TRANSFERENCE

In the period from the writing of *The Interpretation of Dreams* until the formulation of the theories of death drive and repetition compulsion, Freud changed substantially the practical procedure for working with dreams. While originally the client was merely brought to *recollection* of the repressed experiences, the goal now was to get him to *repeat* the events of the past as an immediate experience in the present. This could take place by living the forgotten emotions (hatred, love, impotence, etc.) in the company of the analyst—in *transference.*

Many innovators among Freud's successors have placed more weight on the transference aspects of dreams than he did. Prominent neo-Freudians have claimed that self-analysis is impossible for most people because there needs to be a person from the outside world to whom conflicts can be transferred. An even harder line suggests that it isn't the dream which is therapeutic but its connection to the transference situation. That Freud actually used his own self-analysis as the point of departure for *The Interpretation of Dreams* has been regarded in part as an ingenious exception, or explained in terms of his having a transference relationship to his friend Wilhelm Fliess.

Some examples from various prominent neo-Freudian dream theorists follow.

The German Hermann Schultz, in his dissertation on dreams that initiate a psychoanalysis, has provided the following dream from a twenty-four-year-old woman: *She was lying on the beach, couldn't move from the spot. Anxiety.* The woman had no associations.

The dream is understood in connection with the treatment situation: She has to lie on a couch with the analyst sitting behind her. He can regard her while she can't see him. She is psychologically exposed, just as she is physically exposed on the beach.

Heinz Kohut, a more well-known neo-Freudian, has in *The Analysis of the Self* given this example: A patient dreams that he is *in a rocket, circling the globe, far away from the earth. He is, nevertheless, protected from an uncontrolled shooting off into space by the invisible yet potently effective pull of the earth.* The uncontrolled shooting off into space is regarded as psychosis; the earth symbolizes the analyst; and the gravitational pull represents the narcissistic transference.

Another example comes from the English analyst Patrick Casement's book, *On Learning from the Patient*. A female patient, at a critical point in the analysis, expresses the fear of "going to pieces or going mad." Casement felt that he could help her by telling her that he himself had found lasting strength in daring to face his own deepest fears, including going mad. To the following session the patient brought "a terrible dream": *I was going up a mountain in a cable car. Suddenly it broke down and stopped. I was stuck halfway up the mountain, unable to go any further and unable to go back. I was stranded. What made it much worse was that the door of the cable car kept swinging open. It was all glass in a metal frame—a casement frame.*

The type of metal frame in question is called a casement frame, the same as the analyst's name. Patrick Casement understood the dream as saying that the framework for the analytical situation was threatened, and he should have allayed the patient's fear instead of saying that he, too, could be afraid.

FROM LATENT TO MANIFEST DREAM

While Freud concerned himself almost exclusively with the latent dream, which was arrived at through free association, neo-Freudians have increasingly concerned themselves with what the manifest dream can tell. The American analyst L. J. Saul found that on the basis of the first ten to fifteen dreams which a patient brought for analysis he could characterize the central conflict and the most important aspects of his "neurosis structure." C. W. Reiss, another Freudian, attempted to characterize subjects going from dream series both with and without free association. He was successful in statistically demonstrating a fair correspondence between *personality profiles* obtained with the two techniques.

Other investigations isolated different client groups in order to see whether the dreams differed. Children in puberty as opposed to elderly, schizophrenics as opposed to nonschizophrenics, and so on. And the results were encouraging.

Reiss thought that the manifest dream gave the *skeleton*, or basic outline, of the personality, while weekend associations added *plastic clarity*, and Erik H. Erikson, who shall be discussed in a following section, found that interpretations of respectively the manifest and the latent dream could supplement each other. Meanwhile, analyses of manifest dreams are much more worked out by other theoretic movements and will be discussed in these connections.

DREAMS AND PSYCHOSEXUAL DEVELOPMENT

One of the cornerstone theories in Freud and his successors is that of psychosexual development in childhood. From infancy to age five the child goes through oral, anal, and phallic stages in which sexual instinct and pleasure are associated with the mouth, the anus, and the genitals respectively. These areas are called *erogenous zones*. The child's behavior in these stages follows *prototypes*—that is to say original patterns—for personality traits which can persist throughout life. The early experiences that led to these traits are as a rule thoroughly repressed. Freud called dreams "the royal road to the unconscious." Accordingly, the patterns from these stages must reveal themselves in dreams.

The *oral stage* covers the first and second years of life, when according to Freud the mouth is the primary source of the child's pleasure. The main associations are with ingestion, holding fast, biting, spitting out, and closing; these are the prototypes for later psychological behavior patterns. Ingestion through the mouth is the prototype for greediness, holding fast for stubbornness and resoluteness, biting for the destructive urge, spitting out for rejection and contempt, closing for refusal and negativism. During development the original function modes are channeled via the defense mechanisms so that they are frequently displaced, converted, sublimated, and so forth, and develop into a network of interests, attitudes, and forms of behavior. You can ingest or spit out knowledge, love, or power. Or, as a reaction formation (conversion of emotions), you can "swallow everything raw."

According to this conception, symbols in dreams that are related to eating, biting, ingesting, and so forth, or to derivatives of the original prototypes, can be placed in connection with oral behavior. The Berlin analyst Hans Dieckmann mentions that one of his female patients who at the beginning of an analysis displayed character traits corresponding to "an extreme oral inhibition" used to dream that she *went into empty shops where she couldn't buy anything*, or that she *didn't get anything because other people crowded in front of her*. But around the point in the analysis where her behavior begins to change, she finally dreams about buying what she wants and getting it.

> *I went inside the canteen; it's pleasant there, no work to be done but neighbors whom I meet. We're all happy, and there was somebody who*

recommended an especially nice pastry. I looked hastily down in my purse: yes, I could just afford it. But there were also a couple of rolls which could be sliced and would be nice with liver paste, and for only 1 Mark. My mouth was watering at the thought, and so feeling guilty I spent my last mark and plunged into enjoying the tasty and rare treat.

The *anal stage* is the period in the child's life when he or she begins gaining control over defecation and toilet training is introduced. To "do" can be the prototype for creative work, but also for *primitive discharge reactions* like peevishness and fits of rage.

If the parents praise and motivate the child he will experience joy in creating for himself and others, and the person will be generous and productive. If the parents are strict and negative he will develop compulsive neatness, stinginess, and a need to control—or as a reaction to this, slovenliness, uncleanliness, and wastefulness.

A type of dream I have often encountered in people—particularly women—who are very controlled and have difficulty being spontaneous is where she goes *into the toilet, but just as I sit down I see a man staring in through a window*, or *suddenly a lot of people pour inside*, or *the toilet doesn't work*. In contrast, as a preface to creativity or spontaneous emotional outbursts I have heard about dreams of defecating in the proper place, etc.

It should be recalled that Freud's dream of urinating excrement off of a bench was connected with his creative work. In dreams excrement can be replaced with garbage, and in Freudian symbolism it can also appear as gold and money. Defecation problems can dominate the dreams of those with compulsive neuroses. And in Northern Europe, where character types are designated as anal compulsive, dreams of relieving oneself in a good way are nearly always important and positive.

The *phallic stage* is different for boys and girls. According to Freud, the boy falls in love with his mother, and the love becomes more incestuous as the sexual drive increases. The father is regarded as a rival, and at the same time the boy is afraid the father will geld him. This fear is called *castration anxiety*.

The girl, meanwhile, falls in love with her father (the female *Oedipus complex*) and is jealous of the mother. She isn't afraid of being castrated by the father, but in Freud's opinion she suffers from *penis envy* and puts the blame for this lack on the mother.

In the previous section on defense mechanisms, I used an example from

Charles Brenner that illustrates how a woman's unresolved infatuation with the father can reveal itself in many forms. Likewise the male Oedipus complex can, according to the theory, reveal itself in camouflaged ways.

If one wants to adhere fairly closely to the manifest dream, one can here work chiefly with dreams in which the parents themselves appear, or where sexual advances are made toward persons who are considerably older than the dreamer or have a parental function, such as a nurse or a teacher.

With regard to castration anxiety and penis envy, Calvin S. Hall has established criteria for both men's and women's dreams. These give a good impression of how broad a psychic area the concepts cover in practice. The following criteria apply to castration anxiety in men's dreams: injury to or pain in a part of the body or the whole body as well as to animals or things that belong to the dreamer—or the threat thereof. Something on the dreamer's body is childish or too small. Difficulty in using the penis or phallic objects and in placing things in receptacles or hollow objects. A man displays feminine traits or is dressed like a woman. Criteria for penis envy in women's dreams: acquisition of a penis or phallic objects. The dreamer envies or admires a man's physique, manner, or possessions having a phallic appearance. She displays masculine traits or is dressed like a man.

The phases mentioned here are termed collectively the *pregenital stages*. The subsequent developmental phases—the *latency period* from around ages seven to twelve, and the *genital stage* leading into adult life—are not regarded as such important generators of dream material.

The infantile sexual stages and the reaction patterns associated with them are exhaustively described in Otto Fenichel's authoritative expounding of Freud's theories and are even more accessible in Calvin S. Hall. What is important is that knowledge of these stages' symbolism can provide information about complex character structures in the dreamer.

Those who are critical of Freudian theory and even reject some of the main theses can benefit from a knowledge of these stages when interpreting dreams. An example is the concept of penis envy, which in the neo-Freudian literature refers to a broad spectrum of personality traits in women that can be compared with the dream symbols; it is not necessary to believe that the little girl envied the boy his penis. Correspondingly, it is useful to compare the general description of "anal personality traits" with dreams of defecation, even though it is not supposed that these traits are due exclusively to faulty toilet training.

DREAMS AND PSYCHOSOCIAL DEVELOPMENT

One of the most cited neo-Freudian attempts to carry dream interpretation further was made by Erik Homburger Erikson. Erikson overstepped some of the Freudian boundaries with a new psychosocial development model he termed *epigenetic*, which served as the starting point for his expanded understanding of dreams.

The concept of epigenesis is taken from the biological theory that egg and fetus develop according to certain inherited timetables which operate in conjunction with the external environment, and that for each new development stage a completely new, higher controlling structure is formed in the organism in question. Applied to psychosocial development, Erikson believed that "development" implanted specific resources or *fundamental virtues*, both in the blueprint for the individual's life stages and in human institutions. He thought there existed universal development sequences for the individual human being, and that every society in different ways tried to provide for these stages.

In Erikson's model, human growth and crises are described as a number of fundamental attitudes or stances; development is comprised of eight *ages of life*, each having its characterizing concept.

1. Basic trust versus basic mistrust
2. Autonomy versus shame and doubt
3. Initiative versus sense of guilt
4. Workmanship versus sense of inferiority
5. Ego identity versus role diffusion
6. Intimacy versus isolation
7. Generativity versus stagnation
8. Integrity versus disgust

The first five stages are parallels to stages in the Freudian development model. The last three are Erikson's own, but according to science historian Henri F. Ellenberger, they are clearly inspired by C. G. Jung.

What is new in Erikson's theory of dreams is that like the waking ego these steps are involved in adapting the individual's timetable to the demands society universally places on such critical stages; they try to create a synthesis between the individual's development and the expectations and needs of his surroundings.

Erikson launched his theory in a 1954 article, "The Dream Specimen of

Psychoanalysis," in which he tested it on a dream from Freud himself. The dream, referred to as "Irma's injection," was from the night of July 23–24, 1895, when Freud received the determining inspiration for *The Interpretation of Dreams*. The day before the dream Freud had been informed by his friend and fellow physician "Otto" that a female patient named Irma was not doing as well after his treatment as could be desired.

A large hall—numerous guests, whom we were receiving.—Among them was Irma. I at once took her on one side, as though to answer her letter and to reproach her for not having accepted my "solution" yet. I said to her: "If you still get pains, it's really only your fault." She replied: "If you only knew what pains I've got now in my throat and stomach and abdomen—it's choking me"—I was alarmed and looked at her. She looked pale and puffy. I thought to myself that after all I must be missing some organic trouble. I took her to the window and looked down her throat, and she showed signs of recalcitrance, like women with artificial dentures. I thought to myself that there was really no need for her to do that.—She opened her mouth properly and on the right I found a big white patch; at another place I saw extensive whitish grey scabs upon some remarkable curly structures which were evidently modelled on the turbinal bones of the nose.—I at once called in Dr. M., and he repeated the examination and confirmed it. . . . Dr. M. looked quite different from usual; he was very pale, he walked with a limp and his chin was clean-shaven. . . . My friend Otto was now standing beside her as well, and my friend Leopold was percussing her through her bodice and saying: "She has a dull area low down on the left." He also indicated that a portion of the skin on the left shoulder was infiltrated. (I noticed this, just as he did, in spite of her dress.) . . . M. said: "There's no doubt it's an infection, but no matter; dysentery will supervene and the toxin will be eliminated." . . . We were directly aware, too, of the origin of the infection. Not long before, when she was feeling unwell, my friend Otto had given her an injection of a preparation of propyl, propyls . . . proprionic acid . . . trimethylamine (and I saw before me the formula for this printed in heavy type). . . . Injections of that sort ought not to be made so thoughtlessly. . . . And probably the syringe had not been clean.

This is a very complex dream. Freud devotes thirteen pages to it and has still only scratched the surface. Erikson uses close to thirty-five pages on it. Here I will keep exclusively to the really new aspect of Erikson's dream theory, namely the connection between age of life and social function.

The age of life that the dream was preparing Freud for was, according to Erikson, the seventh age, whose dilemma is generativity versus stagnation. At the time of the dream Freud was thirty-nine years old, and at that age the decisive life task is reproduction. In biological terms this means parenthood, but in a psychological sense it could also be the passing of ideas on to the younger generation. That interpretation is based both on Freud's own many associations and on knowledge of his life and thoughts as they were expressed in his letters to his friend and colleague Wilhelm Fliess.

That Irma was given an injection with an unclean syringe can naturally be construed sexually. And that Freud, as recently as the previous night, had felt inspired to his life's most important work, the injection can be conceived not carnally but as a spiritual insemination. (I have in my own practice encountered in dreams the same coalescing of injection and insemination motifs. One woman dreamed that she became pregnant following a lecture I had given, but then had to get an injection from the doctor in order to hold on to the fetus.) Otto, who had given the injection, can for his part be seen as a disguise for Freud's friend Wilhelm Fliess.

The connection to Fliess is torturous and camouflaged, but it suits Freud's dream-style generally and is hardly odd when considering his eye for the camouflaging propensity of dreams. Fliess had "inseminated" Freud with some of his most important ideas.

Freud and Irma were to a certain degree identified in the dream. Freud had pains in his shoulder just like Irma. Irma's sickness is associated in the dream with something shaped like the turbinal bones of the nose. Freud had been treated for a nasal symptom by Wilhelm Fliess.

Freud had remarked that he could feel an odd homosexual affection for Fliess, and it was in the final letter to him that for the first and last time in their correspondence he had addressed Fliess as "dearest" (*Liebster*). The word *trimethylamine*, as well, could be traced to Fliess, who thought that trimethylamine played a decisive role in sexual metabolism. And Fliess's ideas about the sexual metabolism "inseminated" Freud with one of his most important concepts, namely that man is "constitutionally bisexual."

Moreover, the dream contained a number of birth allusions. It was Freud's wife's *birth*day, and she was actually pregnant. And curiously enough he receives guests, which in German is called *empfangen*, meaning also "conceives."

Erikson's view of the dream is less reductive than Freud's. He sees it essentially as a statement with many facets. He agrees with Freud that infantile wishes supply the energy for the dream, and that one can arrive at a latent dream by means of free association. But at the same time he thinks that the manifest dream material in itself contains valuable information, and that one can combine interpretations of the latent and the manifest dream in a fruitful way. He thinks, too, that every dream contains a transference conflict.

To illustrate the universal character of dreams he—like C. G. Jung—drew parallels to the rites of passage and religious symbolism of other peoples.

DREAM AND AGGRESSION

As mentioned previously, in 1920 Freud inserted in his theory an independent destruction and aggression drive coordinated with sexuality. Among those who have applied this in practical dream analysis is the Danish psychiatrist Thorkild Vanggaard. Of particular interest to Vanggaard is a male aggression drive and its adaptation within hierarchical social structures, male dominance-subjection games, and the sexual symbol language that can appear in them. He has also published an unedited account of a brief psychoanalysis in which dream interpretation played an important part. The book is unique in Freudian literature by being identical with the journal Vanggaard kept following each treatment session. As such it gives us a close look at Vanggaard's own modus operandi.

Vanggaard's analysand was a forty-four-year-old hospital physician called A, who suffered from a "severe neurotic panic anxiety." This manifested itself in, among other things, imaginary heart attacks and hospitalizations. In a dream analysis Vanggaard made him aware that the anxiety attacks were associated with repressed aggressiveness, and by working with this the man was freed of the anxiety symptom.

The anxiety and the repressed aggressiveness were in the analysis connected with two distinct problems: (1) frustration in his sex life with his wife, who didn't want intercourse during premenstrual periods and who demanded that he practice coitus interruptus; and (2) an antiaggressive attitude toward colleagues, which prevented him from exercising the authority demanded by his position and from advancing to the professorship he was qualified for.

Three of A's dreams were considered for analysis. Dream number two was the first in which A's wife of many years had ever appeared: *Lay in bed with the wife. Wanted to have intercourse with her but couldn't get at it because of two disturbing factors—in part on account of a swarm of tiny children that were crawling about on her as in Kai Nielsen's The Water Mother or on The Nile God, and in part because his brother was in another bed in the room.*

Among A's comments on the dream, Vanggaard fastened in particular upon the brother's wife having shamelessly made advances to him, and that he therefore had tried to avoid her. Moreover, there was something "about my father . . . , which had the effect of a warning against the marriage." The dreamer also mentioned that the mother, in contrast to his wife, had "referred to our births as something dreadful." The dreamer himself regarded the children in the bed as his anxiety that his wife should become pregnant. She would not use contraceptives, and he had to practice coitus interruptus as she apparently didn't wish to be "sullied" with his "ejaculate."

At the time of the dream A had less desire for sex than the wife. Vanggaard thought the dream "demonstrated a factor in his mental life which, among other things, is responsible for the braking [the sexual inhibition], namely a forbidding male figure who is a disturbing presence when he is to have intercourse. Here it is his eldest brother, who actually had functioned thus." According to Vanggaard, the forbidding figure could probably also be the father.

Six weeks later, A brought the following dream:

> *He was at examinations and had to expound one of the great equations for cytological corollations in the body, which he has dreamed of previously. His wife was present and among the examiners. If he couldn't manage the equation this time he would die. It was very difficult. But then in some way or other he hit on a solution, and he is unclear as to what it was, but he woke up in a euphoric mood which was very unpleasant and seemed sinister, as the exhilaration was in some manner of an exulting and spiteful character toward all the others. Precisely what the solution was he cannot recall, but he thinks it had to with his having actually given up doing the equation and thereby committing suicide, and that his exulting applied to the others who now had it made.*

Vanggaard here pointed out to A that in principle there was no difference between doing away with himself and taking the life of all the others. The dream thus expressed a violent aggression while simultaneously revealing his fear of it. This led to an admission that he could be very aggressive, as when in writing a textbook he had attacked secondhand viewpoints and made "one head roll after the other." Later it came out how he made a laughingstock of colleagues toward whom he couldn't be openly aggressive. On the whole, A was unable to be aggressive on a personal level but had no problem doing so when it came to dealing with institutions.

Later A and Vanggaard discussed how one of A's assistants, "O," had overstepped some reasonable bounds set for him by A. A was not capable of reprimanding him, but on the other hand came to feel anxiety afterward. To the next session he brought the following dream about his relationship with O:

> He was sitting in a bus beside the driver. The bus wasn't driving very fast. Suddenly O came out on the roadway in front of the bus and lay down, apparently with suicidal intent. A in dismay tried to get the driver to stop the bus, but he did not. Without more ado he ran O over, and as he did so an unpleasant crunching was heard. Then the driver jumped out and now it was he who lay down in front of the bus and was driven over. Afterward A saw that O and the driver jumped about in pain and moaned with terribly mutilated heads. It was a very unpleasant dream.

Vanggaard comments:

> He says himself that immediately this dream gives him understanding of his relationship with O, who irritates him by being ingratiating in an obsequious manner. It has literally disgusted him. He can now see how the dream shows tendencies in himself to subjugate and abuse O, and it has become obvious to him that this contains a sexual tendency besides. The thought of sexuality in relation to other men has always been intolerable to him, but he can now see that he has this in himself. Since this has become clear to him he feels a contrasting serenity toward these questions.
>
> During the subsequent conversation I emphasize for him how against this background it is understandable that it is so difficult for him to give O an in-reality necessary reprimand. For him such a reprimand overflows into one great display of power and sexuality toward O, whence the latter is threatened by both humiliation and maiming. It is this undercurrent of excessive fantasies and impulses that makes him

afraid of himself and his tendencies, so that he desists from the limited displays of aggression reality demands, as in the situation with O.

The upshot of the relatively brief treatment is that A was cured of his panic anxiety. The relationship to the wife, however, remained unchanged.

In his description of A's analysis Vanggaard departs from a conception that Freud expressed in 1920, namely that frustrated sexual satisfaction is directly anxiety-provoking. "A did get rid of his anxiety, without his marital relations changing." Vanggaard concludes it is anger at the sexual frustration he had to live with that produced the anxiety. In Vanggaard the aggression drive hereby takes ascendancy to the sexual.

THE ANALYST'S ROLE AND COUNTERTRANSFERENCE

Deciding weight is assigned to the analyst's power of judgment, because the client's evaluation can be distorted by defense mechanisms. Or, as Freud put it, "The patient's yes or no is not determining for the interpretation's correctness." On the other hand, great openness on the therapist's part is necessary.

Freud recommended that his patients uncouple the critical intellect, so that it didn't brake the "freely ascending" fancies which formed the basis for his association technique. A similar state of relaxedness and "evenly divided attention" was necessary for the analyst as well. For "as soon as anyone deliberately concentrates their attention beyond a certain goal he begins selecting from the existing material; one point remains in the consciousness with particular clarity and others will be correspondingly overlooked, and when making this selection he will follow his expectations and inclinations." Therefore the analyst should "simply listen and not worry about remembering or thinking about anything."

If you want to understand another person's unconscious you have to do it through your own unconscious. This viewpoint has been expanded by the neo-Freudians Thomas French and Erika Fromm, who think that the first step in dream interpretation must be based on empathy—that is, sympathetic understanding and intuition.

A problem that comes into play here is *countertransference*. Freud discovered that it isn't only the client who transfers unconscious feelings to the analyst. In the intense emotional relationship it is unavoidable that the analyst transfers his own feelings to the client. Freud called this countertransference, and the neo-Freudians have different proposals for countering it. The interpreter must now and then withdraw his attention from the "flowing stream of unconscious material and regard it objectively." (But if this occurs before sufficient relevant associative material has been gathered it is referred to as premature closure of the interpretation.) He can then via his interpretation models take his bearings in the material and so correct the error. But he can also, as Patrick Casement and others have suggested, do an *internal supervision*. This was the case with the dream about the mountain railway in which the metal frame (the casement frame) was broken, and Casement realized that he should not have told the client about his own anxiety. The need was not the client's but Casement's.

The classical model stresses trust in the objective interpretation for correcting countertransference, while a continual internal supervision and acknowledgment of the analyst's weaknesses denotes the more modern approach.

In modern Freudian and Jungian psychoanalysis the countertransference is exploited actively and constructively as a therapeutic tool. The analyst can often, with radar sensitivity, sense the feelings the client has repressed and communicate this directly as an interpretation, or implicitly in the therapeutic feedback. When the countertransference reflects the client's actual feelings it is called a *syntonic countertransference*. If it can be felt in the body it is an *embodied countertransference*. If not it is termed *dystonic countertransference*.

Conclusion

Freud was the first in the history of dream interpretation to create a complete psychological interpretation system. Pivotal was that the dream is a wish fulfillment and its function is sleep preserving. Dream contents are turned backward to earlier life stages, and they are a compromise between the unconscious and the ego's defense mechanisms. Their real source of energy is infantile sexual impulses. Neo-Freudians have understood dreams going from transference, ascribe greater significance to the defense mechanisms, and see dreams in relation to a hypothetical independent aggression drive and a model of psychosocial development stages.

The Theories

There is a distinct tendency in Freud and the neo-Freudians—and in most other interpretation systems as well—to have rather lucid theories about the meaning of dreams. What is strange in Freud is that his practical dream interpretations cover a far broader spectrum than his theory, which in particular would reduce dreams to infantile sexual impulses.

The dream in which Freud urinates excrement off a bench could easily be interpreted as infantile sexuality connected with the anal stage, but Freud connects it with his psychoanalytic calling and his task in regard to humanity, nearly as Erikson would have done. An elderly man's dream that he can't turn on a light, which according to Freudian theory can be construed as a failure of potency, is by Freud interpreted as a death dream. Elsewhere he reads a dream image in which a woman bathes in a moonlit lake as a psychological rebirth motif; and a dream of flying expresses longing.

On this basis alone we may rightly assume that Freud's theoretical framework is too narrow to encompass all the many aspects of dreams. But things often take another direction for dream theorists: in their eagerness to have the dream illustrate the theory, they overlook or omit aspects that do not "fit." An example of this is Vanggaard's interpretation of A's dream.

In the dream in which A is in bed with his wife, Vanggaard chooses to concern himself exclusively with a forbidding male figure and the possible relationship to the father. But what about the wife lying in bed surrounded by children like the Water Mother? A ready hypothesis can be that A's sexual inhibition is connected with his experiencing the wife as a mother. The children in the bed can then represent his own infantile sides. But Vanggaard accepts A's own explanation, which from what we have learned could just as well be a defense.

A actually had an association to the mother in connection with this dream. She had always "referred to our births as something dreadful. Psychologically this is a very hostile remark to the son. But this association was not taken up at all. In the dream in which A would die if he didn't solve a certain equation, the wife was among the examiners—in other words, a potential codecider of his death sentence. Nor was this taken up.

In a dream not cited here, A hires a call girl (Christine Keeler). But when she makes sexual advances he experiences disgust. Later he turns her over, against her protests, to a bunch of *very primitive and drunk men* who fall on her *with greedy and pawing hands.* A is amused, and his father laughs and shakes him approvingly by the shoulder. The father would never have done this in reality.

Here Christine Keeler is understood as a cover figure for the wife. Most of the time was spent discussing men's dominance-subjugation problems and A's possible nomination to a professorship.

What is interesting from a dream theory (and naturally also a human) viewpoint is the way the information in the dreams that Vanggaard *hasn't* an eye for corresponds to what he is unable to discern in the conversations on a conscious level. There the wife was discussed almost exclusively on the basis of her mechanical sexual functions; that is, her wish for coitus interruptus and her reduced desire during premenstrual periods. But just as the role of women in A's dreams was underexplored, so was little attempt made at understanding the wife's problems. And what is most astonishing are all the questions Vanggaard did *not* ask concerning relations with the wife.

Vanggaard concludes that "mother has not supplied sufficient grounds for inner psychic conflicts," arguing that the anxiety disappeared without an analysis of the relationship with her. I believe that the lives of A and his wife would have been enriched had Vanggaard not only concerned himself with surmounting the anxiety as a kind of mechanical fault, but also used the dreams to whet A's curiosity about the opposite sex, both as he had originally experienced it with the mother and as it developed later.

The examples in this first chapter demonstrate how it is possible to extract some relevant information from dreams, relocate it in a narrower framework, and exploit it in a treatment whose result is considered satisfactory by the dreamer and the dream interpreter. In social terms, A achieved the same thing as Vanggaard: he became a medical professor (chief physician)—without anxiety.

The treatment of A cannot in itself be regarded as an error of technique, as it is up to the client to determine how deep he wishes an analysis to go. The problem is that interpretations which function in practice (operational interpretations) are elevated to a definitive theory of the nature and function of dreams so the interpreter can close his eyes to diverging scientific investigation, as is the case with Vanggaard when he declares that Freud's eighty-five-year-old *Interpretation of Dreams* is not only epoch-making but "exhaustive."

The tendency to force preconceived theories over available interpretational material has been called hypostatization by Wilhelm Laiblin, a student of fairy tales. In reality it corresponds to what Freud called the "symbolic method of interpretation," a method he opposed in principle.

The development of the Freudian movement has in many respects been marked by greater openness, however. The different models of what dreams actually mean will be related as frames of reference throughout these pages.

A tendency which as early as the 1950s is encountered in neo-Freudian dream theorists like Thomas French and Erika Fromm is that dreams can have several meanings (refer to several areas of conflict at one time). In these theorists the possible interpretations still fall close within the Freudian symbolic understanding: an iron rod is definitely an erect penis, a tunnel is the female genitals, and so forth. But the function of dreams isn't seen as sleep preserving. What dreams are useful for is the solution and integration of emotional problems—"current focal point problems." French and Fromm also believe that dreams have a "cognitive" structure.

The most innovative is Erik Erikson, who thinks that dreams probably get energy from an infantile wish but that they also "suspend the dreamer's isolation, soothe his conscience, and preserve his identity, all in separate and instructive ways." This approach has been called *synthesizing* and approximates what we shall see in Jung. As Erikson conceives it, the dream thus has a constructive and problem-solving function, and it can, as we saw in Freud's dream of Irma, treat several problem areas at one time. The most important here are: transference conflicts, childhood conflicts, and acute life conflicts having to do with social adaptation.

In Erikson's epigenetic development model we can regard the first stages as expansions of Freud's concepts of infantile sexuality rather than a contradiction of them. Basic trust/basic mistrust corresponds to the oral stage, autonomy/shame and doubt to the anal stage, initiative/sense of guilt to the phallic stage, and so on.

While Freud's theory is "father dominated," Erikson places more weight on the mother's role, and he describes a broader sphere of interest than Freud. The child is regarded as being more social than in Freud, and the causal explanations are more complex. If we look, for example, at the anal stage in Freud, it is connected with the child's beginning control over the anal sphincter and the parents' demand for cleanliness. The autonomy in this stage is in Erikson not only a protest against the parents or unwillingness to submit to a potty regime. The child has an inborn desire to make choices, to "stand on his own two feet"; shame and doubt are described not merely as the result of strict toilet training but of hearing "Shame on you!" in general.

If this overlapping of frames of reference holds, we can exploit it in dream interpretation. For instance, we can guess that the woman who dreamed that she always went into empty shops not only has an oral problem in the Freudian sense, but that she also has a basic trust problem. Likewise, if a person has many dreams of feeling shame, then he or she has character traits that overlap Freud's anal character. Naturally this cannot be done uncritically but demands experience and familiarity with the relevant frames of reference, and it must be weighed against other material pertaining to the dream, in which case it would coincide with the theory, the way Erikson describes it.

The most important tendencies in the Freudian theory's development have been an acceptance of the manifest dream's meaningfulness, a greater confidence in the dream's constructively creative potentials, a higher estimate of the ego's role as opposed to the unconscious, and a broader discussion as to how dream interpretation can be used in practical analysis.

Freud's notions that dreams are wish fulfilling and sleep preserving will be considered later in a larger context.

The Empirical Basis

When all is said and done, the empirical material that forms the basis for Freud's *Interpretation of Dreams* is rather insubstantial. Freud didn't want to use dreams from his patients, just as he didn't want to expose himself to the objection "that these are the dreams of neuropaths, from which no valid inferences could be made as to the dreams of normal people." He writes: "Thus it comes about that I am led to my own dreams, which offer a copious and convenient material, derived from an approximately normal person and relating to multifarious occasions of daily life."

Freud mentions in this connection that in the course of his psychoanalysis of neurotics he must "already have analyzed over a thousand dreams"— which isn't especially impressive compared with later dream theorists' material that, as we shall see, often comprises 50 to 100,000 dreams. It should also be noted that Freud never tried being the client, something usually considered a necessity in Freudian dream analysis, and that the scientific literature that was his starting point was very limited.

The meagerness of the material that *The Interpretation of Dreams* is based on is not in itself grounds for rejecting its conclusions. Since the theory was established, both Freud himself and generations of analysts have had opportunity to try it out in clinical practice, and to discuss its inner coherence in a comprehensive scientific literature. A substantial quality in *The Interpretation of Dreams* is the intelligibility of the presentation with its many examples, where not only are we served up Freud's own interpretation but so many authentic details that it is possible to see what he is really doing and not only what is consistent with the theory.

Here the neo-Freudians weigh in short. Their books and articles on dreams are generally of a very high level of abstraction and the practical dream examples are few and far between.

A contributing factor to the beginning transformation of the Freudian dream theories may be a change in the client base and in the forms of neuroses, as is described in the section "The dreamer's ability to integrate," above.

Another significant difference in the empirical basis is that while Freud formed conclusions about the child's development from the material of adult clients, many of his successors have worked directly with children. Psycho-analytical interest has shifted more toward the child's early interplay with the mother, which is of consequence for the interpretation of the transfer-ence. That children's analysts still find the main features of Freud's theories useful says much for being able to infer backward from the dream to earlier development disorders.

The German science theorist K. O. Apel has regarded psychoanalysis, on account of its combination of interpretation and testing of the interpretation in the psychoanalytical situation, as an ideal for the social and humane sciences. Ordinarily, however, the psychoanalytic manner of procuring in-formation is regarded as a weak control method compared with statistical test methods.

With the Freudians the assessment of an interpretation's correctness is based partly on its logical coherence with the theory and partly on its ap-plicability in clinical practice. (In Vanggaard's example the patient is freed of his anxiety, ergo the theory is correct.) Such a method of interpretation is termed *operational*. It has advantages over a literary interpretation method, for example, where you can't go back and see what the interpre-tation triggers in the author. But its weaknesses are obvious.

Historical Background of Freud's Ideas

Henri F. Ellenberger, an American student of the evolution of modern psy-chotherapy, has convincingly accounted for how Freud's (and Jung's) the-ories by and large were all current in the period and formulated by others. Freud's (and Jung's) special talent consisted mainly in forming creative syntheses of what already existed.

The historical background of Freud's ideas is first and foremost positiv-ism, the rationalistic and materialistic philosophy, whose leading figures are Auguste Comte and John Stuart Mill.

In his youth Freud studied with prominent neurology and physiology professors in Vienna who regarded the psyche as resulting from neurological and physiological processes in the brain. Fundamentally, Freud's own conception of the psyche is based on a model for nerve reflexes. He viewed his theory of the *psychic apparatus* as a temporary solution, a "fictitious theory" that he thought would later be replaced by a biologically based theory, whereupon "the psychic phenomena could be studied exactly."

Freud's notion of psychic processes in general and dream processes in particular is strictly causal. The concept of regression, which was used as an the explaining principle for the nature of dreams, he had from Charles Darwin. The instinct theory and the idea that the individual's development reflects that of the species was inspired by another biologist, Ernst Haeckel. And when Freud conceived of dreams as camouflage for embarrassing truths that could be exposed through rational analysis, he was influenced by the philosophers of the Enlightenment, who saw the unmasking of hypocrisy and self-deception as a noble task. This also explains his one-sided conception of religion as illusion.

As it appears from Freud's own commentary on the existing literature, some of the viewpoints he puts forth had been touched on by others. But none of them were argued with his force that dreams had a function. Dealt with were a number of questions as to the emotional intensity of dreams, their relation to the day's residues, and their special symbolic language. An example of symbolic understanding that at times approximates Freud is that of Karl Scherner, a German writer whom Freud quotes in *The Interpretation of Dreams*: In a man's dream in which the top part of a clarinet, the mouthpiece of a pipe, and a piece of fur are lying on the street, the clarinet and the pipe symbolize the male member, while the fur is the pubic hair. In a woman's dream "the narrow space where the thighs come together may be represented by a narrow courtyard surrounded by houses, while the vagina may be symbolized by a soft, slippery and very narrow footpath leading across the yard," and so on.

Not just a positivist, Freud was also influenced by *hermeneutics*, the science of interpreting texts.

Very probably the further development of Freudian dream theory and practice is not only being shaped by new clinical findings, but more fundamentally by an altered cultural and human outlook. Freud was a cultural pessimist and biology oriented. Erik Erikson and many other of Freud's successors are more humanistic and assign greater influence to society and the culture. Freud's psychology is first and foremost a theory of the unconscious. His successors place more weight on the ego's ability to change the world.

2. Jung and the Neo-Jungians

What Jung wrote about dreams—The unconscious in Jung—The nature of dreams—Dream sources in Jung—Dream mechanisms—The living symbol—The archetypal dream symbols—Levels of significance—Interpretation principles in Jung—Important types of dreams—Individuation process and the dream—The autonomous growth processes—Dream and alchemy—Jungian dreamwork—The neo-Jungians (The Jungian schools)—The classical school and dreams—Dreams of call—Dream and death—Problem solving and creativity in dreams—Dream and developmental psychology—Dream and female development—Dream and male development—Waking ego and dream ego—The dream as its own world—Investigations of dream archetypicality—The role of the dream interpreter—The function of dreams in Jung—Freud's and Jung's dream theories compared—The Jungian empirical foundation

What Jung wrote about dreams

Few of the pioneers of psychoanalysis have ascribed to dreams such practical significance as Carl Gustav Jung. In his *Collected Works* there are only four rather brief dissertations that have dreams as their subject proper, plus numerous scattered statements and interpretations. A far richer picture of his work with dreams is to be had from a series of seminars that were taken down in shorthand and later published. Jung didn't claim to have an exhaustive and finished explanation for the phenomenon of dreams. His theories he referred to as working hypotheses whose value must be determined by their usefulness, and codes for interpreting dreams as rules of thumb not to be taken too literally.

Reading Jung is complicated by the fact that his view of the psyche was under constant development and he did not care to revise old texts. As the trailblazing English Jungian Michael Fordham writes, as far as the central concepts are concerned it can be necessary to find "what Jung said once and what repeatedly. Which statements he gave weight and which were intuitions thrown out in passing."

THE UNCONSCIOUS IN JUNG

Jung's concept of the consciousness and the ego's structure wasn't decisively different from Freud's. Where they diverged is in their views of the unconscious and of its relationship to consciousness.

The unconscious was for Jung not simply a chaotic mass of drives and bodily excitations. Pivotal in his model of the psyche is the independent and creative activity of the unconscious in the individual and in the culture. Jung thought man had an inborn array of instincts (a kind of universal program for species-typical behavior), and as psychic counterparts to them an array of *archetypes*—that is to say, universal ways of experiencing. The archetypes are inherited representational *potentialities*, a kind of template that defines the prerequisites for structuring archetypal images and symbols. What is inherited is the archetype, not the image.

To use sexuality as an example, it is an elemental instinct that impels a person into the arms of a partner, thereby assuring the perpetuation of the species. But as archetype it symbolizes the union of inner masculine and feminine forces in the personality, and the consequent potentialities for developing creatively and spiritually.

Jung saw the unconscious as divided into two essentially different layers: the personal and the collective. The personal unconscious is that part of the unconscious containing personal complexes and recollections from childhood, which have been repressed and forgotten because they don't fit in with the notions and moral concepts of the present surroundings. This corresponds in many ways to the layer in the psyche Freud worked with. But beneath this layer is a collective one that contains the archetypes. It is a much older stratum that does not contain elements from the personal life story. They are impacts in the individual from mankind's typical experiences and sum of knowledge.

For Jung man develops from birth to death. The creative activity of the unconscious is expressed in growth processes whose course is natural and independent, the way a grain of corn unfolds according to its own laws (unless there is artificial intervention). The unconscious can correct the conscious attitude in a constructive way; it has a compensatory function.

THE NATURE OF DREAMS

While Freud's conception was that an authority was trying to conceal something from the dreamer, Jung saw the dream primarily as spokesman for the "universal human being in us." To deal with dreams is like sitting down before a being having all of the collective unconscious's knowledge of typical human motives and asking: Now, what do you think of me?

Substantial points in Jung's more optimistic view of the unconscious have significance for his concept of dreams:

1. In the first place, he asserts that the manifest dream—the dream as it is immediately remembered—can comment constructively on the actual situation in the consciousness.
2. Dreams and their symbols are manifestations of growth processes in the dreamer's unconscious that can evolve independently in relation to the consciousness.
3. Dreams can transcend the traditional bounds of space and time, so they reach forward in time and can be vectors for parapsychological phenomena.
4. Not only dreams but also active imagination can have a furthering effect on personality development.

DREAM SOURCES IN JUNG

Like Freud, Jung did not attach much significance to either somatic or external stimuli in dream formation, and he was in agreement with Freud that the dream contained day's residues and material from the dreamer's daily life. He thought too that recollections of the past, including psychologically important events from childhood, appeared in dreams, but he did not assign them nearly the same consequence as Freud.

Still another dream source are so-called subliminal perceptions—impressions that are not registered by the consciousness but are picked up by the unconscious and incorporated into a dream. As an example of such a perception Jung referred to a businessman who was given the prospect of a business deal that on the surface seemed honorable. The following night the man dreamed that his hands and forearms were covered with black dirt. The dreamer then admitted that the deal would involve him in fraud.

But for Jung the deepest and most important source of dream images are the archetypes of the collective unconscious.

Dream mechanisms

Jung thought like Freud that many contents can be "condensed" in the same symbol; that the unconscious expresses itself in wordplay and metaphors; and that different dream scenes or several persons can express the same idea. He used the concept of *contamination* to explain how the contents in the unconscious are mutually connected by an entirely different logic than in the consciousness. For example, a psychotic woman dreamed about an island of silver. The island was herself, she said. "Silence is golden and speech is silver," she explained, and because she talked a lot she was silver.

Jung did not regard the dream as a disguise or facade, and he took particular exception to the dream mechanism Freud called displacement. The apparent disguises in dreams were for Jung associated with the unconscious's very mode of expression; it speaks in metaphors, and these are not concealing but revealing. A woman dreamed the following: *There is a great social affair to which she is invited. She is received by her hostess with the words: "How nice that you have come, all your friends are already here and are expecting you." She leads her to a door, opens it, and the dreamer steps into—a cowshed!* According to Jung, the woman was "well known for her stupid prejudices and stubborn arguments." It hadn't been possible for him to get her to consider whether it was her own and not the others' viewpoints there was something wrong with. Here the dream, in crude and colorful language, seems to be saying: You are bovine and dull. And it "hit home," Jung writes.

Jung did acknowledge that there are dreams where one figure will function as a cover for someone else. But in that case he believed the unconscious had a definite intention with the cover: namely, to shift the dreamer's feelings from the person involved and make him realize that it was really a question of a problem in himself.

While Jung was writing his pivotal work, *The Symbols of Transformation*, which he rightly feared would arouse Freud's displeasure, he had a dream that took place in a mountainous landscape near the Swiss-Austrian border:

It was toward evening, and I saw an elderly man in the uniform of an Imperial Austrian customs official. He walked past, somewhat stooped, without paying any attention to me. His expression was peevish, rather melancholic and vexed. There were other persons present, and someone informed me that the old man was not really there but was the ghost of a customs official who had died years ago. "He was one of those who still can't die properly."

Here Jung regards the elderly man as Freud. "Customs" is a parallel to dream censorship and the rigorous Freudian inspection of dreams. The peevish and melancholic expression also corresponds to Jung's image of Freud, that what Freud got out of his analyses wasn't a source of much joy. The dream's intention, according to Jung, is to downgrade Freud because he still means too much to Jung both personally and professionally. It serves the purpose of getting Freud's influence to die away.

THE LIVING SYMBOL

Jung's conception of the symbol was essentially different from Freud's. While Freud used fixed symbol translations, Jung regarded the symbol as the best possible expression for something relatively unfamiliar. In his practical dream analysis, however, Jung worked with relatively fixed symbolic meanings. As examples, the lion, in innumerable representations over the ages, has been used to symbolize power and sensuality, as air and flying creatures have symbolized the spirit and imagination. These meanings always had to be weighed against a possible personal meaning of the dreamer's. But for Jung the symbol's meaning extends far beyond the cognitional sphere. He regards it as a living and creative entity whose most important attribute is that it can transform the psyche—which is to say it can shift psychic energy from one way of experiencing to another even though it isn't understood intellectually. (See "The autonomous growth processes," below.)

We can imagine a Christian, for example, who on his deathbed presses a crucifix to his bosom and thereby transforms the terror of death into a feeling of acceptance; an African boy who drinks a cup of blood from the adult men of the tribe and experiences that he himself becomes an adult man with all that it implies; or a Pueblo Indian whose life acquires profound meaning and world-embracing significance at the idea that his meditation helps Father Sun to get up every morning.

For Jung such an outlook—however alien it might seem to the modern rationalistic individual—was of tremendous importance for psychic health. He went so far as to define a neurosis, any neurosis, as alienation from the archetypal symbols, a loss of the "symbolical attitude." He saw this corroborated in the instances where primitive cultures had disintegrated under the influence of Western mentality because they discarded the religious symbols and rituals that had provided them with meaning and coherency with a higher cosmic order.

But Jung also thought that loss of the symbolic attitude in the modern individual is compensated for by dreams, which naturally underscore their importance. He found too that working with symbols has a curative effect. Jung saw symbol formation as a manifestation of the tendency in the psyche of every individual to join the forces of the consciousness and the unconscious into a unity, a "transcendent" function.

THE ARCHETYPAL DREAM SYMBOLS

Jung thought that the symbols in religious and ritual ideas, the *cultural symbols*, sprang from even deeper sources than the religions themselves, namely from archetypes. They could therefore appear spontaneously as "natural" symbols in the dreams of people who had never encountered them in the physical world.

Among other examples, Jung mentions a series of peculiar dreams that a worried father received as a Christmas present from his ten-year-old daughter. She had dreamed them when she was eight. Six of the twelve dreams are as follows:

> *1. The "bad animal": a snakelike monster with many horns, that kills and devours all other animals. But God comes from the four corners, being really four gods, and gives rebirth to all the animals.*
>
> *2. Ascent into heaven where pagan dances are being celebrated, and descent to hell where angels are doing good deeds.*
>
> *3. A small mouse is penetrated by worms, snakes, fishes, and human beings. Thus the mouse becomes human. This is the origin of mankind in four stages.*
>
> *5. A drop of water is looked at through a microscope: it is full of branches. This is the origin of the world.*
>
> *11. She is dangerously ill. Suddenly birds come out of her skin and cover her completely.*
>
> *12. Swarms of gnats hide the sun, moon, and stars, all except one star that then falls on the dreamer.*

Jung found no reason to doubt that these were dreams and not waking fantasies; nor did there appear to be anything in the girl's upbringing that could have supplied her with such unusual dream motifs. In nine of the twelve dreams there is death and resurrection, which is a universally occurring religious motif. That the gods appear in a quaternity in the first dream is a theme familiar in eastern religions and philosophies but which does not occur in Christianity. Dream number two, with its pagans in heaven and angels in hell, is reminiscent more of Nietzsche's ingenious transvaluation of all values than of the thoughts of an eight-year-old. Being devoured by a monster and the miraculous rescue is another universal mythological subject. Dreams four and five resemble many primitive myths of the creation of the world, and so on.

Nothing in the dreams appears to have had relation to the girl's personal life; indeed, in their seriousness and archetypal depth they are very different from what one might expect from an eight-year-old girl. So what are the dreams' intentions, their compensatory meaning? If a primitive medicine man had dreamed them they could be variations on the philosophical themes of death and resurrection, the world's genesis, and the creation of man. Or they could be doctrines that young people in primitive societies become acquainted with on initiation into adulthood. But with the little girl Jung found that their intention was to prepare her for an untimely death, which occurred when she was eleven.

Jung stressed that archetypes are not static patterns but dynamic factors. He often found that on sudden transformations of the personality it could be proved that "an archetype has been at work for a long time in the unconscious, skillfully arranging circumstances that will unavoidably lead to a crisis." This can be very distinct in connection with archetypes of the opposite sex, anima or animus. The writer has often seen how over a period of time the feminine figures (the anima) in a man's dreams become more alive and insistent, displaying specific attractive qualities while his wife assumes the backseat. And then "out of the blue" he meets a woman in whom he experiences the dream girl's qualities, and heaven and hell break loose. Without knowledge of the dreams, the conflict between himself and the two feminine ideals would be experienced as events in the physical world that simply happened to him.

LEVELS OF SIGNIFICANCE

For Jung, dreams had essentially two sources. They could be touched off by unconscious impressions and contents, or by creative processes in the unconscious. The latter interested him the most. At a seminar on childhood dreams held in 1938–1939, Jung divided dreams into four categories, according to their *levels of significance*—what is determining for their relation to consciousness:

1. The dream represents an unconscious reaction to a conscious situation.
2. The dream represents a situation that springs from a conflict between the conscious and the unconscious.
3. The dream represents a tendency in the unconscious that strives for changing the conscious attitude.
4. The dream represents unconscious processes in which no connection to the conscious can be found.

Dreams became in that order less and less "everyday" and more and more archetypal.

Dreams belonging to the first category are called *reaction dreams*, with a parallel in Freud's idea of a psychologically significant day's residue. Jung used them as commentaries on the practical restructuring of the dreamer's daily life. Marie-Louise von Franz, Jung's colleague of many years, had a man in analysis who had been in alcohol detoxification for a couple of months. He now wanted to try to manage "a single beer" at a local bar. That night after the try he dreamed the following: *He drove his car up a mountain and got all the way to the top, but there he didn't set the hand brake, and he rolled with the car backward down the mountain "all the way back to the starting point."* The dream was understood to mean that a single beer would cause him to slide all the way back to his starting point, and it was regarded as a reaction dream referring to the specific impression from the previous day.

In the second category a specific current situation giving rise to the dream could not be found. But it was placed in connection with a more general conflict between the consciousness and the unconscious. The following dream sequence from my own practice comes from a twenty-eight-year-old man. He dreamed that

he was in a room where he had lived at home with his parents. A group
of armed men forced their way into his room and sentenced him to death
for "misuse of life." The grounds for the sentence was twelve truths that
were read to him. One of them was "that I hadn't trusted to the unlimited
intelligence of nature." In explanation of this point one of the men ar-
gued that as I in a dream could acknowledge and comprehend truths
which I normally couldn't perceive showed that there was a greater in-
telligence than mine.

We were unable to place the dream in connection with anything from the previous day. He had come to me for advice in a matter concerning his love life. At each therapy session he dutifully presented three or four dreams, which were unusually clear and instructive. But the therapy was hampered by the fact that he didn't "believe" in dreams. The dream above appears to comment on the general problem, that he didn't take dreams and the unconscious seriously.

With the third category we are speaking of particularly meaningful dreams in which the unconscious takes the lead and which according to Jung can make a person change attitudes entirely. The following example comes from a severely depressive American who was a patient of Jung's close coworker C. A. Meyer. He had brought the dream along to the first analytical consultation: *I was trout fishing, not in an ordinary river or lake but in a reservoir which was divided into different chambers. I was fishing with ordinary tackle, flies etc., but I wasn't having any luck. I got exasperated and grabbed a trident which was lying there, and right away I was able to spear a magnificent fish.*

Over several years the man had been in various sanatoriums but without being cured of his depression. He wanted to try a Jungian analysis. When he showed up for treatment he was so paralyzed by the depression that he could hardly speak. His wife had written down the above dream for him.

Ten days after the dream, a gradual alleviation of the depression set in, ending with a complete cure. The treatment continued for a few months and the patient remained psychically healthy until his death. Later we shall have a closer look at the meaning of dreams (see "The dream's dramatic structure," below). Here it should just be remarked that Meyer regarded the unexpected catch as prefiguring the nearly miraculous cure.

In the fourth type of dream it isn't possible to discover a connection to the unconscious situation until much later. The little girl with the peculiar dreams from the preceding section is just such a case. Type four dreams are very rare. They can be decisive for a person's development, and on account of their collective content can be significant to the society in which the dreamer lives. On the other hand, the burden that is placed on persons having such dreams is so great that not everyone can bear it. According to Jung, dreams of this type can precede sudden outbreaks of psychosis or severe neurosis.

An example of collective meaning that became realized is a dream Jung himself had in 1914. He dreamed that *a frightful cold had descended from out of the cosmos.* The dream had an unexpected end when Jung saw *a leaf-bearing tree, but without any fruit (my tree of life, I thought), whose leaves had been transformed by the effects of the frost into sweet grapes full of healing juices. I plucked the grapes and gave them to a large, waiting crowd.*

The dream came at a low point in Jung's life. He had broken with Freud and was no longer accepted in psychoanalytic circles. He doubted his own theories, gave up his academic career, and staked his talent on experiments with himself that he could not be sure were of general value. Given a Jungian interpretation, the dream is saying that the chill he had experienced would nonetheless bear fruit, and that what he could give would be of benefit to many people. As it turned out, Jung's self-experiments during this period were to form the most important raw material for the next forty years' work.

There are examples of the negative effects of a major dream, too. A thirty-year-old man sought out Jung on account of "a nervous breakdown." In advance of the breakdown he had dreamed several times in succession:

> *He is taking a walk in the dunes when suddenly he discovers some black potsherds on the ground. He takes them up. They are prehistoric pot-sherds. He goes home, fetches a spade, begins to dig, and discovers a whole prehistoric settlement, weapons, implements, stone axes, etc. He is tremendously fascinated and wakes up perspiring with excitement.*

The dream can be given the Jungian interpretation that the dreamer dug very far down in the collective unconscious and stands all alone with his fascinating experiences.

It might seem surprising that such a dream can testify to violent processes in the psyche, but the Jungian analytical tradition corroborates Jung's observations. The difference between Jung and the young man is that Jung, through fifty years of work, had the talent and strength of ego to realize the potentialities residing in the dream, and the young man did not.

Jung's basic view that dreams have a purpose made it possible for him to see very different meanings and structures in them than Freud had an eye for. Out of this view evolved a number of practical interpretation principles, the most important of which are:

1. The dream's dramatic structure
2. The dream's prospective and regressive aspects (constructive versus reductive interpretations)
3. The context the dream appears in (the dream's context)
4. Interpretation on subjective (internal) and objective (external) level.
5. Confirming the dream interpretation (testing)

Ahead of any interpretation principles, however, Jung recommended using a phenomenological method: ideally the interpreter had to relinquish all preconceived notions and regard the dream as "a source of information about states whose nature is unknown to him and about which he has just as much to learn as the dreamer."

The Dream's Dramatic Structure

Jung found that most dreams are built up like a Classical Greek drama, and that this structure can provide access to an understanding of the dream. The dream can be divided into formal parts:

The exposition. The dream's beginning. Time, place, and persons are as a rule indicated here.

The complication, or presentation of the dream's problem.

The peripeteia, or climax. A positive transformation of the problem can take place here, but also a catastrophe.

Lysis. The dream's conclusion. The solution of the dream problem is seen, the closing phase of the narrative.

This structure is understood as manifesting a possible development in the dreamer. The introduction and the complication show his present problem, while the peripeteia and the conclusion show the possibilities for getting through it and finding a solution. Especially important in the archetypal dreams is how they end.

If we apply this structural model to the dream from C. A. Meyer's depressive American, it looks like this:

Exposition: *I was trout fishing, not in an ordinary river or lake but in a reservoir which was divided into different chambers.*

Interpretation: Water is regarded by Jung as symbolizing the unconscious. To be in therapy is like fishing in the unconscious. The man had attempted various methods of treatment. (The different chambers containing the water?)

Dream problem: *I was fishing with ordinary tackle, flies etc., but I wasn't having any luck.*

He had tried the traditional forms of treatment but without success.

Climax: *I got exasperated and grabbed a trident which was lying there . . .*

To get exasperated and take an initiative is in itself a momentous step for a severely depressive person who is unable to act. Meyer pointed out besides that the trident is better known in connection with the sea god Poseidon. In some localities Poseidon is a god of healing, but he is also a symbol of the raging elements and thus of the "elemental" emotionality that the dreamer had been lacking.

Solution: *. . . and right away I was able to spear a magnificent fish.*

The possibility of a cure was present back in the culmination. The dream's conclusion underscored that the man would solve his problem.

The Dream's Prospective and Regressive Aspects

The above interpretation as good as says that the dream from the depressive man dealt with a future possibility. This was one of the decisive points in Jung's departure from Freud. When he spoke of a *prospective* (facing forward) aspect of the dream and prospective interpretation he did not mean a prophecy. He saw the dream more as "a preliminary exercise for a conscious future achievement, a proposal for the posing of a problem and an advance combination of probabilities."

He did not deny the value of taking the dream back to traumatic events in childhood (*reductive interpretation*), but it appears clearly from his theoretical dissertations and seminars that Jung regarded this angle of approach somewhat negatively, as something to be gotten through so one can get to what really matters.

The Dream's Context

Jung recommended that *context* be established for each separate element in a dream. By the context he meant partly the associations that attach themselves to the dream element and partly the meanings that can be discovered through comparison with symbolic historical material, i.e., amplification.

Associations

Jung's association technique was different from Freud's smooth swinging from association to association without hanging on to the takeoff idea. Jung did think that free association led the dreamer to his complexes, but he believed that the dreamer could arrive at them just as well by associating from an incomprehensible Russian or Indian railway notice. Free association did not lead to an understanding of the dream's purpose, according to Jung. The dream's purpose was not to point to the complexes but to create distance from them so they could be gotten around in a constructive way.

Symbols point ahead and provide ideas for problem solving. It is a question, therefore, of distinguishing between the associations that belong to the symbols—ordinarily only one or two steps away—and the ones that do not. A simple example from my own practice is the following ultra brief dream from a young man: *Somebody asks: "Are you having coffee?" I reply: "No thanks! I'd rather have tea."* In the dreamer's family, tea was the beverage of habit. Coffee was a luxury enjoyed only when out among strangers. The dream immediately preceded a seminar with persons the dreamer didn't know. Via the dream, he became aware of a resistance to the seminar that he hadn't been conscious of, and a feeling of inferiority toward the strangers (the others' coffee is finer than my tea).

Amplification

Another way to expand the context is by comparing the dream elements with other symbolic material. This is called *amplification* or symbol reinforcement and can be divided into three levels: personal, cultural, and archetypal.

Personal amplifications adhere closely to associations in the Jungian sense. If the dream is about a glass, specific details about the glass must be determined. Is it a beer glass, for example? Let us say it is a drinking glass and that it is standing in Grandmother's room and that a certain type of experience is associated with it.

Symbols can have culture-typical and conventional meanings attached to them. In many languages the word *red* is associated with blood. In Old Norse, blood is called *rodra*, and in Sanskrit it is *rudhira*. The color red is therefore associated with life, passion, strong feelings. In modern society red can be associated with a traffic light meaning stop, while in Indian kundalini yoga it is bound up with a particular area of the body (the root chakra) and thereby acquires a number of special meanings.

The cross, to use another example, appears in Asian mandalas, where a circle divided into four equal parts symbolizes wholeness (see also "The dream series," below). In Christian culture the cross is associated with the crucifixion of Christ. Since the ninth century it has been configured so the transverse piece is elevated above the axis. Symbolically this form carries special meaning for Christians.

Jung found amplification with cross-cultural symbolic historical material particularly useful with archetypal dreams, in which the dreamer has no personal associations. An example of this comes from the Swiss Jungian analyst C. Salles, who had a thirty-two-year-old doctor, called E, in analysis. The doctor played his social role satisfactorily in superficial terms, but emotionally he wasn't the least engaged in his life. The analysis had come to a standstill; the sessions had become so sterile that at length the analyst began to doubt their value.

At this time E had a remarkable dream, followed by major transformations of his personality:

> My skin was strange. It was of a different color (gray). I was made of wax. The air conditioner was turned on, so that I realized that if the temperature increased I would melt. My heart was made of lead. Then I picked up the heart, put it aside, and turned the control of the air conditioner to "warm." As the temperature increased I started to melt and melt, down to the skeleton. By the end, only the skeleton and the heart remained.

Salles amplified thoroughly all of the elements in the dream. Here I will extract the most important.

Wax is a modeling material. Wax figures are not living. They come into being by somebody shaping them. This corresponds to E playing the role others expected of him totally without emotional involvement.

In the dream the artificial (waxy) state is maintained by means of another artificial arrangement, namely the air-conditioning. Heat is often a symbol for emotional warmth. Adjusting the temperature—administrating the emotional energy—plays a large role in the alchemical process, which as Jung demonstrated symbolizes the development of the personality.

In the dream, E chooses to melt himself down so only the bones and the heart are left. To the alchemists the heart is a symbol of healing power. The skeleton is in many cultures regarded as the elemental substance for rebirth. This would indicate that the dream deals with healing and psychic rebirth.

Another parallel to the dream Salles found in a Siberian shaman's account of his call to shamanhood. He had been sick for some time and dreamed that *I was taken to the ancestor and cut into pieces. They threw me into the kettle and I was boiled. They found a bone around the ribs with a hole in the middle. This was the excess bone. One looks across the hole of this bone and begins to see all and to know all, and that is when one becomes a shaman.* Salles found that the shaman and E went through the same transformation processes in their dreams: illness/suffering = dismemberment of the shaman's body/melting of E's wax body; boiling of the shaman/warming of E's room = initiation of the shaman/transformation of E's personality.

There are several other mythological parallels to the heart, to the metal lead, to the color gray, to dismemberment, to rebirth, and so on. The reason for comparing the dream with mythological symbolism from different cultures is that fundamentally they derive from the same elemental substance: the archetypes. Knowledge of the archetypal parallels makes it possible to understand dreams and states of consciousness that are alien and terrifying for the dreamer and so could discourage him from going further with an inner development.

Archetypal amplifications must always be balanced against the cultural and personal. One of my own clients dreamed about a bird that wants to fly out the window. As he had read a little Jung, he thought that it must symbolize the spirit's free flight, as a bird very well might. But closer inquiry disclosed that it had to do with a sickly canary his mother had kept in a cage when he was a child and that this bird would not survive in the open. Here the personal meaning of the bird was the most important.

Jung stressed that dream interpretation could not be learned like a mechanical system. And even though there exist good reference books with indexes of symbolic meanings, their value is limited.

As I've mentioned earlier, the majority of dreams refer to events that made an impression on the dreamer the previous day. This, too, is an important part of the context.

Interpretation on Subjective and Objective Levels

An important feature of Jung's interpretation technique are the rules for how dream figures are seen as expressions of psychic states and complexes in the dreamer's mind (*subjective interpretation*), and how they deal with actual persons in the physical world (*objective interpretation*). Going from his practical experience, Jung set up these general rules:

The objective interpretation is relevant if the dream figure is an important person in the dreamer's life, such as an immediate family member or a very close friend. A subjective interpretation is more relevant when the figure is a distant relation, an insignificant acquaintance or unknown person, a historical person, or a figure of fantasy.

Acquaintances whom the dreamer has a current relationship or conflict with are interpreted chiefly objectively. If the dream figure is seen "photographically" correct, an objective interpretation is more likely than if the dream figure appears distorted or otherwise altered. In these cases there is no question of fixed rules but rather of probabilities and potentialities that must be viewed in connection with the rest of the dream's context.

The following example of a subjective interpretation comes from Jung. One of his male patients dreamed about *a drunken, disheveled, vulgar woman called his "wife."* In reality his wife was totally different. Jung writes, "Clearly, the dream is seeking to express the idea of a degenerate female who is closely connected with the dreamer. This idea is projected upon his wife, where the statement becomes untrue." Jung saw a feminine aspect of the man's own personality in the dream. A similar subjective interpretation could be considered in the Christine Keeler dream from Vanggaard's male patient (see "Conclusion," chapter 1).

On the other hand, dreams can be generous sources of information concerning parents, siblings, spouses, colleagues, etc., that would otherwise be inaccessible. In couples where I have had both parties in therapy, it is striking how dreams from the same night can refer to the same event, and it is possible to see two different subjective attitudes and the slice of objective reality where they meet.

A couple had intercourse one night. It had gone satisfactorily after a few initial difficulties. The woman later dreamed that she was at summer camp and hiked up to a marvelous old castle on a mountaintop. She was together with a group of adolescent girls. *The last and most difficult stretch I see that the rest of the girls are going up by a path of tiny steps running up one pace to the left. As I am about to stumble I dart out to the left in front of the girls.*

Dreams following intercourse often comment on the event if there have been complications. It is also be expected that a Freudian symbolic understanding would be applicable. If mountaineering in Freudian terms stands for the stepwise mounting of orgasm, here a guess might be that she would obtain sexual satisfaction by overtaking the adolescent girl in herself. The man usually ejaculated prematurely, which had a disturbing effect on the woman. To overtake the adolescent girls could also mean to take an adult initiative in the relationship. (A supplementary interpretation is found in "Calvin Hall's theory of symbols," chapter 3.)

In the man's dream he was together with his partner (Inge) *in a theater, waiting for some kind of performance. Now and then there were shots from someplace in the auditorium, and a man was hit in the back. . . . Suddenly Inge discovered him (the gunman), and thanks to that I saw him too. It was a seven- to ten-year-old boy.* The little boy shooting wildly could be an expression for the premature ejaculation whereby the man in the dream, in sexual terms, is killed. The dream reflects the fact that the girlfriend spotted the problem and took the initiative to learn a sexological technique that could preclude it.

Successors of Jung have regarded subjective interpretation as an in-depth interpretation leading to *intrapsychic* change within the person, while objective interpretation is more on the level of the physical world. To the extent that this is true, subjective interpretation would be relevant after a lengthy period of working with self-development, and more relevant in older persons who have realized themselves in the world at large than in young persons who have to live out their problems. A generally accepted rule of thumb is that the objective potentialities of the dream are to be tackled before getting to the interior level.

Confirming the Dream Interpretation

Among the rules Jung pointed out for use in confirming the correctness of an interpretation are these:

1. The interpretation is corroborated by other dreams in the series. One of Jung's patients had a dream in which *the patient's father holds a globe and tries to divide it into two parts of equal size. It is to be done in such a way that there are precisely just as many people in the east as in the west.*

Jung thought of the second day in the biblical account of the creation, where God divides the waters under the firmament from the waters above the firmament, and he interpreted the dream as a bringing to awareness. This interpretation was confirmed when the patient related that he had also had a dream in which *God created the world with lightning and thunder.*

2. A second criterium for the interpretation's correctness is that it says something to the dreamer, it "clicks."

Jung found that it was necessary to "regard a dream interpretation as invalid until the formula has been found that wins the patient's consent." This, however, is a rule of thumb for therapeutic practice, where an interpretation doesn't work if the client doesn't understand it. In terms of theory, Jung often drew far-reaching conclusions when interpreting archetypal dream series. (See the interpretation of the peculiar mythological dreams from an eight-year-old girl in "The archetypal dream symbols," above; and the dream series treated in the section "Dream and alchemy," below.) As with Freud, the patient's yes or no doesn't always decide the interpretation's correctness.

3. A third criterium for confirming the interpretation is that it has an effect on the dreamer and leads to results.

IMPORTANT TYPES OF DREAMS

Jung pointed out certain types of dreams that are especially important: dreams from earliest childhood; dreams at important life transitions, including puberty, mid-life, and death; initial dreams, which open an analysis; and dreams that have significance for the fellowship of man, or dreams of call.

Childhood Dreams

Jung found that the earliest dreams of childhood emanate from the very deepest layers of the personality and are so meaningful that they often foretell a person's fate. Child's dreams are often recalled far into adulthood; this underscores their special significance.

It is difficult to get associations for children's dreams. Jung thought this was because the dreams are generally more archetypal and impersonal than those of adults, and that children often block associations out of fear of the dream contents. As for the remembered dreams, the circumstances surrounding them are long since forgotten.

We will now briefly consider three recalled dreams from Jung's Childhood Dreams Seminar, in order to get a sense of the connection between recalled child's dreams and individual fate.

A forty-five-year-old man recalled a dream he had when he was five or six years old: *I see a pyramid. At the top is a house of glass. Somebody is inside it. When I come closer I see that it is myself.* The dream recurred frequently. All his life the man had been a seeker, a dreamer who had difficulty involving himself in physical reality. He tried being a jurist and became a colonial magistrate. He married. But he couldn't completely involve himself in any of it. He dabbled with philosophy in the hope of finding what he was seeking. He happened upon a book by Jung, and at the age of forty-five he sought Jung out.

Jung found that there was something quite unchildlike about the dream.

It was abstract and archetypal but not neurotic or otherwise questionable. It pointed to the man's other, noneveryday-oriented side.

When the boy in the dream stood at the base of the pyramid he was far distant from this other side of himself. Just as he had been oddly split in his life, so he was in the dream as well.

The image of the glass house atop the pyramid corresponded to nothing the dreamer had experienced in his waking life. On the other hand, Jung found a number of alchemical and mythological parallels that symbolize spiritual transformation. What the dreamer was supposed to see was that he had a kind of spiritual double, a spiritual substance that he should also take seriously and try to emancipate. This dilemma came to color the man's life for forty years, until with Jung he began working on it and regained his peace of mind.

A five-year-old girl's dreams:

> In the first dream I heard my father call. When I got up and went inside my parents' bedroom I saw on top of each of their beds a pyramid of ashes, and on top of each of the pyramids the dead faces of my father and mother.
>
> In the second dream I stood on a desolate open space with nothing but craters. Infinitely far away my father was standing in one of the craters.

Jung was sent these two dreams when the dreamer was thirty years old. They had followed her all her life.

In order to understand the first dream it is necessary to enter into the child's feelings. The fact that the father called during the night seems frightening and weird. "If anyone calls during the night, it is children, not parents." Secondly, the child goes into the parents' bedroom and there, where parental love is, where open arms should be ready to receive, there are two heaps of ashes. Furthermore, neither of the dreams has a resolution (lysis). If the dream had ended with *I rushed to help him as best I could* or *I did what was possible*, you could say to yourself, "Ah ha, there's something the dreamer can deal with. She can at least try." There would be something to work with.

In Jung's experience such dreams had an altogether catastrophic meaning. Shortly after he had received these two dreams, the woman was stricken with schizophrenia. Jung realized that the compensatory function was missing in such cases, or at any rate was reduced.

We have seen a child's dream from a searching soul who found peace with himself, and from a person with an unhappy fate. As a third example let us consider a dream from a great and successful personality—Jung himself.

When he was three or four years of age, Jung had an unusual and fertile dream that preoccupied him for the rest of his life. He dreamed he was in the meadow by his parents' home:

> In the dream I was in this meadow. Suddenly I discovered a dark, rectangular, stone-lined hole in the ground. Then I saw a stone stairway leading down. Hesitantly and fearfully, I descended. I saw before me in the dim light a rectangular chamber about thirty feet long. The floor was laid with flagstones, and in the center a red carpet ran from the entrance to a low platform. On this platform stood a wonderfully rich golden throne, a real king's throne in a fairy tale. Something was standing on it that I thought at first was a tree trunk twelve to fifteen feet high and about one and a half to two feet thick. But it was made of skin and naked flesh, and on top there was something like a rounded head with no face and no hair. On the top of the head was a single eye, gazing motionlessly upward. It was fairly light in the room. Above the head was an aura of brightness. The thing did not move, yet I had the feeling that it might at any moment crawl off the throne like a worm and creep toward me.

Jung's close coworker Marie-Louise von Franz considered the gigantic penislike object to be an underground God standing in opposition to the Christian view of life. In other traditions such a phallus symbolizes a man's "secret genius," the source of his physical and mental power, the giver of all his inspired ideas and his exuberant joy in living.

Jung did indeed, like few others in this century, confront the Christian idea of God with its murkier "subterranean" counterpart. In keeping with the dream, he did possess an extraordinarily fertile creativity and was by those close to him renowned for his tremendous personal vitality.

Initial Dreams

At the beginning of a therapy there will usually be one or more dreams that give an especially representative picture of the dreamer's most important problems, while later dreams often depict more specific aspects of the problem. Introductory or *initial dreams* can be very clear and symbolic in their structure, but often the dreamer manages only a few superficial associations from them. Freud, Jung, and a number of other pioneers of dream analysis agree in these observations.

To the possibility of making a diagnosis by means of the initial dream, Jung added that it could also say something about the prospects for a cure: the treatment's *prognosis*. In the fishing dream from C. A. Meyer's American patient we saw an example of an interpretation of an initial dream with a view to a prognosis.

Another example where it is possible to follow the progress from the initial dream to the therapy's conclusion is from my book *The Feminine in the Man*. A twenty-eight-year-old man dreams that *[a]n obese older woman makes sexual advances to him, and he remains passive. Later he is together with a beautiful young woman in his own car. She has bought tickets for their honeymoon.*

From the dream's context it is reasonable to regard the older woman as a mother figure. The sexual relationship to her illustrates what Freud called the Oedipus complex, and the diagnosis immediately suggested is "unresolved mother fixation." At the same time, the younger woman represents the man's own feminine side and his potential for entering into a binding relationship with a nonmotherlike partner (the honeymoon). The dream's dramatic structure had its negative starting point in the mother fixation, while its positive conclusion indicates the potential for good development. This was corroborated in therapy.

At first glance the above examples appear clear and simple. But at the same time there are many questions they don't answer. How is his problem different from that of other men with Oedipus complexes? How does the dreamer experience it in his daily life? How can he work on the problem in practical terms? And so forth.

Freud, Jung, and other early dream theorists were also in agreement that initial dreams ordinarily don't become understandable until far into the therapy—as far as Freud was concerned, when the first resistance to the therapy had been broken so the patient could associate freely. For Jung it was when you became familiar with the patient's most important complexes and saw the dream in relation to an ongoing series.

The problem also arises as to what dreams appearing near the beginning of analysis are initial dreams. Is it the last dream prior to analysis? Or the first after starting? Or the one on the day the patient phoned the analyst?

Or is it a dream within the first couple of months before the treatment commences? In my view it is a matter of experience—it involves a balancing of the moment of the dream's appearance against its archetypal significance.

There is an inconsistency in the theory that particularly significant dreams from the deep layers of the unconscious arrive spontaneously and independent of consciousness. These initial archetypal dreams on the contrary originate from a very clear and meaningful conscious situation. The German analyst Hermann Schultz investigated initial dreams in thirty-six clients who were in treatment an average of five years with a total of twenty therapists. His conclusion: only half of the dreams produced new prognostic aspects. I think, however, that dream interpreters of Freud's and Jung's caliber would have greater accuracy.

The concept of initial dreams can be expanded to apply to all important life situations where a clear and meaningful decision is made, such as a marriage engagement, the beginning of a creative project, a new walk of life, etc. A number of neo-Freudians have likewise found that if the analyst appears frequently in the first dreams, there quickly develops an aggressively controlling and clinging transference reaction.

An example of an initial dream for a creative project is a dream I had the night after having made the first synopsis for this book:

> *At a pier in the harbor. It was a wonderful evening, warm and with an incredibly beautiful and clear starry sky. Among the others who were standing looking on was a couple of around 55–60 years. I exchanged a few words with the woman, who turned out to be an analyst. In the sky I noticed a certain small star cluster, which came closer as I was standing regarding it. It was a galaxy with myriads of stars. It had a beautiful golden color, and in a rather short space of time you could see a process being played out that must have taken millions of years— perhaps the galaxy's genesis. The suspension of time and space was thrilling and at the start awe-inspiring. The movement inside the galaxy was shaped like two dragons that formed a rotating circle and were devouring each other's tail. One was larger than the other. A woman my own age who was my "wife" turned up and looked too. From up in the star cluster a model ship around 1 meter long and carved in dark Asian wood now came, as it were, sailing down through the air. I reached an arm up and the ship came down right in my hand. It was shaped nearly like a very stout staff. My wife was amazed. I put my arm around her and said that it was quite all right, anything could happen here.*

When I woke up my first association was that the dragons devouring each other's tail are Freud and Jung; but they are also an alchemical symbol. The symbolism is cosmic and archetypal. There is a suspension of time and space. There are two couples that together form an autonomy in a symbol of wholeness.

The ship is a (naval architect's) model, just like my synopsis. It comes sailing right down into my hand, just like the publisher's offer. It dawns on me that anything can happen, and the book did come to have a different appearance from what I had originally imagined. It opened up to new dimensions, and working on it produced profound personal transformation.

Naturally the dream's extraordinary and archetypal character pleased me much, and thinking about it gave me courage to go on when I ran up against obstacles that seemed insurmountable. The association of Freud and Jung as two dragons (with Jung the largest) also recurred in the model ship, which had been fashioned from two pieces of wood. It is Freud and Jung who for me are the two pillars of dream analysis. And the wood from Asia could indicate that the book is made of more esoteric stuff than expected.

INDIVIDUATION PROCESS AND THE DREAM

In Freud's psychology the concept of certain universal human (psychosexual) developmental phases is pivotal. These phases (the *oral*, the *anal*, the *phallic*, and the *genital*) extend from birth to adolescence, and the task of psychoanalysis is broadly to repair what had gone wrong then.

Jung, on the other hand, was especially concerned with the development of the personality that is possible at a more mature age. He believed in a potential inborn development plan, which observes a universal pattern but which within this framework gives the individual his own distinguishing character. The realization of this fulfillment plan he termed the *individuation process*. The individual has within himself, in embryonic form, a transcendent function that can unite the apparent psychic contradictions, the conscious and the unconscious. This ordering and balancing function can be developed through work with dreams.

The model for the inner growth processes in theory looks simple. The adult person, as a step in ego development and social adaptation, identifies excessively with his social role, his *persona*. But in so doing he represses or never becomes conscious of a number of qualities that might be both negative and positive but are in any case necessary for psychic wholeness.

By midlife a person has usually achieved what he or she is capable of in the physical world. He has reached the limit for outward expansion through job advancement and family augmentation. Now, if he isn't to come to a standstill he has to expand inwardly and integrate a number of repressed or unsuspected possibilities into his personality. These aspects to be encountered in oneself Jung calls the shadow, the anima/animus, and the Self. In principle one is confronted with them in that order.

By the *shadow* Jung means a kind of unconscious auxiliary personality. The shadow is usually conceived as a part of the personal unconscious of the same sex as the dreamer. For a man it might be a tramp, a hoodlum, an artist, a homosexual, a Negro, a migrant laborer, or whatever else represents sides of the dreamer that he refuses to acknowledge. For a woman it could be a slattern, a witch, a harridan, a Negress, a bohemian, and so forth and so on. A brother or sister also often appears as a shadow figure. The shadow can also be a more collective figure, such as the devil, or not merely one person's but an entire culture's shadow.

The concept of the shadow is very useful in practical dreamwork. If a man (to use an example from my own practice) who regards himself as very relaxed and unsnobbish persistently dreams about men in pinstriped suits, then in some way or other he must have a desire to be a man of distinction, and he had better try to find out where he is overplaying the aristocrat. Perhaps it's something he thinks people expect of him, but in reality the expectation originates in himself. And if a woman always dreams about a girlfriend whom she describes as gossipy, then she must have a gossipy side herself. Very likely she calls it something else and actually believes that the "information" she is relaying serves a good cause. Implicit in the shadow concept is the idea that we aren't conscious of our own motives.

It often appears that if you give certain concessions to your shadow, then it becomes more cooperative. Say a man dreams about being threatened by a motorcycle gang. It may be that he should permit himself to be more aggressive or simply stand more firmly by his views. It may turn out that in subsequent dreams he begins negotiating with the motorcycle gang and that they aren't as hostile toward him.

In the Jungian model, a coming to terms with the shadow is a condition for being able to work with the opposite-sexed side—*anima* in the man and *animus* in the woman. In the man the anima might be represented by a sister or girlfriend, a gentle virgin or a goddess, a witch, an angel, a demoness, a beggar woman, a harlot, a chum, an amazon, and so forth, and in principle by all of the symbols that are experienced as feminine, such as a cow, a cat, a tiger, a ship, a cave, etc.

The masculine in a woman can appear in a corresponding variety of figures: a brother or a friend, a film star, a boxer, a political orator, or a charismatic religious leader, but also as symbols that are considered masculine: a serpent, a bull, a lion; or as lances, towers, and other phallic structures.

In practical dreamwork these figures are placed in relation to a general theory of certain psychological traits that correspond to the feminine in the man and the masculine in the woman.

If it goes completely unsuspected, complementary-sexedness will show up as, for example, "the temperamental man who is under the sway of feminine drives and is guided by his emotions, or the expert, rational, animus-possessed woman who reacts not instinctually but in a masculine way." But as a person—with the aid of dreams—gradually begins making contact with the complementary-sexed side, it can be developed into a helpful and beneficial aspect of the psyche.

In general terms, the anima is "a personification of all feminine psychological tendencies in the man's psyche such as emotions and moods, prophetic fancies, receptiveness towards the irrational, the faculty for personal love, the feeling for nature and—last but not least—his relation to the unconscious." In other words, a whole series of traits that can shift the man beyond the traditional male role. But if he doesn't exploit these traits consciously they tend to take him unawares as "anima moods" that make him vulnerable and anxious, self-pitying, melancholic and waspish, or sentimental.

For the woman's part, an unprocessed animus can reveal itself as unconscious destructive and self-destructive opinions; as an inner voice that keeps telling her she is no good or that nobody can love her; and so on. Or it can manifest itself in sudden brutal domestic scenes, as coldness and unapproachability, or as semideliberate cynicism that is counter to a woman's more conscious notions about herself. If the animus is made conscious and developed, however, it can make the woman more dynamic, constructive, and full of initiative. It can prompt creativity, build a bridge to the opposite sex, and also effect contact with deeper layers in the unconscious.

A practical example of anima in an ongoing dream series was presented by Jung in lectures he held in the late 1920s on a forty-seven-year-old male analysand. In this man's initial dream he is confronted with his *sister's little daughter*, who didn't exist in reality but only in the dream: *[T]he child looks rather ill. She would not pronounce the name of my wife, Maria. I pronounce that name and ask the child to repeat it, but I really say "Mari—ah—ah," like yawning.*

In this important dream the anima is characterized as an ill two-year-old child, as a wife whose name produces yawns from the husband, and as a sister who is rather indifferent to the dreamer and plays no role in his present life. In subsequent dreams the anima reveals itself as a poor and ill seamstress, as small girls gathering unripe cherries, and as peculiar, nearly hermaphroditic creatures.

The anima and the appertaining traits are depicted in the dreams as sickly, childish, immature, and tiresome. It is therefore no wonder that the dreamer was a hardboiled businessman who had very little time to concern himself with his feelings, and who related erotically to his wife "in the same way as when a couple of times a month he balances his bank account."

After eight or nine months the man dreamed that his wife gave birth to triplets. The first two died but the last survived. Such a dream indicates at least the possibility that his anima could become a more mature psychic factor which could "give birth" to new potentialities in the personality.

An altogether different kind of anima appears in the following dream from a forty-five-year-old male psychotherapist (the example comes from Marie-Louise von Franz's material):

> *I am in an old church together with my mother and my wife. I am to celebrate the Mass as a priest. I am very excited because I have to begin soon, and to add to my troubles my mother and wife disturb me by chattering about unimportant trifles. Now the organ stops, and everybody is waiting for me. I ask one of the nuns who is kneeling behind me to hand me her Mass book—which she does in an obliging manner. This same nun precedes me to the altar. The Mass book is like a board, a sheet of sixteen ancient pictures in columns, one beside the other. First the nun has to read a part of the liturgy before I begin. She has told me that it is Number 15. I turn toward the congregation, although I do not know if I shall be able to decipher it. I want to try all the same. I wake up.*

As he was going to bed the evening before, the dreamer had thought that it was hard to stand alone in life without the support of a church. The dream was (in brief) interpreted as follows:

The mother and the wife (who in reality was extroverted) stand for, respectively, his mother-boundness and an extroverted side of his anima. The nun is the introverted anima. She does not represent an official church, as her Mass book is so strange. The sixteen (four times four) pictures can be understood as "psychic images that your religious anima reveals to you." Jung demonstrated that quaternity is a symbol for the *Self*, the nucleus of the psyche, and the pictures appearing four times four points to psychic wholeness. The people in the church represent the dreamer's own desire to celebrate the Mass himself. In short, the dream can be understood as meaning that he didn't have to observe an official faith. But "if the dreamer overcomes his inner uncertainty, caused by his mother complex, he will find that his life task has the nature and quality of a religious service and that if he meditates about the symbolic meaning of the images in his soul, they will lead him to this realization."

The following dream, which depicts an animus in both its positive and negative forms, is from a forty-five-year-old woman:

> *Two veiled figures climb onto the balcony and into the house. They are swathed in black hooded coats, and they seem to want to torment me and my sister. She hides under the bed, but they pull her out with a broom and torture her. Then it is my turn. The leader of the two pushes me against the wall, making magical gestures before my face. In the meantime his helper makes a sketch on the wall, and when I see it, I say (in order to seem friendly), "Oh, but this is well drawn!" Now suddenly my tormentor has the noble head of an artist, and he says proudly, "Yes, indeed," and begins to clean his spectacles.*

The dream is from one of Marie-Louise von Franz's clients. In outline, it was interpreted as follows:

The two burglars represent a sadistic animus aspect, or in psychological terms *thoughts* that the dreamer torments herself with. This corresponded to reality, for she frequently suffered severe attacks of anxiety during which she was tormented by the thought that people she loved were in grave danger. The deeper meaning of the dream is that behind the anxiety is a creative urge. Both she and her sister had shown a talent for painting, but the dreamer doubted whether painting would be a meaningful activity for her. The dream tells her in an urgent way that she must live out this talent. If she obeys, the destructive, tormenting animus will be transformed into creative and meaningful activity.

Also in this dream, the animus figures represent an element of the collective unconscious, without connection to the dreamer's personal life history.

Jung placed the animus and anima archetypes in a much more elaborate psychological system than it is possible to reproduce here. For example, he set up a series of stages for potential positive metamorphoses of the countersexual side. The first anima stage is symbolized by the biblical Eve, or primitive woman, who represents purely instinctual or biological relations. As prototype for the second stage, Jung sees Faust's Helen, who personifies a romantic and aesthetic level in the man that is still characterized by sexual elements. The third stage is represented by the Virgin Mary, in whom love is transformed into spiritual devotion. And finally the fourth stage, which is symbolized by a figure from Gnosticism: Sophia, who is an expression of the highest wisdom.

For the evolvement of the animus, too, Jung saw four stages. At an early stage of development animus figures appear as primitive muscle men: Tarzan, a boxing champion, or other personifications of raw physical strength. In the second stage the animus figure represents romantic qualities in the woman and the faculty for planned action. The third stage comprises the concept of "meaning" and can be symbolized by a great orator or other personality who knows how to put important ideas into words. As the fourth stage Jung sees the spiritual guide and wise man, such as a Gandhi.

THE AUTONOMOUS GROWTH PROCESSES

Several generations of Jungians have corroborated that familiarity with individuation's formal structure—the shadow, the anima/animus, the Self— is practically useful. Even more important, however, was and is individuation's dynamic process: the inner growth processes (if nothing hinders them) unfolding spontaneously the same way a seed, under the proper conditions, unfolds into a plant.

To prove this in the strict scientific sense is well-nigh impossible, as we aren't capable of completely isolating a person from external influences. But we have already seen some examples of dreams that are hard to explain as externally stimulated (the ten-year-old girl whose dreams portended premature death, the depressive American's cure dream). Jung's primary errand was to demonstrate convincingly the existence of such a process.

Jung made one large experiment after another in order to demonstrate this. In 1912, in the two-volume work *The Symbols of Transformation*, he went through the fantasies of an American woman. In the late 1920s he devoted a two-year lecture series to a man with severe anima problems, and from 1930 to 1934 he examined a thirty-year-old woman's dreams and fantasies.

Jung used a very advanced system, based on his inexhaustible knowledge of archetypal symbols from the most diverse sources, to discover and evaluate spiritual and inner experiential potentialities. The seminars are not easily accessible, and in his eagerness to demonstrate archetypal parallels Jung often departs far from the patient's own account. Always, however, there is an inner thread that can be followed.

Another good example of Jung's conception of independent inner growth processes comes from volume 12 in the *Complete Works*, *Psychology and Alchemy* (1944).

DREAM AND ALCHEMY

In working with his patients' dreams, Jung frequently came across motifs he couldn't understand immediately but that had parallels in the murky texts of the old alchemists. The alchemists thought they could influence chemical substances through psychical magic. Dreams, visions, and meditation played an important role in their work.

In alchemy, metals and different chemical substances had their special symbolic significance. Lead, which was heavy and toxic, belonged to the initial stages in the process in which everything negative and unpleasant in the psyche had to be confronted. Silver was a refined form of the feminine, and gold a refined form of the masculine. Other substances as well, such as sulfur and salt, had male and female symbolic value, and the compounding of them (the *conjunctio*) symbolized the union of masculine and feminine. Innumerable other symbols can be construed from the alchemical texts, for the less the alchemical speculations correspond to a chemistry of the real world, the more likely they are to be projections of inner states, that is, *psychic symbols*.

Many of the alchemists understood that it wasn't so much a matter of producing actual gold, but rather that the complicated processes which were supposed to transform base matter into noble metal were expressions for a refinement of the personality. One of the ways this was manifested is in the distinction between the "vulgar gold" and the "true gold," in which the vulgar gold represents actual material gold while the true gold expresses spiritual development. The different ingredients in the alchemical processes came to correspond to psychic components and states, and Jung found that the collective process of *refinement* was a parallel to his own individuation process.

The Dream Series

The symbols of the individuation process that came to light in dreams were, according to Jung, archetypal. They portrayed a "centralization process," or creation of a new center for the personality. This center Jung called the Self.

In *Psychology and Alchemy*, Jung submitted a dream series that was especially suitable for illustrating his viewpoint. Here he was interested primarily in those images that referred directly or exclusively to the new center, as it comes into the consciousness. Jung found an important archetypal image of the Self in the oriental mandala symbols. The mandala is a kind of magic circle used in religious connections, often richly ornamented and with pictures of the highest divinities in the center or surrounding it. Such mandalas appear worldwide. Jung established their presence in the Christian tradition, among the Aztecs, in Lamaism, and in tantric yoga, and they occurr frequently in the following dream series.

The series Jung had at his disposal consisted of more than a thousand dreams and visions from a young man with a scientific background of an unusually high level. The latter did not include familiarity with the comparative symbol historical material Jung drew upon.

For the book, Jung used only examples from the first four hundred dreams and visions, corresponding to the first ten months' analysis. To avoid the objection that he had influenced the dreams, Jung had one of his pupils, a woman doctor who at the time was "a beginner" in analytic psychology, take over observation of the material for five months. Then followed three months in which the dreamer himself observed his dreams. Only the last forty-five dreams in this series did he have while he was with Jung, and then Jung made no interpretations of the material worth mentioning. The series is excerpted here, with Jung's comments summarized.

As mentioned, Jung normally insisted that dreams be interpreted in a context of associations and placed in connection with the dreamer's concrete life situation. This he deliberately waived in the case in question. Instead he had the series be the context, so that the symbols in the individual dream were seen in relation to their occurrence otherwise. He justified his actions by insisting the dreams formed "a coherent series in the course of which the meaning gradually unfolds more or less of its own accord."

The dreamer's contribution to the process consisted exclusively in his giving it attention, writing down the dreams and visions, and developing them in his imagination. Attentiveness to the process was so necessary because otherwise the unconscious could "send wave upon wave to the consciousness" without any result being produced.

1. Dream: *The dreamer is at a social gathering. On leaving, he puts on a stranger's hat instead of his own.*

Jung explained the hat symbol historically as a sort of leading idea that brings the dreamer's thoughts (the head) to their common denominator, "under one head," which the dreamer submits to. The parallel was drawn to Gustav Meyrink's novel *The Golem,* in which the hero borrows the hat of a wizard (Athanasius Pernath) and thereby shares his attributes. The wizard for his part stands for the unconscious. The interpretation was reinforced by the thirty-fifth dream in the series, where an actor strikes a hat against a wall so that it is transformed into a mandala symbol.

2. Dream: *The dreamer is going on a railway journey, and by standing in front of the window he blocks the view for his fellow passengers. He must get out of their way.*

The train trip is a symbol of the inner journey: the process is beginning to move. The passengers are understood as unconscious content that wants to come into the light, that is to say the consciousness—already illustrating Jung's nuclear idea that the unconscious itself strives to come forth into the consciousness.

3. Hypnagogic visual impression: *By the seashore. The sea breaks into the land, flooding everything. Then the dreamer is sitting on a lonely island.*

The sea is the symbol of the collective unconscious. While the unconscious in the preceding dream was merely insistent, it now inundates the dreamer. Such invasions have something uncanny about them. They are irrational and incomprehensible, Jung wrote, and lead to isolation. Contact with others is disturbed, and energy flows into the unconscious. The vision very likely points ahead—four hundred dreams and visions in ten months is overwhelming.

4. Dream: *The dreamer is surrounded by a throng of vague female forms. A voice within him says, "First I must get away from Father."*

Here it is the anima showing up on the inner stage. The man who turns inward and isolates himself is flooded by the feminine. The father is seen as symbol of the traditional patriarchal and rationalistic intellectual outlook that the dreamer must abandon.

5. Vision: *A snake describes a circle around the dreamer, who stands rooted to the ground like a tree.*

The dreamer draws a magic circle around himself—a mandala symbol. The encircling snake is also reminiscent of the alchemical symbol Uroboros, the serpent devouring its own tail.

6. Vision: *The veiled figure of a woman seated on a stair.*

The unknown woman is an anima figure. The stair played a symbolic role in rites of initiation—initiation into religious mysteries such as the Isis mysteries. The Isis mysteries culminated with the initiate being crowned as Helios, the sun. In alchemy this sun identification is known as *solificatio* and corresponds to the mystic concept of "illumination," a beholding or comprehension of the highest order. Jung estimated that the psychic potentiality the vision reflected lay immensely remote from the dreamer's consciousness at the moment in question.

In describing the dream series, Jung was very attentive to how the encounter with the symbols got them to develop and transmute, so that one had the impression of an advancing process. A flower the dreamer finds by the wayside is connected with an alchemical symbol, "the golden flower," and in the next dream the dreamer finds coins that just like the golden flower are round and made of gold. In the ensuing vision a skull is transformed into a red ball, seen as precursor of a globe in the succeeding vision. On the globe, a woman is standing, worshipping the sun. The sun and gold are related symbols in alchemy.

In a prefatory phase with twenty-two dreams and visions, Jung found six mandala symbols. There appeared in the continued series a particular wholeness and development symbolism that would not have been understandable without reference to alchemy. For example: *Many people are present. They are all walking to the left around a square. The dreamer is not in the center but to one side.* The dream has a parallel in those mandalas that consist of both a circle and a square, and in alchemy where the squaring of the circle symbolizes working toward psychic wholeness, as it appears in the text *Rosarium Philosophorum*: "Make a circle of a man and woman and extract the square of this and of the square a triangle. Make a circle and you will have the philosophers' stone."

In later dreams in the series the circle appears as a clock, as a circle with a midpoint, as a target for target practice, as a clock that works like a perpetual-motion machine, as a round table, as bowls, and so forth. At about the same time, squares begin appearing, in the form of quadrangles or gardens with a fountain in the center. Somewhat later the square appears in connection with a circular movement: people walking around in a square; a magical ceremony (transformation of animals into human beings) takes place in a square room in whose corners are serpents, and people are circling around the four corners; the dreamer drives in a taxi around a square plaza; a square prison cell; an empty square that rotates; etc. In other dreams the circle is described by rotary movement, for example by four children carrying a "dark ring" walking in a circle. The circle also appears in combination with quaternity, as a silver key with four nuts on the four cardinal points, or as a table with four chairs. The center appears to be strongly emphasized. It is symbolized by an egg in the center of a ring; by a star consisting of a platoon of soldiers; by a star that rotates in a circle in which the four cardinal points represent the four seasons; by a pole; by a gemstone; and so on.

Jung found that the dreams contained an increasing number of mandalas. Dividing the four hundred dreams into eight groups of fifty each gave:

I	6 mandalas		V	11 mandalas	
II	4	_	VI	11	_
III	2	_	VII	11	_
IV	9	_	VIII	17	_

Jung described in addition many other symbols for the Self than the ones mentioned here. The dream series concluded with a vision that was "an impression of the most sublime harmony":

> There is a vertical and a horizontal circle, having a common center. This is the world clock. It is supported by the black bird. The vertical circle is a blue disc with a white border divided into $4 \times 8 = 32$ partitions. A pointer rotates upon it.
>
> The horizontal circle consists of four colors. On it stand four little men with pendulums; round about it is laid the ring that was once dark and is now golden (formerly carried by the children [in an earlier dream]).
>
> The "clock" has three rhythms or pulses:
>
> The small pulse: The pointer on the blue vertical disc advances by $1/32$.
>
> The middle pulse: One complete revolution of the pointer. At the same time the horizontal circle advances by $1/32$.

The great pulse: Thirty-two middle pulses are equal to one revolution of the golden ring.

Jung found that the vision recapitulated "all the foregoing dreams' intimations. It seems to denote an attempt at establishing a meaningful whole, consisting of the earlier fragmentary symbols that then were characterized as circle, ball, square, rotation, clock, star, cross, quaternity, etc."

Jung saw the dream as expressing a restoration of harmony in the unconscious, and ascertained that in his life the man actually realized the great potentialities the dreams testified to. It turns out that the dreamer was the renowned nuclear physicist Wolfgang Pauli.

Practical Application of Alchemical Symbolism

What made alchemy especially attractive to Jung was that the practitioners of this hermetic heretical art were individualists who often worked in isolation. Most religious-historical material takes form collectively and is transmitted in codified form, and this means that individual religious experiences—visions, dreams, revelations—are whittled down so they don't offend the tradition. In Jung's conception the imagination of the alchemists was far freer and their material closer to dreams.

Both the above dream series and Jung's later alchemical studies are a rich catalog of ideas that can be used for gaining entry to inaccessible dreams, such as the following dream from one of my own clients: *I go into a chemist's shop where I am to buy some green rejuvenation pills, which are called Vitali something or other.* In dream number fourteen in *Psychology and Alchemy*, we find a parallel: *The dreamer goes into a chemist's shop with his father. Valuable things can be got there quite cheap, above all a special water. His father tells him about the country the water comes from. Afterward he crosses the Rubicon by train.*

The traditional chemist's shop was seen by Jung as the last remnant of the alchemical laboratory, and the special water is compared with the alchemists' *aqua nostra non vulga* (our not-vulgar water) and *aqua permanens* (the eternal water)—that is, a kind of life-giving, eternally rejuvenating water in the unconscious. According to this reference, my client's dream could be seen as an attempt by the unconscious at a renewal and a rejuvenation of his mode of experiencing. (This doesn't necessarily mean he wanted to stay artificially young in the physical sense, the way a neo-Freudian would interpret the dream.)

One of my analysands, a forty-year-old woman, dreamed: *I'm walking around with a beaker of boiling water. Some children are playing underfoot, and I'm in danger of dropping the scalding water.* Jung saw the hermetically sealed retort of the alchemists, which was to be kept boiling over a low and constant flame, as a symbolic instruction as to how one best relates to working with the unconscious. The flame under the retort is the necessary emotionality, or passion, without which you get nowhere. The airtight vessel corresponds to not blabbing to all and sundry about the inner work, and to not blowing off emotional steam, but on the contrary by preserving the inner intensity to supply energy to the transformation process.

As water is the symbol for the unconscious, the above dream can be seen as expressing the woman's way of relating to the unconscious. The fact is that for reasons of ambition, the woman was eager to fire up under the inner process. But the unconscious, the water in the open (!) beaker, is already at the boiling point. The children are unprocessed childish sides that can be injured because they don't know how cautiously the high-intensity contents of the unconscious are to be treated.

JUNGIAN DREAMWORK

According to Jung, dreams can be triggered in part by conscious impressions from daily life and in part by independent creative processes in the unconscious. This gives rise to two different ways of working with dreams: (1) processing current situations in daily life and (2) process-oriented dreamwork.

Processing Current Situations

Here we are speaking of continuous work with the dreams' commentary on concrete problems of daily life, such as the man who tried to drink "a single beer."

Analytical therapy can last from two to five years. One is therefore persistently confronted with the same basic conflicts. Specific types of mother and father figures and particular ways of reacting to them appear, and specific types of shadow and anima/animus figures turn out to be predominant. The dreamer can on the one hand see these figures as parts of himself, and on the other place them in reference to his relationship to the physical world here and now. In that way a transformation of attitudes, experiences, and actions becomes possible.

This practical, down-to-earth side of Jungian analysis also came to expression when Jung trained his pupils. He tried to get them to boil a dream's meaning down to a single sentence, to something simple and graspable that the dreamer could work with until the next session. Jung understood that the dream is extremely complex and virtually inexhaustible of meaning.

Process-Oriented Dreamwork

Here the norm is long-term work with dreams, where instead of here-and-now concrete changes, the aim is a more receptively perceived development of the inner growth processes.

In the normal extroverted Western individual, an extraordinary amount of energy is bound to the consciousness and lived out in the physical world. But when the inner processes need be activated, it is a matter of moving the energy from the consciousness down into the unconscious. Therefore it is important not to talk indiscriminately about what is taking place, as it could lead to a hit-or-miss discharge of emotional energy. The inner transforming images should not be acted out directly in the physical world, but should provide fuel for the inner individuational process. To work on this level is quite difficult. It presupposes a talent for introversion and the capacity for sustaining psychic tension without always having to have immediate and definite results.

Writing Down Dreams

Jung recommended to his clients that they write down their dreams, furnish them with associations and other notes, and as far as possible interpret them themselves. This is in contrast to the Freudian therapy, where you do not write the dreams down because it can detract from the spontaneity of the experience. Jung believed that by writing down dreams, not only has the dreamer followed the inner process to its full length, but he can also go back and see contexts that previously were drowned out in the mass of the material. This practice increases the potential for experiencing a personality development as something that takes place outside the therapy room. It also contains some pitfalls that we will discuss.

Imagination Work in Jung

For Jung, imaginative activity was an important part of working with dreams and the unconscious generally. Just being able to differ from the inner images, to not identify with them but to "regard them with the spiritual eye" was inspiring and could set off a process.

Around 1916, in connection with his own self-therapy, Jung began developing a special technique that he called *active imagination*, which he described in a series of dissertations up to 1933. A thorough and accurate elucidation of the method was made by the Swiss Jungian analyst A. N. Amman. Among others who have described this technique are M.-L. von Franz, Barbara Hannah, Verena Kast, and Jane Dallet. It is now standard technique in Jungian psychology.

The starting point for an active imagination can be any psychic representation whatever that you are motivated to work with. An inner image, a fantasy, a mood, an emotion, a melody you can't shake off—a dream. In practical terms, first the imaginer tries to "empty" himself of extraneous thoughts; then he directs his attention onto the chosen fantasy image, which he tries to fix for as long as possible. It is bound to change at some point on account of a spontaneous association. This is the crucial moment: now the imaginer himself enters into the image, deals with, questions, and reacts in fantasy at the imagined situations that arise.

Active imagination is applied particularly when there are aspects of the dream that seem incomprehensible, or when the ending, the dream's *resolution*, is confused. As an example of this, Amman mentions the following dream from a successful businessman: *He is driving and is stopped by the police. On foot he walks through the town and comes to a poor neighborhood. It is cold and rainy outside. A woman comes toward him; she is poorly dressed, woebegone, and careworn. In passing he receives the impression that she wants to say something to him but dares not.* In active imagination the businessman decides to follow after her. *He lightly touches her arm and inquires: "Pardon me, wasn't there something you wished to say to me?"* She says yes, and together they go inside a nearby restaurant. There she starts telling about her distress.*

Until then the businessman hadn't wanted to admit his feelings, but through active imagination it became possible for him to realize that he himself badly suffered from melancholy and depressiveness, and that this was in stark contrast to the way he experienced himself, which was bound to his outward success.

In Jung the concept of active imagination also covers drawing, painting, and modeling inner images; it can be extended to all kinds of creative activity. He ascribed to the fantasies the same symbolic value and the same function as the dreams, and they could be interpreted according for the same rules.

Another of Amman's examples is the following: *In a dream we find ourselves in a room with four doors. The dreamer has gone through the fourth door without any fruitful result.* The therapist now has a fantasy of going through another door. He emerges in a garden where a woman is sitting; he begins a conversation. He now tells the client what he has experienced and suggests that he try another of the unopened doors.

Active imagination opposed to other techniques

According to Amman, active imagination differs from most other forms of meditation by not having any standardized program or goal. There are no specific relaxation exercises or postures, and you do not guide the experience into fixed paths as in chakra meditation, imaginary journeys, and guided daydreams. As Jung saw it, what was central was that you didn't elevate yourself above the problems but rather entered into them.

Jung found inspiration for his new technique first and foremost in the alchemists' free meditation on chemical processes, and in Eskimo shamans' encounters with helping spirits. The difference is that in Jungian dreamwork the ego plays a much more prominent role. The actively intervening relationship to the unconscious emphasizes the ethical aspect.

Applicability

Jung recommended active imagination in the later phases of an analysis, when the technique could intensify the encounter with the unconscious and speed up the individuation process. He thought, too, that it increased the analysand's independence in working with him- or herself. If there were too many dreams, Jung might suggest replacing dreams with a suitable number of active imaginings, and conversely if there were too few dreams he found that active imagination stimulated the unconscious to produce more dreams. Moreover, it turned out to be useful for eliciting emotions and for an immediate processing of powerful affects.

The method is not useful if the ego is weak, or if there is already a preponderance of unconscious, such as in latent psychoses and borderline psychoses. And the provoking of negative demonic content that the imaginer can't control is to be avoided as much as possible. With Jung's method you also avoid implicating real persons in the fantasies, so it won't have the effect of black magic.

THE NEO-JUNGIANS (THE JUNGIAN SCHOOLS)

Since the 1940s, Jung's analytical psychology has established itself as a professional discipline with an international association and worldwide training institutions. Scientific discussion is conducted at international congresses, in professional journals of high caliber, and as fertile literature from specialized publishers. At the same time there has been a sorting out of diverging attitudes toward theory and practice, with a corresponding alignment of approaches to dreams.

The English analytical psychologist Andrew Samuels distinguishes between three schools: a classical, an archetypal, and a developmental. The *classical* school works more on explaining Jung's theories and expanding on them than criticizing them or conceptually setting new bounds. It puts the main emphasis on the individuation process and its symbolism, on imagination work, and on interpreting dreams. Adhering closely to this is the *archetypal* school, which to an even greater degree than Jung is concerned with the independent activity of the unconscious and the inner images' character of reality. Or as the principal figure in this school, James Hillman, puts it, "Images are the only reality we perceive directly." The third school is the *developmental*. It puts the main weight on analyzing childhood conflicts and on transference/countertransference, while dreams, archetypes, and individuation are secondary—which brings criticism upon the classical school for doing too little for these areas.

An important addition of the developmental school regarding our subject is that not only should dreams be analyzed, but so should the way they are exchanged between client and therapist. It reflects the transference-countertransference relationship and thus also psychological patterns in the client's childhood that it is important to work through. For example, does the client flood the analyst with dreams so he fights a loosing battle to get through the material? Does he hand in dreams like a gift intended to mollify a severe imaginary parent figure? Does he, perhaps in the case of classical analysis, discuss his recorded dreams with notes and footnotes, with literary distance, and without deep emotional experience? Such attitudes always have a *psychodynamic* significance. Samuels sums up this methodical attitude with the words "analyze the patient, not the dream."

There doesn't have to be a conflict, however, between using dreams and concentrated work with transference and/or countertransference, as all dreams have aspects that can be interpreted within the same point of view. This has already been described in chapter 1, on Freud and the neo-Freudians. Beyond that, a certain influence from experience-oriented therapies and other dream-theory movements can be traced, though without it having occasioned more thoroughgoing revisions of Jung's theory of dreams.

THE CLASSICAL SCHOOL AND DREAMS

In contrast to Freud, Jung never assembled a thoroughly worked out account of his view of dreams and their interpretations. Often a lack is felt of truly illustrative examples, or else ideas have been tossed out and never supported by sufficient material. His successors C. A. Meyer, James A. Hall, and Mary Ann Mattoon have each in their way assembled and systematized the dream interpretation rules and modes of working that emerge from Jung's works. Jung and the classical school have thus contributed to some of the most important dream research.

Dreams and the Personal Myth

In the childhood-dreams seminar, Jung mentioned a dream that a girl had at the age of three which "remained as if branded into her consciousness." *A long streak of comets passes across the earth. The earth is set afire, and people perish in this fire; the child then hears the hideous screams of the people and wakes up.* Jung regarded it as a cosmic dream and marveled that a child could concern herself with an archaic notion of the end of the world by fire. A dream interpreter in antiquity would have said that this cosmic connectedness would one day be of import for society as a whole, and Jung added: "Such persons are destined for humanity. Such a collective role speaks against a happy family life. You are torn apart by the collective purpose."

Jung used this and other childhood dreams that pointed ahead to a later incvitability to illustrate the view that "a child unconsciously already has an adult psychology. The individual is already from birth, or perhaps even before birth, what he will later become."

To elucidate his views Jung used concepts like personal purpose, individual destiny, and personal myth. Often this myth was first revealed through extensive work with the individual's growth potentials. Jung's own myth and his mode of working with dreams has been treated by Marie-Louise von Franz in the book *Jung, His Myth in Our Time.*

As an example of an entire life's dreams experienced as the expression of a personal purpose I will use material from the American analyst Sheila Moon, who has published a series of 235 of her own dreams spread out over a period of nearly fifty years. The dream series is especially exciting because the central figure is a woman who in spite of extreme inner difficulties accomplishes many positive things in her life. In one place Sheila Moon says that in her younger years she was close to being schizoid, and graphological and chiromantic analyses describe her as extremely split.

Sheila Moon's mother had lost her first child and was therefore anxious and overprotective. Moon relates very little about her childhood, and rarely mentions it in connection with her dreams. Throughout her life her relations with the opposite sex were difficult. When she was a very young woman she had no success with men and instead became a striver, competing on male-dominated society's terms. She did not marry or have children but instead realized her gifts as a Jungian analyst, teacher, and author. Her life is portrayed primarily through the dreams.

The first dream she relates she calls the Terrible Dream. It came at a time when she was studying for her premedical examinations. The dream begins when she hurtles to the ground from the top of a skyscraper under construction. Afterward she finds herself in a gloomy medieval city. There she meets a redheaded and hotheaded acquaintance and says to him: *"I am dead and in hell and I belong to the Devil." He laughs. I ask him angrily if he has any matches. He nods and pulls from his pocket a handful of kitchen matches. I breathe on them. They burst into flames. Everyone at the table flees and I am left utterly alone in a deserted square in a deserted city.*

Sheila Moon woke up in terror. Later that same night she dreams:

> *I am in bed, in a cell-like room on an upper floor. It is night. Suddenly I realize that a man in a black cape (or wings) is standing on my windowsill. Half afraid and half magnetized, I arise in my nightgown and step onto the windowsill. He stretches out his caped arms (or wings) and folds them around me. Together we step out into the nothingness of the night sky, flying above the earth.*

After the dream, Moon plunged into an anxious depression, recovering only with the help of an understanding Anglican priest. Later she saw the dream as a disclosure of sides in her that were "light years from my conception of myself" as a patient, adaptable, and cautious girl; in the dreams she is practically in league with the devil, or in psychological terms she is possessed by an archetype. The blackness of the cape can stand for the unconscious and depression. The total isolation in the dream corresponds to a profound loneliness she was to live with for many years. The dream testifies to an overwhelming lack of contact and might suggest impending psychosis.

On the other hand, the dream's distinctive symbolism reveals particular potentialities. A Jungian interpretation of the first dream emphasizes Moon's magical abilities. The dreamer's breath can be a symbol of a living intellectual principle, and the fire she lights can symbolize consciousness, transformation, and enthusiasm. The second dream, where she is capable of flying with the help of her animus, signifies on one hand spiritual abilities, on the other the lack of a ground connection. What is interesting in our context is that Jung, in *Psychology and Alchemy*, draws comparisons between the devil and the god Mercury, who was the motive force in the individuation process. So in spite of all the horror, the dream can be evidence of a tendency toward individuation—if the dreamer receives the proper guidance.

It took eight years after this dream before Sheila Moon had the courage to enter therapy. Here was her initial dream: *An evil male figure plotted to destroy a second male figure; an evil male figure tried to find me in a haunted house; an evil brother figure tried to shoot me.* The greatest problem is still "my inner negative masculinity, which tried to destroy me." During this time she was inwardly in an anxious and fearful chaotic state; outwardly she managed work and examinations under inhuman conditions.

Nor is the solution to the dream ideal, for on the inner level she had to kill one side of herself in order to survive. Gradually, however, there did come dreams that showed she was capable of getting the better of the destructive animus that threatened from within. For example, *I am beating about me with a huge club. I knock one young man to the floor.*

With the role men her own age play in the dreams, it is no wonder she had few male friends and that her most intimate relationship was with a man she considered too old to marry.

Moon's dreams in this period (age thirty to thirty-three) continued to be filled with "wars, bombings, falling into abysses, seeing terrible disasters from machines, being lost, disorganized, ostracized. Dreams also gave me some helpers—such as frogs, seahorses, pools with purple fish and grottoes with lovely animals in them, dogs of all kinds and colors and sizes, tiny lambs, tiny wild mice in trees, and one startling dream with a black boy, a black fish, a black hummingbird, all friends." Her ability to fly appeared again in the dreams, when *a lovely male reindeer comes up to me. I climb on his back. He takes my hand (the right one) in his mouth, biting it very gently and smiling at me. I know that if my hand isn't there we can't fly. Then we rise from the street, into air.* Moon interprets the reindeer as a symbol of "imaginative and creative thought, to which I had to surrender my conscious control, my right hand."

Gradually work begins on Moon's feminine side, which also is much battered. She dreams about being crippled for life, and about a stepmother who recommends that she commit suicide.

But while for fifty years the terrible is permitted to come forth and certain negative themes recur (particularly the destructively masculine), the dreams become more and more spacious. More animals appear, as do flowers, music, cosmic and religious themes, and individuation symbolism. The theme of struggle is sometimes replaced by sorrow and weeping. Most of all there appear more women with widely different qualities. The transformation of the feminine in the dreams appears to culminate when Moon is in her mid-forties, particularly under the influence of Jung's wife, Emma Jung, whom Moon consulted during an extended period in Zurich. Her initial dream for this meeting:

> *I wake up in my hut at night. My little black dog is asleep on the floor, and she is bathed in a glowing light. I am afraid and full of awe; I wonder at what can be the source of this mysterious light. I get up and look out the window of my hut. A strongly luminous full moon (larger than in reality) is in the night sky, and its light is covering the dog. On the full moon's face is an awe-inspiring sign of Capricorn: sharp and in clear black.*

In most cultures the night has feminine symbolic meaning, and even though the Self and the moon can be perceived as both feminine and masculine, it is so within a feminine sphere as "the night's son." The awe-inspiring moon was interpreted by Moon and Emma Jung as symbolizing "matriarchal consciousness." And the dream appears to denote a turning point, as the spiritually creative principle in previous dreams had been predominantly masculine. (The moon is naturally a play on Sheila Moon's name.)

Judging from the dream series, the time spent in Zurich and especially the meetings with Emma Jung were a breakthrough; Moon's dreams seem more harmonious than at any other time in her life. Of course, everyday existence in America was different than the atmosphere in Zurich, and this led to some problems. For instance, Moon's analyst in the United States, the prominent Jungian Gerhard Adler, grasped her difficulty in giving free play to her feelings. A dream from this period (forty-nine to fifty-two years) is as follows:

In a mountain landscape with many women, among them myself and several of my female friends. We are making our laborious way up a mountain slope when a gigantic cosmic hand, a Quan Yin hand, white, wonderfully graceful, reaches down from above and appears to lift the skin gently from all of the women, who bent forward are slogging upwards. One and all they must meet their fate alone and naked.

In Jungian terms the cosmic hand in the dream is a boundary-exceeding symbol, and the molting can be seen to symbolize psychic transformation. But we can also see Moon and her girlfriends portrayed as strivers and sloggers—her old model for fleeing from herself. She is depicted as terribly exposed—literally skinned alive—and the dream goes on to explicitly describe the transformation process in even more drastic images, such as being put to death in cruel ways.

Moon survived this psychic crisis and went on to a career as an analyst, a teacher, and an author of Jungian literature. She also revealed a creative side: she wrote a novel for children, which was followed by more. Her studies and self-analysis continued, and at age fifty-four she dreamed: *Harry and I are then in our bedroom, and soon are involved in beautiful and exciting lovemaking. He is tender and passionate and creative, as is our love.*

Out of 235 dreams, this is the only one directly about a successful act of love. Harry was Sheila Moon's closest friend through many years. And so the dream shows for the first and also the last time her readiness to completely give herself outwardly, and perhaps inwardly, to unify inner masculine and feminine antitheses.

In the next dream she relates that *I am the king. A young man threatens me with his sword and I kill him with a dagger.* And in the next: *I meet and talk with a nun.* That the king is threatened Moon sees as expressing that her Self—her inner King—has gotten out of balance. And the encounter with the nun told her that "essentially I am a solitary—not in a neurotic but in a creative sense."

Another dream from this period that she regards as important reads: *I am going some place where the most important person is to be Madame Farnetta, the internationally known medium.* Friends with a knowledge of parapsychology told her that she herself had "psychic" abilities and perhaps was clairvoyant, and I would say that the dreams also point in that direction. But even though she can not dismiss parapsychology as such, she has an aversion to trying out her own abilities of that kind. Instead she regards

Madame Farnetta as a feminine side that could be a medium between the conscious and the unconscious.

Again there comes a period of crisis, and again she manages to channel the energy. A beautiful dream testifies to new inner balance: *I had to make a great mandala, octagonal in shape. Light flowed from it in sweeping rays. I knew it had to do with clues to understanding the mysteries of the Book of the Zohar.*

At fifty-seven years old, Moon continues to deal with many unsolved problems in her life and her dreams. But in general the dream potentials, as I see it, are even more manifold. Only now does she experience being pregnant in the dreams, and correspondingly there is renewed unfolding of creativity and spiritual growth.

Something very moving, both for herself and the reader, is that at age sixty she dreams about a sick woman in her twenties who turns out to be a brilliant painter—and that Moon now looks after her. Thirty years earlier she had dreamed about a young woman who was an invalid for life.

Moon experiences plenty of horrible dreams peopled with repulsive animus figures, along with periods of almost total collapse. But each time she comes away with a consciousness that seems more spacious, more self-accepting, and with an impressive courageous impulse to give herself to the world, for better or worse. As a seventy-year-old she experiences her life as a series of questions and problems that were posed at birth. She feels she has succeeded in answering some of these questions, even if "there are ancestral ghosts still haunting." Still, to the extent that she has held out and found herself, she feels that she has given something to the world.

What is striking in a lifelong dream series like Sheila Moon's is the continuity of the themes, and the persistence with which the dreamer holds on to certain unresolved conflicts while able to take readings of how certain themes develop during ongoing psychological work. Just consider first being overwhelmed by, then the struggle with, and the subsequent—at least temporary—erotic reconciliation with the masculine side, experienced as the demonic bat-winged man's transformation into a flying male reindeer. (The moon dream was preceded, and after an interval of years succeeded, by mythological dreams having the theme of "feminine initiation.")

Jung thought that the experience of having a personal myth, in spite of vital conflicts and human suffering, could provide a feeling of meaningfulness, as the myth isn't an egocentric role but on the contrary a sharing in the common destiny. And so Jungian dream analysis acquires a collective function that extends beyond individual happiness. Thus, a person's problems are not merely the attempts of a psycho-infantile neurotic to become an adult, but rather, by sharing what's in her mind, the fate of all humanity can invest her life and hardships with a dignity that in itself helps give them meaning.

DREAMS OF CALL

Jung's idea of individual destiny has a parallel in the concept of religious vocation. For Jung, becoming a personality was in itself a vocation. Only the person who consciously assents to the inner voice becomes a personality. Jung found myriad examples of cases where, at the critical moment, "a 'saving' thought, a vision, an 'inner voice' came with an irresistible power of conviction and gave life a new direction."

This subject has been taken up by the Jungians Paul D. Huss, who described the symbolism in biblical experiences of *call*, and John Romig Johnson, who investigated the corollary between dreams and vocation in American clergymen and seminary students.

The idea of call is bound up with the choosing of an occupation, and Johnson's study attempted to throw light on whether the choice of profession was an "ego trip" or was significantly attributable to the personality as a whole. He examined new and old dreams from eight would-be and fifty-two ordained clergymen. Of these, twenty-one had been in therapy of some sort. The dreams fell into three main groups: (1) dreams decreeing fate, that is, the choice of calling wasn't free and deliberate but was dictated from within; (2) dreams of crises and crossroads; and (3) dreams of conflict between inner need and social role.

Johnson's conclusion was that dreams generally show a connection between inner psychic need ("the inner myth") and outer professional choice. He found that a number of the persons in his material had dreams in which an inner voice had urged them to enter the ministry. These dreams were the most intense and archetypal, and had been of decisive importance for the life of the person in question.

An American bishop who had not been in therapy sent Johnson a series of dreams of call. A grandfather and two sons of the bishop were clergymen. The three dreams cited below must have been particularly important, as they were recalled many years later.

The first was a nightmare from age six. In it the dreamer saw that *a fearsome priest was in the pulpit preaching and wildly gesticulating. He is told that eventually he would have to do the same thing. He said he wanted no part of it.* That same year some older boys persuaded him to break windows in the school. He steadfastly denied it, even under vigorous interrogation. That night he dreamed

> *the family went to the country to visit my grandparents. In the middle of the main street in the village where they lived stood a towering monument, more like a great triumphal arch but not massive and hulking. Hanging down from the center of the arch was a huge lamp or brazier which was full of a blazing and smoking fire. As I stood there looking at this thing I was filled with an overwhelming emotion—not fear or terror, but something whose name I didn't learn until at the seminary: the feeling of the numinous. It seemed not so much a mere object as a sensitive, receptive being which was aware of my presence. I asked, "What is that?" and someone, maybe my father, replied: "It's the truth." I looked around as we walked on and saw more objects like it in the distance. The next day I confessed everything.*

As an adult, while in his last semester at the theological seminary, he had the following dream:

> *I walked around for a while in a crowd that was milling about like shoppers in a bazaar. And then I saw something which looked like a big black cannonball rolling about on the walks. It neither rolled into people nor ruined the flowers—it was simply moving with violent force and was in the middle of everything. And then I happened to think that this ball was—not Christ—but the icon of Christ. I followed it for a while, then I was distracted and turned away to a little record store. They had a lot of records which I wanted: Bach cantatas, organ music, and so forth. Then I realized I didn't have time to browse nor any money to buy with, and I woke up.*

Another of the bishop's dreams refers to the prophet Isaiah's vocation. The dreamer sees the Lord sitting on a high throne in the temple surrounded by seraphim. The temple is filled with smoke and Isaiah cries out: "Woe is me! for I am undone; for I am a man of unclean lips. . . . Then flew one of the seraphim unto me, having a live coal in his hand, which he had taken with the tongs from off the altar: and he touched my mouth with it, and said, Lo, this hath touched thy lips; and thine iniquity is taken away, and thy sin purged." Thereafter Isaiah becomes the Lord's harbinger to the iniquitous.

I would like to call attention to one of the parallels. The word *grandfather* means literally "great father," just as God is "the great Father"; also, the dream takes place on the main street in the town, where the "great father's" church (temple) is located. The rest of the material nearly speaks for itself.

In the dream from the seminary, the icon of Christ is represented as a black cannonball. It can hardly be an image the dreamer has from his theological schooling. However, Johnson points out the black sphere's meaning as a symbol for the self. Moreover, the dream did indeed get him to feel that he should follow this potent Christ image without any digressions. (We will return to this dream, in a different context, in chapter 4.)

Johnson describes another series of dreams that shows a disparity between the inner call and the ministry:

> *I go back to my first parish church and find it badly dilapidated. The churchyard is also overgrown with weeds. A young man in khaki pants and old shoes is now the acting priest. Some senile old Methodist parson or other is preaching. The young priest uses chocolate cookies for the Communion bread. The whole thing makes me very sad.*

It is understandable that the clergyman is saddened, but unlike Jesus he does not chase the hucksters out of the temple.

Johnson points out that being obsessed by an archetype, which is what a call is, can be less than ideal. It can be negative and degenerate into psychosis, fanaticism, and abuse. This position agrees completely with Jung's thinking; suffice it to recall certain modern historical wars of obsession.

Another form of experience of vocation comes to expression in so-called shaman dreams, which have parallels in the magico-religious traditions of primitive peoples. *Shamanism* is treated in detail by the religious historian Mircea Eliade. Parallels to modern people's dreams have been touched on by Johnson and by the Jung-inspired Jes Bertelsen.

A shaman is a medicine man and magician who is familiar with the healing forces in himself, in others, and in nature. He knows the techniques of ecstasy and can initiate others in them. Shaman dreams have garnered renewed interest in a period when parapsychology is flourishing. (But, as we saw in the case of Sheila Moon, paranormal abilities in dreams can also be understood symbolically as the ability to make contact between the conscious and the unconscious.)

Among primitive peoples the election of shamans often takes place on the basis of dreams, visions, and trance states. Jes Bertelsen, along with other Jungians, has found that such dreams occur in modern people. He takes them to be indications of a vocation as physician or mind-healer. According to Bertelsen, a shaman dream will contain an encounter with an inner guide (a helping spirit) and will point to the technique that the person must use in order to get in contact with his abilities. He takes such dreams more literally than Johnson does, and refers to the fact that among primitive peoples such a dream is an epoch-making experience. "The rest of the man's life is decided in the dream, in that with it he is one of the elected." (Similar traditions are found among yogis where a nonliving guru reveals himself in a dream.) Examples include a dream from a Mongolian shaman and the writer's own inaugural dream as a Jungian analyst.

The Mongolian shaman was initiated in a dream he had while lying in his sickbed. In the dream he is visited by a small slender woman. She says:

> "I am the 'ayami,' your ancestors, the Shamans. I taught them shamaning. Now I am going to teach you. The old shamans have died off, and there is no one to heal people. You are to become a shaman."
>
> Next she said: "I love you. I have no husband now, you will be my husband and I shall be a wife unto you. I shall give you assistant spirits. You are to heal with their aid, and I shall teach and help you myself. Food will come to us from the people."
>
> I felt dismayed and tried to resist. Then she said: "If you will not obey me so much the worse for you. I shall kill you."
>
> She has been coming to me ever since, and I sleep with her as with my own wife, but we have no children.

The election to shamanism is often preceded by a grave illness or crisis. It is a typical motif to make resistance (compare Jonah in the whale's belly), and the call is then experienced as an unavoidable inner compulsion. A no would kill the dreamer.

I was in Jungian analysis for several years. After having been out of analysis for a couple of years, the idea occurred to me to become a therapist. At the time I was undergoing a crisis during which I considered myself a failure. In the final dream before the first hour of analysis

I stood in front of a mirror. I was going to comb my hair. A girl let me go first and stood in back of me looking in the mirror. She asked if I wanted to get in contact with "the living god." A fantastic being was made out in the mirror as in a fog. At first I declined because it was demanding and hideous, even though it was also wonderful. Then I decided to stay. The girl, who at first looked rather drab, now appeared more and more beautiful. She offered me some pills with a "dislocating" effect. I was to look after a four-year-old very sensitive boy. He was to be put in a state of alternately eerie solitude (like being alone in empty space) and marvelous experience—like a state of slumber with dreams. I held him and talked to him and he accepted it. The girl and I were to lie on the floor and perform yoga exercises and other relaxing things. We were nude.

At the time I had no great theoretical knowledge and knew nothing about dreams of call. It was the first time in my own thousands of dreams that a "living god" had appeared; nor had I ever had a dream with such detailed instruction in ecstatic, that is to say shamanistic, techniques.

An example of a famous artist's dream of vocation comes from the painter Marc Chagall. At age twenty he journeyed from Vitebsk to St. Petersburg to become a painter. Being a Jew, he could not leave his ghetto without permission, and as he failed the examinations at a noted art school, he lost his permit. Wanted by the police and living in extreme poverty, he became a success anyway. During that period he had a dream which bolstered his conviction that he was destined to be a painter:

I am in a large room. Standing in the corner is a single bed and I am lying in it. It grows dark. Suddenly the ceiling opens and a winged being descends amid noise and radiance and fills the room with movement and clouds. A rustle of wings dragging. I think: an angel. I can't open my eyes. It's too light, too refulgent. After having pawed through everything, the angel ascends and leaves the room through the crack in the ceiling, taking all of the radiant and heavenly with it. It grows dark again and I wake up.

DREAM AND DEATH

The psychology of the death experience has in recent years been the object of great attention, investigated in particular by authors such as Kübler-Ross,

Raymond Moody, and Stanislav Grof. All of them found that it is important for the dying person to go into the death experience consciously instead of repressing it. Also, certain typical experiences and ideas turn out to arise spontaneously in dying persons and in near-death experiences.

Jung emphasized that the unconscious psyche seems to be little interested in the body's death. Rather, it reacts as if psychic life and the individuation process will continue after death, and as though it prepares the ego for profound transformation processes. It is the Jungians first and foremost who have concerned themselves with how the unconscious, via dreams, relates to the death process. Among those who have made important contributions to these studies are Jane Wheelwright, Barbara Hannah, and Edvard Edinger, who have interpreted the running dream series of dying patients.

The largest overall investigation to date was undertaken by Marie-Louise von Franz in her book *On Dreams and Death*, which supports and expands on Jung's conception. She thinks that the dying person's dreams prepare the consciousness for extensive transformations and for a continuation of the life process. She found that the dreams of the dying contained an unusual quantity of archetypal images, and that they showed thematic and structural similarities to the teachings of different religions concerning life after death. She found parallels especially in alchemy and the Egyptian death rituals, as the Christian religion has no elaborate notions about the death process and life-on-Earth after death.

An objection to the Jungian interest in death dreams is that notions about life after death are wish fulfillment. However, not only does Jungian theory discredit the manipulation of dreams by the wishful ego, but dreams can announce an impending death in the most brutal and undesirable way, as in this dream from a fifty-two-year-old man who was to be operated on for cancer of the bladder: *An ambulance came to take him to the hospital. The driver got out, opened the back door, and there lay—a white coffin.* It turned out that the cancer had spread and he died soon afterward.

While Christians regard resurrection and life after death strictly as divine graces, according to von Franz both dreams and the alchemical and Egyptian parallels represent it in such a way that the individual, while alive, can work on preparing an incorruptible body which survives death. In the religions of the East this can take place through meditation. A sixty-one-year-old Swiss cavalry officer dreamed four weeks prior to a fatal heart attack: *He was once again in the officers' school. There an old corporal named Adam took him down into the cellar of the barracks. (Adam) opened a lead door and the dreamer recoiled with a shudder. In front of him the carcass of a horse lay on its back, completely decomposed and emanating an awful corpse smell.*

Von Franz interpreted Adam as "the mortal Adam." The horse was construed as the death of the body. And finally, "lead" and lead sarcophagi played an essential role in Egyptian death rituals. The dreams of the dying are generally more comforting, however. Von Franz found that death dreams are very archetypal and intense, and that their symbolism in principle is indistinguishable from individuation dreams. But often there are details or a special atmosphere about the dreams that make differentiation possible. With individuation dreams, the contents are interpreted on the subjective level. With death dreams they are understood on the objective level.

In "primitive" religions, death and resurrection are often given vegetation symbolism, by grain growing from a dead body, or by a tree. A man in his forties, after being informed that he had terminal cancer, dreamed the following: *He saw a green, half-high, not-yet-ripe wheatfield. A herd of cattle had broken into the field and trampled down and destroyed everything in it. Then a voice from above called out: "Everything seems to be destroyed, but from the roots under the earth the wheat will grow again."*

Among numerous mythological parallels, von Franz mentions that in Egyptian mythology the corn can stand for "something psychic which exists beyond life and death." A seventy-five-year-old dying man dreams:

> *I see an old, gnarled tree high up on a steep bluff. It is only half rooted in the earth, the remainder of the roots reaching into the empty air. . . . Then it becomes separated from the earth altogether, loses its support, and falls. My heart misses a beat. But then something wonderful happens: the tree floats, it does not fall, it floats. Where to? Into the sea? I do not know.*

Von Franz sees the dream as an image of life's continuation, reminiscent of German legends in which people came from trees and became trees again.

Another important motif is the death wedding. The following dream comes from a fifty-two-year-old doctor in the best of health who approached von Franz with the wish to become an analyst. It was his initial dream:

> *He was going to the funeral of some man who had been indifferent to him; he was just walking with a lot of people in a funeral cortege. In a little square place in the town, where there was a green lawn, the cortege stopped. On the lawn there was a pyre and the bearers laid the coffin on*

it and set fire to it. The dreamer watched without any special feelings. When the flames sprang up, the lid of the coffin suddenly opened and fell off. Out of the coffin sprang a most beautiful woman; she opened her arms and went toward the dreamer. He too opened his arms to embrace her and woke up with a feeling of indescribable bliss.

The dream considerably alarmed von Franz, particularly the feeling of indescribable bliss. Subsequently, however, the man had normal dreams. After one year he broke off the analysis temporarily in order to journey home. There he contracted influenza, which rapidly worsened, and he died—on the way to the hospital—of a heart attack.

Von Franz sees the insignificant man in the coffin as an image of the dreamer's earthly body—a parallel to the decomposing horse in the cavalry officer's dream—and the grassy quadrangle as a symbol for the Self. The grass can be a resurrection symbol, and the fire symbolizes transformation. The beautiful woman who gets out of the coffin is the man's anima. In alchemy an "annealing" of the dead body could lead to an *extractio animae*, when the soul leaves the body. Overall, the dream can be understood as meaning that a higher aspect of the man's anima becomes intermediary for the beyond.

The death anima (and animus) can appear demonically in both myths and dream. An unhappily married man dreamed shortly before his death that he was in church and was to be wed to his wife again. *Suddenly a most beautiful Gypsy woman broke into the ceremony, fettered the parson with ropes, and began to drag him away. At the same time she looked with flaming eyes at the dreamer and said, "And with you I will soon lose my patience."* The dreamer died soon afterward. The parson in the dream is a sympathetic but depressive and conventional man. Von Franz considers the dream to mean that the dreamer's anima is infuriated that he suppressed his emotions and love life.

Death experiences thus seem to be influenced by how life is lived. It might be interesting to see in the previous cases whether earlier dreams, while simultaneously prophesying death, also gave other information. Had the man whose anima got up out of a coffin buried that side of himself in life? And if the cavalry officer's horse stood for the body, had he during his time at officers' school denied bodily needs? This would jibe with the widespread religious notion that one must in death atone for what one didn't do in life.

Von Franz also found dreams that apparently said it was important for the dreamer to reach a higher level of development before he or she died. She saw many correspondences between death motifs in dreams and the religions. Frequently occurring in the dying person's dreams and ideations are gems and diamonds, such as in a younger woman who shortly before dying dreamed that *she found a black bird in a lake. Its eye was a brightly shining diamond.* In alchemy the diamond is an image for the Self, as a nucleus in the personality that cannot—even after death—be destroyed. Von Franz saw the dead bird as symbolizing the body's liberated life spirit.

Among other archetypal death motifs are: separation of the elements as in myths of creation, passages or journeys, crossing water, crossing a bridge with one or more companions, restoring the deceased to a soul or afterlife body, weighing the soul, a court of law, returning to another form of existence, or reincarnation. Also enacted in dreams: struggling with a ghastly intruder, walking through fire and water, and sacrificing and processing the old body in a way that can have parallels to Egyptian mummification rituals.

Von Franz refused to interpret these dreams as exclusively subjective, inner occurrences. She was borne out in this conception of many parapsychological phenomena being connected to the death experience (see "States conducive to psi phenomena," chapter 8). And so this type of dream was for her "a symbolic statement about another reality from which we are separated by a mysterious and dangerous barrier."

Even if you reject the possibility of a life after death, it doesn't shake the clinical experience that persons who work with their death process and relate to the unconscious images become better able to reconcile themselves to death and to the life that remains to be lived.

PROBLEM SOLVING AND CREATIVITY IN DREAMS

After having been long and intensely preoccupied with finding the formula for benzene, the German chemist Kekulé von Stradonitz dreamed of *six shining sparks which danced around in a circle. They turned and twisted like snakes, whereupon one of the snakes grabbed hold of its own tail.*

Kekulé "awoke as if thunderstruck" and spent the rest of the night working on his formula. The formula he arrived at showed benzene as consisting of six molecules arranged in a ring. This was termed the greatest chemical discovery of the nineteenth century and the beginning of organic chemistry.

Robert Louis Stevenson deliberately used dreams when writing. He would work on a story for a few days and then let it lie. Some tiny creatures he called Brownies would appear in his dreams and continue writing the story.

That is how *Dr. Jekyll and Mr. Hyde* came into being. In Jungian terms the Brownies are autonomous complexes.

Marie-Louise von Franz, in the book *Creation Myth*, writes that "dreams are exceedingly interested in creativity"—which is also my own experience. Ordinarily, however, the "interest" doesn't reveal itself by dreams in and of themselves solving the problem, but by their commentary on the dreamer's attitude to the creative process.

In her book von Franz tells about a dream Jung had when he was laboring on one of his major works, *Psychological Types*. He had collected material for the book over many years. He wanted to write it in a rational and refined form so as to convince his opponents, but he couldn't manage the very comprehensive material. Then he had the following dream:

> *He saw in a port an enormous ship laden with goods which should now be pulled into port. Attached to the ship on a cord was a very elegant white horse, absolutely incapable of pulling in the ship, which was much too heavy! At this moment there came suddenly through the crowd an enormous redheaded giant who pushed everybody aside, took an axe and killed the white horse, took the rope and with one pull pulled the whole ship into port.*

After this dream, Jung got up at three o'clock every morning and wrote the whole thing down in a single rush of enthusiasm. The white horse, according to von Franz, represented his plan to write a refined, formal treatise, while the giant stood for the violent emotional engagement which made it possible to hammer such complicated material together.

On the other hand, dreams that apparently deal with creativity can in my experience reflect more general attitudes to life. For example, if a writer dreams: *I have gotten an idea for my new book. It must be simpler and simultaneously more penetrating than my earlier books*, you can't know in advance whether the dream is literally telling about a book he is to begin work on, or whether it is using work with the book as symbolizing working with himself.

DREAM AND DEVELOPMENTAL PSYCHOLOGY

Three pioneers—the Israeli Erich Neumann, the British Michael Fordham, and the German Hans Dieckmann—have contributed separately to Jungian psychology in ways that are relevant for our view of dreams.

Within the Jungian developmental school, Fordham found that the classical Jungians in Zurich were one-sided in concentrating on laying open the mythological aspects of their client material, and to an excessive degree regarded it in light of a preexisting model. In London the interest was increasingly in the client's emotionally charged relation to the therapist, that is, *transference*, and it was felt that Jung's contribution to understanding childhood development was deficient. There were similar developments in Germany.

Fordham thought that Jung, in presenting the client material, neglected the personal and the relationship to the external world, as "living organisms as a whole, and man in particular, cannot be considered only in isolation but are designed to adapt themselves to the objects in the external world."

Jung described individuation in the second half of life. The theory of a corresponding process in the first half of life was established by Erich Neumann. He set up a model of phases in the child's development as Freud had done, but on an archetypal basis. Moreover, he described a number of phases in the woman's psychological development that fill gaps in and supplement the Jungian concept of individuation.

DREAM AND FEMALE DEVELOPMENT

Neumann found that the development of the female consciousness—in a patriarchal society, no less—is essentially different from that of the male. He described seven typical development phases:

1. The self-preserving phase
2. The intrusion of the masculine
3. The self-relinquishment phase
4. Captivity in the patriarchy
5. The encounter with the man
6. The self-submission phase
7. The self-realization phase

As empirical background for his schematic outline, Neuman cited studies of normal and neurotic women in the Western world. In the classical Jungian manner, he compared this material with cross-cultural studies of mythological and ethnological symbolism.

In her book *Kvindelighed i vækst* (Growing womanliness), the Danish

Jungian Pia Skogemann has specified the age corresponding to each phase, and traced the symbolism in dreams of Danish women of today. The *self-preserving phase* occurs during the first three years of the girl's life. Here she is enveloped in a feminine world of experience. The mother is her most important outward contact. Inwardly, development is controlled by the mother archetype. Even the father is experienced as a kind of mother.

The adult woman who is stuck in—is fixed in—the self-preserving phase can't acknowledge other values than the feminine, and when she enters into alliance with a partner what denotes her relations with him will be that he shall beget her children and bring home the food. But who he is as a person and a man doesn't much interest her.

From age three to six there occurs an "intrusion of the masculine" corresponding to Freud's "female oedipal phase." While Freud was concerned with the outer fascination for, infatuation with, and fear of the personal father, Neumann was interested in the inside of the problem, namely the girl's nascent fascination with and fear of her own inner masculinity. This phase forms the background for the experience of the spiritual/religious in fusion with the sexual/erotic "in an ecstatic orgiastic way." But the woman who is stuck in this phase can't confront the man "as an equal partner. What fascinates her is the alien, the unfamiliar, overwhelming in an impersonal masculine form."

Skogemann gives the following dream example from a girl aged one and three-quarter years: *Get afraid of the man . . . played ball in the garden with [maternal] Grandma . . . the man is lying in the grass sleeping . . . Get so afraid if the man wakes up.* The maternal Grandma was understood as symbolizing the Great Mother. The man in the dream was the masculine side of the girl who was not awakened.

A dream from a rather young woman that reflects the *intrusion of the masculine* in an impersonal and overwhelming form follows:

> I am lying in a room in my bed beneath the window. A violent storm is raging outside. We are still only at its edge; farther away it has hurricane force. Later I go out in the storm and see how the roofs of the houses are shaken and lifted. People are worried about the damage it can cause. But somehow or other I'm not afraid of the storm.

Skogemann interprets: "The storm is an archetypal symbol of the male spirit. In ancient Greek the wind is called *pneuma* and means "breath" or "spirit.""

In the biblical account of the creation, God breathed into man's nostrils the breath of life. The wind's force in this dream says something about how strongly the masculine spirit has been activated."

The *self-relinquishing phase* Skogemann sees as the point where the woman starts as a well-behaved little girl in the primary classes of the patriarchal school, while *captivity in the patriarchy* corresponds to adolescence, where the girl gladly identifies with masculine society's feminine ideals and "concentrates on making an impression on the boys." She thereby has difficulty in realizing her own masculinity. Neumann speaks of harem psychology. The woman can also identify with the masculine side so she begins to compete with the man on male society's terms.

A living-through of these three phases was demonstrated by Skogemann in the following dream from an adult woman the night after a conversation about feminine roles:

Together with some other women I come sailing to an island. Soon after we have come ashore we are attacked and captured by some men. I am led inside a room where the leader is, a tall black-haired broadshouldered man. He is sitting on a broad couch where a woman sprawls provocatively. She has reddish hair and is wearing a semitransparent black dress like a negligee. I am placed somewhere else on the couch. Something takes place between the two. He raises her up as in an embrace, but suddenly puts his arm around her throat and strangles her. I look away, but half suspecting that a similar fate is intended for me.

In the *encounter with the man* "she [the woman] becomes capable of confronting the man erotically and spiritually." In the *self-submission phase* "she integrates her animus," and self-realization corresponds to "the encounter with the Self," "the wise woman" in herself.

The dream fragment just mentioned continues with the woman not being raped, but giving herself in intercourse with the man and confiding to him that she enjoys it. Later the woman, who on the island is a captive, is released and the dreamer enters into a relationship of equality with the man who originally wanted to rape her.

Skogemann saw the dream as "a textbook example of the living through of the specified phases in psychological development."

DREAM AND MALE DEVELOPMENT

Jung's typical male client came to him around mid-life, when he had achieved all that he was to achieve careerwise and familywise and his evolvement now led him into contact with his shadow, his inner femininity, and the Self. In my book *The Feminine in the Man*, I have pointed out that Jung's description of male individuation doesn't always cover the situation of modern man. He often enters Jungian analysis at a younger age, he isn't nearly as frozen in his social and family roles, and in our society he can't wait till he is forty to commit himself to the feminine and his emotions.

This is also reflected in the dreams, where he often must start with processing his relationship to the feminine and only then face up to a shadow problem. Frequently the feminine is experienced as dominating. He might dream that *he is made to scrub toilets in a prison camp run by women,* or that *he is bowled over by a women's basis group,* he is *the servant of a nasty brothel madam* or *the pupil of a strict schoolmistress,* or he is *still living at home with his mother,* and so on.

The state such dreams depict I have called *captivity in the matriarchy.* One could also speak of a feminine superego, in contrast to Freud's and Jung's time when this role was usually the domain of a severe paternal authority. Often the modern man defends himself from this captivity by living in a sterile universe lacking a ground connection and naturalness. This state, which I have called the *patriarchal expedient,* can come to expression in a dream like the following:

> *I was in a place I didn't know, sitting on a cornice with my back to a sixth-story attic window. I was freezing and afraid of falling, or rather I was afraid of giving in to an urge to let myself fall. Down in the front courtyard came my sister and my parents. I shouted to my sister to come up and open the window so I could get in, which she did. It was an unpleasant wait.*

The house can symbolize the personality, so the dream shows that the dreamer isn't in contact with himself. And it is characteristic that it is the sister, the feminine in the man, who must help him out of his dilemma. Again, the process begins with a working through of the feminine.

As every man's experience of the feminine starts with the relation to the mother, an activation of the feminine image, if it goes deep enough, will lead back to the earliest phases of life. For orientation in the regressive process I have found Erich Neumann's childhood development phases useful. According to Neumann, during the first three or four years of life the child goes through the following phases (these apply to both boys and girls):

1. A cosmic anonymous phase
2. A vegetative phase
3. An animal phase
4. A magical phallic phase
5. A magical warlike phase

The *cosmic* and the *vegetative* phases extend from the fetal state into the second year of life. A positive cosmic symbolism can be revealed in feelings of unity with all things, of oceanic flowing away in the infinite, transcendence of space and time, cosmic dimensions, and so forth, and negatively in images of cosmic desolation, of being sucked out through a hole in the universe, etc. In the later vegetative phase we have images of verdant landscapes, lush meadows, sheltering trees, and bubbling springs. If drought, scorched or barren landscapes, heaps of ruins, and radioactive or polluted areas predominate in the dreams, then there is likelihood of disturbances in this phase.

The *animal phase* corresponds to the age when the child begins to distance his- or herself from the mother but is still closely bound to her and lives mainly by instinct. With the onset of this phase, more animals appear in the dreams.

In the *magical phases* the child's experience of reality is, as the name says, magical. But the ego is more developed and it moves away from the maternal dominance toward a paternal guidance. Neumann calls this the "transition from matriarchy to patriarchy."

The following dream fragments reflect these phases in a youngish male client:

The cosmic phase: *It was as if time and space were canceled, and I rushed weightless at terrific speed through the most wonderful strata of patterns and colors. It was reminiscent of the section "Beyond the infinite" in the film* 2001.

The vegetative phase: He dreams that his mother is dead, and then about "the perfect hostess": *her womb was symbolized in the drawing by a blooming forest floor, a lush flowery meadow, and a sea floor.*

The animal phase: *Lise and I walked up on a knoll together. A whole lot of horses were standing grazing. Suddenly a huge stallion came leaping down toward me.*

In a dream of the magical phase he meets a Gypsy woman, who *looked at me with hypnotic force. I got dizzy. I was taken up to my friend Leif's apartment in a kind of hallucination. Up there I had to go through a weird and painful ritual. I don't remember the details, but among other things they took the measurements of my erect penis. Afterward I was allowed to rest. A man of thirty-five or forty put his arm around me. He was handsome and masculine in a short sun-colored Greek tunic.* In other words, the magical side of the feminine leads the man from female and mother dominance to masculine initiation.

And finally, the magical warlike phase: *I was at a wedding in the snob style my parents fancy. Suddenly I discovered that I was dancing with a loaded revolver in my pocket.* Until that moment, the dreamer had never been armed in his dreams.

WAKING EGO AND DREAM EGO

Freud described the ego as the part of the id that has been modified by the external world. It represents logical thinking and common sense. Jung defined it as the center of consciousness; that is, a psychic instance with a connection to all the contents of consciousness. Subsequent dream theorists have drawn attention to the constant emotional energy discharge connected with the experience of being one and the same person, of being a specific mind in a specific body: the feeling of ego.

While Jung and especially Freud concerned themselves with dream contents that contrasted with the ego and consciousness, Hans Dieckmann insisted that the ego experience by and large occurred at the transition from the waking state to dream. He was struck by the fact that out of fifty thousand dreams from his clients, plus his own dreams, plus from an inquiry of colleagues, it appeared extremely seldom that the ego identified itself with animals or things. In his own practice he came across only two instances of that sort. One was a female narcotics addict who dreamed she was a flower that could walk; the other was a female psychotic who dreamed she was a vase.

As a principal rule, Dieckmann found that "the dream ego employs the same defense formations, experiences the same feelings and emotions as it would have experienced in a similar situation in reality too. The ego complex possesses, with certain limitations, a far greater measure of consistency and stability, and is largely occupied with maintaining its function even in the dream ego."

According to Dieckmann, the similarity between the waking ego's and the dream ego's mode of experiencing doesn't exclude the occurrence of a certain relaxation of the ego in dreams or contact with repressed contents or new psychic potentialities. On the basis of the preserved ego feeling, the dream ego appears to be well suited to making a bridge to the unconscious contents. It is that part of the dream with which the dreamer can immediately identify himself.

Dieckmann has proposed that at the beginning of a dream analysis, concentration be focused on the dream ego's mode of experiencing and the parallels it has in practical living (objective level). If you buttress the continuity between dream ego and waking ego, the patient becomes more secure at going into the unfamiliar and incomprehensible inner world. Dieckmann stresses that most patients have an ego weakness, and that it is a question of first strengthening the ego and then confronting it with the unconscious content.

In dream series it is possible to follow for long periods how the ego relates to specific recurring complexes. One example Dieckmann gives is from a thirty-five-year-old severely aggression-inhibited policeman. The man came under treatment after being assaulted. Even though he was armed, the policeman did nothing to defend himself, and he constantly dreamed about dangerous aggressive conflict situations that he solved by flight. After fifty-four hours of analysis he dreamed that he climbed up in a tree with two others. Three young girls come walking by and *they looked up and said: "There hang three corpses." Then the Devil appeared, touched us, and we burst into flames. Immediately we were again on the ground again dressed as cavaliers, like Dumas's* Three Musketeers, *and we went off with the girls.*

After this dream "the dream ego began in decisive ways to identify itself with the aggressive and sexual impulses which emerged from the unconscious." Both in school and as a policeman the dreamer had frequently been goaded and made the clown. But a change in this was heralded by the following dream: *I met a colleague in the street who began to tease and taunt me. I became so furious that we began to fight. An older man passed by and said to him: "Aren't you ashamed, you, a strong man attacking someone your inferior?" I told the man to stop interfering, and then we went on fighting.* The policeman, who was very much henpecked, got things balanced out somewhat at home, and his sexual life with the wife improved.

Dream theory explains that the aggressive and sexual impulses which emerge from the unconscious are replaced with ego feelings. In more Jungian terms, you could say that the ego acquires more energy and becomes more spacious by integrating parts of the shadow.

Another example from Dieckmann is described in chapter 1 (in "Dreams and psychosexual development"). It was the case of a twenty-nine-year-old housewife whose "oral inhibition" was canceled in the course of an analysis. This corresponded to a decisive attitude change in the woman's waking life.

What makes the dream ego so important is that it is at once different from and experienced as identical with the waking ego. Dieckmann explains it going from Freud and his colleague Paul Federn: Energy that in the waking state is invested in the body and is used for external doings, during the dream process streams to the dream ego. It is (still in Freudian imagery) like a general who has been given a shortened line of defense and who now obtains greatly augmented battle forces with which to meet the unconscious. Simultaneously, some of the energy is thought to stream to the unconscious and activate potential transformation processes. The dream ego thereby becomes a creative ego connecting the strange dream events with the waking ego.

An important rule of thumb Dieckmann found is that "only when the dream ego registers a problem can the problem enter the person's consciousness." Accordingly, "the analyst who loses patience here and uses behavioral directives receives for his pains symptom displacements, strengthened resistance, or the breaking off of the analysis."

THE DREAM AS ITS OWN WORLD

An independent view of dreams is also met with in James Hillman, who is a representative of the school Andrew Samuels called the archetypal. Hillman saw dreams primarily as a (under)world in themselves, with their own objectives.

Counter to ordinary interpretation procedure, where dream language is translated into the language of consciousness, Hillman proposes that the language of consciousness be translated into dream language, and he calls for "dreamwork on the ego," to see through its "reality." Even though Hillman in terms of method doesn't introduce anything new, his viewpoint is interesting in underscoring the experience that dreams contain something different in kind from consciousness, something fundamentally untranslatable into the latter's language.

INVESTIGATIONS OF DREAM ARCHETYPICALITY

As mentioned, Jung distinguished several types of dreams, some "everyday" and others archetypal, all according to whether they are connected to the personal unconscious or to the collective unconscious. The Israeli analyst Yehezkiel Kluger examined dreams from 218 persons aged eighteen to sixty-two years, the majority of whom were students who had not been in analysis, in order to see whether it was possible to substantiate statistically Jung's dream theory.

Archetypes, according to Jung, are not merely structurally determined but also have dynamic attributes. Jung frequently describes archetypal dreams as more "energy laden" than everyday dreams. If his theories are correct, the following would be predictable:

Dreams that leave a particularly vivid impression on the dreamer contain a greater quantity of archetypal material than everyday dreams. Early childhood dreams are more archetypal than everyday dreams. This is due to the child not having formed so firm an ego. The small child lives more in the collective unconscious than does the adult, who has lived longer and accumulated a correspondingly greater amount of personally unconscious experiences. People in depth analysis have more archetypal dreams than people who are not in analysis, going from the assumption that the collective unconscious is activated during analysis.

As for whether a dream is an archetype, Kluger, in accord with Jung's theory, used the following criteria:

1. Mythological parallel
2. Heightened affect
3. Nonrational imagery or behavior
4. Remoteness from "everydayness"

1. The *mythological parallel* can be qualified by degrees:

A close parallel: *In an oriental temple, giant statues come to life. One says, "The time has come for the battle between Good and Evil for which I have waited for eternity." A tremendous battle ensues between them.* Parallels are Zoroastrianism and the Book of Revelation.

A moderate parallel: *The dreamer slips something into her husband's pocket—his penis, wrapped in Pliofilm. She then has mixed feelings, having accomplished her mission but wondering how it would be able to be put back in use again.* Parallels include the myths of Isis and Osiris, and of Attis and Cybele, with their themes of restoring a dismembered phallus and the problem of its subsequent effectiveness.

A distant parallel: *Flying anywhere I wanted, rising and descending at will.* Parallel: the myth of Icarus.

2. *Affect* can be both positive and negative and vary on the positive side from ecstasy and delight to the pleasant and satisfying, and on the negative side from panic and horror to annoyance. Finally, affect can be entirely absent. But the greater the intensity, the more likelihood of the dream being archetypal.

3. *Nonrationality* is scored according to adherence to natural law and likelihood of occurrence in the dreamer's everyday life. Rational and not unlikely: riding a bicycle, hitting a stone, and falling off. Rational/possible: being chased, caught, and raped. Nonrational: a fish with teeth chasing the dreamer out of a pool and across the fields; a man with a lion's head.

4. Departures from *"everydayness"* adhere closely (in reverse order) to the progression from rational to nonrational.

These categories can then be scored. The use of statistical methods in dream analysis was introduced by Calvin Hall, who will be discussed in the next chapter. In the present connection, Kluger found that it was possible to differentiate with considerable statistical certainty between two types of dreams: archetypal and everyday.

Childhood dreams were 56 percent archetypal. Old dreams that were still recalled vividly were 65 percent archetypal. But dreams that were included solely because they were the most recent were only 20 percent archetypal. In contrast, 38 percent of the most recent dreams of analysands were archetypal.

P. A. Faber, another Jungian analyst, using Kluger's method investigated whether the percentage of archetypal dreams changed in persons who experienced "altered states of consciousness" in the course of the day, either in the form of active imagination over an extended period or through meditation. For this "imagination experiment," twenty-six first-year psychology students were chosen, none of whom had practiced meditation, were actively interested in dreams, or had used *psychopharmaca*, or psychedelic drugs. The participants were selected using an array of psychological tests so that all fell within the "psychological norm." Matched subjects were randomly assigned to either an experimental or a control group.

The subjects recorded their dreams immediately upon awakening during three twenty-one-day periods, so insight into the dreams' character was obtained before, during, and after the work with waking fantasy. During the induction phase, in which the fantasy activity was initiated, the experimental subjects reported to a sleep laboratory for six induced fantasy sessions. After being put in a state of relaxation, they commenced fantasy activity with a neutral, unstructured image such as a meadow, and within minutes invariably began to relate phenomena varying from extremely bizarre, irrational, affect-laden dreamlike imagery on the one hand, to rather bland yet dreamlike sequences closely related to everyday life situations on the other.

The imagery sequences were in no way guided, were entirely spontaneous, and were broken off after fifteen to ninety minutes on the wish of the participants themselves. The control group reported at similar intervals to fantasy sessions, where they listened passively to standardized tape-recorded accounts of fantasy. In order to avoid efforts to live up to expectations, at no stage were the true hypotheses of the experiment disclosed to the subjects.

The dreams of both groups were assessed by Kluger's scale for archetypicality. Prior to the fantasy sessions, barely 4 percent of both groups' dreams were of archetypal character. (The figure is considerably less than Kluger's, which could indicate that the scorers were more stringent in their assessment of archetypicality.) The dreams of the control group maintained this level throughout the experiment. In the fantasy phase the experimental group had no less than 48 percent archetypal dreams, and in the subsequent three-week phase 18 percent.

As according to Jung it is the archetypal dreams that further the independent growth processes, the studies suggest that Jung is correct that fantasy techniques potentially intensify the encounter with the unconscious and accelerate the individuation process. An investigation of the dreams of trained Yoga meditators which Faber carried out also indicated that meditation increases the quantity of archetypal dreams.

Critics of Jungian analysis often claim that Jungian clients dream Jungianly, that is archetypally, because they acquire a conscious familiarity with Jung's theories. This is not corroborated by the Jungians' own clinical experience, here substantiated by Kluger's and Faber's studies, where other factors altogether stimulated the dreams' archetypicality. Naturally, mythological material can be built into dreams via the day's residues that originate in a conscious familiarity, but a covering of that sort would—at least by the trained Jungian dream interpreters I have known—be recognized as such.

THE ROLE OF THE DREAM INTERPRETER

Jung regarded his method as *phenomenological*; that is, the interpreter must not meet up with any preconceived theory. The unconscious content is susceptible to various interpretations, and the dreamer's assent is a condition of the interpretation's being considered valid.

Jung himself "lived with his dreams, carried them around with him, and asked them questions." For example, he got a determining idea for understanding his own childhood dream fifty years later. His interpretations, like Freud's, were creative and undogmatic.

In Jungian analysis the dream is brought to the analyst usually written down. This means that dream interpretation also belongs outside the therapy situation, and that the analysand can gradually acquire a certain skill in interpreting on his own dreams. He or she can go back and find typical motifs and transformations of them and participate in a development process. A pitfall here is that the text is treated like a piece of comparative literature.

In a book on dream interpretation (*Träume*), Marie-Louise von Franz emphasizes self-knowledge as the crucial concept in Jung's dream theory. By this is meant "understanding" and "insight" in a sense which has by later Jungians been regarded as too one-sidedly intellectual. Dieckmann has described how dreams can be used as a shield against coming in contact with the most pressing problems when therapy drowns in "interesting" comments on the dreamer's interpretation. What is needed is more than theoretical discussion: there is question of a rebellion where segments of the younger generation have felt frustrated in therapy with "the old guys," and have begun incorporating more body- and experience-oriented techniques into their therapy.

Like Freud's successors, the neo-Jungians have concerned themselves systematically with the countertransference aspect in dream interpretation. In the late 1960s, Dieckmann and a small group of Berlin analysts investigated countertransference processes in the analysis of archetypal dreams; they found that an inner supervision in the analyst enhances the empathy with the client and the therapy's effectiveness (see "Dream and parapsychology in the therapy situation," chapter 8).

THE FUNCTION OF DREAMS IN JUNG

When becoming conversant with the way in which Jung and successors have worked with dreams, it isn't hard to understand why Jung thought that "the most promising and fruitful hypothesis" was to regard the function of dreams as compensatory—that is, as expedient corrections of the consciousness. According to the Jungians' observations, dreams prepare the mind for solving problems great and small. It appears that features of a "personal myth" can already be read from early childhood dreams, and if dream series are examined during shorter or longer periods the dreams appear to constantly update the consciousness with overlooked items that could further development.

A large number of Jungian analysts confirm that again and again they meet with archetypal themes in dreams which clients couldn't have known in advance, and that such themes have special developmental significance. And both clinical experience and statistical studies show that dreams' archetypicality is not due to influence from the analyst. Seen from this point of view, the unconscious, everything considered, has knowledge that is superior to the conscious.

Meanwhile, the practical application of the *compensation* concept is accompanied by a number of problems. While an older generation of Jungians—such as von Franz, Adler, and, in Denmark, Jolande Jacoby and Eigil Nyborg—has described it as a relatively simple and understandable entity, more modern successors like James A. Hall, Hans Dieckmann, C. A. Meyer, James Hillman, and Andrew Samuels have found it more and more unwieldy. So far no one has incorporated this perception in a general dream theory. James A. Hall found the concept too complex for him to exhaust in his textbook on dream analysis. C. A. Meyer found it problematical that the compensation complex presupposes an instance in the unconscious which is informed precisely as to what is right for the dreamer; and he proposed that also the conscious be viewed as compensatory in relation to the unconscious.

Let us look at what it is that makes the compensation concept so perplexing.

Dreams that Contrast the Conscious

It goes without saying that if dreams brought nothing which contrasted the conscious, they would be totally uninteresting. There is also general agreement that we can learn from most dreams something about ourselves we didn't know. But the older Jungians appear to have stressed the contrasting element in dreams to an excessive degree.

Jung's close coworkers C. A. Meyer and von Franz have understood Jung as meaning that dreams basically have two functions:

1. *A complementary function:* The dream supplements too narrow or too-little-appreciated conscious contents.

2. *A compensatory function:* The dream more purposefully balances out a one-sidedness in the conscious.

Von Franz understands the *complementary function* thus: "Someone or other has met a partner of the opposite sex and has only felt a passing sympathy, and then at night dreams about a passionate love scene with this person." Or a person who has been given a reprimand at work gets revenge by hauling the boss over the coals in a dream.

By *compensation* is meant not only a filling of gaps in the conscious, but also a more purposeful and expedient function. The dream shows a way. We are speaking of a didactic attitude in the unconscious.

Jung mentions that a man who had very lofty notions about his own moral superiority dreams about *a drunken vagabond wallowing in a roadside ditch. The dreamer says (in the dream): "It is terrible to see how deeply a man can fall."* Jung thought the dream was trying to puncture the man's swollen self-regard.

Examples from other Jungians could be a man who dreams that he loses his teeth, interpreted as meaning that he *shall* lose his teeth, in a metaphoric sense, because he is overly aggressive, or a forty-year-old man who dreams that *he sees himself in his girlfriend's mirror as much older than in reality.* Here the aim of the unconscious would be to make him older because his relationship to the girlfriend "was characterized by a much too youthful attitude for his age."

As a general rule for this mechanism, Jung argued that "the more one-sided the conscious performance is, and the further away from the optimum life potentials it leads, the sooner the possibility will arise of there appearing lifelike dreams of strongly contrasting but appropriately compensating contents, as expression for the individual's psychological automatic control." But the more systematized recent inquiry reveals that this contrast function is not the most predominant in the dream (see "Dreams reflect lifestyle," chapter 3), and that the more one-sided the conscious is, the more one-sided will be the dream. If contents appear in the dream that contrast with the conscious, then the dream ego relates to them with pretty much the same defense mechanisms as the waking ego, or as Dieckmann puts it: "The

dream of the sexually inhibited philistine who, lying in bed beside his un-
attractive spouse of long-standing, dreams of orgies with other girls does *not*
exist in reality."

If we regard archetypal dreams as the most contrasting and compensatory,
our experience is that statistically they make up a rather small part of the
mass of dream material. They do not appear as a one-sidedness in the ego
as Jung asserts, but on the contrary open up, for example, in free imagination, relaxation of the ego in analysis, or with the conscious being jogged
more or less out of its usual course.

On the face of it I don't think it is so difficult to explain the above dreams
from a more modern view. According to Dieckmann's theory, the dreamer
from von Franz's example who has a passionate love scene would be very
close to acknowledging that he is infatuated, and the person who bawls the
boss out in a dream is close to being able to feel that he really *is* angry. Nor
can I, with regard to compensatory dreams, see the necessity in construing
the dream as a schoolteacher. Dreams in which the ego says about a vagabond that "it is terrible to see how deeply a human being can fall" after all
reflect very accurately that in the waking state the man is a sanctimonious
person who condemns others, and on the subjective level has himself a
vagabond shadow.

Again, a problem in connection with the compensation concept is that it
presupposes a theory as to what, when all is said and done, is appropriate
for the dreamer. Freud made his wish fulfillment so elastic that it couldn't
be contradicted by asserting that unpleasant dreams were manifestations of
masochistic tendencies; Jung could maintain that if you couldn't directly
see the compensation in the dream, then it had to be sought at a deeper
level. For example, if a person behaves self-destructively, it can't be certain
that the dreams were trying to brake the destructive tendencies. On the
contrary, they could be taking him to further extremes. But then the compensatory could, according to Jung, reside in that "it is apparently more
important to nature that one should have consciousness and understanding
than to avoid suffering." Regardless of whether profound wisdom is embedded in such an observation, it contributes to making the compensation concept so broad that it becomes unmanageable. In any case, it can't be applied
in practice unless the appropriateness be measured out from a frame of
reference that is dependent upon the interpreter's psychological schooling,
life experience, and philosophy.

Jung's remarks in *On the Nature of Dreams* indicate that if the conscious
exerts itself to the utmost in working with itself, and that if you "overestimate

the unconscious" and "shift important decisions and conclusions onto dreams, you will be correspondingly disappointed when the dreams become constantly more meaningless." Jung's successors therefore often emphasize that "dreams don't tell what you're supposed to do." Von Franz speaks of dreams becoming prankish and inscrutable when one doesn't venture to make a choice in a particular life situation and puts the responsibility on the dreams. Seen from this perspective, the conscious *is* compensatory in relation to the unconscious.

FREUD'S AND JUNG'S DREAM THEORIES COMPARED

Immediately it would appear as if Freud's and Jung's theories on dreams are two parallel universes that can never meet. Fundamentally they are at odds regarding the dream's nature, function, and interpretation. While Freud saw the dream's nature as veiling, Jung saw it as revealing. To Freud's wish fulfillment and sleep-preserving functions Jung juxtaposed compensation, and when it comes to interpretation, dreams appear to deal with widely diverging matters in the two systems. Let's examine these concepts one by one.

The Nature of Dreams

Freud's theory that *defense mechanisms* are instrumental to dream formation has been corroborated by Freud's successors, just as a number of observations by neo-Jungians substantiate Freud's theory. In Jungian theory the original psyche is unconscious—the collective unconscious and the archetypes. In the course of the child's development this is superposed on the personal unconscious, which has also been called the Freudian layer, and it is this layer that contains the defense mechanisms. You would therefore expect that when the defense mechanisms are undeveloped, relaxed, or have broken down, archetypal dreams and dreams with primitive drives predominate. This happens to be the case: Psychotics and borderline personalities have more archetypal dreams and more crude overt instinctual drives than nonpsychotics (see "Introduction," chapter 12). Childhood dreams are more archetypal than adult dreams. A general relaxation of the ego during free imagination gives archetypal dreams, and in long-term therapies that process the defense mechanisms there is also seen a progression through the personal unconscious down into archetypal layers.

It is therefore reasonable to assume that dreams from the personal unconscious sphere are influenced by defense mechanisms, and that in all dreams the dream ego brings along a part of its defenses. In his very last dissertation on dreams, Jung also acknowledged that the unconscious can be "distorted" and "biased" on account of repressions, so its "natural symbol producing" function becomes overlaid and distorted. Which is to say that the unconscious in such cases can't produce positively transforming and forward-pointing symbols. Jung did not amplify these reflections. We shall, however.

To include both a creative symbol function and defense mechanisms makes working with the individual dream more complicated, because you constantly have to assess whether the dream content or parts of it come from what Jung called the *objective psyche* or from the ego and the defense mechanisms. In the long run, though, you can better form a picture of the given dreamer's often stereotyped set of defense mechanisms and conversions of affects.

This doesn't mean that you can't do excellent therapy knowing only one side of the nature of dreams—this is actually corroborated by clinical experience. But it means that the Freudian dream interpreter overlooks developmental potentials which might remain untouched or which the client must seek support for elsewhere, and, as far as the Jungians are concerned, that certain defense mechanisms are copartners in all developmental stages. Of course, you can process them with other means than the dreams and still believe that it is the dreamwork exclusively which effects the changes. I have often seen that a newly resolved project, a creative activity, the commencement of a couple relationship, or a fundamental change of attitude is met by the unconscious with a constructive and archetypal initial dream. But soon afterward, when the new initiative is to be realized, punishment and anxiety dreams crowd up, which could be evidence that defense mechanisms don't readily permit a liberation of new life potentials.

A Freudian consideration of the initial dreams would here deprive them of the prospective aspect, while a Jungian conception of the anxiety dreams would indicate that the project could not be realized anyway. This flexible viewpoint could, for example, have been fruitful in connection with Sheila Moon's lifelong dream series. One of the culminating points was a dream in which she had a tender and passionate love scene with her friend Harry. The dream can be perceived Jungianly as a prospective dream, both as a possibility for realizing a close love relationship on the external level and for a new balance between masculine and feminine qualities in herself.

In the next dream, Moon relates, *I am the king. A young man threatens me with his sword and I kill him with a dagger*; and in the next, *I meet and talk with a nun.* As previously mentioned, that the king was threatened Moon sees as expressing that her Self (the king) is out of balance. And the meeting with the nun shows her that she essentially is "a solitary—not in a neurotic but in a creative sense."

These final dreams, as well, were regarded as prospective. But with our present knowledge such an interpretation is disputable. When the relationship to the masculine was such an extremely difficult thing for Moon, as we know it was, substantial psychoanalytical experience argues that the attempt at exceeding the limits hitherto would arouse anxiety and that defense mechanisms would be mobilized. The dreams could be perceived Freudianly as manifesting repression (she kills a man). The source of these defense mechanisms would be sought in childhood, and when Sheila Moon writes plainly and simply that the first four years of her life were good, this would also—and rightly—be seen as a defense. Someone with a harmonious childhood does not have such terrible dreams as Moon's. In no way does this exclude that via Jungian analysis Moon became a very developed, creative, and responsible person. Rather, she was helped along in regions of the psyche that are closed country to the Freudians.

The Function of Dreams

If we understand the compensatory function as a problem-solving tendency in the unconscious, at first sight it looks as though Freud and Jung are irreconcilable in their views. But it isn't that simple. The Jungians have been much preoccupied with the famous examples of problem solving and creativity in dreams found in the literature, as these substantiate Jungian theory. But Freud, as well, found so many well-documented cases that he thought the phenomenon as such was incontrovertible. He also thought that the significance of the conscious for artistic and intellectual work was less than is ordinarily assumed. But according to Freud, it is not dreamwork (condensation, displacement, and so forth) that is responsible for problem solving in the dream. "Preconsciousness" could do an important job in the waking state, and so it was this problem solving that in the sleeping state slipped through the censorship (see "Dream censorship," chapter 1).

As both parties acknowledged the existence of a nonconscious creativity, and that help was available for problem solving through dreams, one might think that the differences are mostly of theoretical interest. There is, however, an important difference in the interpretations. The Freudians take the famous chemist Kekulé von Stradonitz's dream about a snake that bites its own tail (see "Problem solving and creativity in dreams," above) as manifesting infantile instinctual wishes, while the Jungian interpretation fastens upon the fact that the dream *actually* had great creative significance.

Meanwhile, the neo-Freudians have, as mentioned, increasingly maintained that the function of dreams is the solving and integration of emotional problems, that they are constructive, and that they aim at adapting the individual to the surroundings. So just as recent investigations indicate that the Jungians must accept the important role of defense mechanisms in dream formation, it appears as if the Freudians have to accept problem solving, and with it compensatory tendencies in dreams. (Here it ought to be mentioned that compensation can be regarded as a variant of wish fulfillment, in that compensation implies psychologically the wish can be realized.)

While the "nature" of dreams basically is an abstract and theoretical entity, their function is, as Freud expressed it, tied up with the pragmatic question "What is dreaming good for?" In the cases of Freud and Jung it turns out that both are of more service to dreams than the theories permit. Freud's conception of the usefulness of dreams was rationalistic and materialistic and was early embedded in his theorizing. Jung developed his views throughout life. In the early works he compared the compensation concept with the physiological observation that if one organ, such as a kidney, is lost or its activity is reduced, this is compensated for by augmented function of the other organs. In later works the activity of dreams is described more psychologically, and at times metaphysically, as when Jung pronounced that "in dream the Self meditates on the earthly ego." Thus the dream's function is not always to be understood in terms of individual psychology but must also be seen in a broader collective or religious perspective. Which is to say that concepts like individual happiness or psychic "health" are sometimes subordinated to meaningfulness or "purpose" in a larger, perhaps cosmic or natural (ecological) context.

The Dream's Interpretation

As I mentioned in the conclusion of the chapter 1, dream analysis depends on the frames of reference that a given system of analysis permits. We saw how Erikson, going from a broader conception of life than Freud's, was able to find new layers of meaning in the latter's "Irma dream" without canceling Freud's original understanding. Freud understood the dream in the context of his desire for a career and traced it back to infantile sexual wishes, but Erikson demonstrated as well its connection to Freud's social relations. Another example from chapter 1 is Thorkild Vanggaard's analysand A, in whose dreams he saw clearly the elements that prevented A from without fear becoming a professor, while the "father dominated" classical Freudian theory didn't permit Vanggaard to see in them problems with the mother and the feminine. This does not contradict the relevance of the dream analyses, however. On the contrary. For precisely those aspects of the dreams Vanggaard couldn't see corresponded to problems in A that were *not* resolved.

The following is an example of a Freudian dream that could have been enriched by a Jungian analysis. Afterward we shall see Jungian dreams that could have benefited from a Freudian analysis. In *The Interpretation of Dreams*, Freud analyzes a dream from a young chemist:

> *He was supposed to be making phenyl-magnesium-bromide. He saw the apparatus with particular distinctness, but had substituted himself for the magnesium. He now found himself in a singularly unstable state. He kept on saying to himself: "This is all right, things are working, my feet are beginning to dissolve already, my knees are getting soft." Then he put out his hands and felt his feet. Meanwhile (how, he could not tell) he pulled his legs out of the vessel and said to himself once more: "This can't be right."*

With his association method, Freud reached the conclusion that the dream dealt with "whether the cure will work."

As Freud saw it, the man's problem was an infantile sexual fixation. He indulged in a masturbatory sexuality in order to avoid binding relations with women. As to the legs in the dream, the young chemist associated that the previous day he had danced with a woman he was interested in and pressed his legs against hers in a sexual manner. From the associations it further appeared that he was indifferent toward his own analysis.

Freud considered the woman as being "the metal in the retort," and concluded that "if it works with the lady, the cure will work." Using Jung's alchemical studies as a frame of reference, working with the retort can symbolize the analytical work. The personality must get in the retort and be transformed. The connection between the dreamer and a metal to which feminine associations are attached is symbolically the harmonious interplay between masculine and feminine, what the alchemists called *conjunctio*. They understood this union on the inner level. As the man was young, Jung would probably suggest that he was living it on the outer level. Again: If it works with the lady, the cure will work.

Here we see that two apparently contradictory views will in practice give the same result. Also, the expediency of a deeper understanding than Freud's cannot be denied. The dream could be the prelude to a process like the one Jung described in *Psychology and Alchemy*, and it would thus have broader consequences for the man's development and creativity than getting it to "work" with the lady.

It is also possible to imagine that an analyst would discuss the sexuality problem going from the dream, and a possible creativity problem without reference to the dream but from his own personal experience with creativity. The cure would be successful, and the analyst could still maintain the infantile sexuality theory in the dream.

This is an experiment in thought. But from my own extensive experience in psychoanalytical practice it would seem realistic, and a prototype of false corroboration of the correctness of the dream analysis.

In his famous Visions seminars, which extended from October 1930 to March 1934, Jung went through a series of dreams from a thirty-year-old American woman, Christina Morgan Drummond, who was an unusually gifted medium for material from the collective unconscious. Christina was in analysis for only a few months during the fall of 1924. Afterward contact with Jung consisted of intermittent correspondence. Jung was very impressed with Drummond. He found that her material was "a clear descent into the collective unconscious entirely in accordance with the rules." But gradually, as in the course of the lectures he worked down into the material, he realized that the woman had not really been affected by her inner experiences. Possibly she had been too young to keep what was intuitively experienced in the visions in her consciousness after having returned to the United States. Even though he had been given interesting material to work with, he felt that the therapy had been thrown away.

What is interesting in the present context is that if Jung had been more open to the dreams' transference aspect, the therapy would have been more satisfactory. At the beginning of the therapy, Jung processed "personal material, all kinds of small resistances and wrong attitudes, but when all that was cleared up they [the dreams] started getting to the basics." Christina dreamed: *I was going to see a doctor who lived in a house beside the sea. I lost my way and desperately asked people to put me on the right path so that I could get to him.*

Jung interpreted the doctor who lived by the sea as an animus figure, but although he was Christina's doctor and lived beside the water, he refused to see the doctor as a cover figure for himself. Soon after came the following dream: *I was in a boat with some man. He said: "We must go to the very end of the lake, where the four valleys converge, where they bring down the flocks of sheep to the water." When we got there, he found a lame sheep in the flock, and I found a little lamb that was pregnant. It surprised me because it seemed too young to be pregnant.* The man looked after the sheep and Christina cared for the lamb.

Jung immediately saw that it was a big dream. It was remote from the everyday and full of archetypal motifs.

The boat trip has a number of parallels in archetypal hero myths. The four valleys that meet are reminiscent of the four rivers flowing from paradise, and fourfold symmetry is known from temples and urban complexes. The shepherd is seen as a spiritual guide. The sheep that come to the water to drink are familiar from Christian symbolism. Jung saw the lame sheep as a collective symbol of a Christian religion that was no longer viable. The pregnant lamb was Christina, who was still unripe for finding her own religious path.

A transference interpretation could posit the flock of sheep as symbolizing a circle of persons who surrounded Jung and whose shepherd he was; the dream could serve as a caution that Christina was too young to be pregnant with the visions Jung urged her to have. Later Christina envisioned an old man: *I asked the old man: "Why don't you free those slaves of their chains?" And he answered: "I am reading the illuminated book which shows the way." I asked: "Why do you read such a musty ancient volume?" He answered: "It is the book of illumination."* And still later she *spoke to a (blind) old man, asking him why he was chained. He answered: "Your world has refused us. Therefore we are chained. But by our wisdom you shall descend." I walked down these strange steps.*

What the young woman had come to Jung with was in reality an acute problem of the heart. She was married but had fallen in love with another man. The third year into the lectures, a courageous auditor called Jung's attention to this, but Jung maintained that the erotic problem was a minor detail and talked on about the archetypes.

It appears to me that the slaves not loosed from their chains could stand for what the warm-blooded young woman had to fetter in herself. Descending by "these strange steps" corresponds to Jung having introduced her to an active imagination, which led straight down into the collective unconscious. And like the old savant in the dream, the very learned Jung often felt misunderstood by the world.

Against this backdrop it is understandable that in the first dream she desperately sought a doctor; but it was a part of life she should have lived first.

A neo-Freudian interpretation would undoubtedly also have found parallels to the transference in the relationship to her father, and have concerned itself with the latter's influence on her unresolved sexuality. Both the analysis and her youth would then probably have been less frustrated. Best would have been a combination of the two approaches. For Christina's colossal spirituality would most likely have been just as chained by a Freudian analysis as her sexuality was with Jung.

The therapy's aftermath does partly lean in Jung's favor. During the analysis of the dream with the four valleys meeting, Jung asserted that only a great personality has dreams like Christina's. An afterword by the Jungian analyst Henry A. Murray, who came to know Christina personally, testifies that she became a fine psychotherapist and an unusually developed personality. So perhaps the deep effects of Jung's therapy extended far into the future. A brief introduction to the visions' religious aspect is found in Pia Skogemann.

The Frames of Reference

A number of models for what dreams can deal with have been described: Freud's psychosexual, Erikson's psychosocial, and Neumann's archetypal development stages; Jung's individuation process, his religious and alchemical symbolism; the animus and anima stages; along with more recent male and female psychological development models. From the Freudians: aggressive drive, transference, and defense mechanisms. From the Jungians: death symbolism and experiences of call. Furthermore, Jung employed a theory of psychological types in his dream interpretation, and his pupil Toni Wolf has described a special feminine typology. Several more frames of reference could be enumerated.

There is the possibility that these models (1) *supplement* each other (the dream is regarded as having various meanings); (2) *overlap* each other (on some points they say the same thing with different words); and even (3) *exclude* each other (the one being wrong, the other right).

Erikson understood Freud's "Irma dream" in relation to his psychosocial development stages without nullifying Freud's original interpretation. That the dream, according to Erikson, urged Freud to assume some responsibility for the community of mankind adheres rather closely in practice to the concept of dreams of call. But while Freud's and Erikson's models refer exclusively to the external world, the dream could be understood by Jungians in its aspect of an inner spiritual fructification in which Irma is Freud's feminine side (his anima). Erikson does mention this possibility, but he is not in possession of so nuanced a model for understanding as the Jungians. Instead he employs three frames of reference simultaneously without contradiction.

The models for childhood development, as well, are supplemental and overlapping. Erikson added a social aspect to Freud's model. Neumann's models also observe Freud's time scheme, but I have found them able to contain and cover a number of experiential categories of a creative, spiritual, and sensual nature that had no place in Freud's universe.

Although I have stressed the practical value of the Freudians' transference interpretations, in terms of theory they are too narrow. One could mention Heinz Kohut's example of a man who dreams that he is *in a rocket, circling the globe,* where Kohut interpreted the globe as the analyst and the force of gravity as transference (see "Dream and transference," chapter 1).

In a Jungian frame of reference, the globe is this world's realities, and it has a motherly symbolic significance. There is nothing strange in the relationship to the motherly being transferred to the analyst (it is actually implied in Kohut's view of transference), so, practically speaking, Kohut is correct. But it might be objected that the dream represents a general pattern and that it could very well have been dreamed by someone who was not in analysis. The transference theory's weakness is that it makes therapy to a whole world and forgets that dreaming came before psychoanalysis.

Many more examples might be given, but it should suffice to indicate how complex the phenomenon of dreaming is in the light of the frames of reference we have examined. Just as in the case of the neo-Freudian school, the neo-Jungians increasingly stress the possibility that several interpretations can be correct as the same time.

THE JUNGIAN EMPIRICAL FOUNDATION

Unlike Freud, Jung had a psychoanalytical tradition to start from when he began developing his dream theories. At the time when he wrote his last articles it is estimated that he had analyzed close to eighty thousand dreams.

The Clientele

We know that Freud's patients came from the turn of the century's Viennese bourgeoisie and that most of them were economically well off. That Freud saw as much repressed sexuality in the dreams as he did was not simply overinterpretation, for the clients were brought up in a sexually repressed society.

Michael Fordham criticizes Jung for presenting his material as though it were a random selection of the world's population, even though in reality it involved people who "must have singled themselves out on the basis of a number of factors." Usually they were people who had developed themselves considerably; often they were in mid-life, were attracted by Jung's prestige, had perhaps read his books or come to him through acquaintances whom he had helped. The clients were not seriously mentally ill and were often from the upper social strata. Those cases Jung describes most exhaustively are often unusual, creatively gifted persons and ones having spiritual interests.

As the client material of therapists has not been systematically investigated, I must stick to the scattered information it has been possible to gather, and some of it is thought provoking. The classical Jungian Marie-Louise von Franz points out how the clients themselves choose an analyst who suits them. She mentions that "I haven't had a hysterical client in my practice for over twenty-five years." The reason for this might be that von Franz, who primarily places weight on insight in the therapy and who is a "thinking type," according to Jung's psychological theory, is weak on the emotional side. One place this appears is in the example of the man who wanted "a single beer" at the local bar. Von Franz explained to him that she would not play the governess and that he had to try it if he wanted. Another possibility would have been to work through the affects connected with projecting the image of a strict, prohibiting mother onto von Franz. The mountain in the dream that he slides down can actually be understood as a mother symbol. I personally was a product of the von Franz line in Jungian psychology but am a "feeling type." My own therapeutic development rather quickly turned toward integrating the emotional aspects, and the clients permitted themselves to show more "hysterical" sides parallel with my ability to process them.

Dieckmann's examples are often patients with fewer educational and creative resources than Jung's, and Dieckmann was aware that the policeman, the postman, the housewife, and other ordinary people he describes could not match Wolfgang Pauli's sumptuously archetypal dreams but were still in their own way capable of achieving a psychic equilibrium.

Were I to compare Dieckmann's clients with my own, from the descriptions his seem more inhibited. The works of Dieckmann I quoted come from

Berlin during the 1950s and 1960s, from a people who had grown up under severe privations and with a much tougher attitude toward discipline than younger generations of Danes. And so Dieckmann's observation that bizarre identifications of the dream ego appear in only four out of fifty thousand dreams is somewhat under what I have observed in Danes, particularly among people who have had an opportunity to work with altered states of consciousness in one form or another. Dieckmann's clientele on account of a certain uniformity can also have elucidated the very useful theory he advocates, namely the continuity between the dream ego's and the waking ego's reaction modes.

Meanwhile, in the last forty-five years, when Jungian institutions have spread to most countries in the western world, the theories have been able to be tried on a far broader clientele than Jung had at hand. Jungian child analysis has come into being; at hospitals there is work with client groups who would never have sought private help; and Jungian ideas have propagated to other therapeutic movements. The new client basis has led to modifications and developments within the theory but has also substantiated basic features of Jung's discoveries.

The Objective Psyche

The Jungian empirical basis is formed not only by the clients' dreams but also by a very extensive study of symbolic material like mythologies, fairy tales, and religions. The background for this research is the concept of an objective psyche that can't be manipulated by the consciousness and produces archetypal symbols.

Strangely enough, Freud already operated with a universal symbol-forming ability and universal complexes like the Oedipus complex and the castration complex. He had therefore no other choice than to assume the existence of a phylogenetic heritage in man. But he maintained that it was an error of method to concern oneself with these things before exhausting the investigation of the personal level.

Jung's theory speaks only of conceptual *possibilities*, and the structuralistic psychologist Jean Piaget found that formulated in this way the idea could be universally accepted. The theories of neo-Freudian dream theorists like Erik Erikson and Emil Gutheil presuppose such a view, and as Pia Skogemann has described in her book *Arketyper* (Archetypes), it is in keeping with the trend within many modern branches of science.

Jung could therefore term the study of dream images and their parallels in religion, myths, folklore, etc. as comparative psychic anatomy. Seen scientifically, the crux of the matter is when knowledge of symbols in one context, such as the mythology of a remote culture, is transferred to dreams with another context. But here Jung has, as mentioned, indicated methods for testing the interpretations.

Finally, it should be mentioned that Jung was among the first to underscore the special methodological problem in psychology: that the observing subject influences the object being observed. This viewpoint was later justified by the humanistic psychologist Abraham Maslow, who has elaborated a scientific theory that implicates the investigator's personality in the scientific cognitional process.

The Scientific Environment at the Time of Freud and Jung

The turn of the century, when Freud's and Jung's most important ideas were in the germinal stage, was a time of enormous growth in psychological and psychiatric investigation. A wealth of new ideas were under discussion and there was lively experimenting with new psychiatric forms of treatment. But behind this profusion, two fundamentally different world views can be discerned.

By 1850, a rationalistic and materialist philosophy had come to the fore. The other outlook—Romanticism—had been thrust into the background, though a revivification seems to have taken place around the turn of the century. In their yearning for contact with life's more mysterious and indefinable sides, the Romantics had turned to dreams, parapsychology, folklore, fairy tales, and the study of exotic cultures. They saw the imagination as an aid to achieving contact with an inner mystical world, and personality development was regarded as a series of inner transformations.

Both the positivist and the Romantic way of experiencing influenced contemporary psychiatry and the views of modern man. The former was officially accepted, while the latter was practiced more covertly—which mirrors the situation today.

Freud was a declared positivist, and the most important background for his theoretical concepts were positivist scientists and rationalist philosophers. Jung was by training a natural scientist, but his most original ideas were inspired by Romantic poets and philosophers. Among the influences science historian Henri Ellenberger mentions are these: That a person, in addition to his ego, has some part-personalities (complexes) that are different from his self-conception; this notion Jung obtained from Romantic philosophy and fiction. Most familiar was the conception that a person has shadow sides that he or she tries to disregard.

Jung was strongly influenced by, among others, the Romantic philosopher Ignaz Troxler, who saw the life process as a series of transformations. Troxler also maintained that the personality's nucleus was not the ego but what he called "the ego-self." Other important concepts in Jung that were inspired by Romanticism are the "living symbol," which releases dynamic forces in the psyche, and the idea that the unconscious is independent, creative, and has a compensatory function in relation to the conscious. Especially important was the concept that creativity and imagination can stimulate development of the personality.

The Incompatibilities Between Freud and Jung

The theoretical incompatibilities between Freud and Jung can be categorized as: matter opposed to spirit, body opposed to soul, external opposed to inner, environment opposed to inherited potentialities, realism opposed to creative imagination, object opposed to subject. But it is interesting that Freud and Jung, who both thought to encompass the whole truth, each takes a side in an age-old idea-historical conflict that has split, and is still splitting, western man's philosophical outlook; namely, the question of the preeminence of the outer material or the inner spiritual world.

These dichotomies can be traced back through the entire history of our culture. In the Middle Ages the spiritual viewpoint took over completely, while the Renaissance marked a decisive turning point toward a more materialistic attitude. This contradiction is familiar from antiquity, when it separated the two main schools of Greek philosophy. The school at Milet (with names like Thales and Anaximenes) regarded the fundamental question as being "What is the world made of?" Plato and Pythagoras, on the other hand, thought the decisive questions were those of form, pattern, and order.

Jung's hypothesis of the personal and the collective unconscious attempts to be fair. But his interest is mainly concentrated on the doctrine of archetypes, which has its roots in the Platonic conception that the world existed first as purely spiritual ideas, and that the physical world as we know it is a pale reflection of those ideas. Later in his life Jung formulated a theory of a unified world (*unus mundus*) that underlies our perception of psyche and matter and encompasses them both. But Jung at the age of eighty-three wrote in his autobiography: "[O]nly what is interior has proved to have substance and a determining value. As a result, all memory of outer events [in my life] faded, and perhaps these 'outer' experiences were never so very essential anyhow, or were so only in that they coincided with phases of my inner development."

James Hillman found that Jung's concept of the Self as a higher factor is a reflection of our monotheistic cultural view (there is only one God). He proposes many gods, also in the world of dreams, and is thereby probably more in conformity with the current outlook than Jung.

3. Dreams and Waking Lifestyle

Dreams reflect lifestyle—Calvin Hall's content analyses—What dreams typically deal with—Men's and women's dreams—Children's dreams—Calvin Hall's theory of symbols—The interpreter's attitude—Conclusion

Dreams reflect lifestyle

While Freud basically saw dreams as a kind of safety valve for primitive drives, Jung, as mentioned, regarded them as *sources of revelation*. Both assigned the source of dreams to the unconscious. Another of the great pioneers of psychoanalysis, Alfred Adler, thought on the contrary that dreams originate from waking life, and that they show us "precisely the same personality which we find in daily life."

According to this theory, the function of dreams is to solve problems that have not been finished off in the course of the day. As we usually don't understand dreams and perhaps even forget most of them, Adler assumed it was the *feelings* and *emotions* that the dreams arouse which are the essential thing. The dream's "entire purpose is to awaken a mood which prepares us" for meeting daily conflict situations. Dreams are also future-directed.

It is Adler who created the concept of the *inferiority complex*, and he maintained that "the highest law for both sleep and the waking state was that the ego's feeling of worth must not be reduced." The key to dreams of flying, for example, lay in that "they lead from below to above." The picture they give is ease in overcoming difficulties and attaining superiority. They therefore allow us to assume that the person is active, forward-looking, and ambitious, and cannot get rid of his ambition even when he is asleep. Another example: A woman who coveted her sister's husband dreamed that *she danced with Napoleon*. She thereby demonstrated her greater worth as opposed to the sister.

Adler's theories of dreams are not nearly as worked through and detailed as Freud's or Jung's, and the frame of reference he provides for dream interpretation seems rather narrow. However, a great part of Adler's conceptual apparatus has been appropriated by influential authors of dream literature like Montague Ullman and Erich Fromm.

In his book *The Forgotten Language*, Fromm declares himself in agreement with Jung that "we often are wiser and more decent in sleep than in the waking life." But he was opposed to Jungian formulations such as "a person is never helped by what he himself thinks, but by revelations of wisdom which is greater than his own."

According to Fromm, dreams are derived from waking experiences, and when they are wiser than the waking state it is on account of the fact "that the waking state often has a blunting effect on our intellectual and moral capacity."

CALVIN HALL'S CONTENT ANALYSES

The most innovative and influential personality within this school of dream theory is Calvin Hall, originally Freudian-trained but later the director of his own Institute of Dream Research in California. Hall was dissatisfied with the fact that the dream theories were based primarily on clinical experiences from individuals in analysis. He collected over fifty thousand dreams, most from persons not in therapy, found ways of classifying the content, and compared it with information about the dreamer's age, sex, psychological makeup, and so forth. The investigations show that there are clear connections between the manifest dream content and the dreamer's waking personality.

Hall developed—first alone, later with associates Bill Domhoff, Robert van de Castle, and Vernon Nordby—a method he called *content analysis*. Here the dream is treated like a verbal text. It is divided up into elements, which "provides frequencies of occurrence for a large number of dream elements." The method, according to Hall, turned out to be "a) a practical tool for individual dreams, b) a means to statistically verify dream theory hypotheses, and c) a sociological method for investigating dream and lifestyle in larger groups."

Individual Content Analyses

Hall opposed interpreting dreams singly. Although it is possible from a single dream to obtain knowledge of a few character traits in the dreamer, if you really want a picture of his or her personality you need a dream series. Hall found that the dreams fit together like pieces in a jigsaw puzzle. He let one dream shed light on another and compared the information from the various dreams until a total picture of the personality was formed. If a dream didn't fit in with the overall picture, neither did the interpretation, and he had to try a new one.

As an example of this dream series method, in his book *The Meaning of Dreams* Hall went through dreams from two young Americans, William and Gene. William is described as a sensitive young musician who in his waking life is somewhat bashful, not very dynamic, and afraid of girls. Gene, on the other hand, is a pragmatic, robust young man who likes sports, competition, hunting, and fishing. While William is passive and withdrawn and has difficulty accessing energy, Gene is bursting with vitality and gets what he wants.

This difference in lifestyle is reflected clearly in their dreams. William is usually a spectator, while Gene acts. For example, William dreams: *I went to a swimming pool with my mother. . . . We sat on the bench and watched some girls swim. . . . I recognized some of the girls and one that was very attractive. . . . But she didn't pass by.* A corresponding dream from Gene: *I was in swimming with a girl friend. We played around in the water, ducking each other and swimming together. I could feel her pert little body against mine as we kissed each other.*

In six of the dreams Hall collected, William is riding in a car, but only in one of them is he driving. Otherwise he is a passenger in the backseat. In his dreams other people do lots of things but he himself sits and looks on. Why he does nothing in the dreams turns out to be because of fear. In one dream he is *making love to two girls. Suddenly a young, well-built and very handsome man appears and rushes threateningly toward him. Later an older conductor warns him against that kind of involvement again.* And so William's experience is that if he gives in to his desire for girls he will be punished by competitors or reprimanded by fatherly men. His dreams show that he is constantly punishing himself.

Gene, who on the contrary is self-disciplined and is described as a young male animal, in thirteen of his fourteen dreams is involved in strenuous physical activity. He wrestles, shoots, climbs a cliff, skis, paints, catches a sea turtle and stamps on it, rides a horse, tackles another man, and so on.

He embraces his friends, shoots his enemies, and goes to bed with the girls. All of this corresponds with his exciting and vigorous lifestyle.

William is the bookish type who does well in college, in contrast to Gene, who would prefer a practical career.

Hall calls his method diagnosing a personality by means of dreams. In the book *The Individual and His Dreams* he gives this example: "A study was made by a psychologist of 61 dreams reported by a young woman during her 32 months of psychotherapy. He attempted to uncover her principal conflicts and concerns. His approach to the dreams was very subjective and impressionistic, so that the resulting picture of the patient was blurred, confused and chaotic." A content analysis of the dreams discloses that her primary concerns are

> men, sex, marriage and divorce, pregnancy, birth control, and abortion; filth, implements, misfortune, anxiety and money. The dreams about money were related to the lengthy discussions of the payment of fees between the psychotherapist and the patient. The other items suggested that what the patient wanted was a husband and babies, but she was afraid of having her body invaded, dirtied and destroyed by the act of intercourse and pregnancy. Menstruation was a monthly reminder to her of the uncleanliness of the genital regions. Had the psychotherapist focused on her paralyzing fears of body destruction, he might have shortened the length of treatment and increased its effectiveness.

The extensive studies that Hall and his associates conducted through the 1960s and 1970s show that there is a high degree of consistency and continuity in an individual's dreams, even over a long span of time. We have seen this consistency demonstrated in the Jung section on childhood dreams that appear to foresee a person's destiny decades into the future, in connection with Sheila Moon's dreams, and in a number of other dream series. It is a well-known and accepted phenomenon in Jungian dream analysis. But with Hall's method it became possible to demonstrate this in a more objectively scientific manner.

Hall distinguishes three types of consistency in dream series: absolute constancy, relative consistency, and developmental regularity.

Absolute constancy: A man recorded six hundred dreams over a period of seventeen years. The proportion of male and female persons he dreamed about was the following:

Dream no.	1–100	101–200	201–300	301–400	401–500	501–600
percent men	63	61	57	63	62	60
percent women	37	39	43	37	38	40

Relative consistency means that one element appears more frequently than another dream element. In the above dreams there appeared body parts, furniture, clothing, and printed matter. In the six hundred dreams, the incidence of body parts exceeds the incidence of furniture; furniture exceeds clothing; and clothing exceeds printed matter—over a period of seventeen years.

Developmental regularity: Here a change occurs between one period of time and the next, but the change is consistent.

The same man had an increasing number of aggressive interactions with family members. They jumped from 17 percent to 68 percent in the course of the seventeen years. Hall ascribed this escalating hostility to relations with the wife.

These three types of consistency were found to occur in all of the dream series he and his associates analyzed over the years; there was always a considerable amount of absolute constancy but even more relative consistency. Developmental regularities were less common. Hall concludes: "The dreams of an individual are amazingly consistent from one year to the next." As a practical matter, Hall noted that recounting the many repetitions became rather tedious after the first several hundred dreams. It should be added that Hall's material was culled from people who weren't in therapy or working with self-development.

The Scientific Aspect of Content Analysis

Statistical methods of content analysis are nothing new. They have been employed in literature, political science, sociology, and psychology, but Hall was the first to apply them to dreams. In the book *The Content Analysis of Dreams* from 1966, Hall together with Robert van de Castle reviews the problems of method, particularly with a view to converting dream material into "scientific data." Hall names four characteristics of the latter: (1) objectivity and reproducibility, (2) quantifiability, (3) significance for a systematic theory, and (4) generalizability.

A problem Hall discussed exhaustively: Just what *is* understood by a dream? He settled on a very down-to-earth definition: "What a person describes when asked to tell a dream, excluding comments and interpretations." To be sure, Hall realized that experiencing a dream is predominantly a pictorial experience and that the verbal description can't provide the equivalent. Still, the definition is operational and corresponds more to the phenomenon dream interpreters work with than to the dream experience itself. The method requires additionally a classification system that we have seen examples of: the criteria for penis envy, which I mentioned in the Freud section about dream and psychosexual development, is a simplified version of Hall's classification, and the Jungian Kluger's criteria for archetypicality in dreams is another example.

It has hereby become possible to test different hypotheses concerning dreams. Kluger corroborated the theory of archetypes (see "Investigations of dream archetypes," chapter 2), and Calvin Hall confirmed several Freudian hypotheses, such as that men have more castration anxiety in dreams than women (bodily unfitness along with damage to or destruction of something belonging to the dreamer is three times as frequent in men's dreams as in women's dreams). Plus the superego is different in women and in men.

The method also involves the collecting of material from different population groups, to be used as a basis of comparison for other groups. For example, when Kluger made his studies of archetypicality, he wrote to the Calvin Hall Institute and requested a "normal material" of childhood dreams for comparison with his own. A woman

> kept a record of her dreams when she was in her twenties and again when she was in her sixties. Virtually all of the frequencies were the same in the two sets of dreams. There was the same number of males and females, and the same kinds of objects. There was the same proportion of friendly and aggressive interactions with each class of character. There was even the same number of prominent persons and Negroes in the two sets of dreams.

Hall found that often these individual characteristics could be explained psychologically. A businessman sent one hundred dreams to the Hall Institute. The dreams contained many references to women's clothing, and Hall and his associates guessed that the man was a transvestite. This turns out to be the case. A "child molester" who had been apprehended and imprisoned sent a diary with fourteen hundred dreams to Hall in the hope of getting an explanation for his abnormality. It turns out that not once did the father appear in the dreams. Hall guessed two possible explanations: Either the father died or had abandoned the family while the boy was a baby, or he had done something toward the son that made the latter banish him from his dreams. Hall found a dream in which a *bull that seemed to have human intelligence wanted to have sexual relations with me.* He interpreted the bull Freudianly as a disguise for the father and suspected sexual abuse. It turns out that from the age of four the child molester had been forced to perform fellatio on his father.

The longest dream series in Hall's possession comes from a woman psychology professor. It extends from 1912 to 1965 a few days before the dreamer's death. The woman, whom Hall calls Dorothea, dreamed about her parents and siblings with the same consistency for fifty years. The father died when Dorothea was young and the mother died when she was sixty-one. Her four most important dream themes are (1) food and eating, where she didn't get enough in every fifth dream; (2) loss of an object, occurring in every sixth dream; (3) the mother in every tenth dream; and (4) in a disorderly room or someone invading the room, every tenth dream.

Hall diagnosed an "oral" problem (see "Dreams and psychosexual development," chapter 1). Dorothea was the second of eight children and had plenty of opportunity to experience feelings of being ignored or displaced by a new child in the family. She lugged this pattern around with her all her life.

An elderly woman who had been married twice and both of whose husbands had been dead for many years continued to dream about them for the rest of her life. Even though the first marriage had been unhappy, she often dreamed that she was together with the husband in a good and often amorous way. The second marriage she had experienced as happy, but about that husband she dreamed that he was sick or dying or leaving her for another woman.

At the age of eighty-two she has a dream that describes the dilemma she has lived with for fifty years:

> *Two men were in love with me and wanted me to marry them. One was quiet and high-minded and altogether a far nicer, modest person. The other was handsome and flamboyant and took me by storm, simply assuming my consent. I wasn't exactly in love with either, but fascinated and overcome by the second man, and I did say yes and married him, though even then I doubted if I was making the better choice. Then when it was too late I realized what a mistake I had made; my husband was self-centered and arrogant, and once he had me, he treated me with indifference.*

The quiet, high-minded male dream figure is like her second husband. The flamboyant one is like her first husband. She still shows preference for the first one, mistaken though she feels she may be.

Hall concludes that the consistency in the dreams is due to the fact that the personality is a rather stable organization of personal traits, attitudes, and behavior patterns. This can be due to inheritable factors contracted during intrauterine development or development in early childhood. But the reason that a few fundamental themes persistently recur in the individual throughout life is, in Hall's opinion, first and foremost anxiety.

Now and then, however, Hall saw systematic changes in the dream pattern. The reason for this could be psychotherapy, changes due to aging, bodily changes, and sometimes radical changes in the surroundings.

WHAT DREAMS TYPICALLY DEAL WITH

The classification Hall found most essential breaks the dream down according to the following features: settings, characters, actions, emotions. He gave these aspects different symbolic interpretations. We have just seen great individual variation in preferred dream themes, but when you examine the larger categories there are also average ways of dreaming to be found. The *settings* in the dreams are usually banal, familiar surroundings: a living room, a car, a street, a grocery store, a beach, or a restaurant. Exotic and peculiar localities are more rare.

In fifteen out of every one hundred dreams, the dreamer is on a conveyance of some sort that is in motion.

Hall interprets the movement as: "ambition, progress and achievement, breaking family ties, fleeing from something or dying." The nature of the conveyance said something about how the dreamer handles these quantities. If I am driving my father's car, for example, it means independence of him (or of what he stands for). If I can't control the vehicle, I can't control my own progress through life. If it is a big showy car it can be expression for a grandiose self-opinion, and so forth.

The dreams have many recreative settings such as places for dancing and sociability, swimming, and sports, whereas workplaces appear seldom. Correspondingly, dream *actions* are more often pleasurable, entertaining activities than work and everyday routines. The *characters* are more often familiar and closely related than unknown persons. They can both refer to aspects of ourselves and to our connections with the external world, which corresponds to Jung's objective level and subjective level.

Four out of ten persons in the dreams are strangers. The stranger can stand for an alien part of ourselves, or for an unrecognized side of someone we know. If there are many strangers in the dreams, it can also mean that the person is very isolated. This was the case with the child molester. Apart from his mother and sister he had only strange persons in his fourteen hundred dreams.

MEN'S AND WOMEN'S DREAMS

Hall and his coworkers were very much occupied with sexual differences in dreams. It turns out that women are more passive in dreams than men, when by passive it is meant looking, sitting, talking, standing, and the like. Men in contrast are far more active in dreams when it comes to running, driving a car, swimming, dancing, playing ball, and similar actions. A list of the most strenuous actions in men's dreams included *unloading heavy steel rails, digging for ore, working on a boiler, scaling the side of a building, fist fighting and rowing a boat,* and in women's dreams: *moving beds, mixing batter, sweeping stairs, sorting out flowers, taking clothes from a line and carrying dishes.*

These studies were carried out on Americans, and on the whole they cover my own experiences. However, I have in Danish women occasionally seen dream motifs such as *strangling a lion with my bare hands, shoveling coal on a boiler so it's about to explode, stabbing a tyrant to death, shooting a man with a pistol,* and so forth.

Another interesting and apparently universally widespread difference in men's and women's dreams is that in men's dreams there appear on an average two men for every woman, and in women's dreams one woman for every man. This division as to sex is in both boys and girls already present at the age of six. Hall took it as expressing that men are more preoccupied by their relations to men than by their relations to women, while women apportion their interest equally between the two sexes. Other investigations show that men's dreams have more aggressions toward other men than toward women, while women have more aggressions between men and women. Moreover, men have more friendly encounters with women than with men, while women make no such distinctions.

These findings are explained going from Freud's theory of the male and the female Oedipus complex. The boy falls in love with the mother and experiences the father as an enemy, while the woman turns her anger both on the mother and the father. This characterizes the unconscious relations to the opposite sex throughout life.

Men are more often sexual in their dreams than women, and while the roles in women's dreams are often played by mothers, relations, and children. Men dream more than women about unknown men who are identified by their job: a banker, a clerk, a butcher.

CHILDREN'S DREAMS

Boys' dreams versus girls' and children's dreams versus adults' has been investigated by Robert van de Castle, one of Hall's close associates. The girls, and adult women also, are more social in their dreams than boys and men. Girls often describe the face, hair, and eyes of their dream characters, while boys generally describe things by their size, speed, and intensity. Girls' dreams are generally "nicer" than boys' dreams—moods are happier and there are more social events in them. In dreams about animals, girls more frequently have small animals and pets, while boys are more likely to dream about wild animals.

An important difference in children's and adults' dreams is the number of animals that appear. Children less than four years old have animals in 51 percent of their dreams. At ages five to seven there are animals in 37 percent of the dreams. In adults the figure drops to 7.5 percent.

Children more than seven years old who continue to have many animals in their dreams as a rule have less social experience than children who do not. Children moreover dream much more frequently about frightening animals. Lions, spiders, bears, gorillas, crocodiles, tigers, and wolves comprise 28 percent of the animals in children's dreams, while they only comprise 7 percent of the animals in adult dreams. As children mature they dream more and more of animals that can be steered and controlled.

Most dream investigators think that animals symbolize instinctual impulses. It follows that the many animals in children's dreams reflect their greater spontaneity, their less stable egos, and their difficulty in directing their own impulses.

Parents may be alarmed by their children having anxiety dreams, but it is quite normal. The American author Patricia Garfield has compiled a list of themes (bad and good) and their frequency in children as found in a survey of 247 dreams:

Bad dreams

1. Being chased or attacked   77
2. Sensing something scary   28
3. Injury or death   26
4. Damage or loss of property   9
5. Being frustrated   5
6. Falling   5
7. Other   8
     158

Good dreams

1. Enjoying nice activity   30
2. Desirable possession   15
3. Outstanding performance   9
4. Being important   7
5. Adventure   7
6. Media hero (Superkid)   7
7. Eating delicious food   6
8. Friends with an animal   4
9. Being loved   3
10. Flying   1
     89

CALVIN HALL'S THEORY OF SYMBOLS

Hall developed his own cognitive theory of dream symbolism. He believed the symbolic process is a part of the ego's intellectual system. A young man's dream: *I attempted to turn on the water faucet. I then decided to call a plumber. I discovered that it was a lady plumber. She turned the faucet, and immediately water flowed. At this point I awoke, having a nocturnal emission.* That the dream leads to a seminal emission makes it reasonable to assume that it is sexual. As the dream represents the male sexual organ as a water faucet that can be turned on by a female plumber, it suggests that the dreamer has a mechanical conception of sex.

Quite a different natural and sensual attitude toward sex is depicted in another dream: *In the dream I was lying in bed in the cold, dull morning. Suddenly the sun rose and the room seemed to fill with warmth. I had an ejaculation.*

For Hall, dreaming is like thinking in images. The symbols are concepts translated to imagery. A pistol never stands for the male sexual organ in itself, but it can, in a very concise way, show that a man has an aggressive conception of his own sexuality. Correspondingly, a man can dream about his mother as a cow and it would represent in the simplest way his conception of the mother as a nurturing person. Symbols are thus not disguises but a kind of mental shorthand: My mother is a cowlike person, ergo let her appear as a cow in my dream.

Hall, like Jung, repudiated Freud's theory that symbols are disguises. Yet we have heard many good arguments that defense mechanisms are often involved in dream formation. Hall reasoned (and Jung has done the same) that Freud's disguise theory doesn't explain why a dreamer may have a disguised dream of an incestuous relationship one night and a perfectly obvious dream of incest the next night. But as we know, this is rather seldom. And what Hall's own investigations do show is that the individual's dream themes are on the whole monotonous and don't suddenly take new turns.

Hall also lacks the important Jungian dimension of the symbol as an energy transformer that can touch off growth processes in the psyche. In Jung, the most important thing isn't the intellectual understanding of the symbol but its emotional charge. On the other hand, Hall has convincing examples of the value of his theory, and I myself have found that it functions well in practice *together* with Freud's and Jung's. Let us apply it to a couple of the earlier examples.

Previously we viewed an American bishop's dreams from the point of view of their testifying to his vocation as clergyman (see "Dreams of call," chapter 2). Hall's method might show a new dimension to this call. In the first dream a "wildly gesticulating" priest is associated with the call. In the second the call emanates from a "triumphal arch" that is a victory monument for a war, and in the third Jesus is represented as a cannonball. If this is the typical imagery in the bishop's dreams, we could add to the earlier interpretations that he must have conceived his call in a rather warlike and fanatical way. Now we know nothing of the bishop's waking lifestyle, but my own experience with thousands of dreams tells me that Hall's method would function in principle.

In Wolfgang Pauli's alchemical dream series one can clearly see reflected his own techno-scientific waking lifestyle (see "Dream and alchemy," chapter 2). Few people would dream about the individuation process in symbols about "squaring the circle" or see the Self as an exceedingly complicated technical construction: the cosmic world clock. For others the grand harmony might have revealed itself as contact with a talking wise animal, as a cosmic space full of undulating colors, an ecstatic sexual union, and so forth.

In the Jungian section about interpretation on internal and external levels, I mentioned one of my female clients who dreamed that she was going to visit a wonderful old castle on a mountaintop (see "Interpretation principles in Jung," chapter 2). At the final stretch she had to go up a difficult path of tiny steps. Her problems with the ascent I understood Freudianly as an orgasm problem. It might be added that the dream was simultaneously a beautiful archetypal dream. The mountain hike was by Jung regarded as an image of the individuation process, and the wonderful old castle could be a symbol of the feminine Self. I think that both the Freudian and the Jungian interpretations describe sides of the woman's reality. A Hall interpretation, meanwhile, would say that both parts are to a certain extent experienced, as a blend of pleasure (vacation) and performance (the steep ascent), in contrast to a letting go, for example. This too is correct.

THE INTERPRETER'S ATTITUDE

While the Freudians maintain that dreams cannot be interpreted without transference to an analyst, and the Jungians think that interpreting dreams is extremely difficult to learn on your own, it is Hall's "conviction that anyone who is able to follow a few basic rules can interpret dreams." Here the interpreter must accept the following premises:

1. The dream is created by the dreamer's own mind. By "mind" Hall means first and foremost the ego and its defense mechanisms. The dreamer himself is the playwright, director, and actor. The dream is an entirely subjective product. It gives an exact picture of how one perceives reality; that is, how one sees oneself, others, the world, one's own impulses, and one's own conflicts.

2. To dream something one must have thought it (in the waking state).

3. The dreamer can disclose more than one conception of himself or the world.

4. The dream is an organic whole. By this it is meant that the separate elements can only be understood in the context of the whole dream. The separate symbols' meaning must be weighed against their placement in the dream. The interpretation is based upon series and according to Hall "can be very precise and objective if one approaches the task in a scientific manner."

In *The Individual and His Dreams*, Hall puts forth a method for the individual to follow. He sets up tables of a large number of feelings and ways of relating to oneself and others. He is undoubtedly right that if the individual keeps to the formula he will obtain rather astonishing information about his waking lifestyle and his view of the world. The method is a positive move toward taking dreams out of the consultation room and making them a tool for the layman. It can also help professional dream interpreters in checking their own interpretations. On the other hand, the attitude toward emotions and the psyche is rationalistic and disregards Freud's and Jung's findings that analysis and intellectual understanding are seldom enough to create change and transformation.

Contingency Analysis

In his latest book, Hall took cognizance of a criticism which has been aimed at the content analyses: that they separate the dream into elements and thereby destroy its unity and coherence. A method for countering this he calls *contingency analysis*. Here you don't try to see only the separate elements but also whether there are typical "constellations" among several elements. For example, do animals appear in a child's dreams causing more fright or acting more aggressive than usual? In another instance, a man is disturbed if he has intercourse (most often with an older woman) in a dream. Moreover, dream elements such as tunnels and tubes, rear ends, pressure or tightening, dirt, stink, brown, etc. appeared with unusual frequency in eighty-four dreams from a young man. All can associate to defecation.

Most psychoanalysts sum up typical traits and linkages in dream series, but Hall's method provides the possibility of testing the impressions and checking for countertransference.

CONCLUSION

There can be no doubt that this third branch within modern dream analysis fills a gap, and especially that Calvin Hall's investigations document the connection between dreams and waking lifestyle. The movement hasn't had such great influence as Freud's and Jung's ideas, but it is on the other hand buttressed by prevailing tendencies in the latter's successors.

Erik Erikson thinks that dreams, aside from other facets which interest him, have a "style of representation," that they represent a person's lifestyle. Also the Jungian Hans Dieckmann's description of the continuity between dream ego and waking ego parallels Adler and Hall. It must be emphasized that waking lifestyle is not the same as consciousness. It instead refers to how you actually conduct yourself and experience the world. A person can be aggressive, for instance, but experience his own aggressiveness as a defense against others' hostility.

The Nature of Dreams

As representatives of this school, Alfred Adler, Erich Fromm, Calvin Hall, and Montague Ullman think that dreams contain material that has been experienced in the waking state. None of them is so sustained in his theory formation as Freud and Jung. Hall, who is the most systematic, deliberately abstained from developing a unified theory, partly because he thought there was still too little accessible knowledge in relation to the complexity of the phenomenon dreams, and partly because he thought that prematurely stated theories create barriers and inhibit innovation. On the other hand he thinks that theories can provide useful guidelines. The discovery that a "child molester" had repressed incestuous experiences with the father is due to Hall having very Freudianly assumed that a bull is a father symbol.

Hall considered Freud's and Jung's theories the most useful. The conception of the nature of dreams is revealed especially in the conception of the symbol. Hall and Fromm, like Freud and Jung, advocate the existence of universal symbols, while Adler and Ullman believe that symbols are private.

In Adler, symbol interpretation is determined by associations and by his special frame of reference. In Ullman, only the dreamer himself can determine what the symbol means. Hall is alone in placing the main weight on the symbol's intellectual meaning. Fromm, like Adler, stresses its ability to induce feelings and moods.

Hall thinks that symbols have one distinct meaning for the individual dreamer, while Fromm advocates their having several possible meanings simultaneously. As Adler sees it, dreams are not determined by a single event but by many events. They are therefore to be understood on several levels at the same time.

His view of the symbol notwithstanding, Hall operates very much with defense mechanisms, both conceptually and in practice. He uses Freud's concept of punishment dreams and thinks that the ego's fear contributes to the dreams' monotonousness. Fromm's conception adheres closely to this idea. Ullman demonstrated that Adler works with Freudian concepts like condensation, displacement, and regard for representability, even though this is at odds with the fundamental theory. Adler moreover pointed out that it is important not only which symbols appear in the dreams but also which ones do not, as this shows what the dreamer excludes from his life. This viewpoint is corroborated by the one-sidedness in the lifelong dream series Hall studied.

The Function of Dreams

While the theories on the nature of dreams can seem somewhat diffuse and full of contradictions, within this school of dream interpretation there is excellent agreement as to the function of dreams. Hall concluded from his investigations that dreams give a rather dreary picture of persons; they deal more with their anxiety and problems than with joys and successes. Of course, this is because their task is problem solving—they are the result of good, hard, and creative mental labor in the sleeping state.

When we dream frequently about intimates it is because we are emotionally involved with them, whether the emotions are love, fear, anger, or a combination of these feelings. But as an important rule, *we seldom dream about persons with whom we have stable and satisfactory relations*—only when feelings toward a person are problematic do we dream about them. The reason we don't dream about our successes, according to Hall, is that they don't create tensions in the mind. Tensions are a prerequisite for thinking and dream activity.

Ullman writes that dreams take "our emotional temperature and point at causes and contexts." Fromm and Adler, too, think that dreams help solve unresolved problems. Here there is an alignment with the Jungians and a number of neo-Freudians. Even though Freud didn't advocate this concept, he nonetheless used dreams for psychoanalytical problem solving. On a pragmatic level there is in spite of everything something that unites the theories we have described. At the same time it must be admitted that there are important differences in both the nature and the manner in which it is supposed that dreams solve problems. It depends on how dreams are actually interpreted.

The Dream Analysis

Calvin Hall posits that there are a number of basic conflicts which tend to manifest themselves in human life and dreams: conflicts between love and hate in the parent/child relationship, between freedom and security, right and wrong, masculinity and femininity, and life versus death. Hall's system appears to adhere closely to Freud's, and there are many good observations, but the system is far from being of the same format as Freud's. One of the objections of existentialist Medard Boss to Hall's statistical investigations is that they can't be used in working with the dreams of the individual. Here I disagree. The statistical classifications are frames of reference on an equal footing with others, and they can be useful both in psychotherapy and for the layman's dream understanding.

Knowing that every third dream a child can recall deals with being hunted or attacked can perhaps take the edge off the parents' anxiety, so they don't make more of a normal occurrence. (Naturally it says nothing about how they are to respond to the child.) And if the dreams of someone in his forties start containing more childhood settings than those of the twenty- to thirty-year-old, it can be practical knowing it is a natural part of the life stage he or she is in. Regressive dreams of this kind appear much more frequently in persons in their forties and fifties.

As I mentioned earlier, Hall, with whom I occasionally compare material, reports that in men's dreams there are normally two men for every woman. What does it mean if this ratio is no longer present? In the Jungian view the feminine in the man is usually activated at impending transformations in the psyche, and often these are accompanied by radical fluctuations of mood and emotion. In dreams taken down over two weeks, a thirty-nine-year-old man found nine women to four men—in other words, a marked predominance of the feminine. During this period the man was depressive, felt tired, and complained of being almost unable to sense his body. A month later when he again recorded the normal ratio of two men to one woman in his dreams, the perception of his body, his energy, and his zest for life began returning. Such a preponderance of women in a man's dreams thus seems to be experienced as an imbalance and a loss of ego, but it can be necessary to the development process.

Hall didn't think there was anything "esoteric or mysterious in dreams." In support of his theory he made use of the fact that the greater part of the dream material is fairly everyday, while the alien or bizarre (the archetypal) is relatively rare. As the archetypal material is so loaded with meaning and binds so much energy, it makes up in quality for its infrequency. In ignoring this Hall loses much.

As an example I will mention dreams that Hall treats in a section on life versus death. He cites a series of dreams from a sixty-eight-year-old man who had lived an active and outgoing life. He was now seriously ill and had been forced to give up his work, but found it difficult to accept his new state of living. He dreamed: *I was back in Yugoslavia, the land of my youth. I am waiting for a train. I attempt to catch it but the train rolls away again. I continue on, wading through water until I come to a flour mill. I see large fish and think that it is probably good fishing.*

Hall sees in his missing the train the man's experience that life is passing him by because he no longer has the agility to seize and hold it. Given the man's situation, this is a reasonable interpretation. But then Hall also sees the water, the mill, and the thought of good fishing as an expression of the youthful vitality the man tries in vain to recapture.

A Jungian interpretation would see the water as an expression of the collective unconscious, and the fishing we have already come across in the dream from the depressive American businessman. In another dream the man swims like a fish in a stream while thinking: Others are younger and stronger than me but I swim better than them anyway—and in this Hall sees the urge to compete with younger men. This undoubtedly is an aspect of the symbolism. In Jungian terms, he is better at swimming in the unconscious (the water) than younger men; he has a greater possibility of going in-depth with himself than when he was younger. Immersion in water also has parallels in baptism and spiritual rebirth.

In a third dream *the man is in a church, and three ladies serve him whiskey.* Hall mentions that the word *whiskey* means "water of life" and again sees it as expression for the man's desire for rejuvenation. But in the Jungian understanding the water of life is the same as the alchemists' *aqua permanens* (see "Dream and alchemy," chapter 2) and thus represents the self and the goal of individuation. Spirits once more underscore the spiritual aspect in the dreams. The same with the church and the three ladies: the dream stands for rejuvenation and transformation, and the threefold feminine is often seen in connection with portentous archetypes such as the three Fates who have sway over life and death.

The negative picture Hall gives of our dreams can therefore be linked with some profound and edifying aspects that he is unable to see. His viewpoint is nonetheless consequential. Many dreams immediately appear negative—but that is the way it looks from a consciousness afraid of a transformation for the better.

Even though Adler in theory clung to the inferiority complex as the main theme of dreams, in practice he opposed interpretation by rules. He regarded dreams as a manifestation of the dreamer's creative abilities that make it possible to view everyday problems in an unorthodox way. The interpretation of dreams, as well, requires artistic inspiration.

Erich Fromm's frames of reference aren't as clearly defined. His symbol interpretation is reminiscent of the existentialists, who are discussed in the next chapter. Montague Ullman thought that only the dreamer himself can decide what a dream means for him. All three agree that the previous day's events are of decisive significance for any dream, compared to Freud, who claimed that the day's residues are projection screens for infantile wishes, and to the Jungians, who think that even though they are the most frequent, everyday dreams are not the most important. Hall isn't interested whatever in the day's residues.

Ullman opposed that anybody could be an expert in others' dreams. Only the dreamer's personal understanding is determining for an analysis. He developed a technique for dream analysis in self-help groups, where the leader/counselor is looked upon as less authoritative than in psychoanalysis.

Like Hall, Ullman contributes to making dreams communal property. That these efforts initially come from analysts who are better at seeing parallels to waking life than plumbing the more perilous depths of the unconscious may be natural enough, but it shows at the same time that dream analysis can be beneficial on several levels.

The Empirical Basis

The idea that dreams act prospectively and are problem solving was suggested as early as 1913 by one of Freud's successors, Alphonse Maeder. It was soon appropriated by Jung and later by Adler and his successors, and by the neo-Freudians. Melanie Klein and a number of laboratory dream researchers embrace the theory, which thus has a very broad clinical tradition behind it. The greatest change with regard to the empirical basis came, however, with Calvin Hall's analytical method.

Around 1970, Hall and his associates had analyzed fifty thousand dreams. In the beginning his predominant interest was in persons who were not in therapy. He thereby contributed to expanding dream investigation's human material without it necessarily altering basic assumptions about dreams. An examination of the examples given in this chapter, and of Hall's material generally, doesn't indicate that "normal" people have inner conflicts that are essentially different from neurotics'. Perhaps they are a little better at closing them off and making do outwardly, but many of the dreams we have seen in the two psychoanalytical chapters are of quite another quality when it comes to depth.

Hall expanded his analyses to very disparate social groups dispersed over widely various societies, cultures, and subcultures. The one-sidedness in Hall's conception of dreams naturally can't avoid influencing his statistical scoring systems. Hall investigates particularly the dream ego's actions, and generally it takes place without Freudian associations and Jungian amplifications. Which is to say that the dreams' symbolic aspect is not sufficiently taken into account. As an example, men's dream egos have more sexual actions and experiences in dreams than women's. Symbolic sexuality has not been counted in; but as we have seen, both sunrises and plumbers can be very sexual in dreams, and it could well be that women generally are better at experiencing the erotic in images. Some sources of error have been investigated by the Danish psychologist Erik Schultz.

The Philosophy

In philosophical terms, this school is predominantly rationalistic and materialistic in its essence. Common sense is an important concept for Adler, Fromm is Marxist oriented, and Ullman is interested almost exclusively in dreams' everyday aspects. Hall, who adheres to Aristotle's dream theory, doesn't think there is anything mysterious or esoteric about dreams. When Hall finds mainly negative themes in dreams, it is reminiscent of Freud, who thought that what was possible and realistic in a therapy was to transform "neurotic misery to common misery." All in all, however, this movement is more humanistic than Freud's, and it nurtures confidence in the dream's creative potentialities.

4. Existential and Phenomenological Dream Interpretation

INTRODUCTION

Existential dream analysis has its roots in the works of German philosopher Martin Heidegger. Heidegger's basic idea was that although science "investigates all of the things and relationships that are, that is to say existence, it has forgotten to account for what existence is." What Heidegger wanted first and foremost to get rid of was a number of divisions between ego and world, subject and object, inner and outer, because these divisions make us "foreign" to the solidarity that exists between these apparently separate worlds.

Existential philosophy is closely bound to a method: the *phenomenological* method, which was founded by the German philosopher Edmund Husserl at the beginning of this century. Here one of the basic ideas is that one must be open toward phenomena as they immediately appear and avoid all theoretical abstractions. This ideal is not new in dream interpretation. Jung maintains that his scientific method is phenomenological, and he writes time and again that in working with dreams one ought to forget all technique and theory and regard that which is being presented as something completely new and unknown. Calvin Hall and Vernon Nordby assert that they began their investigations of dream contents without any preconceived ideas about what they would find. And when Freud introduced his method of free association it was precisely a means for avoiding arbitrary symbol translations and theorizations. At the same time, we have seen that these interpreters nevertheless arrive at theories and frames of reference which could be both enriching and constricting.

The dream interpreter who has attracted the most attention by bringing existential philosophy and phenomenological method into dream analysis is the Swiss psychiatrist Medard Boss. In the United States two pupils of the Freudian defector Karen Horney, Harold Kelman and David Shainberg, have worked with the method, and another prominent name is the humanistic psychologist Rollo May. Phenomenological interpretations are also often seen among the Jungians, who, however, don't make it a decisive theoretical factor.

Existentialism and phenomenology have also influenced experiential methods, which shall be discussed in the next chapter. Here my main point of departure will be taken from Boss's theory and working method.

MEDARD BOSS'S PHILOSOPHY AND THEORY

Martin Heidegger constructed a special language that was supposed to overcome the artificial divisions humans set up in the world, and this language was appropriated by Medard Boss. Boss calls his method *Daseins*-analysis. According to the Norwegian philosophy historian Arne Næss, *Dasein* can be translated as "person," but the idea behind the concept is that you mustn't think of a person as a finished, closed thing, but rather understand him from his special way of *being:* his *Dasein* (there-being). Heidegger's concepts are so special that even trained philosophers usually translate them to normal language, even though some of the effect is then lost. That is what we will have to do too.

The Heidegger and Boss specialist Walter James Lowe has stressed the Heidegger concept of "being-in-the-world" (*in der Welt sein*) as pivotal in Boss. It can best be understood as a state where the person "is on intimate terms with," "at home in" life, in contrast to being alienated. Boss thinks that people are originally "open," but that this openness becomes impaired. The basic gist of his therapy is to recover this openness and regain the feeling of being positively present in the world.

According to Lowe, Boss's use of the concept being-in-the-world has a threefold purpose. *Fundamentally* it unites the spheres of life that normally appear dissociated from each other; *diagnostically* it tells something about a client's way of experiencing the world; and *normatively* it makes it possible to determine whether a person is realizing "the full potentialities of his being," the "actual meaning and aim of his Dasein."

THE PHENOMENOLOGICAL METHOD

Medard Boss's method appears primarily as a reaction to overinterpretation and cliché-ridden theorizing analyses. Boss means to reawaken the sometimes dulled senses of the dream interpreter. He wants to let "the dream phenomena unfold, to allow them to tell their own story" instead of "letting everything be something else than what it is." The danger in interpreting at all is that it does violence to the poetic effect the dream might have in itself. "A causal explanation can never pass for the experience itself."

Boss's method appears to be simple. Say a person dreams about a dog. It is a matter of not straightaway interpreting the dog as a sexual symbol or as expression for the dreamer's animal-like traits. The interpreter must simply let the dog be a dog, and then let this phenomenon stimulate thought. The dog differs from a stone or a plant, say, by being a warm-blooded animal. It is the tamest animal known. It is on account of its instinctuality less free than man and more enslaved, etc. As a *first step in the interpretation* it is now a matter of opening the dreamer's eyes to the idea that some of the qualities mentioned are potentialities which might touch on his own waking existence. The *second step* is to get the dreamer to tell as precisely and detailed as possible how he reacts and feels toward the dream phenomenon in question. Does he approach the dog happily, react with indifference, or flee from it in terror? When you have gotten an exhaustive description of these two things, then Boss thinks you have understood what it is possible to understand.

The key concepts in Boss are the *unlived possibilities* the dreams reflect, and the *dreamer's bearing toward* (bearing oneself toward) the world and life.

Boss gives this example of a dream interpreted first Freudianly and then by himself. A twenty-four-year-old psychology student dreamed

> that the fiancée of a friend of his had just died of cancer. The dreamer had felt distant from his friend ever since the latter's engagement. The dreamer was shocked and saddened at the news of the young woman's death. After going to her funeral he found himself with other mourners in a self-service restaurant. He searched anxiously for some dessert or sweets but could not find anything of the sort.

A Freudian psychoanalyst had interpreted the first part of the dream as an unconscious death wish toward the young woman, prompted by his friend's engagement to her. The second part was interpreted as a regression to the oral phase. This interpretation the dreamer did not feel struck by, and according to Boss it had no therapeutic effect, so he sought a new analyst.

Boss placed weight instead on the young man's *bearing* in the dream. He felt genuine sorrow, which was not indicative of a death wish but rather that the friend's engagement had "attuned him to the theme of loving commitment." Even though the dreamer himself wasn't ready for a love relationship, he could experience it through the friend. To lose the possibility made the dreamer's universe contract to a self-service restaurant. Here the sweetness in a woman's love was replaced by sweet dishes, but even that was only present as something to be longed for.

Boss sharpens our attention toward the positive bearing: that the dreamer feels genuine sorrow, and that he has the possibility of giving himself in love. In my own experience too, such a shift in attention can be determining as to whether it becomes possible for the dreamer to feel himself as being a valuable and accepted person.

Boss mentions another dream from a twenty-year-old recruit in the Swiss army. The dream was collected by someone other than Boss himself and is intended as a practice example:

> *I crawled through the streets and killed a woman by strangling her with a cord. It wasn't the only murder that night. In all I committed three murders, just for the fun of it. The other two women I stabbed instead of choking. After a long time I got caught and, in spite of my stubborn denials, was sentenced to death by hanging. I woke up terrified just as they were slipping the noose around my neck.*

The dreamer was not in therapy. He showed no visible neurotic or psychosomatic symptoms nor was there anything particularly striking in his character, Boss writes. He had female acquaintances, and in the waking state did not think of murdering them.

Nevertheless the dream, in Boss's and also in my own opinion, was most suspect. Of all the conceivable ways of behaving toward women, this man in his dreams was only capable of killing them. And for fun into the bargain! Boss demonstrated that the one-track behavior was diametrically opposed to a normal, mature love that recognizes all the potential for life in partner.

In terms of method, what Boss does is normatively describe what ought to belong to mature love, and he interprets the dream going from what it does not contain. In the preceding chapter I mentioned that Adler and Hall also looked at what was not in the dream.

Hereafter the first therapeutic step Boss would take was to ask the dreamer whether he had anything against women in the waking state. According to Boss's experience, he would gradually, and in ever greater numbers, remember concrete situations from his life hitherto which had contributed to narrowing his register of feelings toward women so drastically. This would get him to realize that adult women had always stood in the way of his possibilities for developing into a normal self-assured adult man, and therefore he wanted to do away with them. This inevitably leads back to the realization that there was something wrong in relation to the mother. Either that *she* had obstructed the dreamer's development in one way or another, or that his own infantile fixation to her had done so. In any event, his psychological field of vision from infancy onward would be restricted so that he could only see women as dangerous, venomous creatures who deserved to die.

The causal explanation itself of the man's dilemma is entirely Freudian. But one of the things Boss has against reducing a dream like this to traumatic events in childhood is that it can hinder the dreamer from realizing that what is happening in him is happening here and now and isn't merely a past event he has no responsibility for.

THE INTERPRETER'S ROLE AND THE DREAM

In Boss's dream analysis it is clearly a question of expert as opposed to layman, and different levels of interpretation are possible, all according to what it is thought the client can take. In reality, Boss writes, his therapeutic exploitation of the dream is nothing more than what Freud called *resistance analysis*. Boss follows Wilhelm Reich in putting special stress on processing the ego's defense mechanisms. If one concentrates on that exclusively, then according to Reich the id contents (the unconscious contents) would come to the surface in an orderly and natural way. "If you do the opposite the analysis will inevitably end in terrible chaos."

Boss's method is therefore extremely gentle. He uses the dream to see what open wounds he must avoid jabbing an analytical knife into. If an anxiety-neurotic woman dreams, for example, that some force started tearing her pet turtle apart, thereby inflicting unbearable torture on her, he then advised the therapist not to use his magical analytical force to tear her dream apart and thereby inflict on her an unbearable pain. Boss placed much stress on how an analyst should present his or her analyses to the dreamer.

A thirty-year-old single man suffered from depression and difficulty in making human contact. One night he dreamed *I was standing at a hot dog stand. I had just finished ordering a hot dog and was having a pleasant conversation with the vendor, when a young woman appeared beside me and began to snuggle up to me. I became violently afraid of her and ran away as fast as I could, even forgetting to take along my hot dog in the rush.*

Nothing would be easier, of course, than to make the hot dog into a symbol for a penis or a pseudopenis. But, Boss writes, it would "preclude a paramount insight," namely that the therapy had taken the client to the point where he could eat in a public place, regardless of his being unable to relate erotically to a woman. To be sure, the hot dog–symbol could have many meanings and frames of reference that should be brought to the patient's attention. But what Boss wished to use as the point of departure is the contact with "the jolly hot dog vendor," and that the dreamer ate in the dream, actually assimilating something "fleshy." He preferred addressing the dreamer in an interrogatory form, and proposed the following "questions":

1. "I think it is wonderful that, at least while dreaming, you allow yourself the deep sensual pleasure of eating a juicy hot dog, and that you are bold enough to enjoy it right out in public, at a stand on a busy square."

2. "On the other hand, don't you find it at all strange that when a woman approaches you in a highly erotic way, you see her only as a frightening, anxiety-producing creature?"

3. "Are you aware of the extent to which anxiety overwhelms you in the presence of the young woman, forcing you to run away and preventing you from enjoying the sensual pleasure of consuming the hot dog in peace?"

4. "What is it that you concretely fear, in your waking life, about the sensual, erotic presence of women?"

A thirty-year-old woman began analytic treatment on account of frigidity. She related the following dream:

I was supposed to decline a Latin noun, one of the ones whose masculine ending disguises its feminine gender. I was supposed to decline it with an adjective, so that the feminine endings of the adjective would betray the true gender of the noun, despite its masculine forms. But I had a

*hard time performing this task; in fact, I never managed to finish it.
Even while I was dreaming I wasn't sure just which word was involved.*

The therapist understood the Latin feminine noun, which was concealed in back of a masculine ending, as a parallel to the woman herself hiding her femininity behind a masculine manner. Other details in the dream indicated that the woman was far from grasping what this implied. First, the problem was presented to her in a "dead language." Second, her femininity could shine through via a tacked-on "adjective." Third, she wasn't clear as to where the demand for femininity came from, but she behaved like an obedient schoolgirl toward a strict invisible schoolmaster. Fourth, she wasn't up to the task.

The woman would probably have found a traditional symbolic interpretation very interesting, and she would have thought it over. But her problem was that an intellectualizing attitude blocked her emotional contact with herself. Boss suggested that the analyst simply reformulate the dream with a slight emphasis of the feminine/masculine gender problem. From then on it was important that he find the most positive content in the dream, and he was unstinting in his appreciation of it.

1. "As a person who doesn't know what to live for in your waking life, might not the appearance of a task in your dreaming state signify a first step toward a freer, more meaningful existence?"

And then:

2. "On the other hand, does it not strike you as strange that in your dreaming you are given a task so separate from yourself, involving only a word from a dead foreign language, and that the task entails highly abstract, intellectual labor, namely, a grammatical declension?"

When the patient became aware of her distance from the Latin word in the dream, she spontaneously recalled a lot of things back in early childhood from which she had been similarly distant. And she began understanding how her parents had influenced her to this.

Then Boss, like the Freudians, operates with defense mechanisms and varying degrees of integration ability in the ego. What is new is that he introduces a method of communicating the interpreter's insights in the most expedient way. The technique resembles a therapeutic method called *reframing*.

The idea behind reframing is that the value of any attribute or attitude whatever depends on the framework in which it is used. By placing an apparently negative content within a new frame, it suddenly becomes positive. In my experience this method is especially suited for motivating people to work with negative dream content. All things considered, any knowledge of how a message is communicated so that it is received is good to have for a dream interpreter. The cautious approach that Boss recommends becomes all the more imperative the graver the psychic diagnosis a dream exposes.

An example of such a tactful interpretation of a schizophrenic's dream is given in chapter 12.

As phenomenology deals with experiencing immediately, the notion of interpretation is already a stumbling block. Younger phenomenological dream theorists have described the therapist's role as that of an *illuminator* who gets the dreamer to see what *actually* takes place in the dream, who helps by shedding light on overlooked nuances, who "comes with suggestions" or "draws attention to." Here stress is laid on "the spontaneous and creative as opposed to the compulsive intellectualizing of experience," which is seen as a typical neurotic trait. It is a matter of "lifting out" an aspect of the dream and seeing what sets it in motion, and then letting this process determine the next step in the interpretation. This is in several ways close to the Jungian method, in which client and therapist sit face to face and carry on a dialogue.

DREAM SERIES AND PERSONALITY DEVELOPMENT

Like the Jungians, Calvin Hall and many neo-Freudians use Boss's running dream series to measure whether the patients are making progress in their therapy and personal development.

Boss treated a thirty-year-old depressed and impotent mechanical engineer over a period of three years. His 823 dreams were sorted into well-defined phases, in which certain themes predominated practically to the exclusion of others. Boss could follow an orderly and progressive development from phase to phase.

In the first six months the man dreamed only about turbines, cyclotrons, cars, airplanes, and other machines. Then he began to dream about plants, trees, vegetables, and flowers. This botanical phase was followed, after a long dreamless interval, by dreams teeming with animal life—in the beginning about injurious insects. During a six-month period there were more than a hundred insect dreams; then came a long period in which toads, frogs, and snakes dominated the picture. The first warm-blooded animal to shoulder its way into his dreams was a mouse, which scurried into a mousehole. The first human turned up in dreams after two years of therapy. It was an unconscious gigantic woman in a long red gown who floated in a large pond beneath a transparent layer of ice. Half a year later he dreamed "that he was dancing at a country fair with a woman who was also wearing a red gown but was, unlike the earlier dream figure, wide awake and full of life."

The first sign of improvement in the man's waking life occurred when he began dreaming about plants. At that moment the feeling that life was totally without meaning began to give way. Moreover, his impotence vanished at the moment lions and horses began appearing in his dreams.

A different kind of dream theme was used by Boss to evaluate the progress of a twenty-six-year-old female medical student's course of therapy. Three months into the therapy, the woman dreamed that *my teeth had become rotten and broken off,* and eighteen months later she dreamed once again that *all my cutting teeth are missing.* But twenty-seven months after the beginning of therapy and four months after its successful conclusion she dreamed: *I'm looking into the mirror. I see that in many of the gaps, the tips of new, larger and stronger teeth have already broken through.*

The Nature and Function of Dreams in Boss

A psychoanalyst by the name of Schrötter was cited by Freud for the following experiment: he hypnotized a number of persons and asked them while in a trance to dream of specified sexual activities. One hypnotized woman was asked to dream about lesbian intercourse with a female friend. In the dream in question *she met the friend, who was carrying a traveling bag with the inscription "For ladies only."* It was obvious to both Schrötter and Freud that the traveling bag symbolized the woman friend's genitals.

Boss simulated these experiments and "hypnotized" five women—three healthy and two neurotic—and asked each of them to dream about a specified male friend who was in love with her and came walking toward her nude, aroused and clearly with sexual intention. The three healthy women had dreams that in all details corresponded to Boss's suggestion. Upon awakening they related the sexual dream experiences without embarrassment, even with delight. With the two neurotic women it was a different story. Boss's suggestion induced anxiety dreams with markedly altered content. One of these women dreamed that *a uniformed soldier, a complete stranger to her, had come toward her holding a handgun. While playing with his weapon he had almost hit her; she had been so frightened that she woke up.* Boss took it that the woman's experiential world was so "infantile, narrow and fear-drenched" that not even in dreams was there "place for a sexually aroused, desirous lover."

Naturally this anecdote doesn't demonstrate anything concretely, but it gives a picture of Boss's conception of the dream. It is akin to Hall's dream-work (the child molester who didn't dream about his father), and it states why Boss judged the dream by what *doesn't* appear in it.

What separates Boss most radically from Freud and Jung is that he denies the existence of the unconscious. He doesn't think it is possible to speak of an intrapsychic system that "makes" the dream, neither a dream censor nor a collective unconscious. Both concepts presuppose a kind of intelligence in the unconscious that on certain points is superior to the conscious. Boss on the contrary thought that the waking state is superior to the dream in intelligence, horizon, and freedom of choice. The great therapeutic value in dreams lies in that the dream events press in on the dreamer with a sensual and emotional force, with one intense event following the other at a rapid pace. This means that in dreams one is confronted with one's problems much more powerfully, and aided by the dreams the trained therapist can point out corresponding but as yet unrealized potentialities in the dreamer's waking life. Boss states nothing about the extent to which dreams have a natural function. He simply ascertains that they can be used for a therapeutic purpose.

Boss has about the same conception of the continuity between dream and waking ego as we have seen in Hans Dieckmann, and which is also borne out by Calvin Hall's investigations. Even in extreme transformations of the ego into, for example, a floor cloth or a many years younger or older person he found that ego perception—the feeling of being me—was preserved. In his long career as a dream analyst he saw only one exception to this rule, and that was in serious mental illnesses (schizophrenias). Even there he thought that the person had felt a similar loss of himself in the waking state.

Boss considers dreams as being events of another order but having the same quality of authentic reality as the waking state. The background for this is the philosophical assumption of the impossibility of separating the experience of the thing from the thing itself. Reality is what we experience as real, and in dreams we experience events as just as real as in the waking state. It is only later, from the point of view of waking experience, that the dream is declared to be less real. Boss acknowledges, too, that the dream has a forward-pointing prospective aspect, and that it can deal with as yet unrealized potentialities.

Phenomenology compared with other methods

Undoubtedly the phenomenological method fills a gap in the analytical tradition, and for someone schooled within a particular movement, becoming acquainted with it can be liberating. Boss's criticism of Freud and Jung is based first and foremost on the fact that their interpretations don't do justice to the immediate experience of the dream. Freud has given one of the dreams in *The Interpretation of Dreams* the title "A Beautiful Dream," yet Boss asserts that Freud's treatment of it made it "something unshapely." The woman who dreamed that *[s]he is in the sea, rising and falling with large threatening waves. The waves finally assume the shape of a beautiful orchid and become calm. Her anxiety subsides* might reasonably feel that the immediate experience of the dream is betrayed when her neo-Freudian analyst regarded it as "denial of anxiety by means of a fantasy of high aesthetic quality."

A phenomenological understanding of the dream would if anything open her to the fact that she was capable of experiencing such tremendous natural forces (within her), and that there was space for a priceless and rare flower in her dream universe. Such an understanding would possibly motivate her to further work with herself—more than a Freudian rap over the knuckles.

As far as I can see, it isn't so much a matter of the "right" or "wrong" interpretation as of different perspectives of the same phenomenon. A Jungian interpretation would regard the dream as archetypal with development potentials. Only a closer knowledge of the context can determine which interpretation is the most expedient.

In the example in which a twenty-four-year-old psychology student dreamed that his friend's fiancée had died of cancer, Boss rejected a Freudian interpretation that emphasized an oral problem in the dreamer. That the student broke off a Freudian analysis does indicate that the analyst hadn't taken the resistance into account. But the interpretation can still have been correct. According to a Jungian analysis, the friend's fiancée could represent the dreamer's own feminine side, which had been "engaged to" the friend. That is to say, the feminine way of relating to the friend is dead. This could be viewed as a positive development potential. Or it is the friend's anima (the girlfriend) he has been in love with. Going from this it would be possible to form a picture of the young men's relationship, the way I have described it in *The Feminine in the Man.*

The long dream progression from the depressive, impotent engineer is, incidentally, remarkably similar to the progressions I described in *The Feminine in the Man* without being acquainted with Boss's series. Like the engineer, in these progressions the men start with a rather narrow and mechanical consciousness, after which they run through, so to speak, the entire phylogenetic scale in a vegetative and an animal-like phase on their way toward a new humanity. Boss's case, however, appears to be far more severe than mine, just as the dreams in his are correspondingly extreme.

The best argument for letting the dream stand on its own poetic aura has in my opinion been given by Erich Fromm, when in *The Forgotten Language* he describes the symbol's effect. You dream, for example, that you see yourself in a deserted and impoverished neighborhood on the outskirts of a city just before dawn, and when you awaken it occurs to you that "the feeling you had in the dream was precisely the lost and gray feeling which the day before you tried to describe to your friend. In less than a second the symbol describes vividly and exactly something which words could not reproduce," Fromm writes. "It is like having to explain for someone the difference between red wine and white wine. The best is to let the person taste."

Nevertheless, some of the most important psychological discoveries in this century, namely Freud's and Jung's, were made not merely by experiencing dreams but by interpreting them.

Boss's distinctive communication technique that I have compared with reframing, i.e., recasting the contents to other frameworks, suggests a dimension in dreams that isn't contained in any of the earlier methods. In accepting the method we must acknowledge (contrary to Boss's own postulates) being able to take the dream contents out of the frame in which the dreams' own structure locks them and obtain information about the dreamer that is excluded in other systems. We could even—although no one has done it yet—use the relationship between "frame" and "contents" as a basis for personality studies.

HIDDEN INTERPRETATIONS

The principal idea in phenomenological dream theory is that you mustn't base your dream interpretations on any abstract theories but rather must let the dreams speak their own language. Yet in Boss especially it becomes clear how problematic this strategy is. Boss opposes Freud's and Jung's symbolic constructions. But he himself philosophizes on, for example, the dog as creature and its meaning in dreams. It was warm-blooded and not cold-blooded, it was obedient and enslaved, etc. The hot dog in a thirty-year-old single man's dream was something "fleshy and animal-like, rather than something bloodless from the vegetable kingdom."

This isn't so different from the Jungian way of working with problems. The difference is that Jung didn't leave it up to the individual analyst to figure out important traits in a dog, but tried to form an empirical basis for the symbolic construction by collecting a large amount of material on notions about the dog from myth and folklore. This can in part prevent the analyst from projecting his own complexes onto the dog, and in part open for broader possibilities of meaning than he had the fantasy to conceive. Freud, for his part, tried to avoid the analyst's haphazardness and make the analysis more objective by using free associations from the dreamer.

It also seems strange that Boss argues strongly against speaking of animals' sexual symbolic meaning, considering that his mechanical engineer stopped being impotent when horses and lions began appearing in his dreams. Boss was highly selective and hypostatizing when characterizing the individual dream elements. In innumerable places his personal outlook and philosophy form the basis for dream interpretations. For example, in interpreting the woman-murderer dream he makes his basis the assumption that "a human *Dasein* is attuned to pleasure whenever it is allowed to." But this was precisely Freud's original assumption. Later Freud added that a person is also guided by a destructive death instinct. This is naturally open to discussion, and it is Freud's strength that he does discuss it and presents his premises so they can be criticized. Boss on the other hand tosses it out like a given phenomenological truth about the human *Dasein*, and simultaneously asserts that no special value system is taken as the basis for this assumption.

The American author of a number of books on psychology and phenomenology Eugene Gendlin has examined one of Boss's interpretation examples: "In one patient's dream published by a Jungian analyst (H. K. Fierz), the patient dreamt that *the analyst is performing surgery on him. Then an unknown white-haired man appears, cuts two pieces of his own flesh out of himself and grafts them onto the dreamer's abdomen. Thereby the dreamer's life is saved.*"

The Jungian interpreter saw the white-haired man as a symbol for the archetype "the old wise man." Boss, who was opposed to this interpretation, regarded the old man as a "possibility" in the dreamer for becoming a "masculine, mature, selfless, helpful fellow-man." Boss labels the patient's bearing (to submit to surgery) as "purely passive," while the Jungian sees it as positive that he accepts aid from something greater than his ego. To characterize the old man, Boss selects concepts including "selfless" and "masculine," but he could also be called "courageous, insensitive to pain," and so on. The operation can be characterized as "painful, bloody, unusual, expensive, dangerous, usually done by men, and constituting an emergency, etc."

In working with interpretation one of the most difficult things is to not jump to conclusions and load the material with one's own biases. With dream texts this tendency is reinforced by two things: 1) the interpreter often has countertransference, and 2) the symbol appeals to feelings and to our own unconscious images that we project into the dreams. Time and again in training situations, in groups, at lectures, and in my own analyses I have seen prematurely concluded interpretations.

Here phenomenology is an aid to self-criticism and to attentiveness to the "given" experience. On the other hand, the antiauthoritarian bearing readily results in the interpreter unconsciously putting his own value systems into the dreams. If you don't have a clear conception of your frames of reference, they unconsciously seem merely a view of man, a philosophy of life, a bias, a countertransference.

THE EMPIRICAL BASIS

The existential-phenomenological method of dream interpretation has fewer adherents than the previously discussed methods. Nor does it have nearly as comprehensive a literature. The empirical basis becomes accordingly smaller. Boss's interpretations are extra difficult to test, as he rejects in principle the validity of scientific methods in human relations. He doesn't think that a method like Hall's laboratory experiments with dreams, for example, provide any truth about the phenomenon, as he thinks that it can only be understood qualitatively.

Boss's personal empirical basis is the analysis of nearly one hundred thousand dreams, and there is no question as to his being an expert and inspired interpreter. If you evaluate his clientele on the basis of the examples in his most important works on dreams, it is clearly a question of the sorriest clientele in this book. This will be corroborated in the chapter on dream and psychosis. The faintness of ego in his clients possibly forced him to invent his gentle interrogatory technique. Thus it is particularly useful in dreamers with a weak ego, or when approaching vulnerable areas in a person's psyche.

Among the many trained dream analysts I have met there wasn't one who didn't take into account how much a client can "take." Boss's method is buttressed by having been the first to incorporate this concern.

FREUD'S, JUNG'S, AND BOSS'S IDEAS COMPARED

The American professor of religious history Christine Downing has compared the ideas behind Freud's, Jung's, and Boss's theories. She finds an essential joint endeavor among them, namely the surmounting of an egocentric and overly controlling attitude to life. Freud showed this in, among other things, the concept of narcissism, which he regarded as a form of death. Likewise Jung with his conception of the Self as a natural instance preeminent to the ego.

Freud had contact with a predecessor of Boss, Ludwig Binschwanger, and Jung had a correspondence with Boss. They were originally positive toward the phenomenological endeavors, but as Jung later wrote to Boss: "In spite of all existential philosophy the opposition between ego and the world, subject and object, is not annulled. That would be too simple." And when I myself have not made use of Boss's conceptual apparatus it has to do with the view that words like *I* and *thou*, *inner* and *outer*, which have grown out of life and language, are probably more viable than concepts that have originated from a philosophical mind. I have gone the way of many others who originally were trained in one particular school of dream analysis. At first Boss's theories had the effect of a liberation from the straightjacket of systems. Later I discovered that both Boss and I had taken Freud and Jung more literally than they themselves had done.

5. Experiential Dreamwork

INTRODUCTION

Even though the dream theorists in the preceding chapters have placed the
main emphasis on understanding, insight, and interpretation, they have also
been very much interested in the emotional experience in dreamwork. In
Freud's therapy the emotional experiences came in through recollections of
events in childhood, which the clients accessed when lying relaxed on the
couch in free association. Freud used a term associated with ancient Greek
tragedy, *catharsis*, or purification through suffering: the audience experienced an emotional release through their vicarious involvement in the
drama. And when Freud later so strongly emphasized transference, it was
precisely to get the client to relive what was repressed as an actual experience in the present.

In Jung the experiential acquired weight through his active-imagination
technique, and through connecting dreams to actual experiences in daily
life. Archetypal symbols he also saw as laden with emotional energy. A
pitfall of free associations, however, is that they are often supplied without
real emotional involvement, and a weakness in Jung's active imagination is
that the fantasies can become merely the objects of interesting interpretations, which occur "off the top of the head" without one being emotionally
affected, let alone released.

The phenomenological method reacted against overinterpretation and advocated experiencing the dream as it presented itself. But in practice—like Freud's and Jung's interpretations—it could be somewhat one-sided, intellectual.

The early dream interpreters were conscious of the value of emotional experience in therapy, but younger therapists have sometimes been criticized for not giving it the proper attention. This gap has been closed by the so-called experience oriented and emotionally releasing therapies. In this chapter the main emphasis will be on gestalt therapy, and psychodrama shall be discussed. These methods, along with body therapies, "esoteric" methods, and dreamwork involving birth experiences and consciousness-expanding techniques, will be discussed in later chapters and place more weight on experience than on understanding.

GESTALT THERAPY AND PERLS

The most influential of the newer experiential therapies is *gestalt therapy*, which to a high degree uses dreams in the treatment. Gestalt therapy was founded by the German-American Fritz Perls. He was schooled as a psychoanalyst with body therapy's great pioneer, Wilhelm Reich; with the classical Freudian Otto Fenichel; and with the more existential-oriented Karen Horney. Later Perls affiliated himself with a newer therapeutic movement called humanistic psychology.

Perls's principal work is the book *Gestalt Therapy* from 1951, in which together with associates Ralph Hefferline and Paul Goodmann he developed a new theory of personality and a new therapeutic method. Perls's theory and practice is exhaustively described by the American gestalt therapists Erving and Miriam Polster, and concisely by the Danish psychologist and gestalt therapist Ville Laursen. Of especial interest to us is a verbatim transcription of a series of dream seminars that Perls held in California from 1966 to 1968, in which he did practical work with clients in groups. Parallel with this he accounted for his theories on psychology and therapy in general and on dreams in particular. A more recent introduction into gestalt therapeutic dreamwork is the American gestalt therapist Jack Downing's book *Dreams and Nightmares*.

Perls took the name for his therapy from gestalt psychology, which posited that people don't experience in parts but in wholes, in *gestalts*. When you look at a picture, for example, you don't spell your way through it but see all of it at once. In music you take in the melody rather than the single tone.

Perls regarded the personality as a "self-regulating organization," an "organism." Naturally there is an interplay with the surrounding world, but it is the organism that sorts out and shapes its experiences and actions. The organism always works as a whole. It isn't a putting together of individual components but a coordination. Disturbances in the "organismic balance" create "incomplete" gestalts.

Perls regards the organism as spontaneously creative and thus able to complete gestalts, re-creating balance. If the gestalts aren't completed, on account of pressure from the surroundings or excessive self-control, states of tension arise that can become chronic and disturb the growth of the personality. The aim of gestalt therapy, then, is to complete the incomplete gestalts. This act liberates energy so that the natural development process and the organism's self-regulation can resume. In practice the releasing of a gestalt is always accompanied by powerful emotional discharges, and these discharges are the cardinal point of gestalt therapy. Intellectualizations and abstractions are gestalt therapy's number one enemy.

For Perls, maturity is moving from the support of the surrounding world to self-support. There are several personality layers that have to be worked through before one becomes an "authentic" person:

1. The cliché layer, or as-if layer. All communication is superficial, meaningless, and contactless, an exchange of empty phrases.

2. The role-playing layer. Here you pretend to be someone different than you are: more important, polite, tougher, the nice little girl, the good boy, etc.

3. The no-way-out layer, or neurotic layer. Normal defense mechanisms and role playing are no longer functional. You attempt a kind of antiexistence, avoiding feelings of real anger, real love, real grief, real happiness. Now you stand face to face with yourself as a human although very split entity. And you don't know a way out of the impasse.

4. The implosive layer, or death layer. This is the nucleus of the neurosis. All the vital energy, the emotions, and the needs that have been denied for so long can now be felt. It's as if the energy contracts and compresses. You are under tremendous pressure, and implode into a state of deadness.

5. The explosive layer, or life layer. The energy gets moving, explodes into grief, anger, orgasm, or joy in living. You are now free to feel, to experience, to be responsible.

The crux of Perls's therapy is to get the person to be present here and now, to constantly be aware of what is actually taking place in the personality. The consciousness of what someone is really experiencing, feeling, and sensing is in itself curative. Perls calls it *creating a continuum of awareness*, and this continuum is a prerequisite for the organism's self-regulation. As far as most people are concerned, the continuum is broken by "holes in the consciousness," and the holes are stronger the more neurotic we are. In the meantime the holes are always visible, in any case to those who don't have them. They reveal themselves as a "phobic attitude," as "avoidance."

All of what we have excluded from our experiential sphere, both in others and in ourselves, we experience as frightening, and we do everything to avoid a confrontation. This leads to alienation and self-impoverishment. The most important expedient in the therapy is therefore to again and again frustrate the person until he stands face to face with his own blockages, with his inhibitions, with his manner of avoiding.

Perls believed that you can't repress a need. What you can repress is the *expression* of it, and "Anything unexpressed which wants to be expressed can make you feel uncomfortable." He advocated group therapy and thought that individual therapy was outmoded. Two important ingredients in the therapy are "the hot seat," for whomever wanted to work with him, and "the empty chair," where the client in his imagination could put a person with whom he wanted to have dialogue. (The profuse weeping that resulted is the reason Perls was the first to make Kleenex obligatory in psychotherapy.) Perls appropriated the empty-chair technique from Jacob Levy Moreno, the originator of psychodrama. But while Moreno, so as to get a person to play out his inner complexes, let other group members have roles in the skit, the occupant of Perls's hot seat played all of the roles himself.

PERLS AND THE DREAM

While Freud termed the dream the royal road to the unconscious, Perls called it the royal road to integration. The dream was "[t]he most spontaneous expression of human existence," its "concentrated reflection." It was an "existential communication"; that is, a message as to how the dreamer should relate to his life.

According to Perls, every dream that can still be recalled contains an incomplete situation and can therefore be made the object of gestalt therapeutic work. All of the various parts of the dream can be regarded as fragments of the personality, which is projected away from the ego and into the different dream elements. Due to the phobic attitude, we try to avoid contact with them and so become alienated from ourselves, and the conflicts among the dream elements reflect conflicts in the personality. "Understanding the dream" is to realize what you are trying to avoid. You achieve contact with the projected parts of yourself by identifying yourself with them, by "becoming them," really feeling yourself as the hideous frog, as the little devil, as the mood in the dream, as the dead things—or the living ones. This could be accomplished through role-playing.

Perls's favorite example of identification was a patient who dreamed that he *is leaving my [Perls's] office and goes into Central Park. And he goes across the bridle path, into the park.* Perls asked him to play the bridle path. He answered indignantly, "What, and let everybody shit and crap on me?" Perls could, however, also relate to a dream element on its own terms: that is, emphasize the bridle path as expressing directionality, leisurely movement, beauty, etc., so the client doesn't remain caught in the negative projection: to be shit on.

For Perls the ideal is to "learn through discovery." He opposed interpretations, analyses, and explanations. Verbal contact is torn out of our total experience of ourselves and the world. It can never pass for experience. In order to get the wholeness you also have to observe body attitudes, movements, and body sensations. "A good therapist" doesn't listen to "the content of the bullshit the patient produces, but to the sound, to the music, to the hesitations." Instead of interpreting, give *feedback*, not only on the client's sentences but everything you see and sense in her.

JEAN'S DREAM: A PRACTICAL EXAMPLE

As a practical example of Perls's dreamwork I have chosen the most important sections from a session with thirty-one-year-old Jean, with whom Perls did group work. I make a running commentary on Perls's technique. The last three commentaries come from Erving and Miriam Polster, who have also considered this example. In this session, Jean plays herself, a piece of cardboard, and her mother.

The dream starts with Jean and her mother in something that could be a New York subway. They are standing in front of a chute:

> [I]t was sort of muddy, sort of slippery, and I thought, Oh! We can go down this! and well, sort of on the side, I picked up a leftover carton—or maybe it was just flattened out or I flattened it out. At any rate, I said,

"Let's sit down on this." I sat down on the edge, kind of made a toboggan out of it, and I said, "Mom, you sit down behind me," and we started going down. And it sort of went around and around (quickly) and there were other people it seemed like, waiting in line, but then they kind of disappeared, and we were (happily) just going down and around and it just kept on going down and down and down, and I was sort of realizing that I was going down kind of into the bowels of the earth.

And every once in a while I'd turn around and say, "Isn't this fun?"— it seems, although maybe I'll discover I didn't have that attitude either. But it seemed like fun. And yet I wondered what would be down at the bottom of this—going, turn and turn, and then finally it leveled out and we got up and I was just astounded, because here I thought, "Oh my God, the bowels of the earth!" And yet instead of being dark, it was like there was sunlight coming from somewhere, and a beautiful . . . oh, kind of like a . . . I've never been to Florida, but it seemed like a Florida kind of Everglades, with lagoons, and tall reeds, and beautiful long-legged birds—herons—and things like that. And I don't remember saying any-thing particularly, except maybe something like, "Who would ever have expected this!"—or something.

After Jean tells the dream, "Fritz" talks for three or four minutes about dream theory, philosophy of life, and morals. Then working with the dream continues:

Commentary	Dreamwork
	F: You are now on the chute. Are you afraid to go down?
	J: *(laughs)* I guess I am, a little afraid to go down. But then it seems like . . .
	F: So the existential message is, "You've got to go down."
	J: I guess I'm afraid to find out what's there.
	F: This points to false ambitions, that you're too high up.
	J: That's true.
	F: So the existential message says, "Go down." Again our mentality says, "High up is better than down." You must always be somewhere higher.

The chute is regarded as a projection. A dialogue is started.

J: Anyway, I seem a little afraid to go down.

F: Talk to the chute.

J: Why are you muddy? You're slippery and slidy and I might fall on you and slip.

F: Now play the chute. "I'm slippery and . . ."

J: I'm slippery and muddy, the better to slide and faster to get down on. *(laughs)*

F: Aha, well what's the joke?

J: *(continues laughing)* I'm just laughing.

F: Can you accept yourself as slippery?

Jean gets in contact with her own slippery side.

J: Hm. I guess so. Yes. I can never seem to . . . Yeah, you know, always just when I think I'm about to, you know, I say, "Aha, I've caught you now!" it slips away—you know, rationalization. I'm slippery and slidy.

In a minute Jean happens to think of the cardboard she is sitting on.

A new projection is taken up.

F: Can you play this cardboard? If you were this cardboard . . . what's your function?

J: I'm just to make things easier. I'm just kind of lying around and leftover, and aha, I have a use for.

Fritz decoys the unsuspecting Jean into seeing her own suppressed side.

F: Oh—you can be useful.

J: I can be useful. I'm not just leftover and lying around, and we can make it easier to get down.

F: Is it important for you to be useful?

J: *(quietly)* Yes. I want to be an advantage to somebody . . .

F: Is that enough for being the cardboard? . . .

J: Maybe I also want to be sat upon. *(laughter)*

F: Oh!

THE DIMENSIONS OF DREAMS ■ 163

J: What is that part in the book about who wants to kick who? I want to be pitied, I want to be scrunched down.

By getting her to repeat and by involving the group, Fritz intensifies Jean's awareness of the new experience. Fritz points out Jean's body language. Jean turns the anger onto herself. Fritz supplies the intention as the psychological mother.

F: Say this to the group.

J: Well, that's hard to do. (loudly) I want to be sat upon and scrunched down ... Hm. (loudly) I want to be sat upon and scrunched down. (pounds her thigh with fist)

F: Who are you hitting?

J: Me.

F: Besides you?

J: I think my mother, who's turning, who's behind me and I look around and see her.

F: Good. Now hit her.

J: (loudly) Mother, I'm scrunching down upon—(hits thigh) ouch!—you (laughs) and I am going to take you for a ride (laughter) instead of your telling me to go, and taking me wherever you want to, I'm taking you along for a ride with me.

F: Did you notice anything in your behavior with your mother?

J: Just now? (laughs)

Fritz conveys his impression of the situation so Jean becomes conscious that she is still afraid of the mother. Fritz amplifies the experience, which Jean in a flash gets hold of.

F: I had the impression it was too much to be convincing ... It was spoken with anger, not with firmness.

J: Hmm. I think I'm still a little afraid of her.

F: That's it. You tell her that.

J: Mom, I'm still afraid of you ... but I'm gonna take you for a ride anyway.

F: Okay. Let's put momma on the sled. (laughter)

Then Jean imagines that she and her mother are sledding down the chute. Fritz starts a dialogue.

Here it becomes obvious that Jean has inherited her evasive action from her mother. Jean is afraid.

Fritz catches Jean by her body language.

"Mom": Don't worry. I've got it all taken care of. *(decisively)* We're having fun. I don't know where this is going, but we're going to find out.

J: I'm scared!

"Mom": I think I—don't be scared. It's going down and down and DOWN and DOWN . . . *(softly)* I wonder what's going to be down there. It'll just be black . . . I don't know what she says.

F: What's your left hand doing?

J: Right this instant?

F: Yah. Always right this instant.

J: Holding my head. I'm—

F: As if? . . .

J: not to see?

F: Aha. You don't want to see where you are going, don't want to see the danger.

Jean nears the death layer.

J: Umhm. *(softly)* I'm really afraid—of what will be down there . . . It could be terrible or just blackness or just maybe oblivion.

Fritz goes along with the resistance and encourages her to explore the experience of the death layer. It looks as if Jean eludes the negative in the experience; it gets too exciting. This is probably what prompts Fritz's next remark.

Fritz again points out an "avoidance."

F: I would like you to go now into this blackness. This is your nothingness, the blankness, the sterile void. What does it feel like to be in this nothingness?

J: Suddenly, nothingness is I'm going down, now . . . So I still have a feeling that I'm going down, and so it's kind of exciting and exhilarating . . . because I'm moving, and I'm very much alive . . . I'm not really afraid. It's more—kind of terribly exciting and . . . the anticipation—what will I discover at the end of this. It's not really black—it's sort of going down, somehow there's some light, where it's from, I don't—

F: Yah. I want to make a little bit of a shortcut here, to say something. Are you aware of what you are avoiding in this dream?

J: Am I aware of what I am avoiding?

F: Having legs.

J: Having legs?

F: Yah.

J: Legs to carry me someplace.

F: Yah. Instead of standing on your legs, you rely on the support of the cardboard, and you rely on gravitation to carry you.

Fritz gets a dialogue going between Jean and her mother. The mother says that Jean can't take care of herself.

F: Stand on your legs now, and encounter your mother, and see whether you can talk to her.

J: *(softly)* I'm afraid to look at her.

F: Say this to her.

J: *(loudly)* I'm afraid to look at you, mother! *(exhales)*

F: What would you see?

J: What do I see? I see I hate her. *(loudly)* I hate you for holding me back every time I wanted to even go across the aisle of the damned department store.

"Mom": *(high-pitched)* Come back here. Don't go on the other side of the aisle.

J: I can't even walk across the damned aisle. Can't go to Flushing when I want to go on the bus. Can't go to New York—not until I go to college. Damn you!

F: How old are you when you play this now?

J: Well, I'm . . . in the department store, I'm only anywhere from six to ten or twelve—

F: How old are you, really?

J: Really? Thirty-one.

F: Thirty-one.

J: She's even dead.

F: Okay, can you talk as a thirty-one-year-old to your mother? Can you be your own age?

J: *(quietly and firmly)* Mother, I am thirty-one years old. I am quite capable of walking on my own.

F: Notice the difference. Much less noise, and much more substance.

J: I can stand on my own legs. I can do anything I want to do, and I can know what I want to do. I don't need you. In fact, you're not even here if I did need you. So why do you hang around?

Fritz tries to get her to finish off the incompleted situation with the mother, and it is this contact which makes her cry, because it is in contact that real stimulation can arise.

F: Yah. Can you say goodbye to her? Can you bury her?

J: Well, I can now, because I'm at the bottom of the slope, and when I come to the bottom I stand up. I stand up and I walk around and it's a beautiful place.

F: Can you say to your mother, "Goodbye, mother. Rest in peace"?

J: I think I did tell her . . . Goodbye, Mother. *(like a cry)* Goodbye! . . .

F: *(gently)* Talk to her. Go to her grave and talk to her about it.

J: Goodbye, Mom. You couldn't help what you did. It wasn't your fault you had three boys first, and then you thought it would be another boy, and you didn't want me and you felt so bad after you found out I was a girl. *(still crying)* You just tried to make it up to me, that's all. You didn't have to smother me . . . I forgive you, Mom . . . You worked awful hard. I can go now . . . Sure, I can go.

Attention to the dreamer's body is important. If she holds her breath it will keep her from feeling and inter-

F: You are still holding your breath, Jean.

J: *(to herself)* Are you really sure, Jean? . . . *(softly)* Momma let me go.

F: What would she say?

J: I can't let you go.

vening in her personal mobility. Here Fritz tries to help her to liberate herself from the projection and get her to identify herself with the fixation process rather than shoving it one-sidedly onto the mother.

F: Now you say this to your mother.

J: I can't let you go?

F: Yah. You keep her. You're holding on to her.

J: Mom, I can't let you go. I need you. Mom, I don't need you.

F: But you still miss her . . . don't you?

J: (very softly) A little. Just somebody there . . . what if nobody was there? . . . What if it was all empty, and dark. It's not all empty and dark—it's beautiful . . . I'll let you go . . . (sighs, almost inaudible) I'll let you go, Mom . . .

F: I'm very glad that we have this last experience—we can learn such a lot from this. You notice this was no play-acting. This was no crying for sympathy, it was no crying to get control, this was one of the four explosions I mentioned—the ability to explode into grief—and this mourning labor, as Freud called it, is necessary to grow up to say goodbye to the image of the child.

Fritz's work with Jean and her dream contains the most important elements in his therapeutic program: working with the projection and the dialogues, attentiveness to body language, practicing the feedback technique, working through the personality layers that Perls's theory contains, completing important gestalts, and so forth. What stands out particularly in this piece of dreamwork, as in the theory, is that Fritz again and again gets Jean to face her blockages, her manner of avoiding. The laughter and the "Oh, isn't this fun?" attitude is Jean's special elusive tactic. During this role-playing dispute (in Freudian terms the laughter could be a reaction formation), anxiety, anger, and grief appear gradually as the therapy advances.

Fritz starts by getting Jean to play the slippery chute and then links the slipperiness to the laughter:

F: Aha, well, what's the joke?

J: (continues laughing) I'm just laughing.

F: Can you accept yourself as slippery?

The next dream element, the cardboard box, leads Jean down into deeper layers, namely to the realization, in flashes, that she is willing to let herself be sat upon and be scrunched if it can give her a feeling of being good for something. Fritz passes on feedback to her body language, which reveals that she turns her aggressions inward (hits herself), that some of the aggressions in reality are intended for the mother, and he then gets her to amplify them. Jean now directs both anger and anxiety at the mother. Although she repeatedly slips back to role-playing, Fritz takes her back every time to the blockage: the neurotic layer.

When Jean gets on the chute she sleds straight into the no-way-out layer. During this process it turns out that the mother adopts the superficial "Isn't it fun?" attitude, while Jean herself is scared. The mother is the controlling part of Jean:

"Mom": Don't worry. I've got it all taken care of. *(decisively)* We're having fun.

This experience leads further to the death layer and finally to an emotional explosion, anger, and grief: to the authentic life layer.

DREAM AND PSYCHODRAMA

Perls's personal style has been conceived as a kind of individual therapy in groups. In the above example, Fritz and Jean are entirely in the center, while the group by its simple presence intensifies the experience. In *psychodrama*, a form of therapy developed by the Rumanian-American psychiatrist Jacob Levy Moreno, dreamwork also has an important place, and group members join in actively. Moreno's method has been further developed by his associates Dean and Doreen Elefthery.

Like Medard Boss and Fritz Perls, Moreno affiliated himself with humanistic psychology and was inspired by existential philosophy. Moreno was supposedly the first to use concepts like *group therapy* and *encounter groups*, and it was originally he who introduced role-playing, the empty chair, and numerous other techniques that Perls also uses. Perls receives more space in this book than Moreno not because I regard him as a more important or more pioneering, but because his method is more flexible and because he has shown how techniques from psychodrama can be incorporated in other kinds of therapy.

A psychodrama is always a group event, and it is built up slowly and

methodically according to Moreno's and the Eleftherys' directions. First
there is a group discussion about who is to be the lead (*protagonist*), then
a conversation phase in which the theme is selected, then a warming-up
phase. Only afterward does the drama itself begin.

Among the most important basic techniques are role-playing, doubling,
soliloquy, and exchanging roles. These are surrounded with a number of
highly structured procedures that effectively lead the person in and out of
the roles. After the skit, the members of the cast relate how they experienced
their roles. Then there is a *sharing*—that is, all of the participants can tell
(share with the others) about experiences from their lives that remind them
of the psychodrama. No interpretation is allowed during this phase.

Dreams can be a starting point for psychodrama, using either a single
element or the whole dream. If the work is to be with the whole dream, the
lead begins by playing that she is lying down, dreaming. She tries to recall
as precisely as possible the mood before slumber, the room, the previous
meal—anything and everything that can activate the *recollection*.

The dreamer can identify herself with different figures in the dream by
playing them. At the lead's request, chosen persons in the group perform
as *auxiliary egos*, playing father or mother, for example, or a third dream
figure. Group participants who have no roles can step in and give their
version of any role (*understudying*). Furthermore, the lead is constantly un-
derstudied by a "double." The following is an example from the Norwegian
psychotherapist Eva Røine. A woman whose husband had committed suicide
dreams that she was

> in a room full of gloomy people in mourning. Especially fixed in her
> memory was her sisters' appearance. They were wearing white capes and
> resembled "big flapping agitated birds." A funeral march was played.
> The room was large and decorated in red and gold, "almost like a gala
> performance."
>
> Suddenly she saw her deceased husband in a coffin beneath a large
> canopy. Beside the coffin lay a golden crown glittering as in a fairy tale.
> But as she walked past it and sat down on a humble stool she saw that
> the crown was cardboard.

The dream is then dramatized with auxiliary egos, doubles, role exchanging, and other techniques demanded by the story. Sisters and relations are
called up from the group to perform. A man plays her former husband in
the "coffin." After the suicide the woman had begun an affair with a new

man, thus an auxiliary ego is asked to sit on a chair outside the dream stage itself.

Through soliloquy the woman reflects on the situation: "It's strange that I don't feel the least bit bereaved. After all, it's my husband's funeral, and I was totally paralyzed by despair. Now I feel nothing."

Here she assumes contact with the "sisters." They are instructed to flap about as she had seen them. The reaction does not fail to appear: "I guess I see you demanding that I should cry. You look like real doomsday angels. But it's a sham, I tell you. *[aggressively]* It's all a sham. And look, how he enjoys it!" The woman points to the "corpse," whom she has been asked to trade roles with.

> *The woman (as her deceased husband):* I'm genuinely happy to see you all here. It's just as I had imagined it. Charming grief. A perfect performance.
>
> *The woman (as herself):* How strange, that not until now after your death can I see what an actor you were. There I was going out of my way both day and night trying to understand you, and you were going around with that ridiculous cardboard crown. You mustn't think you can do that to me one more time!
>
> *A woman from the group begins to double:* I've already got a new husband.
>
> *The woman:* Sure, I've got a new husband. Well, only a lover. If only you'd known that, my chaste sisters!
>
> *The double:* The thing which pains me is that I don't think this new relationship can last . . .
>
> *The woman:* You *(to the corpse)* are still a scary nightmare.
>
> *The double:* I'm transferring a whole lot of irrational reactions onto my lover . . .
>
> *The woman:* No, that's not it. I actually think he has many of the same tendencies. Not that he's an actor, but he also has depressions, and then I get so scared. I'm afraid the whole thing will repeat itself!
>
> *The double:* And that I can't manage one more time.
>
> *The woman:* I won't make it one more time.

In a longer psychodrama, which includes many memories from childhood and marriage, memories that in themselves explain why the woman was a patient, the story ends in a scene where the woman turns her back to the new man and asks him to come again later when she has gotten a better hold on herself. In the last phase of the psychodrama the woman shows good insight into what she has experienced earlier, even though she has never previously in the dream seen her husband as an actor and king of fools.

The above psychodrama is an example of how the leading character interprets his or her dream in a meaningful way, and how seeing the dream played out stirs up relevant feelings and thoughts. We also see how the double can weigh in with propositions that the leading character can either accept or reject. The dream is experienced entirely on the objective level, but in the Eleftherys' psychodrama the various dream elements can also be understood on the subjective level.

Naturally it often happens that understudies can't identify themselves with the roles but "project their own fixed emotional positions" into them, or they use the roles to gain insight into their own problems (*acting in*). Yet it is known among directors that, if it doesn't get the upper hand, precisely these persons or inappropriate fancies give very effective help, because transference processes can activate even deeper conflicts in the leading character and the coactors. It should be noted that in group therapy the coactors, too, can derive benefit.

A further description of dreamwork in groups is found in chapter 14.

PERLS'S DREAMWORK COMPARED WITH OTHER METHODS

Perls's theories about the nature and function of dreams as existential messages and their function filling in gaps is a direct extension of his psychology, and of therapy in general. He puts them forward in *Gestalt Therapy* as axioms and then leaves it up to the reader to determine whether they hold in practice.

Perls's therapy is inspired by many sources. The conception of the organism as self-regulating, the belief in its wisdom, and that dreams are meaningful communications to the dreamer adhere closely to Jung's view. To see dream figures as aspects of the dreamer himself is very Jungian, and when the client plays and makes dialogue between these aspects it is an expansion of Jung's active imagination, with techniques that considerably amplify the emotional experience. Perls's method also departs from Jung's in that the dreamer can identify himself with all of the dream elements, whereas Jung gave the ego in the dream an especially prominent position.

Working with defense mechanisms comes originally from the Freudians, but Perls in his dream seminar reduces Freud's complex system to a single defense mechanism: avoidance.

Erving and Miriam Polster have described gestalt therapy's view of dream symbols as being "creative expressions of self rather than unconscious disguises of troublesome life experiences." Here there is no one-sided attitude, and in practice Perls time and again comes around in back of the dream's level to traumatic events in childhood.

Even though Perls draws on many sources, his theories are not a creative synthesis of the experiences of predecessors. He is a specialist in emotional release and resistance processing, but there are many fruitful aspects of the previously described methods that he does not exploit. Perls opposed free associations because they jump "like a grasshopper from experience to experience, and none of these experiences are ever *experienced*, but just a kind of flash, which leaves all the available material unassimilated and unused." It is in the intensified work with this overlooked material that Perls brought a truly new dimension into therapy and dream interpretation. However, as we have seen, this in no way excludes the possibility of working in the Freudian manner with chains of associations, or that as with Jung you simply go one or two links out in the chain of associations and then let this throw light on the dream's meaning.

Moreno thought that he himself began where Freud left off. In the only exchange of words he had with Freud he expressed the difference thus: "You [Freud] analyze people's dreams. I give them the courage to dream again." The anecdote exemplifies the essentially creative in Moreno's view of dreams.

Whether you concretely choose to tackle a dream from an experience-oriented method can depend upon many factors. The Jungian Edward Whitmont mentions a young female analysand who dreamed of *a landscape dominated by a centrally located, brilliant, square-shaped quartz crystal. A voice was heard saying: "It is the four in red."* Then she dreamed that *she considered whether or not to eat breakfast.*

In a classical Jungian understanding this would be an individuation dream, and the client turned up with a "correct" Jungian interpretation and was quite proud of it: the motif of the center and the crystal being the *lapis*, the philosophers' stone, the four representing wholeness and red corresponding to a stage in the alchemical process (*rubedo*), and so on (see "Dream and alchemy," chapter 2).

Whitmont, who saw the woman as intellectualizing, had her play the crystal. As the crystal, she said: "I feel hard, immobile, straight and tense. I cannot move, and I resent being pushed around by other people." When she asked the crystal what it wanted, it replied: "I want to be released and

taken out of the box I have been put in. I feel confined there and scared."
When she was asked to "stay" with those reactions, there came a stream of
associations. The quartz crystal reminded her of her father's mineral collection that he had fussed over, and further that with his overcritical and
pedantic manner he had stifled her own artistic sensitivities. The number 4
was associated with the grading system in elementary school, where the
mark was entered in red ink by a teacher who reminded her of her father,
and the breakfast made her recall that she was often so afraid of school that
she couldn't eat her breakfast. The client's experiential work and free associations pointed to performance anxiety as the central problem. And with
her refined interpretation it could be expected that the dreamer would try
to live up to the father's and the teacher's norms instead of freeing herself
from them.

Whitmont did not exclude the validity of the individuation symbolism,
but he thought that the personally unconscious material which was associated from the dream had to be experienced on the here-and-now level before
you could go on to the understanding level.

A strength of the gestalt therapeutic method is not only the ability to
bring the dreamer into contact with feelings, but also that it stimulates the
dreamer's creative potentials in the waking state. The gestalt therapeutic
literature contains many examples of dreams that with a psychoanalytical
interpretation seem rather dreary, but nonetheless give occasion for encouraging work.

Erving and Miriam Polster provide the following example from a woman
dreamer: she jumps *from a high diving board into a devious swimming pool*
which empties itself of water as she plunges toward it. Now we don't know
the dream's context, but as a thought experiment let us consider it as isolated
and an initial dream. Then it could be understood to mean that the dreamer
would like to hurl himself out into the unconscious (the water), but the pool
empties itself and the dreamer will be killed in the plunge.

It could also be that a grave diagnosis is underlying and the prognosis
for therapy poor. Naturally it is important for the therapist to know this, but
for the dreamer it can be a crushing blow to the hope of improvement and
so remove the motivation to do something about the problem. The therapist
had the woman talk

> to the tricky swimming pool, she played the disappearing water, she
> dove from the board, she became the pool, filled again and shining. and
> finally became a lone swimmer who slipped out at night to swim in the

unoccupied pool. Through these many guises she came also to know more about her own sexuality, ephemeral, untrustworthy and private but also full and gleaming.

Experience therapy releases a creativity in the waking state that the dreamer lacks. The consciousness thus comes to complement the unconscious. But the gestalt therapeutic method also gives rise to a number of critical considerations of the dream's theoretic and therapeutic natures. The dream's context in the Jungian sense, with all that it implies of insights and constructive working aspects, is not taken into consideration: the dream's objective and subjective levels; what took place the day before; the practical consequences of the dream in relation to the surroundings here and now (that is, not only with regard to intrapsychic conflicts and the dreamer's inner bearing). When Perls sneers at the Freudians with remarks like: "You can chase your childhood memories to doomsday, but nothing will change," it mustn't be taken too literally. There is hardly a therapy where the client to such a degree bobsleds back into childhood and is encouraged to work off affects in relation to the parents. (Jean and her mother, for example.)

With the theory that all dream elements are (equal) projections of the dreamer's ego, Perls loses the important information that resides in the dream ego's differentness from all other elements in the dream, and as we have seen earlier it is the ego in a dream that can be used to evaluate which conflicts the waking ego is ripe to take up.

This leads us directly to question the expediency of going in back of the client's defense mechanisms at the pace that Perls does. As far as I can see there is the danger that although the repressed contents do surface into consciousness (in gestalt lingo, "an uncompleted gestalt shows up at the ego's boundaries"), this content can be too emotionally charged to be integrated in one mouthful. Then the result might be, as we have learned from Freud, a displacement of the emotional intensity onto a surrogate. A typical example could be a man who bawls his mother out while she is sitting in the "empty chair" while his consciousness is not yet capable of containing that anger. As soon as he is outside the consulting room he starts to think that it is an unsympathetic therapist who puts feelings on him he doesn't have. The anger is now displaced onto the therapist and the man breaks off the therapy. But the anger can also be taken out on the spouse, the children, or other blameless persons.

Perls on the contrary thought that the protracted course of a psychoanalysis only teaches people to "become better at being neurotics." His dream seminars were often a once-only affair, and he made it emphatically clear that he took no responsibility for how the participants would use their experiences. I have myself worked with live-in courses where the dreamwork was combined with gestalt therapy and psychodrama, and found it very valuable. But it has been my experience that the effect is greatest if the emotional release is associated with processes of longer duration, and many therapists today are of the same opinion. In an intensive course it is quite possible to within a week see progressions in dreams that would otherwise take much longer to obtain.

At one live-in course where I was therapist, a man started off with dreams in which *he killed various animals in a rather brutal way.* In later dreams at the course he began relating in a friendly way to animals, letting them out of their cages, and so forth, and *gradually the animals began mating with each other.* Parallel with this, *his contact with women in the dreams changed from that others got the girls to that he himself went to bed with them.* This corresponded to very powerful and liberating affect experiences during the span of the course. But when a few years later he approached me for individual therapy, his dreams showed the same picture as at the start of the course. The problem was that he could not feel any support from his immediate surroundings for the emotional release. The resistance of the surroundings and his own defenses forced the released content down into the unconscious again as soon as he was without therapeutic support.

The combination of gestalt therapy and psychodrama with more prolonged individual therapy has many advantages. It can be used to break through cliché acquired associations and premature interpretations and in that way elicit a spontaneous material that is closer to the dream's reality. This, together with other associative material, can then be incorporated in a dream interpretation that uses the methods described in earlier chapters. If via dreams you keep tabs on a client's progress, and if you register the dissolving of defense mechanisms and work with transference, then you have a good possibility for inserting an emotionally releasing therapy at the exact moment when the dreamer is ripe for it. I have described this elsewhere in connection with a male client's work with a mother complex.

The example given here is from a woman dreamer who was in therapy with me and who was strongly defensive. The defensive attitude toward men was reflected in the dreams. Her relation to men was at the outset formal. Very correct persons would often appear: priests, administrators, men wearing impeccable gray suits, etc. When erotically attractive men began appearing, other women ran off with them. For instance, *Peter, whom I am in love with, drives away with another woman.*

Slowly, she herself began approaching the erotic: *I'm lying in bed with a man. We both have our clothes on.* From there followed dream motifs in which male therapists made sexual advances. This brought to light an episode from a few years previously, when a therapist had disclosed that he was sexually interested in her and therefore thought it best to break off the therapy. A workthrough of the affects surrounding this occurrence surmounted her unconscious anxiety that I, too, would misuse the analytical situation. After some time she had dreams that, camouflaged or directly, dealt with incest situations. In one of the explicit dreams she *lay in her own (present) bed. Her father was lying beside her. There was something sexual in the situation. He seemed awkward.*

In Freudian terms the repressed female oedipal situation (in love with the father) could here be confronted with the dream ego. The transference had reached the point where I could hug and support her physically without her being afraid of "attempted incest" on my part. I saw this as a good moment for her to refresh her feelings for the father by having a dialogue with him in the empty chair.

THE INTERPRETER'S ROLE IN EXPERIENCE THERAPY

Back in the preceding chapter it was questioned whether dream experts should "interpret"—that is, be a kind of translator from one language to another—or whether their role simply was to buttress the dreamer's own experience. It was concluded that the phenomenological interpreters in practice *had* frames of reference, but that these could readily have an under-the-surface effect. The problem becomes even more acute in *experience therapy*, where it is a therapeutic principle to give "feedback" but where, as Perls puts it, you "never, never interpret."

Perls's attitude had its background in his familiarity with how psychoanalytical interpretations can become mechanical and sterile and, contrary to the intention, become a defense against authentic experience. His method really is, when applied well, a splendid means of avoiding intellectualizations. Nevertheless, both Perls and the gestalt therapeutic literature show that there is at least as much interpreting as in psychoanalysis, except that the interpretations are more concealed and the danger of manipulation is thereby all the greater.

To use the work with Jean as an example (and it is by no means atypical), the interpretations stick out a mile. In the first place the entire dream seminar is embedded in a theoretical lecture. Interposed between Jean's dream interpretation and the dreamwork itself is Perls's three- to four-minute talk about dream theory and moral/philosophical reflections on the desirability of settling accounts with impossible goals. Immediately afterward he asserts, as if it were a divine revelation, that the dream is an "existential message" that points to false ambitions.

The remark that Jean doesn't rely on her own legs but instead counts on the support of a piece of cardboard manipulates directly the dream content. If she stood on her legs on a slippery chute she would get into trouble.

The seminar is chock full of interpretations of behavior and dreams that obviously refer the contents back to Perls's therapeutic favorite postulates, such as in connection with another participant: "Now you notice already the hole here in her personality," "now we have got here the typical top-dog, underdog situation," "now this is a point which we would call the impasse," and so forth and so on.

At this point I would like to introduce another definition of the concept of interpretation. In his book *Poets and Demons* the Danish poet-philosopher Villy Sørensen in one place understands interpreting as "an unconscious organizing of the emotional life about certain central values and symbols." According to this broad definition, interpreting is a part of the way we comprehend life. We inevitably interpret and use interpretations as the basis for what we do and what we perceive.

Understanding the dream means realizing when you are avoiding the obvious, Perls said at his dream seminar, and by that he meant that an analysand's most important blockages rather quickly become obvious to everyone except the analysand himself. Perls's theory predicates also that there is always a particular gestalt that is more insistent than all the others. It is natural to assume that there is one particular experience that it is most important to get out at a given moment. Therefore it is necessary that the therapist is not only as open as possible toward the client's signals, but also that he has a strategy.

Perls's method gives a clearly better possibility for exploring what is happening in the client here-and-now than a plain and simple verbal analysis, and the spontaneously surfacing material gives a corresponding possibility for correcting the strategy. But precisely because the client constantly tries to "avoid," and because the therapist's role very much consists in luring him out on thin ice, the therapist doesn't get the direct feedback from the client as when an interpretation is put under discussion.

Psychodrama also gives unique possibilities for exploring the dreamer's experience of different elements. Understudying, especially, is excellent practice for a dream interpreter. As mentioned, understudies are used when the lead character together with the group tries to explore what he really felt in a given situation, in back of his "immediate," often cliché-like and defensive experience. The understudy enters into what the dreamer "really" experiences; in the broad sense of the word, that's an interpretation. As all group members have the possibility for putting in their bids, the individual has plenty of opportunity for studying everything he himself hasn't the fantasy to imagine, and thereby also for exploring the limits of his own interpreting skill.

Nor is there here any guarantee whatever of "objective" interpretings of a dream. The psychodrama is built up slowly and structuredly, and there is the necessity, for reasons of time and to not inundate the protagonist with material, for sticking to rather simple dreams or scenes from them. If it isn't to be derailed the therapist must form an overall view of the situation and have a strategy.

And so the conclusion must be that the experiential therapies on the one hand open up for the exploration of hitherto inaccessible aspects of the dream material, but on the other that the therapists, if they do not acknowledge their own strategies, theories, and interpretations, make themselves and their clients victims of manipulation.

Just as with the other dream interpreters, we must be careful not to take Perls too literally. Also, experienced gestalt therapists dissociate themselves from the antitheoretic attitude that reduces therapy to oversimplifications, smart tricks, and primitive "action."

THE EMPIRICAL BASIS AND THE PHILOSOPHY

It is said of Perls that he prepared the way for popular psychotherapy. It is indisputable that gestalt therapy and psychodrama have contributed to bringing dreams to a broader public than the psychoanalytical mainstreams and thus made our experiential foundation more comprehensive. The short group sessions are less binding and not as economically burdensome, and it is possible that the group members being spectators to a therapist and client in action has made dreamwork more democratic.

The dreams from these persons are not any less blocked or resource filled than those of psychoanalytical clients, and nothing indicates that the laws governing the dream activity are fundamentally different. Perls claimed— without providing examples—that the existential messages in dreams become clearer if you are capable of identifying with those parts of yourself that are projected in the dreams. This idea corresponds to Jung's that a dream analysis can bring you closer to the Self, and confirms what all the other dream theorists have found: that the dream reflects evolvements in the personality.

Experiential therapists have to a great extent embraced humanistic psychology, whose scientific theory is best described by the movement's founder Abraham Maslow. Maslow lays stress on the personal experiences of scientists as the basis for their theories. In his major work on motivation and personality he writes, "science is man-made rather than being an independent, nonhuman, or in-itself 'thing' with its own built-in rules. The laws, structure, and formulations of science rest not only on the nature of the reality which it discovers, but also on the nature of the person who makes the discovery." Thus the expansion of science can be furthered by curiosity and the creative urge but can also be hindered by the security-seeking, defensive, dogmatic, and methodological attitudes of the researchers. Not a few of the contradictions we have seen in dream analysis are determined by such factors.

Meanwhile, humanistic acknowledgments as regards the motives of scientists have undoubtedly influenced the scientific climate toward greater tolerance among and merging of different schools.

Philosophically, both Perls and Moreno are influenced by existentialism. And they adhere to the romantic line, which essentially sees dreams as revelations of a higher wisdom and as stimulation of growth processes. Perls's emphasis on the reality of the here and now is also influenced by Japanese Zen Buddhism.

TENTATIVE CONCLUSION CONCERNING THE NATURE OF DREAMS, ASSOCIATIONS, AND SYMBOLS

I have now delimited and described five mainstreams within modern dream investigation. We have found that all of them make essential contributions to the understanding of the phenomenon of dreams without any of them having a patent on the truth.

To go back to the example in which a woman dreamed of a landscape with a radiant quartz crystal in the center, a classical Jungian would see the individuation symbolism as the message proper of the dream. In Jung's opinion, free associations did not lead to the dream's meaning. They led to complexes—which could just as well be arrived at "by associating from a Russian railway sign." Although there is some truth in this, from my experience it just as often happens that in-depth experiential work, via widely ramified fantasies, associations, and discharges of affect, elicits material that more obviously fits in with the dream's logic than the first or second link of a chain of associations. These first links can on the contrary appear superficial, even though they are not irrelevant for understanding the dream. This implies the theoretical and practical consequence that the dream is compounded in a more complex way than in the classical Jungian system, where it refers to a developmental tendency or gives a didactic hint.

Neither would the nature of dreams be able to be contained in the Freudians' more or less reductive system of reference; nor in Hall's "cognitive" understanding, Adler's emotions theory, Fromm's notion that the dream speaks for itself; nor in Medard Boss's normative existentialism, which doesn't implicate associative material. Neither is Perls—for whom the dream concludes a gestalt when the five layers of the personality have been worked through—adequate for our understanding.

True of all of the interpreters we have dealt with is that they regard the symbol as a complex entity, although their understanding of this complexity isn't altogether congruent. While Freud regards the symbol as an "overdetermined" disguise and Jung sees it as an energy transformer, Hall asserts that it is a compressed stenographic language. With Boss's recasting technique it became clear that the meaning of symbols can be wrested free of the dream's structure, and in the experiential therapies they became the channel that permits exploration of here-and-now affects at a far deeper level than do the others.

With our present knowledge we can only assume that dreams are brought about in a form that at best can compress just as many kinds of information as the different theories we have been able to extract from them, and that the individual dream can at once be seen as a whole with a dramatic, symbolic, cognitive, and disguised structure, and at the same time combine with a far more ramified network of associations and contexts than the theories up till now have supposed.

How a theory of the nature and function of dreams should be phrased will be considered later. But before that there are still a number of frames of reference and modes of understanding we must have a look at. First, though, some important results of the latest laboratory research into sleep and dreams.

6. LABORATORY RESEARCH WITH SLEEP AND DREAMS

REM sleep and non-REM sleep—External stimuli and dreams—Is the dream an actual phenomenon?—The course of a night's dreaming—The psychological significance of the amount of dreaming—Biology and physiology—Learning and unlearning in dreams—Laboratory experiments and the mainstream of dream interpretation—Still another perspective

REM SLEEP AND NON-REM SLEEP

In 1953 the American M. D. Eugene Aserinsky together with sleep researcher Nathaniel Kleitman discovered that infants, and later adult experimental subjects, at regular intervals performed rapid eye movements while sleeping. If the subjects were awakened during these times, they usually could remember a dream. This phase of sleep is called REM (*Rapid Eye Movement*) sleep.

If brain wave activity is measured with an *electroencephalograph* (EEG), it shows lower frequencies and higher tension patterns in the dream phases than in other sleep phases. Brain activity is high and closely approximates the waking state in alarm or anxiety. Moreover, REM sleep is accompanied by a particular neurophysiological pattern. Heart rhythm, pulse, blood pressure, and respiration are irregular. The muscles of the body are more relaxed than during other forms of sleep; the muscles of the head and neck lose nearly all tension, while small muscles in the face and fingers now and then make rapid movements. Men may have full or partial erections during REM sleep, while it has not yet been technically possible to observe corresponding sexual stimulation in women, although it must be assumed to occur. Strangely enough, it is possible during sleep to maintain alertness toward certain sounds. For instance, a mother during the deepest phases of sleep can hear her child while closing out other sounds. Aserinsky and Kleitman's discovery became the start of an experimental era in the history of dream investigation.

A number of certain new data about dreams was rather quickly produced: under normal conditions, REM sleep = dreaming.

It appears as if the mechanisms for the regulation of sleep and waking states are already developed at around six months of gestation. REM sleep constitutes 50 percent of a newborn infant's sleep and even more of a premature infant's. The amount of REM sleep diminishes with the years. In young people it is around 25 percent of sleep, a level maintained through the middle years, after which the amount of dreaming declines slowly. The dreaming time for normal adults varies between 18 percent and 33 percent of sleep, but for the individual the amount of dreaming is remarkably stable from night to night, regardless of what takes place in the course of the day (apart from illness and use of medication). Most of our dreams are in color.

There are four different forms of brain wave activity during sleep. They are, respectively, descending stages 1, 2, 3, and 4, which is the deep-sleep threshold, and ascending stages 4, 3, 2, and 1, which occur in reverse order. REM sleep is always stage 1 sleep, closest to the waking/sleep threshold. These stages are gone through four to six times a night, in cycles of ninety minutes' duration. Falling asleep is accompanied by a dream five to ten minutes in length. The next dream which occurs, nearly ninety minutes later, is somewhat longer, and so on until the last dream of the night which can last thirty to forty minutes.

At the start of the laboratory research it was thought that there was mental activity only during REM periods. Later it was discovered that it also applies to non-REM (NREM) stages. But NREM activity is less dreamlike. It more resembles a relaxed conceptual thinking. It isn't as rich in images or as emotional and illogical as dreams, and the themes are often taken from the person's daily routines.

At the transition to REM sleep, the processes that give dreams their dreamlike quality are increasingly active. Gradually, as we get further into the REM period, the dreams become more lively and emotional, bizarre and dramatic, more anxiety provoking, violent, and "distorted," qualities that also become increasingly pronounced after ten minutes into the dream.

It turns out that animals, too, have sleep patterns that resemble humans', and that dream activity has come into being as the animal species have evolved. NREM activity is known from primitive mammalian species that are known to have evolved 200 million years ago, while REM sleep arose

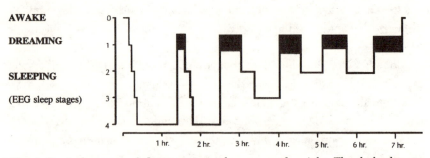

Fig. 1. Typical pattern of sleep stages in the course of a night. The dark plateaus are dream stages. These become longer as the night progresses.

in somewhat higher animals whose history goes back around 150 million years.

EXTERNAL STIMULI AND DREAMS

One of the most common charges that skeptics have put forth against psychological interpretations of dreams is that the dream "in reality" is nothing but a reaction to external and internal stimuli; for example, indigestion, a ringing alarm clock, etc. All of the dream theorists we have so far dealt with have rejected this. And now, with the new possibilities of the sleep laboratory, it has been repudiated again and again. Calvin Hall has summed up and exemplified the results thus:

> For example, the following dream was reported following the utterance of the word *Help* in the ear of the sleeping person: *I was driving along the highway at home. Heard yelling and we stopped. A car was turned sideways on the road. A man crawling out. Said he wasn't hurt. He told me someone was under the car. I helped turn the car over. There was a woman badly cut. We took her to the hospital.*

This dream is in keeping with the experience of hearing a cry for help, but the details of driving along a highway, the overturned car, the badly cut woman and the unhurt man, and the trip to the hospital are all supplied by the dreamer.

Moreover, it has been demonstrated repeatedly that the stimulus, whether it be an alarm clock ringing, a car backfiring, a cold wind, or a numb arm, is not experienced in a dream as it actually is but is distorted in some fashion. The ringing alarm is represented as church bells or the siren of a fire engine, the backfiring car is heard as a pistol shot or an earthquake, the cold wind is experienced as a trip by dogsled through the frozen north, and a numb arm is felt to be a snake curling itself around the dreamer's chest. The same stimulus may be experienced in a variety of ways by different dreamers, or by the same dreamer in different dreams. In one experiment a wax candle was placed in the hand of the sleeping person on two different occasions. The first time he dreamed he was playing golf, and the second time that he was trying to lift a bar in a physical training class.

IS THE DREAM AN ACTUAL PHENOMENON?

The laboratory experiments have also shed light on a question that perhaps seems surprising but which has often been raised by skeptics: Is the dream an actual phenomenon at all? Is the dream a phenomenon that occurs at the moment of awakening, or a fantasy that arises after awakening and is erroneously ascribed to the REM period?

The following are a few experiments that indicate the opposite. William Dement, the American pioneer in this area, incorporated various external stimuli in a running dream process. As expected, these stimuli appeared camouflaged or transformed in the dream, but it turns out that the period of time between the external stimuli corresponds accurately to the length of the corresponding dream sequences. (This doesn't exclude fantastic leaps in time between the individual dream sequences.) The object of another experiment was to hypnotize the subjects into telling their dreams while they were taking place. In 87 percent of the cases the dream reported in the sleeping state fit precisely with what the dreamer could recall after awakening.

This is in contrast to Freud's conception in *The Interpretation of Dreams*. Here I would add that persons in shock, in near-death states, or during mystical experiences can have so many and intense experiences within a brief space of time that it exceeds all normal limits. Thus the psychic potential appears to be present and can therefore presumably also come into play in dreams, even if this is hardly what is most usual.

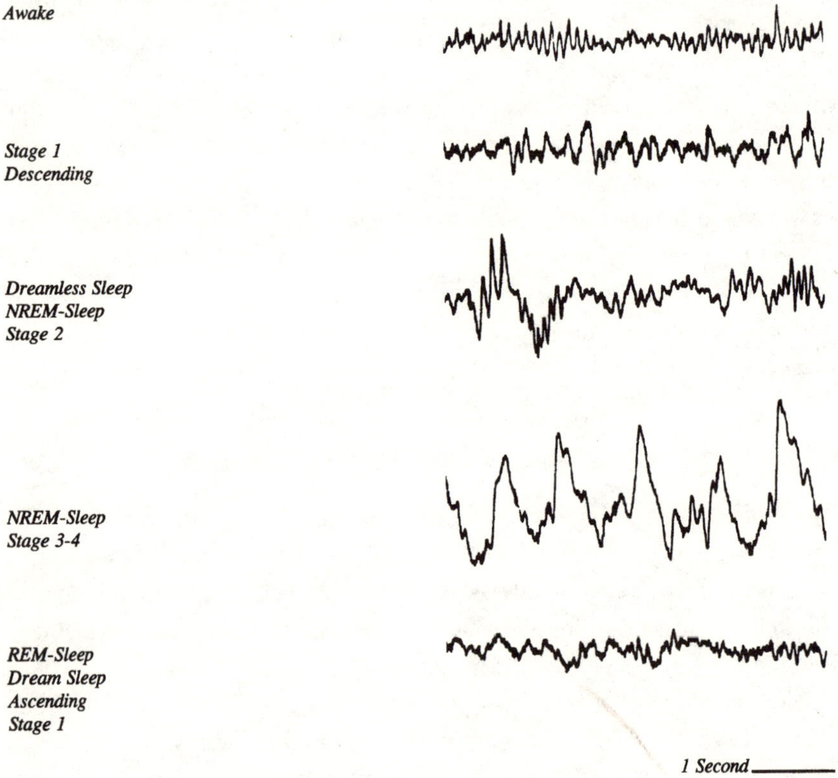

Awake

Stage 1
Descending

Dreamless Sleep
NREM-Sleep
Stage 2

NREM-Sleep
Stage 3-4

REM-Sleep
Dream Sleep
Ascending
Stage 1

*1 Second*_____

Fig. 2. Since the early 1950s patterns of sleep and dreaming have been investigated in the laboratory. An important tool for this is measurement of the brain's electrical activity. (Electroencephalogram = EEG). There are four stages of sleep (see chapter 6), characterized by gradual increase of brainwave amplitude and a just as gradual decrease in the frequency.

THE COURSE OF A NIGHT'S DREAMING

Not many analyses have been made of dream themes as they unfold in the course of a single night from sleeping to awakening. The studies that are available point to a certain pattern. Different investigators have found that the dreams during the first half of the night concern themselves with current experiences and in the last half of the night slip backward into the individual's life history, resuming the attention to current problems toward morning. A specific theme often develops through the night, alternating between unpleasant tension-augmenting dreams and tension-releasing dreams that are reactions to the unpleasant ones. Rosalind Cartwright, one of the most significant of the young laboratory researchers, corroborated these findings and added that the morning's dreams have a problem-solving tendency.

Cartwright has given some illustrative examples of the course of a single night's dreaming. She describes two subjects, both male medical students in their early twenties, who are found "in good physical and psychological health." Neither of them has any special interest in dreams, and they normally remember only one dream a week each. The laboratory procedure, meanwhile, got both of them to recall five dreams in one night. Here follow the cited dreams in excerpt.

The first subject, Jerry, is described as a "tall, rangy farmboy," a "young Jimmy Stewart type, rather shy and unsophisticated."

Jerry's first dream *was not very dreamlike. He was trying to figure out where the EEG electrodes went. He tried connecting them himself in various ways, but without success.*

Dream number two is still close to external reality: *He was driving in lab assistant Mr. H.'s car together with Don, another subject. There was some confusion in stopping at an intersection, because the stop sign was turned around the wrong way.*

Common to the two first dreams is "confusion about the right way of doing something, and the absence of a person of authority who 'knows how.' " In dream number three *Jerry goes inside a library to return a book, but has great difficulty finding out where to take it.* Here Cartwright finds the first symbol condensation. The library reminds Jerry of his undergraduate days but also resembles the hospital where he would be pursuing his medical studies. It is understood as standing for his educational institution. Again the dream deals with confusion and the absence of an authority figure (the librarian) who could be of help.

In dream number four Jerry sits *making mud pies. The day was pretty, bright and sunny. A girl helps him mix the mud, and he pats it out into little round patties.* The dream is understood as a tremendous regression and wish fulfillment: "Oh, to be a child again, sitting in the sun, with nothing more complicated to do or learn than making mud pies with a little girl helper."

In dream number five *four-year-old Jerry is in his childhood home being given a bath by his mother. She pulls his earlobe and washes the inside of his ear.* He remembers that the last time Rosalind Cartwright woke him he put his hand behind his neck and felt some pimples. And he gave himself the good advice to wash more often—just as his mother would have done. In the dream he experiences himself as passive but angry.

Cartwright had routinely cleansed Jerry's earlobes with acetone before installing the electrodes. The mother in the dream is regarded as a symbolic condensation of the "female-helper-mother-knowledgeable-authority." Jerry told later that he had a problem of always insisting on learning to do things for himself. In the laboratory prior to going to sleep he had tried feverishly to plug the electrodes in the right jacks before Cartwright turned up. Cartwright concludes that the three first dreams worked with anger because Jerry's shaky sense of competence was threatened by the complicated laboratory arrangements and reminded him of earlier instances of his ineptitude.

Some weeks later Jerry was asked to read and comment on his dream journal. He thought that the dreams followed from his trying to figure things out for himself and not being sure he could do it. This problem was real for him now that he was living in a big city (Chicago) for the first time. But he had always been like that, he said. He remembered how his father made him keep a secondhand car running for him. He had to keep trying, robbing parts from junk cars, but he could never win.

Don, the other subject, "in contrast to Jerry was from a big city. He was sensitive, intellectual, and humorous, a Woody Allen type." The first dream took place

> in a boarding house, where there were little grates in the floors and walls where everyone could see into everyone else's room. Nobody liked one of the tenants, and a sharp, very pushy, very bossy person killed him. He got some paper to get rid of the body in. His girlfriend, long black hair, stocky, not at all pretty, got some sort of liquid. The man organized everybody into helping him, and everybody had to rub the liquid into this paper which he unrolled.

This dream report was more developed than normal for the first REM stage. Cartwright found that the dream combined two anxiety-provoking reality situations. The first is the sleep laboratory itself, as the peculiar boarding house where everyone could be observed. The pushy leader is the lab assistant Mr. H., and his black-haired girlfriend Rosalind Cartwright herself. The paper is the EEG paper, and the gluey liquid the collodion used for applying the electrodes. The other anxiety-provoking situation is one Don had talked about while being prepared for the experiments. In his anatomy class the cadaver of an adult male had been presented for dissection, wrapped in brown paper. Here was a parallel between himself, who was to be dissected spiritually in a dream laboratory, and the cadaver in an anatomy lab. The boarding house that is the setting for the dream he recognized as the one where he lived. This got Cartwright to ask herself: "What is going on here that is also making him anxious about sleeping or death?"

In the next dream Don is together with

> *somebody he had gone through high school with. In a bad black neighborhood they were followed by a couple of middle-aged black junkies. They go into a drugstore to phone Don's father, but the operator doesn't understand him. Don tries and tries but doesn't get through. Don is a bit nervous himself, and this rubs off on the friend. The two junkies are degenerate low-class types, a bit drunk and very nasty.*

The dream becomes still more involved and ends with Don and the friend being trapped.

The third time Don is awakened he has dreamed he *was sitting in an open-air café in Paris . . . just a nice frosty fairy tale. A very large café with many, many tables. Everything expensive. There was the "noble Duke of Something." I look out over the street, sipping Bordeaux.* Cartwright regarded the dream as a wish-fulfilling solution to the threat in the preceding dream, which is a parallel to Jerry's dream about playing with mud pies.

In the fourth dream Don is *with another kid on a horse in a ground-level apartment. The horse goes into the kitchen, opens the refrigerator and takes two ice cubes in its mouth. Then they ride out in the park and each picks up a very good-looking girl. Don's girl gets the horse to go faster by jamming the point of a fountain pen into its rump.*

And finally in the fifth dream:

> *[I] go to see Barbara Streisand with some girl from my class here at school. She is not very pretty and not very nice also. The reason that I took her to the concert was that she had a car. We arrived late and there were no parking spaces. We started back and got into some sort of accident. One reason was that it was packed with 150-story buildings. I had never seen these before and was so shook that instead of turning I hit a wall.*

When Don woke up in the morning he couldn't remember the first dream, until he was reminded that it took place in the boarding house. He then told that he had just moved in. It was the first time he was living away from home, and the boarding house was "full of homosexuals." He felt that he should move out, and had even considered going back home to his father.

The homosexual motif forms the nucleus in Cartwright's understanding of the dreams. The first and second dreams reflect anxiety about homosexuality. Dream number three represents an escape from the problems. In dream number four Don rides into an apartment with a guy, which again is regarded as a homosexual motif. The horse is "cooled off" with ice cubes, and they then find two girls in a park. Even though his girl is pretty she "behaves according to a more masculine sex role by jamming the horse in the rump with something sharp to make him go faster." And finally in the last dream he "experiences being surrounded by large phallic figures and loses control." The rhythm in this series is that the anxiety starts in dream number one and culminates in dream number two. Dream number three is regarded as escape, dream four as neutral, and dream five as unpleasant.

Cartwright believes that a discussion of whether the dreams are complementary or an extension of waking life would oversimplify the interpretation. In Don's series, for example, the anxiety dreams correspond to Don's waking life, while the dream about going to Paris is complementary. It is also concerned with a real future, as Don was saving up for a trip to France, and Cartwright assumes the dreams, like waking consciousness, can think both backward and ahead in time.

Cartwright concludes that the first dreams of the night relate rather directly to current worries, the following ones involve past situations, and the last are concerned with contemplating solutions.

Jerry and Don did not take part in therapy or other dreamwork. They came back a year later to participate in another laboratory experiment.

In Jerry's first dream of this series he was eight or nine years old and struggling with an algebra problem he couldn't solve. Don's first dream dealt with "his ambiguous sex, passivity in the face of being taken advantage of, turning to authorities for help and finding that they are not much help." The results correspond with Calvin Hall's long-term investigations of dreams: They don't change unless we do something serious about the psychic conflicts they reflect.

THE PSYCHOLOGICAL SIGNIFICANCE OF THE AMOUNT OF DREAMING

If you awaken the subject each time an REM stage begins, it is possible to reduce the amount of dreaming sleep without decreasing the normal sleep time.

Ernest Hartmann, who is known for one of the most ambitious attempts at amalgamating the enormous quantity of data that has come to light since the beginning of REM research, found the following negative effects of REM deprivation: irritability, difficulty in being attentive, gaps in and distortions of the ego's normal defense functions, problems in interplay with others, and that repressed impulses and conflicts sometimes broke through to consciousness. None of these effects is particularly extreme, however, and REM-sleep deprivation does not ordinarily lead to chaotic or psychotic states in daytime hours, as many believe. A single subject, which Cartwright describes, became rather paranoid, and another, contrary to his usual behavior, cheated a waitress. But there were also persons who felt fine and who became more creative than normal.

For ethical reasons, studies of REM-sleep deprivation have only been carried out over brief periods and primarily on "normal" subjects. In connection with chronic depression, a study of forty-three patients revealed that half of them improved markedly after seven weeks of REM deprivation.

The first measurable effect of REM deprivation was that the subjects attempted to make up for the loss by reducing more and more the interval between REM stages. If after five or more nights REM deprivation ceased, the subjects' amount of REM sleep increased in relation to the normal level. These two findings were taken as evidence of a biological need for REM sleep.

Cartwright discovered later that a number of persons instead of *rebounding* from lost REM sleep were able to *substitute* it by having dreamlike sequences just before REM sleep set in. In the period with REM deprivation it turned out that the "substituters" functioned pretty much as usual, apart from a slightly increased level of activity so that they got more done. The "rebounders," in contrast, had more difficulty managing their day. Psychological tests showed that it was a question of widely different personality types. The "rebounders" were externally oriented, reality-bound, and rather fantasy-poor. The "substituters" were more equally attentive toward the demands of the inner and the outer worlds, and they showed no change on their tests before and after REM deprivation. Surprisingly, the substituters had better test results after REM deprivation. They got more in touch with their inner feelings and fantasy resources, and according to the study became more evenly balanced personalities.

Hartmann compared persons who slept little with persons who slept much. He found that the first were generally "smooth, efficient persons with a tendency towards handling stress by keeping busy and by denial." The "slugabeds" were worried types, chronically somewhat depressed or anxious. This group also included creative persons.

Great sleep need was typical of the "tortured genius," while effective practical persons—administrators, political leaders, etc.—tend to have a low sleep requirement.

The indication is consequently that dreams have a creative function.

Persons good at remembering dreams are psychologically similar to the long sleepers, while those poor at remembering dreams resemble persons with little sleep need. The long sleepers' dream life has more sex and aggression, while their waking life has less. As their sleep contains more and more REM, as the night progresses they get a disproportionate amount of REM sleep, and as REM sleep is tiring it may possibly produce exhaustion. People are perhaps familiar with this phenomenon when they sleep late on weekends.

Some experiments indicate that REM sleep is of positive significance for the control of stress and anxiety. For example, REM-deprived persons react to a horror film with greater anxiety the second time they see it than persons who have the opportunity of sleeping in the interval. Material of personal and emotional relevancy is recalled more poorly upon REM-sleep deprivation.

Stimulation of dream recall and of the interest in dreams appears to influence the social and psychic situation. For example, a group of subjects awakened during REM stages was made to tell their dreams and the next morning repeat them to an experiment leader. Another group was awakened in NREM stages. They got just as much therapy as the first group but their dreams were not discussed. The dream rememberers clearly made greater progress in the therapy, after both psychological tests and independent clinical evaluation. They also did better on the social level.

BIOLOGY AND PHYSIOLOGY

The development of a number of advanced scientific techniques has given new knowledge about the brain's biochemical activity during sleep. The rapidly growing literature on the subject has been insightfully gone through by American psychiatry professor Harry Fiss. Here it can be mentioned that experiments with animals have successfully localized two centers in the brainstem that have special significance for REM sleep (locus coeruleus) and NREM sleep (Raphé nuclei). Once the regulating centers are functioning, however, other brain structures become involved. Damage to the locus coeruleus makes REM sleep cease in animals, but the animal can still appear as if it is living out a dream, for example that it is attacking an imaginary enemy. Damage to the Raphé nuclei leads to complete insomnia. Correspondingly, there is in the locus coeruleus a large accumulation of biochemical substances that promote dreaming, and in the Raphé nuclei ones which inhibit sleep.

In the beginning it was believed that relatively simple biochemical systems controlled dream life and sleep, but the picture is becoming ever more complex.

Dream researchers Robert McCarley and Allan Hobson have, on the basis of neurophysiological studies, put forth a theory of dream formation that they call the *activation-synthesis* model: During REM sleep the sensory impression from the surroundings are strongly limited. But the brain is kept constantly going from within by an "activity" having no specific "motivation." The activation comprises both the sensory system and the motor apparatus if the "command signals" go over into dream activity instead of waking activity.

The experiential intensity in dreams corresponds to an intense activation of corresponding nerve-cell systems during REM sleep. The dream's predilection for visual impressions and images is associated with the likewise intensive activation of the visual system's and the eye's motor apparatus.

It is possible that information about the body's movements in dreams (the dream ego is walking, running, or dancing, for example) corresponds to an activation of the same system that sets body movements going in the waking state. Higher cerebral regions controlling instinctive behavior are also functioning, among them systems associated with anger and defensive behavior. Regions of the brain associated with recollection and memory work in the same manner as in the waking state, but also independently.

The very different form dreams have appears due to the fact that more cerebral systems can be working simultaneously than in the waking state. And the many more neurophysiological combinations possible corresponds to the manifold nonsensical combinations in dreams.

That humans and other mammals have a sleep cycle that brings the sleeper on a par with the waking state several times in the course of the night has by biologist Frederich Snyder been taken as manifestation of a "sentinel" function. A more renowned biologist, Lyall Watson, found support for this hypothesis in the fact that subjects who are awakened abruptly during REM sleep are alert and quickly orient themselves, while subjects who are awakened in an NREM stage "display confused and often self-repetitive thinking, and even a certain amnesia."

It has also been suggested that the fetus's "long periods of internally stimulated activity account for the rapid growth and coordination of the cerebral and central nervous system of the higher mammals." REM sleep, which controls over eight hours of the infant's life after the sixth month, effects a "veritable storm" of stimuli. As early as the eighth month the fetus has an activated cerebral cortex in areas where later thought processes, perception of spatial relations, and various complex tasks are handled. According to Snyder, REM sleep has a function in the evolution of the species and is coresponsible for human supremacy.

Montague Ullman thought that vigilance in the human species has a "more refined and sophisticated social nature." In the dream process the organism assesses the effect of recently disturbing events. The dream carries out a scanning of the brain's memory layers in an attempt to connect the actual experience with past experiences. The vigilance process is at first of an exploratory nature and tries to assess the consequences of the material in question. Secondly, resources are mobilized to deal with the alarming event; that is to say, the dream is also directed toward the immediate future. "The dreamer can have the necessary resources for a creative solution or can seek refuge in his habitual defense reactions."

LEARNING AND UNLEARNING IN DREAMS

A very large number of researchers have in widely different ways demonstrated corollaries between the amount of REM sleep and the ability to learn new and difficult tasks in both humans and animals. To enumerate a few, patients with speech defects (aphasia) have a greater amount of REM when their speech function is improved. In humans difficult, frustrating problems and traumatic experiences lead to increased REM sleep, and a whole series of studies have shown that something similar is true of animals during new learning processes.

Harry Fiss, on the basis of a survey of the literature, concluded that REM sleep consolidates ego functions such as learning, mastering situations, remembering, and problem solving. This is called "the adaptation hypothesis for REM sleep."

A newer theory of the function of dreams combines neurophysiological observations of brain functions with computer theory. This theory was put forth by two American molecular biologists, Nobel Prize winner Francis Crick and Graeme Michison, who link theories concerning memory's various functions with dreams. The gist of Crick and Michison's theory is that "dreams are necessary in order to stabilize memory, which takes place through a reverse learning process that can fittingly be called *unlearning*. In the dream phase the brain disconnects the normal input channels and consciousness and continually generates memories by means of randomly created activity patterns. When a pattern—a memory—is produced in this way, the learning process is turned into an unlearning process, and the electrochemical strength of the memory is weakened. The dream is gradually forgotten, perhaps after you have dreamed the same dream or parts of it several times." An argument in favor of dreams helping us to forget superfluous memory material is that we only remember an insignificant fraction of our total dream quantity.

Corroboration for this theory has been found in the American researcher John Hopfield, who has experimented with simulating the brain's memory structure and unlearning technique on a computer. Hopfield found that a computer, which learns in the same manner as the brain, accidentally produces "false memories which appear as illogical and hallucinoid conglomerations of correct memories." If these are not sorted out, the network's memory capacity will gradually be exceeded. Something corresponding would thus happen in the brain if false and incorrectly combined memories weren't sorted out.

The theory is interesting, but it also has many weaknesses. The simulations are carried out on a computer whose capacity is at least ten thousand times less than the human brain's and which with regard to a number of qualitative traits is far inferior to it. Is it at all possible, scientifically or otherwise, to contain the superior system's structure in that of the inferior?

That we should forget the material we dream about is also made doubtful by the fact that the persons who do not work psychodynamically with dreams have by and large the same recurring motifs. These "hallucinoid conglomerations" only disappear if fundamental transformations of the personality occur.

If intellectual unlearning can take place in dreams, it must therefore take place simultaneously with and not instead of the other psychological functions that have been suggested for dreams.

LABORATORY EXPERIMENTS AND THE MAINSTREAM OF DREAM INTERPRETATION

Laboratory experiments and advanced technology in general have in part led to a number of supplementary conceptions of the nature of dreams, and in part contributed to the reinforcing or rejection of old theories.

An argument favoring that dreams have a function is the simple one that "a so commonly occurring involuntary activity, which under normal conditions takes up far more time than sex, for example, must be of vital importance for the brain's functioning," and that it might be coresponsible for mankind's survival. Other functions suggested for dreams are a vigilance function, information processing, and unlearning of memory material.

Very few investigators have claimed that dreams have no meaningful biological and psychological functions. Interest has concentrated in particular on the adaptation hypothesis. Another theory, which was put forward by Hartmann, is that the dream reestablishes the mental functions after the trials and loads of the day.

In the early days of laboratory experiments there was a tendency to reduce dreams to side phenomena of physiological processes, but it has become more and more obvious that this doesn't hold. Today the predominant attitude is expressed in phrases like "nobody who has experience in collecting, investigating and interpreting dreams can doubt that dreams often express a person's basic feelings and indicate his problems," while the more enthusiastic liken the dream process (without interpretation) to effective psychotherapy.

The basic concepts of laboratory research are for the most part derived from clinical and psychological practice, and the most important results of laboratory studies are still the light they throw on the already described mainstream within dream interpretation.

Freud, both in *The Interpretation of Dreams* and in a dissertation on dream and occultism, touched on the fact that during sleep there could be unaltered repetitions of the day's actual events; such dreams he called "night fantasies." They were given no place in his theories but have presumably been NREM thoughts. The theory that dreams are sleep preserving and come about when a dangerous wish is triggered from the unconscious is invalidated by the fact that dreams are a perfectly regular phenomenon that sets in independently of the dangerousness of the unconscious content. Freud imagined, however, that in advance of a dream there would be a long preparatory period—maybe hours—of unconscious thinking, which would then suddenly break through to consciousness like fireworks.

Apart from this there is more support for Freudian ideas. Most laboratory researchers stick to the importance of the defense mechanisms for dream formation, and as we saw in the examples of Don and Jerry it is possible that the defense mechanisms are gradually weakened in the course of the night but are reinforced if contents too problematic are allowed to break through. The fact that most dreams take place during REM sleep, in which the body displays signs of sexual stimulation, makes it understandable that Freud was able to find sexual associations for most dreams.

When recollection and memory, as we have seen, neurophysiologically function in a way that is independent of the waking patterns, and moreover have more energy available, it supports the idea that dreams contain repressed memory material from childhood that otherwise is inaccessible. The neurophysiological studies also showed that many other cerebral functions are active when we are dreaming. So Freud's theory that all dream material is of an infantile sexual character can't be the entire truth.

Not only animal experiments but also observations of brain-damaged accident victims and of infants born with only the brainstem and lacking higher cerebral functions show that primitive parts of the brain, reckoned as the phylogenetically oldest, are responsible for REM sleep, while NREM sleep is associated with the functioning of higher cerebral regions. The French brain researcher M. Jouvet has therefore put forth the hypothesis that the function of REM sleep is to organize and program instinctive behavior, and that complex inherited behavior patterns are the basis for dream formation. It is a parallel to Jung's theories that dreams get material from the collective unconscious, which represents mankind's past and evolutionary history. And the very great dream activity of infants and fetuses can be seen as a parallel to Jung's theory that "the child is first enveloped in the world of the archetypes." It also supports Jung's theories about inherited psychic structures.

McCarley and Hobson's idea of a physiological brain activity without any specific motivation as the prompter of dreams has an analogy in Jung, who imagines that psychic energy is not bound to a particular structure but is free energy. As the brain during sleep doesn't have to process so much sensory data and external stimuli, and as brain activity is powerfully increased during REM sleep, attention can be directed toward data that is generated from within. This seems consistent with the Jungian Hans Dieckmann's theory of a creative dream ego that has more energy available than the waking ego with which to process contrasting contents (see "Waking ego and dream ego," chapter 2). Just as the Jungian Yehezkiel Kluger has done measurements of dreams' archetypicality, laboratory researchers have set up scales for the assessment of how vivid and emotion laden, different and dramatic, alarming and distorted dreams are, and so have unwittingly corroborated the Jungians' conception of the archetypal in dreams. It can be demonstrated that the further into the dream, the more archetypical it becomes. That dreams balance the psyche without our interpreting them can be seen as supporting Jung's theory of autonomous processes and the compensation concept. But that we become irritable and less sociable with REM-sleep deprivation could also point toward a safety-valve function in the Freudian sense, or Perls's theory that they finish off incomplete situations. All three explanations may be valid simultaneously.

There is a tendency within most branches of dream analysis for the younger generation to be more tolerant and less dogmatic than the older. The laboratory researchers, too, as the latest arrivals, are usually more open to the use of several interpretation models on one dream.

The Empirical Basis and the Philosophy

As we have seen, laboratory research has altered dream interpretation's empirical basis in important ways. Dreamers who are awakened in the middle of the night should theoretically not have the same possibility for tinkering with their dreams by rationalizing them and making them more acceptable as people who can wait days before getting to a therapist and telling them. Nevertheless, studies have shown that laboratory dreams are milder and contain fewer of the aggressive and sexual contents that dreamers normally try to repress than "home" dreams, which are told to a therapist.

The explanation for this presumably lies in the fact that therapy is more reassuring for the dreamer than the laboratory. The therapeutic client gradually learns to open himself without being rejected or quashed morally. He learns that he doesn't need to defend himself so strongly against the unconscious content if he feels secure with the therapeutic companion. Conversely, these observations indicate that the therapeutic client does not cheat with his dream reports, the way some skeptics at times claim. On this basis we must assume that laboratory dreams primarily present us with the unconscious's superficial layers.

What gets the most attention are the aspects of dreams that fit in with Adler's and Hall's theories. The Jungian analyst Jane Dallet has rightly ascertained that the theories mainly focus on dreams' function in the domination of and adaptation to the surroundings. They are seen as problem solving, information processing, and ego strengthening in a sense that is not especially profound. Dallet has demonstrated the connection between the newer American dream theories and the materialistic utilitarian values she thinks characterizes American society (and that American psychology is based on).

STILL ANOTHER PERSPECTIVE

One of the questions that has created and is still creating the greatest barrier between analytical schools and generations is whether the dream is contrasting to or an extension of waking life. In connection with Don's and Jerry's dreams, Rosalind Cartwright points out, however, that dreams from the same person can more or less contrast the consciousness. And in Hartmann's studies of persons with respectively great and little sleep need, it turns out that the long sleepers have greater contrast between dream and lifestyle when it comes to sex and aggression than persons who only sleep a little. We must then assume that the long sleepers have more imagination both in dreams and in waking life than others.

Also the Freudians' concept of different degrees of integration ability in the waking ego, and the Jungians' studies of dreams' varying degree of archetypicality, suggest that the contrast/noncontrast discussion is too simple in relation to the dream phenomenon's complexity. Furthermore, we must ask ourselves whether the professional interpreters' different degrees of creative support to the integration of dream contents—in contrast to stiffened frames of reference—play a role in what is considered as contrasting with the waking consciousness and lifestyle.

Cartwright explained the phenomena that accompany REM-sleep deprivation with a hypothesis that Jung once put forth: "The dream is a mental process which is present at a low level all the time," but we are only able to register it when the right conditions are present: when our attention isn't flooded by external stimuli. Meanwhile, REM-sleep deprivation increases brain activity sufficiently for the dream to overstep the threshold of consciousness at other times: in NREM sleep or in the waking state. This made Cartwright assume an equilibrium (homeostatic) function in the psyche, which sees to it that we in any case dream an appropriate amount, which is a parallel to Jung's compensation concept.

David Foulkes, an American laboratory dream researcher who has worked out a scale for the evaluation of the fantasticality of psychic contents, on the basis of a large investigation concluded that around 25 percent of the waking state is of a dreamlike (regressive and/or hallucinoid) nature. Other investigators think that there is an inner regulation of waking fantasy at intervals of 72 to 120 minutes amidst the realistical thinking, and that functions identical to REM sleep occur in the waking state.

Is it this dreamlike activity that pushes to the fore when persons poor in fantasy become more creative during the day if deprived of their dreams at night? Is it this activity that is working when analysts listen with "free-floating attention," as Freud suggested, and is it that activity we make contact with when a good interpretation strikes home or some experiential work gives a feeling of release? We must also ask ourselves whether the concepts of the consciousness and the unconscious are too rigid a pair of opposites to describe the fluid transitions between dreamlike and rational psychic activity.

In any case, creativity seems to be one of the most important key concepts both for the dream and for the consciousness that concerns itself with it. This also appears to be true based on the fact that Freud's and Jung's theories, which to a large degree were developed in work with dreams, are among the ideas that have most inspired psychology and cultural activity in this century.

In the following chapter we will look at a number of frames of reference and dream theories that today are considered alternative.

7. DREAM AND THE BODY

DREAM CONTENT AND BODY STATE

Investigations into the relationship between dream content and bodily states
are still considered alternative science, so that very little material on the
subject is registered in the international psychological and medical data-
bases or in the literature. As mentioned, a good deal is known about REM
sleep and the physiological and biochemical processes that accompany it.
But this does not give us much understanding of the content of dreams.

It has been found that somatic symptoms can be statistically correlated
with specific dream contents. There is, for example, an apparent relationship
between hypertension and repressed hostility in dreams. Among a small
group of women it was found that there is more erotic activity in dreams but
also more discomfort and overt hostility during menstruation than between
menstrual periods. Investigations of this sort are extremely rare, however.

The abovementioned investigations concern themselves with statistical
probabilities. When confronted with the individual person's dream we have
to balance our interpretation in keeping with its context, and nothing is
given with certainty. For example, a twenty-six-year-old woman dreamed: *I
am together with my mother in an exotic wooden house. To get out to the
house we have to jump from island to island. There is a tide: during the day
the islands are lying exposed, at night they are nearly covered by the water.*

When we arrive it is high tide. This was dreamed the night before ovulation at the time of her first desire to be pregnant, and the dream was without precedent in her three-year analysis. The mother can symbolize the woman's own motherliness; the tide, which is controlled by the moon's phases, the female menstrual cycle; and the flooding, fructification. It is also conceivable that the body was notifying her of the possibility for fructification in a dream. The literature also contains examples of a pregnancy's inception appearing in a dream before it was ascertained in waking life.

The body's reaction to medications can occasionally be reflected in dreams. A fifty-year-old woman dreamed the following: *My mother was in the hospital. All at once she vomited blood. A great lump of clotted blood along with a lot of guts floated about in the mess which was on the floor.* The woman was feeling very badly at the time, with fatigue, headache, and emotional imbalance. The next day she began bleeding from the vagina, and it dawned on her that she had neglected her regular hormone treatments. The dream's macabre character departed essentially from her normal dream-style. She received a hormone treatment and dreamed three days later: *A young woman phoned. She was going to have a baby in a couple of days. I was pregnant too. I was hanging some clothes on the clothesline out in a yard while joyfully thinking how fantastic it was to know that in a couple of days you would have a child. (The light was warm rosy-golden.)* In keeping with the dream, she was now in far better spirits and full of optimism. The presence of the younger pregnant woman could have to do with the fact that the hormone treatments were an artificial rejuvenation cure.

Dreams like these underline the necessity of being aware that other than psychic factors influence dream content, and that it doesn't do to rush into psychological overinterpretations. The symbolism in dreams about the body can be complex and difficult to predict. There is no tradition making possible a broad comparison of clinical material and dream interpretations. This is the initial difficulty of any research.

DREAM AND THE BODY IN FREUD AND JUNG

Following from his materialistic outlook, Freud regarded the body and sexuality as the source proper of all psychic energy, and thus every dream is concerned ultimately with bodily needs. The following mechanism applies: In sleep the possibility for living out bodily needs through physical action and movement is blocked. Motor energy is turned inward and via "the psychic apparatus" converted to wish-fulfilling dream fantasies, which serve a safety-valve function.

Freud's theory that the development of consciousness during the first years of life is attached to experiences around body zones—the mouth (the oral stage), the anus (the anal stage), the genitals (the phallic stage)—reflects the conception that the psyche evolves from the body, and that the ego originates from a "body image." Yet Freud was not able to see any direct connection between dreams and the somatic state in practice, and he thought it necessary to maintain a psychological fiction theory. That is, in order to understand dreams one had for the time being to act as if they were purely psychic in nature and dealt with psychic problems.

Jung, with his synchronicity theory, postulated the existence of a universal oneness behind the spirit and matter that fundamentally united them (see "Psychological theories concerning parapsychological phenomena," chapter 8). This hypothesis he used primarily in his studies of parapsychology, where he found that there existed a curious gap between the mind and the body. Contrary to Freud, Jung viewed this gap from the side of the spirit and marveled that "we get so unbelievably little direct information about the body from within, and that . . . the unconscious . . . very seldom refers to the body, and if it does always in the most indirect way." In this way one could have an advanced fatal disease in a certain part of the body without suspecting it through dreams. Now and then, however, it was possible for a trained physician or therapist to diagnose certain organic diseases on the basis of dreams.

Dream and Organic Disease

A doctor, T. M. Davie, submitted to Jung the following dream from one of his patients: *Someone beside me kept on asking me something about oiling some machinery. Milk was suggested as the best lubricant. Apparently I thought that oozy slime was preferable. Then a pond was drained, and amid the slime there were two extinct animals. One was a minute mastodon. I forgot what the other was.* Jung did not hesitate to say that although there were numerous psychological derivatives in the dream, it pointed primarily at some organic disturbance. The emptied pond he interpreted as the damming up of the cerebrospinal fluid circulation. Jung's interpretation turns out to be a striking description of an illness that was diagnosed later as periventricular epilepsy.

In another example a seventeen-year-old girl dreams about *coming home at night. Everything is as quiet as death. The door into the living room is half open, and I see my mother hanging from the chandelier, swinging to and fro in the cold wind that blows in through the open windows.* And later: *A terrible noise broke out in the house at night. I get up and discover that a frightened horse is tearing through the rooms. At last it finds the door into the hall, and jumps through the hall window from the fourth floor into the street below. I was terrified when I saw it lying there, all mangled.*

Jung found, apart from the gruesome character of the dreams, a number of traits that point to a grave organic disease with a fatal outcome. Here it should be mentioned that symbolically the mother can be understood as the nature-bound life of the body. In the image of the mother hanging from the chandelier the dream says that the body is destroying itself. The horse, as well, can stand for the body and biological life, so the second dream is saying nearly the same thing as the first—only in a different image. The interpretation was soon confirmed.

Other older dream theorists have on occasion described dreams that informed about impending organic illness. One of Medard Boss's female patients dreamed three nights in succession: *A Balinese sickness demon revealed itself to her and forced her to sit on an overheated central heating pipe, and she experienced an intolerable burning pain between the legs.* The third night she woke up with fever and acute inflammation of the bladder.

Neo-Freudians who have investigated psychosomatic disorders consider pain a compromise solution between intruding repressed material from the unconscious and self-punishing repressed forces in the psyche. We have from Emil Gutheil this example from a forty-four-year-old man who suffered from migraine: *I am speaking with one of my woman neighbors who proposes an outing. I think how inconvenient it would be to go on a trip with two women. Then I am overcome with affection for my wife and dash up and hug her. I wake up with a severe headache.* Here the patient's "headache" is that he in reality wanted an outing with two women, and the feelings of affection for his wife can be regarded as eagerness to pacify her. We see here yet another example of the Freudian conception of defense mechanisms and reversal of feelings (reaction formations) in dreams.

Gutheil found, incidentally, that themes of cannibalism and devouring corpses or living animals in dreams appear particularly in patients with migraine accompanied by nausea: *I am devouring my mother . . . I wake up with nausea and headache.* Or: *I am eating a live white rat.*

French and Shapiro, two other neo-Freudian analysts, were involved with psychic causes of rheumatic joint disorders. They supply the following dream from a young woman with rheumatic fever and acute arthritis: *I was held captive in a large apartment by my mother. My arms were tied to my sides like in a straightjacket. I was allowed to go about in the apartment, but I mustn't go outside. The only thing I was given to eat was sugar cubes. It appeared to be my mother who was holding me captive.* The dream came shortly before an attack in which her arms became stiff and painful. The woman associated that her mother was "keeping her tied to her apron strings."

In my book *The Feminine in the Man* I have described a more general connection between bodily state and dream symbolism. As a person's relation to his own body is largely determined by life's early phases, whose symbolism often reveals itself in dreams, it is possible via this route to obtain hints about the body's status. The symbolism of these early phases is described in the section "Dream and male development," chapter 2.

If the negative symbolism of the cosmic or vegetative phase is predominant in the dreams, there will often be phobias in relation to the body, allergies, bizarre bodily symptoms, generally reduced resistance to illness, poor physical bearing, etc. Or its diametric opposite, that the body seems totally unreceptive toward minor physical ailments (colds, etc.) because the psyche is split off from the body, which runs on its own like an insensible machine. The symbols can be reactivated in pressured life situations, during grave illness, and before impending death.

If the positive symbolism is in the foreground, then the probability is of a good health and a good relation to the body generally.

Cosmic symbols, when they are positive, can mean that a person has not really been born into his body; that is, he or she is not properly grounded. An example is this dream from a twenty-eight-year-old woman: *It is night. I am hovering out in space together with an unknown young girl named Margueritta. She says to me that we have to go down to earth and live through all the material things before we can free ourselves of them.* The activation of repressed contents from a later animal phase of individuation, which can produce a more or less opulent fauna in dreams, often opens up to bodily spontaneity and self-expression.

DREAM AND THE AMPLIFICATION OF BODY SYMPTOMS

The Jungian Arnold Mindell, who for a period of years was himself seriously ill, has developed a method for working with somatic symptoms and dreams.

In light of many years' experience, he asserts that he has never encountered a case where a symptom's "process" hasn't been reflected in a dream. In his view a sickness is often part of a person's individuation process, and "the soul is expressing an important message through the sickness."

A starting point for Mindell's work is the observation that people, contrary to common sense, have a tendency to worsen bodily symptoms. If a scab itches, you scratch it and thereby open it. If your eye hurts, you press on it, and if you have a stiff neck you bend your head back so as to feel the pain. Mindell therefore concludes that the body tends to reinforce pain, and he utilizes this phenomenon in his therapeutic method.

In itself, there is nothing revolutionary about the method. The technique originated with Wilhelm Reich. It has been used by Alexander Lowen in his bioenergy exercises, and Perls often has his clients reinforce a bodily sensation in order to get them in contact with their emotions. For example, he would ask a group participant to reinforce a tension behind the eyes with the result that the person broke into tears.

What is new in Mindell is that he more specifically applies the method in connection with dreams. A patient was dying of stomach cancer. He had severe pains in the abdomen. Mindell got him to "amplify" them. Suddenly, at the peak of his pain, the man shouted out: "Oh, Arny, I just want to explode. I've never been able to really explode!"

"My problem," the patient explained. "is that I have never expressed myself sufficiently, and even when I do it's never enough." For a long period afterward, Mindell had him work with "exploding": the man would make noises, cry, shout, and scream entirely on his own initiative. The upshot was that his stomach pains disappeared and he lived three years longer than expected. Shortly before entering the hospital the man had dreamed that *he had an incurable disease and the medicine for it was like a bomb.*

Another case is the little girl who came to Mindell with a rapidly growing tumor in her back. She was dying, and her family was ready to say good-bye to her. The girl told Mindell about a dream in which she *let go of the safety fences around a very dangerous lake.* Afterward she lay down on the floor and said she wanted to fly. Thinking of the dream, and with her doctor's permission, Mindell removed a corset she wore to support her back (the safety fence). Then they both played like they were flying. At one point the girl wanted to fly away "to another world, a beautiful world where there are strange planets," but then changed her mind and wanted to come down and play with Mindell. "The other world" Mindell interpreted as death, and understood the dream and the fantasy to mean that she should be allowed to play and move about freely. The little girl recovered rapidly and her tumor disappeared.

The Norwegian psychodrama therapist Eva Røine gives an example that is in line with Mindell's. A woman dreamed about *some sort of a garden or yard for patients. They were all very ill and sitting in bathtubs where the front piece was missing.* The woman tried playing the bathtub. She bent forward with her arms stretched out as if they were the edges of the tub. The distance between her hands represented the missing front piece. Just as the woman *was* the bathtub, she felt as if all the strength left her. It felt, she said, as if fluid (water, blood, strength) was streaming out of her. The leader warned her that she ought to take a vacation. She didn't listen to his advice and shortly afterward suffered both a physical and a psychic breakdown, followed by a prolonged illness.

Mindell's point of departure is the active imagination of Jung. But while Jung worked almost exclusively with mental ideation, visualizations, and inner dialogues, Mindell expands this to include body sensations and movements.

The work has four phases:

Phase 1: Self-exploration. The person is lying completely still. He feels the symptom—forgets all thoughts about it and only feels. If there is a slight trembling he concentrates on the pains around this trembling: where they come from, do they feel hot or cold, do they radiate, have a special geometric form, is there differing pressure, shifting location and intensity, etc.

Phase 2: Amplification. When the symptom has been experienced and registered without preconceived notions, the person lies completely still and tries to amplify it. He must not do anything whatever to reduce the discomfort.

Phase 3: Channel changing. If the above instructions are followed, at some point the limit of toleration will be reached. According to Mindell, there will then occur a shift from a proprioceptive channel to a visual channel. The person sees *a knife blade in the pain's center, for example, fire in the throat infection, an iron clamp in the stomach, a bomb in the tumor, a drummer in the headache, and so forth.*

Now the experience is amplified in this channel, for example by developing the image through active imagination or gestalt therapy into a dramatic plot.

Phase 4: Completing the work. At a certain point the person will feel that the work is finished (corresponding to Perls's finished gestalts). This is a subjective evaluation. Very often he or she will feel better and possibly have gained an insight. This change of state can then be worked into a more general understanding of the person's life situation and incorporated in the dream interpretation.

Mindell's clientele was broader than that of most psychotherapists. His experience stems from his private practice, from seminars with professional therapists, from psychiatric wards, and from hospitals with normal, psychotic, physically ill, and dying patients. The clients in the examples mentioned were persons who would not have sought him out or interested themselves whatever in psychology if it hadn't been for a serious physical illness. This may be the explanation for their very few, very short, but also very essential dreams that make possible such a simple diagnosis.

THE DREAM ELEMENTS' LOCATION IN THE BODY

I agree with Mindell and the Danish dream theorist Jes Bertelsen that in principle a connection to an area of the body can be found in any dream. In my opinion it may be a question of a connection between the entire dream and the body area, but often different dream elements are bound to different areas in the body to a greater or lesser degree.

Some dreams, especially anxiety dreams, are on waking accompanied by localized body sensations: the throat constricts in terror, the dreamer feels a dull pain in the stomach, there is tension in the neck, or he gets a headache. But the body sensations can also be positive, like orgasmic sensations, relaxation, calm, and well-being.

In other instances the connection between dream and body is perceived on waking when the dream can't immediately be recalled. If you now go through the body in your mind and focus on a particular area, suddenly a recalled dream image might appear, followed by a longer dream. Or a forgotten dream can, as it were, be let out of imprisonment in the body, if you do relaxation exercises or meditate on particular body areas. For example, one morning I woke up with tensions in the neck but no recollection of any dream. I got up and did an exercise where the shoulder and neck muscles are held in tension for approximately thirty seconds. Following this excess tension, a momentary relaxation appeared and a dream, which written down would have filled four sheets of paper, welled up into the consciousness. Another time a sexual touching brought the memory of an erotic dream. Other dreams of mine have been saved from oblivion through chakra meditation (see "Dream and meditation," chapter 9). Also, later in the day a body sensation can be induced that forms the channel for the recollection of a dream.

One example of work with a dream element's location in the body comes from a young female client: *I was to visit some man or other, and he had a lot of Alsatian dogs which growled and barked. I was afraid of them. They were shut up in a wooden cage, but it was as if they could get out anytime.* The dream clearly deals with anxiety. The dogs can symbolize male drive and sexuality and can express a suppressed aggressiveness in the woman herself that she is afraid will get loose. But on interpretation it wasn't possible to locate the dream problem in relation to the previous day's events. Was she anxious because she had danced with a somewhat pushy fellow? Did it have to do with a conflict at work? Did it have to do with her boyfriend? Or was it a spontaneous popping up of unconscious content?

I asked the dreamer to imagine that she was again standing in front of the cage with the dogs, and then try to feel where in the body she felt her anxiety. It was in the abdominal region a little below the navel. Just then she could recall that she had had exactly that feeling in the stomach during an episode with her boyfriend. She had been furious but kept her anger in check for fear of losing him. She had also had this bodily sensation in connection with conflicts at her workplace, but not so strongly. After having made this realization, she played a furious Alsatian dog. It took some overcoming to get out of the nice-girl role, but the role of furious Alsatian dog made her far more vivacious, and the stomach pain disappeared. Having this image and this body sensation in mind also made it easier for her to use the dream in her daily life.

BODY SHAPE AND DREAM SYMBOL

The possibility also exists that symbolic dream and fantasy structures are so meaningful that they reflect the entire physical organism and shape of the individual. Alexander Lowen, the founder of bioenergetic therapy—which is based on Ernst Kretschmer's theories of the connection between character and body type—in his book *The Denial of the Body* gives the following example: One of his female clients related that at the age of eleven she discovered her body and her sexuality, and a year later—with violent guilt feelings—began masturbating intensely. During this whole period she had the persistent fantasy that *she was riding on a horse which was better than all of her girlfriends'*.

Lowen interpreted the horse in her fantasy as symbolizing the body, particularly the lower body. On account of her guilt feelings, the girl tried to split off the insistently greater physicality, and this was clearly readable in her body. "From the waist down the girl was heavy, hairy and darker. Above the waist she was slender . . . the lower half of the body gave the impression of sexual maturity . . . the upper half of her body appeared innocent and childish."

Parallel with this theme, one of my woman clients dreamed she *was riding on a stiff-legged horse that was named Victoria.* Apart from having a Victorian attitude toward sex, she also had an unbending lower body and felt her legs as wooden posts.

Here I should point out that the horse is a symbol having many meanings, and that not all horses in dreams symbolize the body. Also, the meaning of the symbol must as always be weighed against the importance of the context in which it appears. In Lowen's client the horse appeared in a fantasy that recurred again and again in one of the most important phases of life, the transition to adolescence, which underscores its essentiality.

DREAM AND KINESTHETIC SENSE

The American psychologist Barbara Lerner thinks that one of the functions of dreams is to strengthen the body image and the sense of movement: the kinesthetic sense. Lerner cites investigations that show with great statistical certainty that REM-sleep deprivation leads to false sense perceptions and dissolution of normal body image. An example is this experience by a "dream deprived" person: *His face and hands were covered by spider webs. He could both see it and feel it. He tried to wash it off but couldn't, and finally shouted for help.*

When we are dreaming, there are no movements of the large muscles, and the inhibition of movement during sleep (that is, being tied to the bed) appears to increase physical activity in the dream. In contrast, we do *not* dream during phases of sleep in which muscle movement occurs, such as in somnambulation.

Lerner's theories are inspired by Hermann Rorschach. In experiments using his psychological ink-blot test, REM-sleep deprivation led to an increase in kinesthetic fantasies, which should then mean that the missing movement in dreams must be compensated for in waking life. Correspondingly, inhibition of movement increases the number of kinesthetic fantasies. Thomas French, too, found that muscles and joints that are inhibited in the waking state often are active in dreams. In Lerner's and Rorschach's words: "The fantasies the body doesn't allow itself in waking life it lives out in dreams, and one of the functions of dreams is to maintain the kinesthetic sense and the body image."

Other laboratory researchers have tried having people walk around in the laboratory every time they were awakened out of an REM phase. But the movement could not replace the need for REM sleep. Thus, movement training and maintenance of body image cannot be the only function of the dreams.

Lastly, it should be mentioned that dream recollection seems to be coded to the body position on awakening, so that a dream is easily forgotten if the dreamer wakes and changes position.

Collectively these observations contribute to understanding why in practice we can see such distinct connections between dream and body language.

DREAM AND BODY LANGUAGE

One of the problems surrounding associations to dreams, as mentioned, is that dreamers learn rather quickly how to supply associations that are relatively innocuous and at the same time fit into the dream interpreter's frame of reference. A good way of obtaining associations that haven't first gone through the ego's filter is by observing the body language while the dream is being related and then working with it subsequently. Descriptions of this practice are to be found scattered in the gestalt therapeutic literature and in Mindell. Here I shall give examples from my own material.

A dream sequence from a fifty-year-old man: *I am tearing down a large scaffolding that my father has built.* To tear down what the father has built up expresses father-rebellion. But the dreamer maintained that he *had* made the rebellion against his father he was supposed to, and that he was "completely clarified" on that point.

As he was telling the sequence, he sat with his hands folded, gazing heavenward into the ceiling. This made me remind him that his father had been a member of a religious sect, and he admitted that not only had he encountered much false piety during childhood, but that he still had a strong aversion to people who were holier-than-thou. This, then, was the emotional background for the dreamer's father-rebellion, and the body language seemed to reveal that he too considered himself saved.

A forty-year-old woman dreamed that she *was married to her father. A number of complications arise, and the dream ends with her feeling such a terrible emptiness that she wants to commit suicide.* As the woman was telling the end of the dream, she gestured twice with her hand as if stabbing herself in the solar plexus. During work with the dream we talked about her father's death, which she "had practically felt as a deliverance." I asked her: "Are you certain of that?"

> *N:* Yes. He died in the arms of his mistress, and I was so happy that she had relieved me.
>
> *OV:* But when the dream says that you are married to him, then weren't you mad with jealousy?
>
> *N:* No, on the contrary. I thought it was so beautiful.

It turns out that the anger she previously turned inward as suicide thoughts she was able to turn outward as rage directed at the father and the mistress. The further dreamwork got her on the track of her anger toward the father, anger that she turned toward herself (the dagger in the solar plexus). Also a talk about the dagger's symbolic meaning together with the feelings that were attached to the solar plexus came to play a role.

Example number three relates a dream sequence from a thirty-eight-year-old man: *I am meeting Ida.* To Ida the dreamer "associated" that she was a girl whom he could relate to personally without sexualizing. Ida was named three times in the course of the conversation. All three times, and only those times, the dreamer unthinkingly scratched himself in the crotch.

Holding or pointing to the stomach, the heart, or other parts of the body, clenching the fist, picking at the ear, rubbing the nose, massaging the lip, opening and closing the body in numberless ways, holding the breath or breathing rapidly, looking in a certain direction. These signals are often nearly invisible. A change in the look; the relaxation of a body part, particularly the eyes, the jaw, the mouth; an indefinable change in ambience— all can be spontaneous expressions for emotions and experiences that are closely connected with the dream's meaning. The dream interpretation can be integrated with whatever system is being used to decipher body signals.

The associations that body language gives to the dreams can be quite unperceived by the dreamer himself and at the same time have considerable clout, so the dream interpreter must use them with circumspection. They can reveal things that the dreamer is unprepared to go into, and inexpedient defense reactions can be provoked by calling attention to them. Therefore it is often better to let the dreamers explore body symbols themselves, to let them "learn by discovering."

Also, a deepening or reinforcement of the movements or body postures that accompany a particular element in the dream narrative can produce associations we otherwise wouldn't access. This often proves to be the case. One example: Some time ago I worked with a woman who was pregnant in a dream group. She was in the ninth month and wanted to give birth at home, but the infant's head was turned the wrong way. A lengthy dream included the following sequence: *My father and mother had abducted my child* (the expected baby, which she knew was a boy). *They had conspired so that I couldn't get in contact with him!* The woman couldn't get any associations whatever to the dream. It seemed totally absurd that her parents or her relationship with them should be able to create problems.

As she related the sequence, she was sitting with wide-open eyes and one hand in front of her face in a horrified gesture. I asked her to assume the same position and concentrate on what had happened. Different associations came up. Her maternal grandmother had never accepted that her mother was pregnant with her out of wedlock. But the woman herself had invited her mother to look after the child and herself immediately after the birth in order to bond her to the child from the start. The associations went on with feelings of anxiety, insufficiency, and rejection. To remain sitting in this position also brought her in contact with different body sensations, which I asked her to examine and amplify. There now occurred some subtle changes in her air. As she was telling the dream, her face had alternately assumed a facadelike smile and a look of anxiety. Her expression softened, the eyes and mouth showed dejection, the musculature in jaw, neck, and shoulders relaxed, and she went through feelings of rejection, anguish, and insufficiency in quiet succession.

Afterward, when I pointed out to the group how important it was that such inner processes be allowed to take their course, it turned out that no one had noticed what had taken place. Some had actually been rather impatient and tried to break into the therapy with interpretations, which in themselves were good enough but which were on the point of distracting the dreamer's attention from the inner emotional/bodily continuity. So, these processes can outwardly be very undemonstrative. It requires time and sympathetic understanding, and words often divert attention from authentic self-contact.

That same night the infant turned to the normal position! The woman had dreamed that *she had contact with the boy while he was in her womb. She coaxed him gently and asked if he didn't want to "come down" (be born). And he said yes.*

DREAM AND TOUCHING

In my experience tactile contact can be a very valuable part of a therapy, if consideration is given to the client's individual requirements and possible contact anxiety. A light touching, a hug, a supportive arm around the shoulders, massage, healing, and so forth, can with the correct timing perform small miracles. In gestalt therapy circles this is understood, whereas in classical psychoanalysis, daylong seminars could be devoted to discussing the opportuneness of shaking the client's hand.

To be touched in a dream can frequently be translated as to be *emotionally* touched, in contrast to merely understanding or realizing. If in a dream a woman is touched by a man, it corresponds to getting in closer emotional contact with the inner psychic content (her animus), or to the masculine in her surroundings. Likewise with other figures and complexes in dreams.

An interpretation such as this will often be borne out in the course of the work. But it can also be of benefit to understand the touching patterns in dreams more concretely.

A woman in a dream group related a dream where *my mother is holding me. It's suffocating. I feel disgust.* It was the first time the dreams had displayed negative sides of the relationship to the mother so overtly. A dredging in the dream made a strong impression on her and she burst into tears. The dream was told in a group, and I asked whether she wanted somebody to hold her. She did, and a female group participant put her arms around her. The dreamer (D) at first gave herself over to it. But then there was a hint of tension in shoulders, neck, and jaw, and a flicker of distaste around the mouth. I imagined what was taking place in her: Now Mother is suffocating me again. It's disgusting. I am ashamed of feeling that.

> *OV:* Do you feel distaste?
> *D:* Yes.
> *OV:* Do you want her to let you go?
> *D (sighs in relief):* Yes.

As men did not appear as negatively in her dreams, I walked over in back of her and asked her to feel how close I could get before it was unpleasant. It felt good to her that I placed my hands supportively on her shoulders. But I did not try to hold her in my arms. There was nothing wrong in principle with the female group participant's "acting in," because it gave the dreamer the possibility for discovering in a concrete way some emotions and sensations in herself that she had not suspected.

On the basis of my experiences, I would advance the hypothesis that the dream ego's relationship to physical touching often either directly or symbolically reflects the waking ego's attitude to touching. More generally, tender touches and contact in a love relationship, in therapy, and in sensuality training can yield dreams that correspond to the positive symbolism for the earliest phases of life (cosmic and vegetative symbolism and eating symbolism).

DREAM AND BODY THERAPY

After years of working with his technique of amplifying bodily symptoms, Arnold Mindell came to the conclusion that "All dreams talk about, one way or the other, body conditions . . . about physical diseases . . . about all physical gestures (facial expression, vocal pitch, pace, etc.) . . . all your communications to others." He pointed out that there are problems that can remain untouched in straight psychotherapy unless the body is involved. My own experience is that qualified body therapy (such as Rolfing, kinesiology, bioenergetics, rebirthing) can accelerate psychic growth processes, and that it can be seen in the dreams. You must always be attentive to whether the consciousness can manage to integrate the contents that are released in body therapy, and whether in accelerating the process there are inexpedient side effects.

Rolfing

Rolfing is a depth massage where the muscles and connective tissue are restructured so that the body's configuration and carriage become more harmonic. The method is known for its strong physical and psychic effects.

The American Rolfer and psychotherapist Karl Krackhauer found that dreams process and develop the Rolfing experience, and that they accelerate the therapeutic process. Krackhauer thinks that alterations of the dreamer's waking experience of the body are accompanied by corresponding changes in his experience of his body in dreams. He saw too that the new body experiences in dreams can have a symbolic meaning that reflects psychic growth processes.

Krackhauer regards dreaming as a less controlled state than waking. The

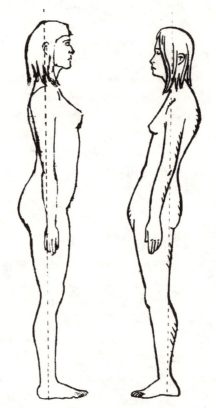

Fig. 3. Dreams can reflect bodily states and effects of body therapy. This is seen in connection with body psychotherapy, in which in-depth changes in bodily structure and posture are accompanied by more physical dreams. See Chapter 7.

dreamer can come in contact with traumatic body experiences in childhood; the body experience in the dream can be a reflection of the waking state; or the dream can provide the "awakebody" with a "pre-play" of experiences and activities to come.

Krackhauer has described a therapy he did with a young woman (Lilith). The first year they worked with psychotherapy without Rolfing, and it is interesting that in this period (thirty dreams were analyzed) the body played a very small and mainly indirect role in the dreams. In a few cases the dreams might deal with pregnancy, paralysis, or death, but only as states without closer reference to the body *experience*. In a single dream half a year into the therapy, after the woman had begun experimenting with her sexuality, she had a more specific body experience. She dreamed that she was menstruating and *I discover that my clitoris is actually a little translucent pyramid. It's glowing with an inner light. I'm so happy I have my own pyramid—a source of power and magic.* The young woman had not had many really enjoyable or orgasmic sexual experiences, and she protected herself from sexual advances by being forty pounds overweight.

In the second year of therapy, Rolfing was added to the treatment, and here the body figured in a significant way in more than twenty dreams. The work with the body brought her in contact with childhood experiences that had left their mark on her body. In one dream Ida Rolf, the founder of the method, is doing preliminary Rolfing on her. It takes place in a bathtub. Ida Rolf says: *"I can see by the way you hold your shoulders and chest that you had a very unhappy childhood."* *I get very upset and start to cry.* *"I didn't know I was unhappy at the time, though."* *I'm very upset and keep protesting that what she said is not true.* Later in the dream, Ida Rolf continues: *"Karl (Krackhauer) Rolfed you and Fritz Perls Rolfed you, and they both said the same thing about your shoulders."*

The woman's shoulders had been permanently frozen in a suspended position, but in this period the Rolfing work relaxed her chest and shoulders considerably. It also got her to relinquish some of her defense positions. She revived traumatic childhood situations, in which her constantly depressive father had sat with his head literally on her shoulder and confided to her his desire to leave the family or take his own life. She had defended herself against "the painful contact" by turning her shoulders into a block of wood.

After ten months of Rolfing, Lilith has the following dream:

> *I walk through an exotic Egyptian-like marketplace . . . I move my body in an undulating rhythm to the drums and flutes resounding from the bazaar . . . I feel how my hip is connected to my leg and how my leg is connected to my foot. I feel the place radiating from deep in my stomach where the upper part of my body is connected to the lower part. I have a sense of this spot being my "center." I refer to it as the "connection between two worlds." I am filled with awe at the range of my movements of my body as an integral part of who I am. . . . [I am] feeling my whole body spreading outward from my deep stomach muscle . . . I'm feeling very whole and strong, and I start getting energy rushes from deep in my pelvis.*

Krackhauer understood the "connection between two worlds" as an approaching integration of body and emotion on the one side with intellect and control on the other.

There is no doubt that as the day's residues the dream absorbs Rolfing jargon—such as the word *integrating*—into its language. (The subtitle of Ida Rolf's textbook on Rolfing is *Integration of Structures*.) Nevertheless, there is a detailed working in of bodily sensations and body consciousness the like of which I have never seen in thousands of dreams without body therapy.

The symbolism in Lilith's dream was not only corporeal but also very spiritual. Where in the dream Lilith's shoulders are Rolfed, Ida Rolf appears as a *large imposing woman . . . very magical and very intimidating. She's like a sorceress; her ankles and feet meet at a point as if she's a genie who's just come out of a lamp.* Later in the dream, Ida Rolf flies *like a whirlwind through an Arab market in Cairo. She is looking for a magic potion to make for me . . . gliding through the air . . .* and Lilith is pulled along. With great difficulty Ida Rolf finds the vital ingredient for the potion: *bird wings . . . with black and gold feathers.* Then Lilith is put in the bathtub again and over her objections is fed the potion and Rolfed by Perls, who is *very big, also looking like a genie just out of a bottle.* The idea of a spirit that is let out of a lamp or bottle is archetypal. Arnold Mindell describes it in the book *Dreambody* as body experience shut inside the body organs; moreover, it is possible to contact the experience, in the East often by meditation.

The dream series, like much other body work, points to the fact that the more we immerse ourselves in the body experience, the more we get into the spiritual dimensions of existence. In this way we suspend the traditional Western dichotomy of body and spirit.

Here it should be mentioned that the word *dreambody* doesn't have entirely the same meaning in different authors. In Mindell it refers to a kind of subtle energy body that forms a bridge between spirit and body. Krackhauer uses it more in the sense of the dream ego's body.

The writer, in connection with a Rolfing treatment, has had dreams referring to a suspension of blockages both psychic and physical. For example: *I was together with a big boy who got Rolfing. Some "watertight bulkheads between parts of his personality disappeared." It was like a basin where the water could flow freely between different parts.* I woke up with a pleasant, relaxed sensation of energy flowing freely in my body, and it happens to have moved into psychic regions that had been closed to me.

Kinesiology

Kinesiology is a body therapy that works with a system of energyways in the body (see also "Dream and chakra symbols," chapter 9). According to this therapy, the energy between these paths must flow as freely as possible The treatment consists of dissolving blockages by manipulating certain points on the body.

There exists no literature on the subject of dream and kinesiology, but I have had the opportunity to follow dream series in twelve clients who were receiving kinesiological treatment. An illustrative example is a twenty-one-year-old man who had a double blockage between the right and left sides, which disturbs rather basically the energy circulation. The dreams he brought to the first five or six treatments had a common theme: *lakes that were dried out, polluted, completely without life, or covered by glass.* The blockages gradually began to be dissolved and simultaneously the dreams changed character. He dreamed that he *found accessible and pure water, and came to lakes and streams where there was a hope of catching fish.*

After four months and the twelfth kinesiological treatment, he dreamed: *My girlfriend and I are standing beside a lake. It is lush and green around us. I am fishing. I catch two eels and am very glad. One of them slips down into the boot of my girlfriend. I am afraid and try to get it out.* In Jungian terms, the living processes in the unconscious (the water) had ceased in the initial dreams. The procurement of pure water is apparently the image of the therapeutic process. Regarded psychoanalytically, the change in symbolism over four months is radical. The eel in the girl's boot could well be a sexual symbol, and with this new shift he goes from the frying pan into the fire.

Another dream comes from a twenty-seven-year-old woman who had a blockage in the left half of the brain and was in kinesiological treatment. She dreamed that she *rode the train many times between East Germany and West Germany. The car had three chairs on the right side, but on the left side the seats were missing.*

Finally this dream from a man who was in bioenergetic therapy: *It is at night and I am among a group of people around a bonfire. We are nude except that I am wearing shoes and socks . . . (later) It gets colder . . . (later) I take a warm shower and take off the shoes and socks.* Naturally the symbolism of the shoes and socks could be dealt with from a Freudian, Jungian, or phenomenological point of view. The dreamer's own comment was that he had worked his entire body through bioenergetically. He had now come to some tensions in the ankles and was working with the feet, becoming alternately cold and warm.

CONCLUSION

The growing acknowledgment of a connection between the psychology of dreams and body processes makes it ever clearer that dreams can be understood in many dimensions. New experiences underscore the fact that the interpreting consciousness's horizon is determining as to what information from the dream can be made accessible and usable. In the section on dream and laboratory experiments, I took up how problematical it has become to use the terms *conscious* and *unconscious*, because it appears that the boundaries are more fluid than the old dream theorists assumed.

This becomes increasingly obvious. At the moment a person registers a body sensation, he has body consciousness. But if the body's signal is unable to be integrated in an existing interpretation of the world, it subsides meaninglessly back into the unconscious. In the infancy of psychoanalysis, a body signal had to be so strong that it produced a physical illness before it could be given a place in the psychoanalysis and with it the dreamer's consciousness and self-understanding. Today a far greater spectrum of bodily expressions are taken account of in the consciousness.

As in most areas where the younger generation is taking over dreamwork, the body therapists are more open in their interpretations than the old theorists were. Even though Krackhauer didn't construct a theory from them, he does use interpretations that have Freud, Jung, the existentialists, and Perls as their premises. In my own dreamwork, all of the above methods are applied, depending on what is most fruitful at a given moment. It therefore must be made an important point of theory to form creative syntheses of different approaches to working with dreams.

In the dream a dialogue between the conscious and the unconscious develops primarily in three ways:

1. Working with the body starts processes that are automatically reflected in the dream.
2. Augmented awareness of and interest in the body sharpens attentiveness to wholes and details in the dream, which reports on the status of the body.
3. Work with the body provides the dream with a language via the

day's residues, so it can communicate the body status to the consciousness in a readily understandable way.

Moreover, different kinds of new evidence suggest the following dream functions:

1. To register organic illness and inform as to possible remedies
2. To maintain the body image during sleep and compensate for inhibited movement
3. To confront the dreamer with traumatic body experiences in childhood and anticipate new body events.
4. To reflect the dreamer's attitude to bodily touches.

8. Dreams and Parapsychology

Examples of precognitive dreams

President Abraham Lincoln was very interested in parapsychological phenomena and dreams. One evening he was discussing dreams and premonitions with Ward Hill Lamon, who wrote his biography. A couple of other persons were present as well, including Mrs. Lincoln, who remarked at her husband's solemn mood and lingering on the subject of dreams. Lincoln replied: "I had a dream the other night which has haunted me ever since. . . . Somehow the thing has gotten possession of me, and like Banquo's ghost it will not [lie] down." Lamon jotted down the unpleasant dream immediately after Lincoln had related it:

> There seemed to be a deathlike stillness about me. Then I heard subdued sobs, as if a number of people were weeping. I thought I left my bed and wandered downstairs. There the silence was broken by the same pitiful sobbing, but the mourners were invisible. I went from room to room; no living person was in sight, but the same mournful sounds of distress met me as I passed along. It was light in all the rooms; every object was familiar to me; but where were all the people who were grieving as if their hearts would break? I was puzzled and alarmed. What could be the meaning of all this? Determined to find the cause of a state of things so

mysterious and so shocking, I kept on until I arrived at the East Room, which I entered. There I met with a sickening surprise. Before me was a catafalque, on which rested a corpse wrapped in funeral vestments. Around it were stationed soldiers who were acting as guards; and there was a throng of people, some gazing mournfully upon the corpse, whose face was covered, others weeping pitifully. "Who is dead in the White House?" I demanded of the soldiers. "The President," was his answer; "He was killed by an assassin!" Then came a loud burst of grief from the crowd, which awoke me from my dreams. I slept no more that night.

A few days later, Abraham Lincoln was assassinated.

Such a dream that predicts a future event is called a *precognitive dream*. As usual when events and stories of that sort are cited in the parapsychological literature, the testimony is from firsthand sources whom there is no immediate reason to doubt—if the subject didn't happen to be parapsychology. On the other hand, the events can be difficult or impossible to verify.

On October 21, 1966, an immense heap of coal slag in the Welsh mining village of Aberfan avalanched and buried the local school. One hundred forty-four persons were killed. The following week the English psychiatrist J. C. Barker placed in a nationwide newspaper an appeal to people who felt they had received parapsychological information about this tragedy. The response was large. After a thorough process of elimination, thirty-five accounts remained that Barker felt were reliable. In twenty-four of these cases the person had told his precognitive experience to someone else before the slag avalanche occurred. Twenty-five cases dealt with dreams. In one of them a telephone operator in Brighton helplessly spoke with a child who came walking toward her followed by "a black, billowing mass."

A little girl, Eryl Mai, told her mother the following dream: *I dreamed I went to school and there was no school there. Something black had come down all over it.* She said to her mother: "Mummy, I'm not afraid to die, because I shall be there with Peter and June." When the mountain of slag slid down over the school two days later, Eryl Mai, Peter, and June were among the 116 children who were crushed or buried alive.

In addition to foreknowledge, a number of other parapsychological phenomena (*psi phenomena*) are connected with the dreams. The concepts, which overlap somewhat, are: out-of-body experience in dreams (*lucid dreams*), thought transference (*telepathy*), chronological coincidences of physical and psychic events (*synchronicity*), extrasensory perception (*ESP*).

SCIENCE AND PARAPSYCHOLOGY

Acknowledgment of the existence of parapsychological phenomena has been and is still very problematic in our culture, especially in a scientific context; to be at all concerned with parapsychology can lead to mudslinging and exclusion from the "respectable" scientific community. The fear of discrediting the psychoanalytical movement was an important reason for Freud's noncommittal attitude toward occult phenomena; as for Jung, his acceptance of them led to isolation and accusations of being unscientific.

An important breakthrough in parapsychological research was made in the 1930s with J. B. Rhine's use of statistical methods and thoroughly controlled laboratory experiments. The following are among the experiments with which he demonstrated ESP phenomena:

He used a deck of twenty-five cards divided into groups of five cards each. Each card was marked with a sign: a star, a square, a circle, a cross, two wavy lines. The experiment was carried out in the following manner: In each series of tests, the deck of cards is dealt eight hundred times without the subject being able to see the cards. He is asked to guess the cards as they are put down. The odds for a correct answer are 5:25. The result, calculated on the basis of very large numbers, showed an average of 6.5:25 correct answers. The probability of a random deviation of 1.5 is 1:250,000. Some subjects gave more than twice as many correct answers. On a single occasion the subject guessed all twenty-five cards correctly, at the odds of 1:298,023,223,876,953,125 (!). The spatial distance between the experimenter and the subject was in other experiments increased from a few meters to around 6.5 kilometers, without it influencing the result (synchronized clocks were used). Another experiment consisted in asking the subject to guess a series of cards that would be dealt within a shorter or longer period. The time factor was increased from a few minutes to two weeks. The result of these experiments gave odds of 1:400,000.

Something interesting with these experiments is that a prerequisite for their success was a certain enthusiasm. Upon repeating with the same subject the interest dropped and with it the frequency of ESP phenomena.

After that, innumerable experiments were carried out by scientists who were and are recognized in fields other than parapsychology. The American dream theorist Montague Ullman, from an examination of the literature, concluded that today there is overwhelming documentation for the existence of parapsychological phenomena.

Because most parapsychological phenomena are by nature nearly always unique and unpredictable, the most difficult point in connection with scientific substantiation is to find experimental situations that can be recreated. One of the factors that contributed to the crisis and break between Freud and Jung in the years 1910–1914 was Freud's negative conception of parapsychological phenomena. Freud was skeptical at the time and feared that an interest in occult phenomena might jeopardize psychoanalysis being recognized as a science. But less than two years later, experiences with his own clients convinced him that the existence of occult phenomena such as telepathy could not be excluded, and he encouraged psychoanalysis to take up the scientific challenge. He thought, "If telepathy exists as a phenomenon then one must assume that it is a rather frequent phenomenon, the difficult verifiability notwithstanding."

Cross-cultural investigations have shown that the belief in parapsychological phenomena exists in nearly all cultures; this suggests that it is a question of actual experiences. The same applies to the innumerable reports of precognitive dreams that have been sent to recognized American and British journals of parapsychology. A study carried out on 433 American college students showed that 111 had experienced dreams they considered precognitive.

The German parapsychologist Hans Bender carried out systematic studies of precognitive dreams. In that connection an actress sent him her dreams for twenty years. Among her possible precognitive dreams was one from May 5, 1966: *She dreamed of a costume which she was to have for a certain role, and made a drawing of it. Its most outstanding feature was that the collar was missing.* On May 4, 1967, just such a costume was delivered to the actress. Another time she dreamed: *She was in a department store to buy a woolen jacket. She found one in a beige tone and the saleswoman brought her three, one after the other. But all three were too small.* One year later she received a beige jacket as a present, but it was too small. She returned it, but twice it was replaced with a jacket that was too small.

There is general agreement that precognitive and telepathic dreams adhere in time rather closely to the corresponding external event, usually within twenty-four hours, but that is not always the case. In the example of the actress, the mysterious coincidence was that the occurrences fell almost a year to the day after the dreams.

The general tendency in the extraordinarily large number of reports of precognitive dreams is that they are submitted as isolated occurrences. They appear not only in the parapsychological literature but have also absorbed psychiatrists, psychoanalysts, and therapists of various schools, for it would seem that the therapeutic situation is advantageous to the occurrence of parapsychological phenomena. In connection with natural catastrophes and major disasters (for example, Aberfan and the loss of the Titanic), it has been possible to obtain somewhat larger material to work with.

Of special interest for the scientific substantiation of the connection between dream and psi phenomena are a series of laboratory experiments carried out by Montague Ullman. The experimental setup and the statistical calculations have been described in detail by Ullman himself. The procedure was briefly as follows:

The subjects were placed in a sleep laboratory and their sleep and dreams monitored with EEG. All dreams and associations were tape-recorded. The "target material" was twelve prints of famous paintings. On a given night one of these was randomly selected and looked at by a "transmitter" subject in a room at a distance from the sleeping subject. At a later point three independent outside judges were sent the dream transcripts and the twelve potential target pictures and asked to rank the targets according to which of them was closest to the dream.

In a preliminary experiment it turned out that the one transmitter was with great statistical probability incorporating more telepathic material than the other into the receivers' dreams. As a result of this experiment the dreamer and the transmitter were selected who together had the greatest incorporation of pictorial material in the dream, in order to see whether it was possible to repeat the success. When the two worked together, the odds for achieved telepathic influence on the dream was 1:1,000.

The following example involves the randomly chosen target *The Sacrament of the Last Supper* by Dalí. It shows Christ at the center of a table surrounded by his twelve disciples. There are a glass of wine and a loaf of bread, while water and a fishing boat are seen in the distance. Excerpt from S's first dream transcript: *There was one scene of an ocean . . . it had a strange beauty about it and a strange formation.* Excerpt from S's second dream transcript: *I haven't any reason to say this but boats come to mind. Fishing boats. Small size fishing boats . . . There was a picture in the Sea Fare Restaurant that came to mind as I was describing it. It's a very large painting. Enormous. It shows, oh, I'd say about a dozen or so men pulling a fishing boat ashore right after having returned from a catch.* Excerpt from S's third dream transcript: *I was looking at a catalog . . . it was a Christmas catalog. Christmas season.*

A number of similar experiments that suggest probable telepathy in dreams were carried out by Calvin Hall's coworker Robert van de Castle and Stanley Krippner in collaboration with Ullman.

PSYCHOLOGICAL THEORIES CONCERNING PARAPSYCHOLOGICAL PHENOMENA

To explain the phenomenon of telepathy theoretically, Freud likened it to large insect societies in which it is unknown how "the common will" is created, but where it is possible to imagine a "direct psychic transference path." Telepathy could then be conceived as a primitive (archaic) mode of understanding between separate individuals, belonging to early stages of evolution but still functioning in the individual's unconscious and in agitated masses.

Jung took Rhine's experiments and his own experiences as manifestations that the psyche was capable of overstepping the normally accepted bounds of space and time. As a collective designation for parapsychological phenomena he introduced the concept *synchronicity*. By this he understood the coincidence of a psychologically significant inner occurrence with an external event where there is no reasonable external causal relation.

Jung mentions as an example the following occurrence from a younger woman who was in treatment with him. She told him a dream that went as follows: *Someone had given her a very valuable piece of jewelry, a gold scarab.* (The scarab is a kind of beetle that had high symbolic value with the ancient Egyptians, who used it as the prototype for countless jewels.) As the woman was telling the dream, Jung heard a soft tapping at the windowpane. He had the feeling that something extraordinary was happening, turned around, and saw that a beetle was trying to get in. He opened the window and captured it. It was a rose chafer (*Cetonia aurata*), which is the closest thing to a golden scarab found in Switzerland, and with the words "Here you have your scarab" he showed it to the woman.

Synchronicity can be the simultaneity of two events that are connected not by an external cause but by their common meaning. The meaningful coincidence could also occur at a distance. For instance, the Swedish mystic Emanuel Swedenborg had a vision of a great fire in Stockholm while he himself was somewhere else. It turned out later that the fire had actually taken place at the same time as Swedenborg's vision. Finally, the psychic state could coincide with a future event, such as in precognitive dreams.

What may be hard to grasp but at the same time innovative in Jung's

theory concerning parapsychological phenomena is that he did not regard
them as a result of cause and effect. He imagined that in back of our perceiving the psyche and matter as separate phenomena lay a nebulous "psychoid" world of unity comprised of the archetypes in the collective
unconscious.

Jung's theory implies—for telepathy, say—that it is not I who sends a
thought to N. N., but that the collective unconscious almost simultaneously
generates the same experience in me and in N. N. All of us, according to
our contact with the archetypes, are able to a greater or lesser degree to
experience that sort of connection. Jung's concept of a world of unity (*unus
mundus*) was taken from medieval philosophy. But his ideas about significant chronological coincidences have many parallels in recent thinking in
biology and quantum physics. Jung, as mentioned, spoke of an "absolute
knowledge" in the collective unconscious, and in this was undoubtedly inspired by the alchemists' notions of a world soul (*anima mundi*), which
contained every information as to what had happened and was going to
happen in the world. It was just such a knowledge Swedenborg, for example,
had been in contact with in an altered state of consciousness.

In the esoteric tradition, which will be discussed in the next chapter,
parapsychological phenomena are explained as coming from a "higher consciousness"—that is, a kind of cosmic spirit or world soul having unlimited
intelligence and from which it is possible to tap knowledge.

For Jung the setting for synchronicity was always that an archetype had
been activated. Synchronistic phenomena require that you are in an
emotion-laden state and have a lowered threshold of consciousness. This
encourages activation of archetypal material. Rhine's experiments were difficult to repeat because the enthusiasm and thus the emotional intensity
dropped off with repetition. Gifts of prophecy are effective primarily because
they played on emotion: by touching unconscious leanings, they stimulated
interest, curiosity, expectations, hope, and fear.

Stanislav Grof has also been intensely occupied with parapsychological
phenomena, which are experienced frequently when working with psychedelic substances and techniques. He uses Jung's conceptual apparatus but
finds that Jung didn't go far enough. Synchronistic phenomena do exceed
the limits of statistical probability, Grof thinks, but the traditional
(Newtonian-Cartesian) natural laws aren't violated. He calls synchronistic
phenomena *first degree psychoid experiences. Second degree psychoid experiences* include poltergeist phenomena, ghosts, and spiritistic experiences.
Third degree experiences are described especially in the yoga tradition: peo-

ple can live without food, water, or oxygen, or can fly or suddenly demate-
rialize or materialize, travel in time, and so on. All of these radically
challenge our conception of reality.

STATES CONDUCIVE TO PSI PHENOMENA

Inherent in Jungian theory is that parapsychological experiences are bound
to the collective unconscious. This is why they most frequently appear in
archetypal situations; that is, at the important life transitions, such as birth,
puberty, conjugal life situations, midlife crises, and death, and during creative processes and at important collective events in culture or society.

A renowned newer researcher into the child's early object relations, René
Spitz, thinks (like Freud) that parapsychological registrations take place via
the evolutionarily older autonomous nervous system, and that this registering ability is lost in connection with the development and stabilizing of the
ego. This view is buttressed by Marie-Louise von Franz's observations that
parapsychological sensitivity is also lost with an ego-stabilizing analysis.
But no position is taken on the possibility that the ego structure, at a later
developmental stage where the ego personality is firmly established, is again
softened so that the parapsychological sensitivity can be integrated and
brought under control at a higher level. It is a difficult balance.

It is also well known that the ability to register and accept all kinds of
supernatural phenomena is greatest in people living in contact with nature
and is least in intellectual urbanites. Von Franz has also pointed out the
necessity, under conditions of nature, of being able to rely on intuition,
particularly in hunting societies where dreams are used to predict where
game is to be found. Ullman thinks that under primitive conditions the
aptitude for precognitive and telepathic dreams performs a vigilance function.

By and large there is agreement among psychoanalytical investigators that
parapsychological phenomena are particularly in play between people with
intense emotional bonds; that the contents touched are more meaning-laden;
and that transition stages and other intense life situations are conducive to
them. The same applies to the psychoanalytical situation, with its intense
living through of emotions and psychic boundary transgressions. Ullman
found that telepathy took place especially in situations of crisis where the
emotional distress was so great that it could surmount any barrier.

So the difficulty in repeating experiments with psi phenomena is understandable, as usually they are contingent upon spontaneously experienced

life crises that can't be re-created in a laboratory. The neo-Freudians especially have been occupied with the pathological side of telepathy and the ESP phenomenon. Nearly all of the authors underscore its significance for the transference/countertransference process, and that the clients often attempt to strike at particularly vulnerable areas in the therapist. In this case, according to Ullman, it is a question of inhibited compulsive patients who have a very strong need for contact but who at the same time desire to maintain distance. With the "telepathic maneuver" they show the therapist, without taking responsibility for it, that they know his secrets.

I myself and several of my colleagues have occasionally experienced borderline psychotic clients who via their dreams have sensed conflicts in their therapist that they couldn't have had any conscious knowledge of but which could be used to consolidate resistance to the therapy. A woman who had worked for many years with schizophrenic children told me that they often communicated telepathically with their parents when the latter couldn't otherwise be reached. The neo-Freudian Jan Ehrenwald has been occupied exhaustively with the parapsychological phenomena in psychoses.

It is also largely agreed that altered states of consciousness promote psi events. The Freudian Emilio Servadio found that telepathic dreams and hallucinations make up 90 percent of all instances of telepathy. Other investigations of precognition find the most reliable instances in connection with dreams, meditation, hypnosis, trance, influence from psychedelic substances, as well as in psychotic states. It therefore isn't strange that dream interpreters and therapists in general have a special interest in parapsychology.

SYMBOL AND DISGUISE IN PARAPSYCHOLOGICAL EVENTS

While traveling with her mother, sixteen-year-old Louisa Rhine spent the night in a town in Arizona. Toward morning she had the following dream, which she told to her mother upon awakening:

> I was back in Los Angeles. I saw our neighbor standing in his front yard by an open grave. I went over to him and asked what had happened. He told that Elaine (his little daughter) had been hit and killed by a car. Then he held his arm out—palm up—and brought his fingers up in a crushing motion and said, "Her head was crushed just like an egg."

Later the same morning when she and her mother were standing in line at the post office, a Mexican man told the postmaster about an accident that had just happened outside, in which another Mexican had been hit by a train and killed. The man said to the postmaster, while making precisely the same crushing motion as the neighbor in Louisa Rhine's dream: "His head was crushed just like an egg."

In looking at this and several of the other parapsychological dreams referred to, a consistent feature is that some of the details in the dream correspond very realistically to the actuality they say something about, while others don't agree. What agreed in this case were the hand movement and the words about the crushed head, whereas the persons and the place did not.

In order to understand this we ought to see it in connection with the fact that parapsychological phenomena usually arise from "altered states of consciousness." They are not logical and rational but are characterized by the unconscious's way of thinking. In Jungian psychology such divergences are regarded as symbolic, and the symbols are again expressions for compensatory processes that it is of value to interpret and process.

Freud thought that occult phenomena could be interpreted in the same way as dreams and other unconscious material, and he regarded divergences from reality as displacements, condensations, and so forth—in other words, as expressing a kind of "dreamwork." And the hypothesis has been advanced that dreams, just as they exploit past experiences and day's residues, also use future events as building blocks in their individual messages to the dreamer.

DREAM AND PARAPSYCHOLOGY IN THE THERAPY SITUATION

Not only did Freud think that telepathic phenomena observe the same laws as other unconscious processes, he also suggested that they be utilized in the dream analysis in the same way as associations. Freud's "telepathy hypothesis" has been of some significance for his successors, and it can be used in practice regardless of whether telepathy is regarded as being real or a powerfully energy-charged fantasy.

In *Dream and Occultism* Freud gives examples of the analytical application of the telepathy hypothesis. A man who according to Freud "was in no way occultly infected" dreamed on the night of November 16–17 that his wife (by another marriage) gave birth to twins. The next day he received a telegram to the effect that his daughter gave birth to twins around the time he had the dream. At first it didn't appear so telepathic, because the substitution of the daughter by his former wife in the dream could have been a displacement. The fact is the dreamer wasn't very happy with his present wife. He didn't want to have children with her because he didn't think she could raise them sensibly, and he hadn't had intercourse with her for a long time. The daughter, on the other hand, he was very close to, and "he knows that she loves him fervently." And so it was not inconceivable that he had the unconscious wish to marry his daughter and have children with her rather than with his present wife.

What argued for telepathy was that the daughter "was probably thinking very much of him during the ordeal." Besides, the delivery had been expected a month later, and the last time he saw the daughter twins had not been mentioned. Freud's interpretation was that the dreamwork usurped the telepathic message and tried to camouflage the unconscious wish to put the daughter in the wife's place. Thus psychoanalysis can help to detect telepathic phenomena that would otherwise go unrecognized.

Freud took no final stance on whether it was a question of telepathy. What was important was that it could be integrated in the dream interpretation.

Jule Eisenbud, one of the neo-Freudians who has worked with Freud's telepathy hypothesis, gives the following examples:

"A young married woman passes out while entertaining some guests and comes to hours later with tetraplegic paralysis. At the same moment, 10:30 p.m., a former lover dies of a heart attack." The woman had expected that the former lover, a wealthy elderly man, would leave her a sizable fortune. But his will disclosed the unrealistic nature of this fantasy. If his death had caused her violent psychic regression, then it told in a very clear manner of her expectations of people and especially men. The uncanny coincidence could also be interpreted as a violent aggression on the woman's part, and not until it stepped forth into the light was the therapy truly effective.

And another example: "A young man is deeply depressed in connection with an unhappy love affair. When the woman he can't obtain marries without his knowledge, the depression lifts as if by magic at the same time as the marriage. When he later learns what has happened, the depression returns." The telepathic occurrence seems to indicate that the man unconsciously wished to be free of the relationship—while he consciously desired to remain stuck in the unrequited love.

In Jungian analysis as well, parapsychological phenomena are assigned great practical significance. Both Jung himself and a number of his successors have described how in many cases synchronistic factors play a decisive role in curing a client.

In the late 1960s a highly regarded group of Jungian analysts investigated countertransference processes in the analysis of archetypal dreams and made surprisingly many parapsychological finds. Over a period of two years working with clients' dreams, the analysts registered their own associations, emotions, and bodily sensations regardless of how irrelevant or even disturbing they seemed. It turned out that not only in the clients' but also in the analysts' own unconscious, archetypal processes took place that were helpful in getting beyond blockages and blind spots that made it difficult to feel their way into the clients. This was especially obvious when working with archetypal material and in emotionally strained situations.

Often the analyst has only to mention the emotion, thought, or fantasy he has—he need only to be aware of it—for the client to spontaneously give expression to a parallel fantasy in himself. Such experiences are regarded as synchronistic, as ESP or as telepathy.

A female client with a severe neurosis dreamed: *I have moved into a house. There was also another woman . . . a man forced his way in and wanted to rape me. I ran away to get help. When I got back to the house the man and the woman were gone. I was very frightened in the dream and woke up exhausted.* The dream came after 147 hours of analysis in which the woman had run away from any confrontation with her problems, the sexual ones in particular. The analyst regarded the dream as another escape attempt. He felt a slight annoyance and thought: "In reality one ought to do like Hades, grab her and hold her." (Hades is the Greek god of the underworld, who raped and abducted the mother goddess Demeter's innocent young daughter Kore and took her down into the underworld.)

The analyst's next significant inner image was a meaningful dream he had when young: *He was in a grotto. In back of a grille living people were representing every conceivable way of being together sexually.* Just then the client blurted out: "There was a glass wall in the house. I experience nearly everything as in back of a glass wall." (Glass wall and grille are symbolically very close.) The analyst now recalled how at the time of his dream he had been greatly helped by a woman analyst's acceptance, and he now altered his approach for the rest of the hour to motherly solicitude while saying nothing about his associations. The next day the client phoned him up and said: "The glass wall is shattered. After the last hour I had a flood of sexual fantasies . . . incidentally, you were included." The archetypal pattern regarded as active here is the myth of Demeter, Kore, and Hades. The mutual background of analyst and client was a strict puritanical upbringing in which all sexual impulses were suppressed.

A phenomenon familiar to many Jungians and which at times has its simplest explanation in parapsychology is that a dream sets off a fantasy or train of thought in the analyst, and which then turns up in the next dream as if the analyst had continued dreaming along the same track as the client.

The following is an example from my own practice. A thirty-eight-year-old man dreams: *Father has sexually attacked me. It's disgusting.* The dreamer asks me how it could be that this theme didn't turn up until three years into the analysis. I mention his predilection for young girls. Recently he had had an affair with a considerably younger woman, but now for the first time has become infatuated with one his own age. Could it be that he has had to repress his anger at the father's (symbolic) incest against him so long as he himself has erotic relations that can be experienced as father-incest on his own part? He hastened to say, "Yes, the next dream warns me against going to bed with E (the younger woman)"—and she happened to be in an incest therapy group.

The conclusion the Jungian analysts could draw from their experiment was entirely in Jung's spirit: that in order to help a client the analyst must put his own unconscious processes in order. If some thought persists, however illogical or unreasonable, and especially if it is emotionally charged, it may manifest a powerful store of energy that must be taken seriously.

Jung's experience of the rose chafer rapping on the pane as a woman client is telling a dream about a golden scarab is an example of a synchronistic phenomenon that was of great significance for an analysis. The woman had an over-rationalistic and intellectualizing attitude that made her very closed, but the incident got her to change attitudes.

Phenomena of that sort are not altogether seldom in analysis sessions. I remember a dream that made me exclaim "but that could be called a psychic defloration" just as a pink azalea dropped onto my desk. Or a client who was telling a dream that included an automobile collision, and just then cars were heard to collide down in the street.

INFLUENCING THE FUTURE THROUGH DREAMS

If dreams say something about the future, it is tempting to exploit them to change it in a favorable direction; this theme has often been treated in the parapsychological literature. A case published by the Society for Psychical Research concerned a woman who dreamed *that her child was injured while playing by some railroad tracks.* She forbid the child to play there, and later an accident happened at precisely the place the dream had indicated.

The Dutch Jewish psychiatrist H. E. de Zoete has described dreams he had before and during the Second World War in which he was warned of the outbreak of the war, the bombing of Rotterdam, the suffering the Jews would be subjected to, and the actual circumstances surrounding the SS raids that would take place in the area where he was concealed. The premonitory dreams prompted his fleeing with his family.

Robert van de Castle has collected a large number of examples of dreams that led to increased monetary incomes. The example here is a dream from a highly placed British official in Kuwait, Lieutenant Colonel H. R. P. Dickson. He had it sometime in 1937.

One day there was a violent sandstorm that made a hole beside a palm tree growing in Dickson's compound in Kuwait. That night he dreamed that *he approaches the hole and finds a sarcophagus. Upon opening this, he finds a shroud which he touches and causes a beautiful maiden to rise up to life. At that point he is aware of strangers shouting in the desert, who come and seize the sobbing girl and try to bury her alive. He chases these men away.*

Dickson consulted a Bedouin woman who had a reputation as a prophetess and dream interpreter. She told him that the girl symbolized riches beneath the sands of Kuwait, and the strangers were "men from across the sea" who wanted to prevent him from discovering the riches. He was to get a British drilling crew (who had futilely drilled for water for two years) to drill beside a lonely palm tree in the Burgan desert. At first the drilling crew scoffed at him, but he held firm in his intention. In May 1938, by a lonely palm tree in Burgan, the drilling crew found the great riches symbolized by Dickson's beautiful dream maiden—oil. The find was of a magnitude that had international consequences.

Van de Castle tells of persons who systematically used their dreams to play the horses or the stock market—successfully, mind you. Among many examples, is this dream from an eager stock market speculator and university board member in 1963: *I am telling a woman that Freeport Sulphur is going to go up for a period of five years.* During the period 1963–1968 he bought what he could afford and the stock rose steadily, and he sold at a profit. Later he followed advice from a vice president in the company and again bought shares. But this time he lost money.

The unconscious exploitation of dreams to play the horses and the stock market is remote from the Jungian outlook. This could bring to mind Jung's descriptions of the alchemists who wanted to produce the vulgar gold and those who sought the true gold, spiritual riches. Even though I myself would hardly resist the temptation to dig up a million dollars in vulgar gold, the danger in manipulating the unconscious is that we lose the very information that could compensate the unconscious outlook and help it over a one-sidedness that in the long run is unfortunate.

There are parapsychological studies that indicate dreamers are not capable of changing the portended event even if they try. On the contrary, the dream's prophesy sometimes comes to pass during the attempt to annul it. Of 191 such instances, Louisa Rhine found only 3 in which going against a dream was successful. This is not corroborated by psychoanalytical experience, where many dreams deal, for example, with the death of close relatives without them dying in reality. Now it is probable that people who don't normally work with their dreams tend to remember the archetypal dreams, which according to Jung's theory to a high degree overstep the space/time boundaries. And often those dreams that are experienced as precognitive are of a special intensity and verisimilitude. But the most important reason that prophetic dreams often come to pass might also be that the dreamers take the dreams too literally and are not able to work with them as symbolic-psychological phenomena.

The psychological theories I have described imply that spontaneous parapsychological phenomena arise especially when the ego relinquishes too much energy to the unconscious, or when communication on the conscious level is blocked. And as a principal rule I think that parapsychological phenomena are manifestations of energies that lie beyond the ego's control; that psychological and developmental information is embedded in them; and that if the meaning is integrated the phenomena in question will often cease. To illustrate this I will describe some presumably synchronistic phenomena and a dream I experienced in 1982 when I began writing my book *The Feminine in Man.*

One day in mid-September 1982, I was standing in the kitchen in my office when water suddenly started spraying from a leak in the pipe under the electric hot-water heater. It turned out to be a corroded joint between two pipes. A few days afterward I discovered a moisture stain on the ceiling. This time it was the upstairs neighbor's washing machine that was defective. A few days later the dishwasher overflowed. Next it was my kitchen sink that became clogged, and soon the drain in the bathroom. Finally, a faucet was inadvertently opened in the scullery, with resultant flooding. Characteristic of all of the incidents was that they were discovered early, so the water damage was minimal. And I didn't remember being subjected to even isolated plumbing casualties for several years.

Coincidentally with this, lightbulbs began going out, fuses started blowing, electrical installations broke down, and so on, which often happened when I was about to embark on a creative project. The strange thing was that every time I discovered flooding I wondered whether I shouldn't write a book about the psychology of the modern man. On October 3, 1982, I dreamed:

> I was out swimming with a group of younger men. The place resembled the French Atlantic coast. We were a ways out and couldn't touch bottom. Back in there was a splendid wide sand beach. The sun was shining and we sported in the water.
>
> All at once I sighted a gigantic wave, maybe 20–30 meters high. It had risen up foaming and would break when it had come far enough in. It was a grand sight with the sun glinting in the spray. For a moment I was fascinated, but then I realized the danger and warned the young man beside me that it was spring tide. Our only chance was to dive under the wave, if we were to avoid being carried out by the tremendous undertow.

The dream continued on the sea bottom, where we waited together with an older instructor for the wave to draw back. The dream corresponded to the violent flood of ideas for the book that tumbled over me, and as soon as I started writing them down the synchronistic phenomena would stop.

Even though it is highly improbable to experience seven plumbing casualties in two weeks when for numerous years there had been nothing of the sort, it is still not sufficient material for a proof of parapsychological phenomena. But what applies here as in all other practical life questions is that if you always had to go around with statistical tables in your back pocket then it wouldn't be life. The individual situation is unique and you've got to make a choice.

In this case the dream seems to show what the synchronistic phenomena dealt with. But how are you to relate to a dream that deals with disaster or the death of someone close to you?

In a psychoanalysis in which a large part of the work consists in freeing a person from the influence of parent fixations so he or she can be adult and independent, such a development is often accompanied by dreams of the parents' death without them dying in reality. Here the best meaning would as a rule be gotten by understanding the dream on the subjective level. Also, if a mother dreams that her child is about to fall out of a window or be hit by a train, to use a terrifying example, my advice would be to first work with the dream on the inner level.

Generally children in dreams can be understood as either creative sides (they represent unused development potentials) or childish tendencies. So if Johnny is about to be hit by an express train in his mother's dream, she must work with the unused development potentials Johnny symbolizes in herself. Does she experience him as a sensitive boy? Is he independent and spontaneous, creative or practical? Is he loving? Can he speak his thoughts? And so forth.

Furthermore, she must look and see whether something in herself is, like an express train, quashing the development potentials Johnny represents. If she works in this way it is not my experience that the dream will come to pass. If she in contrast surrounds him with hysterical safety measures, these can actually manifest an urge to dominate that can engender a misfortune-bringing counterreaction. On the objective level the express train could also symbolize a quashing attitude to the child.

What is problematic in this whole discussion is that we can't say with certainty that a dream is precognitive unless it actually comes to pass, so it is impossible in the individual instance to prove that something has been averted.

A man who had begun analysis with me was after four months of therapy involved in a traffic accident, on September 9, 1983. After the accident he thought of the following dream, which to his astonishment was dreamed on September 9, 1982—one year before to the day:

> [I]n an attempt at passing on a curve, two cars collided head-on. One stopped upside-down in the field, gutted by flames, also the surrounding area scorched. Walk around it and look for traces of the occupants. Did they get out, or were they burned up? Find no traces at first; the flames were intense on the driver's side—suddenly there is something, there in the driver's seat—an amorphous mass, reddish yellow, practically a melted cheese with a head, the head is normal, nice young man—slowly, he now comes to and looks down his battered, singed body so as to find out how much is left of him. He has the use of one hand and passes it over his body, also down between his legs to see if anything is left there; there is, enough for there to be something one day. I think that the reason

*he couldn't be removed immediately is that he was too badly injured. I
look at one of his knees to see whether there are holes from the hypodermic
syringe, to ascertain whether he has been given anesthetic injections by
the rescue team. At the start of the dream I'm standing outside looking
at the man, but gradually I myself become him.*

The dreamer himself found many parallels between the dream and the
symbolic incident:

1. The date of the dream is the most obvious parallel.
2. His own traffic accident was a head-on collision with himself behind
   the wheel of his car.
3. His coming-to reminds him of the dream. First he was, as it were,
   completely outside his own body and felt like a spectator to the
   event. Then slowly he comes down in the body, what he experiences
   as the peculiar melted cheeselike substance that becomes a real
   body. The spectator role stops, and just as in the dream he becomes
   the person who has been in the accident.
4. In the accident he had the use of one hand while the other was
   badly injured (the same hand as in the dream).
5. He got a small tear in one knee of his blue jeans. In the dream he
   looks for a perforation from a hypodermic injection.

That the accident takes place a year from the date and that it is a head-on
collision is not necessarily parapsychological. It could be construed as an
unconscious arrangement; that is, he has an unconscious self-destructive
tendency that at first is reflected in the dream and later is lived out.

The other details are more difficult to explain in a rational way. Psychologically the car is an ego symbol. The dream can be interpreted as meaning
that his ego drives away without consideration for other people or for other
parts of himself, and that in the long run this will lead to a violent confrontation, at the worst a manic psychosis. On the basis of such a dream it would
be wise to reorganize the ego's style and to drive with caution.

What can particularly give occasion to understand the dream as parapsychological is the detailed and amazingly realistic elaboration of the central event without any intrusion whatever of other psychological symbolic
details. There is on this point perhaps a parallel to death dreams, birth
dreams, psychedelic dreams, and psychotic dreams. But why didn't he have
so revealing a dream while he was in therapy with me? Here what happened

was that the shock experience and prolonged hospitalization to such a degree gave food for thought that it was a turning point in the dreamer's life.

CONCLUSION

One of the biggest difficulties in achieving scientific recognition of parapsychological phenomena is that emotional states and attitudes that are a prerequisite for them can't straight away be re-created in laboratory experiments.

Both Freudians and Jungians think that parapsychological phenomena are especially associated with intense life situations. J. B. Rhine's experiments show that the statistical probability for parapsychological phenomena wanes as the enthusiasm wanes. Krippner found that positive expectations are a prerequisite for the success of telepathy, and that if the experiments are repeated by skeptics the result will often not be favorable. But if this is so then the gulf between adherents and skeptics will enlarge, as the experiments are a success for the former and a fiasco for the latter.

In practical daily living a skeptical attitude toward parapsychological phenomena can be in place, and there are many reasons for this. Their bizarre quality makes it easy to forget what practical significance they have for *me* here and now, and it is a commonly used defense mechanism to escape from concrete problems by talking about interesting occult phenomena. When it comes to prophesies, Freud was aware that fortune-tellers are skilled at expressing their clients' wishes—so skilled that one more than willingly believes in them.

A number of parapsychological phenomena also turn out on closer scrutiny to be unconscious registrations. Another pitfall is called "reading back." This is a form of false inference. Its point of departure is an actual event that resembles something you have dreamed, and as you think more about it you imagine that other later experiences are congruent with the dream.

Or it may be that you have forgotten certain thoughts you once had and which appear in a dream as parapsychological. Freud imagines, for example, that the man whose daughter gave birth to twins could already at an earlier visit have thought that she looked as if she were going to have twins, or had calculated a month off but then forgot it again.

Something also experienced in psychology is that if your attention suddenly is zeroed in on a certain phenomenon, you see it everywhere but just hadn't noticed it before. Skeptics could also assert that, in connection with my having at a certain period in my life experienced plumbing casualties and water damage, an inundation complex was activated in the unconscious that was demonstrated by my dream about the tidal wave.

These and a good many other exceptions can be considered reasonable enough in the individual case. But the most common exception to parapsychological experiments is that it is a question of humbug. Here one must, in Ullman's words, consider the reasonableness of assuming collusion, dishonesty, and self-deception of gigantic proportions in a long series of investigators with the finest imaginable training and recognition in scientific areas besides the parapsychological. Are these stubborn accusations of deception and self-deception a manifestation that there are no longer tenable scientific arguments against the existence of parapsychological phenomena?

As for working with dreams, acknowledgment of parapsychological phenomena implies a sharpened sensitivity in the interpreter. They supply us with still another frame of reference and are open for still another dimension in the associative material. Besides, they are an essential challenge to the outlook that dominates Western science.

9. ESOTERIC DREAM UNDERSTANDING

INTRODUCTION

The word *esoteric* means "for the specially initiated." It covers a broad spectrum of mystical-religious and occult schools and forms of meditation whose conception of reality our culture has difficulty accepting.

In the previous chapter I described mainly spontaneous oversteppings of the normally recognized limits of consciousness. Under esoteric dream understanding I will discuss the more deliberate exploitation of parapsychological phenomena via specially developed techniques such as meditation, energy body theories, lucid (astral) dreams, healing, prophetic techniques, and so forth. Dreaming is closely bound to the esoteric, and the dream itself can be regarded as an altered state of consciousness.

DREAM AND MEDITATION

Explained simply, meditation is a form of double consciousness. Normally thoughts, feelings, and plots run through consciousness automatically without our reflecting on them. In meditation you observe the inner process while it is elapsing. Meditation can be combined with concentration on a specific topic, a feeling, or a symbol, so you register both the object and consciousness's reaction to it.

The new potentials in the sleep laboratories have inspired a number of researchers to investigate whether meditation (yoga and transcendental meditation) are independent neurophysiological states between sleep and waking. The majority think this is the case. The brain wave pattern is most reminiscent of the falling asleep stage, and techniques are being developed to more clearly distinguish the two stages from each other. There is, however, a single investigation undertaken by skeptics that has been unable to verify the results.

It is fairly certain that meditation increases the number and length of remembered dreams. The Jungian P. A. Faber found in a small group of trained yoga meditators that there were more archetypal dreams than in nonmeditators. This is also my experience, with myself and with my clients who meditate. It appears especially clearly in the dreams if a person does only a little daily meditation and then for a limited period, such as at a course, meditates intensively around the clock.

Among the many different forms of meditation I will here be concerned with the so-called *chakra system* of tantric yoga. This is because meditation according to this system has in recent years become rather widespread in the Western world, and because associated with these meditations are symbols and psychic development stages that recur in the dreams.

DREAM AND CHAKRA SYMBOLS

Sometime in the late 1920s Jung met with an odd development in a treatment. After a few introductory misunderstandings between him and a younger female client, she presented him with a very peculiar series of dreams and drawings, and parallel with this a just as peculiar series of changing bodily symptoms. Her first dream in the series was that *a white elephant was coming out of her genitals*. The dream made such a strong impression on her that she carved an elephant out of ivory.

Shortly afterward her uterine mucus membrane swelled up in a state of infection that shifted from place to place and resisted all treatment. Then abruptly the symptom vanished and there appeared instead a hypersensitivity of the bladder. In the ensuing period she drew a series of colored symmetrical flowers that resembled mandalas, and now the symptoms affected the colon only to gradually ascend to the upper sections of the small intestine. The symptoms again vanished but were replaced by a strange sensitivity of the head. It felt as if the top of her skull grew soft and opened, and that a bird with a long sharp beak pierced through this fontanel all the way down to her diaphragm. Whereupon violent emotions erupted, which signaled that instead of isolating herself she now began to hurl herself into living her life.

At first Jung didn't understand anything of what was going on, but the patient constantly assured him that in spite of the symptoms she was feeling better and better. At one point in the treatment Jung happened upon a book that gave him insight into the connection between the bodily symptoms on one hand and the symbols in her drawings, fantasies, and dreams on the other. It was John Woodroffe's book *The Serpent Power*, about the symbolism in tantric yoga.

Tantric yoga takes its point of departure in ideas about man having a subtle energy body, which is neither spirit nor matter but a state in between. Such notions are universally widespread but are described in different ways. In the Western occult tradition it is known as *ethereal bodies* and *auras*. It is also familiar in the Orient as *energyways* that can be influenced through acupuncture and foot-zone therapy. With the shamans the energy body is a soul or double that can go on journeys outside the body. With the Christian saint it reveals itself as a halo, and in everyday use we speak of a person's radiance. The energy body can be conceived as the cause of bodily symptoms and the source of dream images. In tantric yoga and also in other forms of meditation the energy body is experienced as a system of inner centers or energy vortexes called chakras.

The chakra system isn't described consistently in the different traditions, but always included is a series of energy centers superposed on each other along the spine. In the Western occult tradition there were formerly five chakras. In the Hindu and Lama tradition, which today is the most influential with us, seven (or eight) chakras are included. There are variations in the exact location, presumably in accordance with what experiences the school in question desires to produce in the persons meditating. Beyond the seven principal chakras are a multitude of more or less significant auxiliary chakras, which in old tantric texts can reach a total of up to eighty-eight thousand.

Jes Bertelsen describes the chakras with two main aspects, corresponding to two different functions of dreams. One is the continuous balancing of bodily and psychic energies, the other is the chakras as expressions for levels of development. It is especially the latter—the chakra system's reflecting bodily, psychic, and spiritual development—that is treated in the literature, as what is described is how the energy is awakened in the lowest chakras and ascends toward the higher ones. But the Irish meditation teacher Bob Moore and others have pointed out that all of the chakras are functioning from birth, and that psychic development is also connected with the energy balance between the individual chakras.

The following description of the chakras is based on a number of sources of whom Jung, Bob Moore, plus Jes Bertelsen—who was inspired by Jung—and Rudolf Steiner are the most prominent. But also Sir John Woodroffe, historian of religion Mircea Eliade, and others have helped to clarify the concepts. Arnold Mindell has described the chakra system in relation to physical illnesses. The examples are for the most part from my own material, and some of the dreams are my own.

Here I will enumerate the chakras with both their English and Indian (Sanskrit) designations, and Jung, Moore, and Bertelsen all locate them as follows: the root chakra, *muladhara*, the lowest segment of the spinal column corresponding to mid-sacrum. The abdominal chakra, *svadhistana* (or the Japanese *hara*), four fingers' breadth below the navel. Solar plexus, the *manipura* chakra, just under the breastbone. The heart chakra, *anahata*, opposite the thymus gland on the breastbone. The throat chakra, *vishudda*, at the thyroid gland. The forehead chakra, *ajña*, at the pineal gland opposite the area between the eyebrows. The crown chakra, *sahashara*, at the top of the head to a couple of centimeters above it.

The germ of psychic development and individuation lies dormant in the lowest chakra and is symbolized by the coiled "kundalini" serpent, which is also the symbol of the goddess Shakti. At the individuation process's beginning this dormant energy is awakened: "the kundalini serpent rises" and ascends toward higher centers. Thus each chakra comes to symbolize a set of human qualities, feelings, attitudes, interests, and development potentials, so together the seven chakras comprise the human totality. The description of the individual chakras and the symbols associated with them can thereby be infinitely ramified. The chakras are symbolized by different animals; by lotus flowers with different numbers of petals; by the four elements; and so on. Particularly important is that the colors of the spectrum symbolize the chakras' "energy vibration," so the warm and slow red colors are lowermost and the cold rapid violet colors uppermost.

Jes Bertelsen has developed meditations by which important dream symbols can be associated with specific areas of the body. Here he found that the dreams were evenly distributed in six body areas, which corresponded fairly accurately to Wilhelm Reich's classification of the so-called muscle armor. This is made up of six main zones whose distribution corresponds roughly to the location of the six lower chakras: the eyebrow region, the mouth-throat-neck belt, chest-heart-shoulder-arms, diaphragm–solar plexus, mid-abdomen, and pelvis-genitals-legs.

Looking at the developmental side of the dreams, according to Bertelsen there will be fewest dreams from the highest chakras, but when placed in connection with bodily regions they appear to be more evenly distributed in the upper and lower parts of the body.

It was a coincidence of bodily symptoms and psychic states in a woman client that put Jung on the track of the chakra symbols.

In the first dream Jung mentions that a white elephant came out of her genitals, and shortly afterward she had an infection of the uterine mucus membrane. Then the symptoms moved up into the bladder and further via the intestinal tract up into the solar plexus area.

Jung interpreted it in accordance with tantric tradition, as meaning that the kundalini serpent or the goddess Shakti had been awakened and rose from the root chakra up through hara to the solar plexus.

Next came the feeling that the skull opened and that with its beak a bird penetrated from the top of the head all the way down to the diaphragm, which was interpreted as the god Shiva who from the crown chakra moved down through the forehead, throat, and heart chakras to meet with and fecundate the goddess. Simultaneously there came a dream series that could only be understood going from the chakra symbols.

The Root Chakra

The *root chakra* represents the material aspect of existence. It is the attraction of the basic physical benefits such as food, clothes, money, career, and power. It is the security inherent in house and home, father and mother, the latter's representatives, social conventions; the outer and external in life, success and fiasco, the body as such, and also the genitals and the feet. It corresponds to the anal zone in Freudian psychology. The psychic and spiritual play an inferior role. As it represents the vital earth connection—the person's "ground"—it is a very important chakra to keep in balance with the rest. It is also called an expressive chakra.

The root chakra is associated with the element earth. It is symbolized by a four-petalled lotus flower and by the color red. Its most important animal symbols are in India the elephant, and in Western symbolism the horse. They stand for all the energy invested in daily life's practical goals. The same with conveyances such as bicycles, cars, buses, trains, etc. Other of its animals are snakes, insects, and reptiles, seen as symbolizing primitive, deeply unconscious instinctual impulses. If daily life stagnates into routine and monotony, refuse appears, corpses and dead things, prisons, uniforms, regimentation, concrete, deserts. Transformation in this chakra can be heralded by dreams of earthquake, buildings collapsing, the death of parents, fecal material, plowed fields, and so forth. The root chakra corresponds to the genitals and the lower part of the digestive tract. It includes urinary, bladder, and prostate complaints, and kidney ailments and arthritis.

Numerous dreams containing the above symbols have appeared in the foregoing sections: showdown with mother and father, horse symbolism, physical death, and so on. In this chapter we will see mainly dreams that do not resemble what we have seen previously. That is to say, dreams that are associated with the higher chakras.

The Hara Chakra

The *hara chakra* is connected with the element water, and in Jungian psychology likewise to the encounter with the unconscious (in yoga nidra symbolized by "a state of unconsciousness"). This is a familiar occurrence in a therapy. In the yoga tradition it is said that the sleeping goddess in the root chakra is awakened by the guru, the spiritual instructor. In the root chakra one is sustained by conventions and assuming the parent's attitudes. In the hara chakra the experience of people, of oneself, of opinions, and of standpoints becomes more fluid.

An important symbol of the element water is the devouring sea monster Makara. The unconscious is experienced as devouring: If you lose control, do you lose your mask and your social identity? Do you become psychotic? Experienced positively, this chakra can be symbolized by fish and game. It can be a vessel of water, symbolizing the unconscious, or a lake. It can be dammed up in basins or bathtubs or enclosed in an alchemical retort, all manifesting the various ways of relating to the experience of the hara chakra. It can be purifying, or it can be fructifying rain. Jung pointed out that in many religions the first initiation to spiritual development takes place "by baptism with water."

Sexuality could be connected to the root chakra, where it is experienced as a strictly instinctive and automatic impulse. In the hara chakra it can be dangerous, voracious, and demonic on the one hand and fusing and oceanic on the other.

Other symbols in this chakra are a lotus flower with six petals and the color orange, which is more intense and luminous than the root chakra's red color.

We have already seen a number of dreams with water symbolism that all dealt in different ways with the conscious's encounter with the unconscious and unknown processes at their onset: Jung's example from the alchemical book (see chapter 2), the dream of the tidal wave (see chapter 8), the watertight doors which were opened (see chapter 7), and an angler's unexpected catch (see chapter 2). In all cases it was a question of unconscious processes—psychic, developmental, creative, or bodily—that streamed to the consciousness and gave it new life. And for someone interested, these dreams could obviously be supplemented with meditative or body-therapy work with the hara chakra.

Here I will just mention a dream in which the chakra symbolism is directly connected with meditative work: *I go from the ground floor up in the second story in a house. I walk into a completely orange room where an unmade double bed is standing.* The dream comes from a thirty-eight-year-old woman who in connection with a change of partner experienced a very powerful flaring up of her sexuality. When she meditated on the dream she became sexually aroused.

The Solar Plexus Chakra

The solar plexus chakra is associated with the element fire. First of all, fire symbolizes emotions and passions. Fire can be used to light at night, to make tools, melt solid materials, transform produce into edible food, and so forth. Symbolically it expresses man's potential for processing and transforming psychic raw materials.

In working with the solar plexus chakra one is confronted with the task of liberating violent feelings, with all the resulting complications, to tame them and make them into tools for a psychic and spiritual transformation. Jung thought that only a few individuals had the courage to venture to do this. The symbolism is known from the alchemical process in which the retort is kept over a constant and controlled flame. This can in turn be compared with the controlled therapeutic working with feelings and emotions. Sacrifice and sacrificial animal can likewise symbolize the giving over of oneself to transformation in the solar plexus.

Fire appears frequently in dreams when the dream ego goes into panic. That a movie theater is burning or your hair or clothes catch fire and you try every means to stifle the flames can express that you aren't ready for transformation. In such dreams you are trying to control violent emotions or to escape from them. But if the new inner situation is met in the proper way, the fire can in subsequent dreams be brought under control and be used.

Other symbols associated with the solar plexus chakra are a ten-petalled lotus flower and the color yellow; also wild animals such as lions and tigers, etc., which can symbolize violent emotions.

Here I will mention a couple of fire dreams from a fifty-one-year-old woman who had no familiarity with meditation and chakra symbolism but whose hands were drawn to the "correct" chakras as she told the dreams:

> [S]he was in an indoor swimming pool, where together with some boys she was supposed to pull out a large elephant that had fallen in the water. The door to the boys' locker room opened and out came a lot of youths and boys. The youths were carrying harpoon rifles. Suddenly there was a tremendous explosion. A lot of flames and bits of steel that whizzed around the men and boys. There was chaos. They rolled about among each other and blood spurted.

The dream ended with the boys being saved and with she and a group of men and women helping make order and clean up after the explosion. A man said, with a mixture of wonder and consolation: *The living are already smiling—that's how it goes.*

The dream is full of violent emotions. The elephant, the swimming pool, and the explosion can be seen as respectively the root chakra, the hara chakra, and the solar plexus chakra. The dream is full of threatening phallic symbols: the elephant's trunk, the youths' harpoon rifles. The explosion could correspond to a violent aggression toward men, which she had at the time. But seven days later she dreamed the following: *I lay on my back like a cross. From a star in the sky came some rays and struck right in the "cross" of my chest* (solar plexus). The dreamer experienced it as a dream about giving oneself. This violent turnabout is characteristic of the solar plexus chakra, and Bob Moore connects to it the key words *fear* and *love.*

Among the diseases that are connected with this chakra, Mindell mentions abdominal cramps and ulcers, diabetes and certain forms of cancer. The word *hypochondria* means "under the breastbone."

The Heart Chakra

The *heart chakra* is associated with the element air, birds, airplanes, breathing. Jung demonstrated that air, in the various cultures, is the symbol for the breath and the spiritual. The wind in dreams can represent a fructifying element, because it is an agent of pollination in flowers and plants. The spiritual principle can also reveal itself as a storm that topples everything. If there is very little spiritual movement, the air in dreams can be experienced as thick, so you can't make headway or move your arms.

Dreams of flying can deal with fantastical, creative, or intuitive ways of experiencing. You can be transported by airplanes or fabulous animals. Dreams in which you fly by yourself can be manifestations of "transcendence," for the ability on the spiritual level to overstep what consciousness normally can imagine. But it can also testify to a lack of ground connection, unrealistic reverie, and self-aggrandizement.

Other symbols are a lotus flower with twelve petals and a bestiary of light-footed animals like gazelles or deer as well as unicorns, where horns or antlers symbolize spiritual antennas.

Several years ago I had the following dream:

> A hot summer day. I was bicycling along a path in the woods. The path led to a lake that I thought was so shallow I could wade through it. But it turned out to be deeper than I had figured, and suddenly I couldn't find any way to get ashore. A young deer with a small rack of antlers appeared before me. It started leaping in toward land so as to show me the way. It apparently knew a fording place. I followed it in, and meanwhile it had become a big fully grown stag with an immense rack that stood looking at me. At first I was afraid, but on looking closer it turned out that we could speak or at any rate communicate intelligently together. It made signs that I should follow it.

For some time before this dream I had experienced "righteous indignation" of such an intensity as I had never permitted myself before. The anger assumed dimensions that culminated in a dream about *a city that is wiped out by a nuclear attack.* I now realized that the feelings which at one point had been fruitful and set a lot of necessary changes in motion gradually deteriorated into something self-destructive. Henceforth I worked on pulling back all projections of anger, and the stag dream heralded a period in which I found peace of mind. The dreams testify to a moving of energy from the hara and solar plexus to the heart chakra.

The heart chakra's key words with Bob Moore are *joy* and *sorrow.* Here you relinquish your ego. It is also called the self-development chakra, and the color green, symbolizing growth, is connected with it.

A thirty-eight-year-old woman who worked with chakra meditations dreamed the following: *I'm together with Karsten in a lovely green clover meadow. It turns out that the clover is all four-leaf clover. And we decide to stay there.* The woman's own association from the four-leaf clover, besides luck, was the fourth chakra. She dreamed about the night when Karsten from the dream had proposed to her and she had said yes. They had made love, and she had felt very happy and had given herself more than any time before. During this period she had especially good contact with her heart chakra.

The heart chakra represents the psychological potential for elevating yourself above your emotions and passions and experiencing them impersonally, from a higher spiritual level. Jung illustrates it with Paul's words: "It is not I who lives, but Christ who lives in me." The chakra indicates the place in the individuation process where the ego receives its first inklings of the self. In the yoga tradition the divine reaches down and touches the disciple.

A fifty-six-year-old woman dreamed that she was in a room and that

> *in the adjoining room was a man who could cure me. I turned toward a half-open door next to a bookcase and asked: "Why are you just standing behind the door? Is your emanation so powerful that you can cure me through the door, or is it more than I can take if you come in here?—So try coming in."*
>
> *He replied: "Do you dare for me to come in?"*
>
> *"Yes."*
>
> *He came in and stood opposite me. My hands could feel his powerful emanation. "Might I touch you?" I extended my hands over toward him and felt the emanation even more strongly, like a compelling force. "What happens if I touch you? Will I be absorbed by you?"*
>
> *"No, touch me by all means," he said. When I had touched him the magnetic field and the force spread over me. The image vanished.*

The woman, who was a practicing Christian, periodically for nearly one-and-a-half years, had worked with Revelation 3:20: "Behold, I stand at the door, and knock; if any man hear my voice, and open the door, I will come in to him, and will sup with him, and he with me." Being touched is symbolically to truly feel "touched" by something, and that the door was beside a bookcase could testify that there was now a shift from bookish theological insight to direct experience.

Following this dream the woman felt so well that a three-year course of therapy could soon be concluded.

The heart chakra is also connected with abilities for perceiving others' invisible energy emanations and out-of-body experiences.

From the heart chakra onward there appears an essential difference in Jung and the esoteric conception. Jung thought that heart chakra experiences, the being receptive for impulses from the self, were the highest Western man could and ought to attain. But Jung did not meditate himself, and others who actually have worked with meditation think that it is not only possible but also that it doesn't need to be harmful or questionable for a modern Western individual to have experiences corresponding to the highest chakras.

I will save the discussion of principles until the conclusion of this chapter and for the time being concentrate on the phenomenology of the higher chakras; that is, whether it is possible to have experiences with the symbols, mental states, and bodily sensations that are described in the Eastern tradition, and how they appear to the person who has them. Whether energy emanations, seeing auras, and out-of-body experiences are "actual" or merely psychic phenomena I will leave to the reader to decide.

The Throat Chakra

The *throat chakra* is associated with "the element of sound" and the cosmos. It is also called the ethereal center or "the completely purified." This is where you begin hearing sounds that are perceived as reflections of vibrations in the cosmos: the tinkle of delicate bells, as it were, singing in the ears, "the music of the spheres"; or you hear authoritative voices or have "dreams of call" (see chapter 2). So the ear and hearing play an important role.

The value of listening to your own interior can be underscored in dreams with a pearl in the ear or a costly earring, for example. Cosmic dreams and dreams with otherworldly ethereal structures also have connection to the throat chakra.

The elephant or the horse, and perhaps the automobile, which we saw in connection with the root chakra, recurs as a symbol, but here the animal is white to express that the drive is purified and transformed. Again it represents a powerful motivating force, a nonmaterial force, but also spiritual promptings, inner necessities that sweep away rational and materialistic objections. The psychic is experienced as just as real as matter was experienced in the root chakra. Or in psychological terms, all projections are pulled back.

The color blue and the spiritual feminine are associated with the throat chakra, in India symbolized by the goddess Kali and in Christian religion by the Virgin Mary, whose headcloth is blue. Physical ailments connected with this region include speech disorders, hoarseness, and throat infections.

I myself have had dreams with throat chakra symbolism when completing manuscripts, when the material was assembled and gone over and it was a question of extracting all private feelings—for example, in connection with the concluding stage in the writing of this book:

> *Down on the street in front of "my" building, where I live and work. I see to my astonishment that the neighborhood has been completely re-built, in a charming blend of large airy buildings of glass and painted steel construction and newly thoroughly restored old buildings. All of it is brilliantly colorful. There are many people in the street and the weather is grand. I glance back at "my" house. It appears as an ethereally vi-brating structure. Now I see it and now it is invisible. A woman Jungian analyst and another woman who practices meditation are waiting for me in a new white sports car.*

My own interpretations and associations perceive the dream as "over-determined" with throat chakra symbols. There could be a reference to my book in the creative synthesis of the many building styles, and in that the throat chakra is connected with expressing oneself in words. If the house is a symbol of the personality, its ethereal structure points at an expansion of my experiential spectrum corresponding to the throat chakra's phenomenology. The spiritual feminine is symbolized by the woman Jungian analyst and especially by the meditating woman, who has access to areas of experience beyond what Jung would accept for Europeans. In my imagination the white sports car, with its lighter and quicker getaway, was a parallel to the white elephant of the throat chakra. For a two-week period preceding the dream I meditated much and had reactions in the throat region.

The Forehead Chakra

The *forehead* (pineal) *chakra* is associated with the element of light but also with its opposite, darkness, and the color black. The light symbolizes enlightenment, elevated consciousness, and clarity of sight, while the darkness stands for the cosmic primeval darkness and experience of unity.

The forehead chakra refers to levels of consciousness where the spiritual is not only equivalent to the material but is experienced as more real. In yoga nidra the meditator imagines a small golden egg in the middle of his forehead and hypnotizes himself with the words "I am consciousness in equilibrium, I am not body, I am not thoughts, I am not feeling, I am not sensory impressions, I am not will, I am not name, I am not karma, I am consciousness living through all this."

It is also called the guru chakra and the "third eye." In this chakra one can learn to halt the stream of inner images and empty the mind so that altogether different categories of experience can penetrate into the conscious. The ordinary experience of time and space can be gone beyond so that one feels moments of eternity and being in other dimensions. Associated with this is the experience of a life after life, seen in connection with near death experiences and consciousness-expanding techniques.

The most important symbols are, in the Indian tradition, a lotus flower with two petals "white as the moon, shining with a gleam of perfect meditation," plus the colors gold and indigo. For instance, a man who had meditated on the forehead chakra dreamed that *he saw his brother-in-law enveloped in a white flag with gold and indigo stripes.* He was not familiar with the symbolism.

Jes Bertelsen has on the basis of an alchemical text found a number of symbols corresponding to chakra experiences. Among them are the rotating celestial sphere and the clock, which in the forehead chakra express the contradiction between eternity and temporality.

When light appears in dreams associated with the sixth chakra, it has the character of a special light, a special intensity. Naturally light can appear in ordinary dreams, but Jes Bertelsen mentions that a criterion for whether it is specifically a throat and ajña chakra dream is that awakening feels like a narrowing of consciousness. This corresponds to near-death experiences in which feelings of aversion can accompany the return to normal consciousness. An example from Marie-Louise von Franz gives the intense mood of such a dream. The dreamer was a Protestant clergyman a few days before his death: *The clock hand which has just moved now stands still. A window opens in back of the clock and white light streams in. The open window becomes a gate and the light a luminous way. I walk out along this way of pure light and disappear.* Here we see the contradiction between the clock as symbol of temporality and the eternity in back of it. One of the most common elements in near-death experiences is encountering an intense light, "an indescribable radiance which in no way hurts the eyes." The parallel to the forehead chakra is that this too is an acceptance of death: in psychological terms, the annihilation of the ego.

Even though Jung is skeptical toward forehead chakra experiences as such, he mentions in his commentary on a Chinese alchemist that mystical light visions implicitly combine the greatest imaginable energy with profoundest meaning, and that he had had clients whose own "light experiences" had led to fundamental changes in their lives.

Bertelsen writes that an ordinary dream about the sun can be transformed to a light dream from the forehead chakra, in that one looks at the sun and thus becomes a light-filled consciousness. An alchemical symbolism, which according to Bertelsen is bound up with the throat chakra, is a blue bird that drinks from a crystal well of blood. The bird belongs to the forehead chakra, and the blood and the crystal well to the root and hara chakras. In other words, the forehead chakra in order to function must be connected with the lower chakras. This is reminiscent of Jung's woman client in whom a bird with a long sharp bill penetrates through the fontanel all the way down to the diaphragm. A skull can symbolize both the death experience and the head's essence. Bertelsen mentions a dream having *a stair down which blood flowed. At the top was a skull whose eye sockets were mirrors in which an alien dimension was reflected.* After this dream the dreamer became ill from a blood infection that resulted in meningitis and came close to dying.

The eyes and sense of vision are generally important symbols. A key concept is "clear seeing," which can be understood either as the ability to discern mentally with a "higher" consciousness unenveloped in personal illusions, or occultly as the ability to see "mentally" or read auras. These transformations can often be preceded by visual disturbances. One night I dreamed that

> *I witnessed a total eclipse of the sun. I was amazed that my eyes weren't damaged by looking at the sun. At the precise moment the sun began reappearing with radiant light I had a clairvoyant vision: four men wearing phosphorescent green colors came walking from the free port down through my childhood street. Each carried a large lighted candle. One of them was Jesus. The men revealed themselves in luminous nimbus colors. My father, who was standing alongside, could see nothing.*

Here we have the play of light and dark, the radiant light that isn't harmful, plus the seeing auras, elements that connect the dream to the forehead chakra. The dream came after the conclusion of a two-year meditation program that culminated with intense meditation on the head's chakra. At one point I had strong visual disturbances. After the dream it might happen that a client, when I felt an especially strong empathy with him or her, more or less dissolved before my eyes in vibrant radiant colors, something I had never before encountered.

The Crown Chakra

The *crown chakra* represents the most potential for spiritual development in man, who here has elevated himself above all contradictions. This chakra corresponds to an experience of being one with the divine and is connected with states of mystical union or permanent enlightenment that are ascribed to Jesus, Buddha, and other great initiates.

Ordinary mortals can have flashes of such experiences, or dream about them, but usually it will be a manifestation of pathological states or be prompted by consciousness-expanding substances; it would be difficult to connect them to the rest of the personality. Experiences in this chakra are fundamentally ineffable. The crown chakra is developed automatically through working with the other six chakras.

Important symbols are a lotus flower with a thousand petals and the color mauve. The union of all opposites is portrayed in the image of the divine wedding of Shiva and Shakti, or in the alchemical texts by the royal couple's death and rebirth and in their "chemical wedding." The spiritual enlightenment can also be symbolized by a diamond body.

It is interesting that Jung in 1944, during a grave illness and after, had visions that symbolically belong to the highest chakras, without he himself mentioning this connection. "It seemed to me that I was high up in space. Far below I saw the globe of the earth, bathed in a gloriously blue light," he writes in his memoirs. Out in space he caught sight of a tremendous dark block of granite. He saw a black Hindu in the lotus position and a door to a temple surrounded with a wreath of bright flames that shone from innumerable tiny niches. The vision continued with an experience of his entire earthly existence being stripped from him.

In other visions Jung experienced eternal bliss and witnessed a divine wedding of Hera and Zeus, all of it with supernatural intensity and power. On waking he had the characteristic experience of being narrowed in, that the material world was crude, unwieldy, too concrete. The nurse told him later that it was as if he were surrounded by a bright glow. It looks as if Jung, who would halt development at the heart chakra, experienced these higher states in connection with a heart attack.

LUCID DREAMS

In his book *Astral Projection* from 1962, the English author and parapsychology enthusiast Oliver Fox writes, "I had the dream which marks the real beginning of my research:

> *I dreamed that I was standing outside my home. On glancing casually at the paving stones I discovered that they had all changed position, and the long sides were now parallel to the kerb instead of being at right-angles to it. Then the solution flashed upon me: though this glorious summer morning seemed as real as real could be, I was dreaming. Instantly the vividness of life increased a hundredfold. Never had sea and sky and trees shone with such glamorous beauty. Never had I felt so absolutely well, so clear-brained, so divinely powerful, so inexpressibly free! The sensation was exquisite beyond words; but it lasted only a few moments, and then I awoke.*

As I was to learn later, my mental control had been overwhelmed by my emotions."

A dream like this, in which the dreamer has the experience of being awake when he is dreaming, is called a *lucid dream*. Oliver Fox's dream contains features typical of this phenomenon.

Definition and Literature

The term *lucid dream* was introduced in 1968 by the English parapsychology researcher Celia Green, author of the book *Lucid Dreams*, but the experience itself is old and worldwide. It is also known as a wisdom dream, astral projection, and out-of-body experience. It is described by the French orientalist Hervey Saint-Denys, the Russian philosopher P. D . Ouspensky, the American clairvoyant Edgar Cayce, and the mystic Carlos Castenada. The phenomenon is cultivated as a step in the Tibetan yoga's program of spiritual training. Psychologists and parapsychology investigators have aslo taken up the subject.

It can be objected that perhaps a lucid dream isn't a dream at all but a fantasy in the awakening stage, or that it is merely an ordinary dream in which you think you're awake. But this supposition is rejected by lucid dreamers because the experience is so special. The only valid criterion is subjective.

Beyond the experiences of intensity, beauty, and freedom that appear in Oliver Fox's dream, the lucid dream phenomenon can form the point of departure for parapsychological, consciousness-expanding, and religious experiences. In it may lie unexploited therapeutic potentials. And as a borderline phenomenon it discloses new facets of the essence and function of dreams.

Techniques for Maintaining the Lucid Dream State

If one is interested in the possibilities residing in lucid dreams, there exist techniques for initiating and maintaining the state, and there is considerable agreement among the different authors as to how this should be done.

Most persons experience initial stages to lucid dreams, and Celia Green mentions four ways by which so-called prelucid dreams can be recognized:

1. By emotional tension, especially via anxiety dreams that repeat themselves. For example: *[I] am about to be hurled off a cliff . . . and then there's something inside me that says: "You mustn't be afraid. It's only a dream."*
2. Experiencing something incongruous in the dream. In Oliver Fox's case, that the paving stones turn the wrong way
3. Analytical thought in the dream. For example, that the dreamer realizes the unnatural quality in an echo that picks out separate words from what he says and echoes them repeatedly.
4. Lucidity arises spontaneously. The dream is experienced as just as real as the waking state, but you suddenly become aware that you are dreaming.

If after waking you analyze your dreams for incongruities, it has been demonstrated that the critical attitude can be incorporated in the prelucid dreams so they develop into lucid dreams. If a lucid dream is successfully initiated, the state is very difficult to maintain. On the one hand you can easily slip back into ordinary dream-sleep, and on the other, overly keen inspection can result in awakening. As we saw in Fox's first lucid dream, it is easy to be so overwhelmed by the dream's intensity that it wakes you up. So it is a matter of keeping the intensity under control.

Another common obstacle to the prolongation of lucidity is called "false awakening." This phenomenon seems to be much more frequent in connection with lucid dreams than with ordinary dreams. The dreamer apparently looks back on the dream experience she has just had and thinks she is awake. The practiced lucid dreamer Patricia Garfield gives the following example:

> I dreamed that I turned on the light by my bed. I looked at the night table beside me, observing the red of the lampshade, the glow of the light on the leather-top table—all was as in a waking state. Yet I suspected something. I reached out my hand and rapped vigorously on the tabletop. Quite solid. I decided that the experience was real because I could feel it. So concluding, I continued to dream in the usual manner.

Another measure that seems to be useful in maintaining lucid dream states is to look at a body part, such as the hands, in the dream. The effect is possibly due to the fact that the dreamer's body is among the most stable elements in a dream. In cases of frightening dreams it is suggested that you say to yourself: It's only a dream, nothing can happen. The emotional tension that can lead to awakening is thereby reduced. *Autosuggestion* is mentioned as being able to initiate lucid dreams.

Lucid dreams appear to be most easily realized when awakening from the last dream of the night. In Tibetan yoga, however, you practice going directly from the waking state into the dream and preserve continuity of consciousness.

Deliberate Work with Lucid Dreams

Lucid dreams are by many writers likened to out-of-body experiences, and they are often described as parapsychological journeys in time and space. One of Fox's accounts is of "Elsie," a sweetheart from his youth with a natural talent for "astral projection" who intentionally visited him while he himself was in a lucid dream: *Suddenly there appeared a large egg-shaped cloud of intensely brilliant bluish-white light. In the middle was Elsie, hair loose.* According to Fox, the next day Elsie told him "I did come to you" in his room while he was dreaming of her. Even though she had never been there in reality she could describe the room in detail.

Another use of lucid dreams is as an access to religious mystical experiences. This has been described by the American psychologist George Scott Sparrow in a book about how lucid dreams can be used to obtain clear light experiences on the lines of those described in Tibetan yoga as symbolizing the highest enlightenment. Sparrow avoids occult speculation about whether the consciousness can actually leave the body during lucid dreams and finds that the experience of reaching another religious plane of consciousness can just as well be understood in Jungian terms as "projections in the dreamer's own self."

In a lucid dream Sparrow saw light from space strike the Earth and approach him: *I wait until the lights are directly overhead. Then I know that it is time to close my eyes and meditate. Immediately a tremendous energy wells up within my body. I try to surrender to it. As I do, light begins to fill my vision. There is a tremendous sense of warmth and love, which continues for a good while.* Sparrow recommends that one meets the lucid dream with an "ideal"; that is, has a religious or ethic attitude toward the unconscious content. It becomes no longer a question of "How beautiful was the experience?" but of how it relates to the ideal. For Sparrow it is a Christian ideal.

Opposed to this is more of a supermarket attitude to lucid dreams, such as with the American author Patricia Garfield where the phenomenon is used for a rather uncritical pursuit of thrilling experiences.

Sparrow draws interesting parallels between lucid dreams and meditation. Lucid dreams can yield the type of experience normally obtained through deep meditative processes and partly, because you are simultaneously undergoing and observing, be regarded as a double consciousness. It is Sparrow's observation that "surrendering to a higher experience" is a key concept in developing lucid dreams, just as with meditation.

Finally there is the possibility that lucid dreams can lend themselves to a kind of intensified active imagination. My first forehead chakra dream began: *I am shut inside a room where a man wants to assault and torment me. I wake up with a stomachache.* Immediately on awakening I worked with the dream's context and bodily sensations, but without the stomachache going away. I succeeded in going back in the dream and influencing it: *I couldn't find out how to get a dialogue started, but then I thought that the bully was, after all, a part of myself, so I had to be able to enter into him. It worked. I now experienced myself as both persons in the dream, and I definitely didn't want to assault myself.*

The dream continued:

> *I am at a party in some large banqueting rooms. It seems trivial and absurd. A beautiful oriental woman in a black silk dress seizes me softly from behind. She leads me, in a dancing movement in which our bodies, as it were, melt together, to the exit. Outside it is a marvelous spring morning with sprouting fields and growing weather, an otherworldly mood of beauty and intensity. Suddenly it dawns on me that it must be*

*a dream because in reality it's winter, and I realize that I can work with
it. I now see the sun rise just above an avenue of trees in full bud. I
concentrate on seeing the sun and am myself transformed into light.*

In that period I was meditating on emptiness and on the forehead chakra.
(My efforts got the stomachache to vanish.)

OTHER ESOTERIC FRAMES OF REFERENCE

The esoteric domain covers a large number of other approaches for working
with dreams: astrology, tarot, healing, aura reading, clairvoyance. Here I
will just mention dreams in connection with the Chinese book of oracles *I
Ching*, which was very popular with Jung and his coworkers.

The *I Ching* contains sixty-four prophecies in symbolical language and
directions for what actions are expedient at a given time. The appropriate
prophecy is arrived at by tossing five sticks, or more usually three coins,
according to certain directions. Jung explains the connection between the
toss of the coins and the divination going from his theory of temporal coincidence: *synchronicity*. It is a meaningful coincidence between the person
asking the oracle and the corresponding prophecy. Exhaustive explanations
have been given by Marie-Louise von Franz and Jolande Jacoby.

If the *I Ching* is supposed to give comments on a dream, it is recommended that you throw on the same day you have had the dream, as what
is in question is a temporal coincidence.

CONCLUSION

In this chapter I have outlined some dimensions of the nature, function, and
interpretation of dreams. Esoteric dream understanding gives important new
perspectives. Its weakness is the one-sided treatment it gives. Often personal associations, contexts, and frames of reference are overlooked. However, it appears possible to view esoteric dreams from other approaches,
and in this way we can integrate them in the mass of knowledge presented
in this book.

Esoteric Dream Theory

A key concept in esoteric dream theory is *higher consciousness*, a cosmic or
divine consciousness in possession of inconceivably vast amounts of infor-

mation. The concept is akin to Jung's "absolute knowledge in the conscious" and the alchemists' omniscient world soul. Jes Bertelsen thinks that the experience of higher consciousness gives far more lucidity, light, and accuracy than the experience of the collective unconscious, and he thinks that it is possible to get a more permanent contact or direct identification with what he calls the wisdom in the unconscious than Jung did.

Jung and his successors focus on the obvious danger of self-aggrandizement and inflation illustrated in the belief that a person can become directly identical with wisdom. At the same time they dissociate themselves from the concept of higher consciousness. Adherents of higher consciousness have found it necessary in order to describe categories of experience different from those Jung outlines, and to help understand the nature and function of dreams, symbol formation, and the symbolism of the chakra system.

As Jes Bertelsen understands it, "the dream mechanism" is in certain respects a kind of radar that scans the personality both psychologically and bodily, and in attempting to correct and regulate the inexpedient state of affairs reveals imbalances or one-sidedness. In *The Psychology of Western Meditation* he depicts symbols as garbled information from the higher consciousness. The garbling is due to the fact that the mass of information in the higher consciousness can't straightaway be contained in a lower level of consciousness.

Even more than in Jung, one gets in Bertelsen an experience of dreams being didactic messages to the dreamer, but there is less commitment to interpreting the human instance that decides what is the didactic element and what is not. A decisive point in Bertelsen is that understanding the meaning of dreams does not in itself lead to higher consciousness. If you follow the tempo of the dreams' growth processes it will go too slowly. Bertelsen proposes that you "transfer consciousness's much higher tempo and rhythm to the unconscious," and the means for doing this is meditation. He distinguishes between a "general openness" toward the unconscious—as in Jung, where the unconscious has the lead—and a more "specific openness" that can further a specific desired development.

The Dream Interpretation

"Study yoga. You will learn immensely much from it, but don't use it," Jung wrote to his contemporary Europeans. "An Indian guru can explain all of it to you and you can imitate all of it. But do you know *who* uses yoga? Do you know how you yourself are constituted?"

It is my own experience that by practicing yoga or meditation people can stay floating above deep conflicts and split off important parts of their own personalities that later come up in an analysis. If a person has done this, it may be because he or she sees no other way out of a conflict and psychoanalytical methods appear too exclusive, too terrifying, or too one-sided. Therefore I think it is fruitful to view the interest in Eastern meditation as expressing a lack in our culture.

Today, when thousands of people practice one system of meditation or another, there is more experience at hand than in Jung's time. There are also efforts toward adapting meditation to Western ways of life. In Bob Moore's system, development comes about first and foremost through the balancing of chakras. Quick results are not aimed at. Most of Moore's meditations contain both a specific and a general openness toward the unconscious. Jes Bertelsen has designed meditations that work with Jung's shadow and anima/animus concepts, and we saw that George Scott Sparrow integrated his clear light experiences in a Western Christian ethic. Lucid dreams can be used in active imagination. But still the aggregated experience of Eastern meditation and Western psychology is limited. And there are pitfalls in using chakra symbols and meditation.

The published material doesn't indicate the reasonableness of excluding lucid dreams and experiences associated with the higher chakras from our theories of dreams. On the contrary, what is wanting in the literature is some descriptions of when they are relevant and when not. Here are a few guidelines.

Chakra Symbolism and the Dream's Context

Just as with the other frames of reference mentioned in this book, it is important always to balance them against the dream's context. Chakra symbols are archetypal, which is to say they only appear in a relatively small portion of the dreams. As we have seen in the chapter on Jung, associations from symbols can come from different layers of the personality. They can be archetypal, culturally determined, or personal. Moreover, they have many meanings. A yellow car can refer to the solar plexus chakra, but in a case where the dreamer's father was run over by a yellow car in reality it more likely is bound up with the traumatic childhood experience. And the relevant interpretation of a parrot isn't necessarily that it is a symbol of the heart chakra. Especially not if the dreamer associates that a parrot keeps parroting the same sentences.

Also important is whether the symbols comment on events from the previous day; for example, that the dreamer drove home in a yellow taxi after his sweetheart had broken up with him, and so forth. If every sardine tin in dreams is a "hara" symbol and any disheveled sparrow corresponds to a "heart" experience, the dream can be robbed of its creative multiplicity; its quality of spontaneous experience be castrated and the chakra system reduced to seven boxes that all manifestations of life can be stuffed into.

It is important to see which facet of the symbol it is relevant for the dreamer to work with. To walk through a wall in a dream can, seen esoterically, stand for development of "astral consciousness," but it can also be interpreted more simply as "to break through to another aspect of one's personality." To fly can be lack of ground connection, and so on.

Moreover, you must see whether parallel with the dream there are body experiences that point in the direction of the chakra, whether special meditation exercises have been performed, and how the dream relates to other dreams in a series. It also appears that changes of attitude connected with our daily lives can trigger a particular chakra symbolism, even in dreams associated with the highest chakras. For example, when I dreamed about Jesus and about seeing auras I had indeed meditated very intensely on the head's chakras. But the dream wasn't triggered until I had changed my view in a certain matter from suspiciousness to something more trusting and philanthropic. To see a person washed in colors can symbolically express that you have an eye for emotional nuances.

Lucid Dreams

In the literature on lucid dreams, discussions of possible negative side effects from this form of work are seldom. Sparrow deplores the overemphasis in the popular literature on the ability of dreams to be manipulated. Fox thinks that excessive and immature preoccupation with lucid dreams can lead to psychosis and physical exhaustion. And it might be added that an egocentric influence on the dream content can lead to the distortion of a possible compensatory element, so that by this technique positive growth potentials and regressively psychotherapeutic material is increasingly split off. It is imaginable that the fear which in following Garfield's advice you avoid by saying "it's only a dream" could have been a spur to working with problematic areas in the psyche.

The double consciousness in lucid dreams can indeed be a kind of meditation experience, but I find it can also symptomize a powerful split—a schizoid tendency—in the psyche. In such cases it can be especially important to work with the lucid dream's symbolism.

An example of an interpretation that is connected with the dreamer's daily life and developmental background Garfield gives to the dream where a woman raps on the tabletop to feel whether it is real. She had wondered whether, after all, the affection a friend had been genuine, and it was that theme the dream took up: "It must be real because I can feel it." Looking at Oliver Fox's dream of Elsie, one could, with the neo-Freudians' telepathy dreams in mind, ask whether there is an emotional barrier between the two with an attempted illicit transgression.

It is my experience that lucid dreams often appear in people who have creative and spiritual potentials. But just as often there are problems with the ground connection and practical daily life. For example, if a person lucid dreams: *I float out of my body and see myself from above*, it isn't just an interesting out-of-body experience. It would be appropriate to ask whether the person in question has such experiences in the waking state, whether he or she is really present in his everyday reality, and if there are mental lapses. In the latter case, driving a car should be discouraged.

In my view the esoteric aspect in most cases is combined with the ordinary rules of dream interpretation, which have been gone through earlier in the book. In the yoga tradition, development starts in the crown chakra. In tantric philosophy the god and goddess Shiva and Shakti are united at the world's beginning, just as the individual can experience at the crown chakra's level of consciousness. On the cosmic level the creation of the world consists, so to speak, of a fall through the chakras' consciousness levels from the spiritual down to the material world of things, corresponding to the root chakra. The yogi has to do this development in reverse in order to get back to the original experience of mystical union. Following this analogy, the little child starts in the higher chakras and "is born" slowly through ego formation down into his body and into the world.

Difficulties in adapting to surroundings, as well as traumas, fear, disease, and near-death experiences, can disturb ego formation and the contact with external reality, so that the child's consciousness remains suspended in an archetypal fantasy world. In this case there can occur experiences from the higher chakras that are hard to integrate in the consciousness. A forty-year-old female client had the following dream, which is full of sounds and voices:

I was five years old and sat in front of a large musical instrument (something like an organ), which contained within it all the tones and voices in the whole world. I pressed some of the buttons and the loveliest music came out of the instrument. To the right there was a rectangular black rocker key. I pressed it, but just then behind me to the right there was a warning woman's voice that forbid me to do it. But then from the right side there was a man's voice that broke in and answered the woman's voice: "Just let her press the key, she's big enough." "No," replied the woman's voice, "for it leads straight to purgatory." "But," I replied, "I already know 'das Fegefeuer.'" And so I started rocking up and down with the dangerous key, and the instrument played even more and more beautifully—the tones were a grand and tremendous harmonic peal. I can best describe it as the music of the spheres.

For a period I (the analyst) had concluded each session with a ten-minute guided fantasy journey through the colors of the rainbow, one at a time from red to violet and back again. The day before the dream I had the woman meditate the colors on the corresponding chakra body locations without mentioning chakra symbolism, which for that matter was completely unfamiliar to her. The dream reveals an unusual talent for contact with the collective unconscious, but the dream ego's age is five years old. A large part of the woman's emotional life was actually, on account of grave traumatic events in early childhood, "fixed" at the five-year stage. It is an unusually splendid throat chakra dream but it does not express maturity.

A creative and socially well-functioning man in his middle years dreamed that *he was God, and he was struggling with a devil child.* To *be* God is a crown chakra dream, but this has the problem that the dreamer is struggling with a devil child. Shortly afterward the man got encephalitis, which he recovered from without harm.

It makes good sense to simultaneously view the dream from a Freudian angle as a violent regression to magical notions of omnipotence belonging to the period before the superego is established. The mother used to say, when he misbehaved, that he was "wicked," and the dream most likely leads him back to the struggle with his own inner devil child. There were in this man three things which could be determining for him, of all people, having a crown chakra dream: he had near-death experiences as a child, as a youth he had taken ten to fifteen LSD trips, and he meditated.

I have in a few cases also seen very beautiful light dreams inaugurate the onset of schizophrenia.

Jung saw clearly the force for generating spiritual development inherent in the various Eastern forms of meditation. But with his method the unconscious very gradually drew his pupils into a development process in which each dream revealed an increment of that process, whereas the orientals had worked for centuries on their meditation techniques and "therefore had amassed many more symbols than Westerners could digest."

If chakra meditation leads to premature opening up of unconscious contents that are fear-inducing and can't be integrated, dreams can provide good hints about the ego's attitude to the unconscious contents and its defense mechanisms. During a course of meditation that activated especially the lower chakras, a woman dreamed: *I am in an unfamiliar city. To my horror I discover that everywhere snakes are slithering in the streets. I don't know where to go. Then a whole line of street sweepers turns up and they sweep away the snakes.* Here the snakes express a strongly repressed sexuality, and the street sweepers represent a bombastic defense that was immediately mobilized.

With such experiences there is the risk that a person who could slowly and cautiously have gone into a development process comes to a standstill.

The Empirical Basis and the Philosophy

It is hard for me to determine how the psychoanalytical clientele differ from people who work with meditation. That it's cheaper and less binding to take part in meditation courses than to be in analysis naturally plays a role.

The empirical material probably acquires a distortion if you interpret dreams mostly in connection with intensive meditation courses, for there will be far more archetypal material than normal and fewer dreams that reflect waking lifestyle. Corroboration of the dream interpretations is also problematic, because the defense mechanisms often don't really take hold until you get home and are all alone in having to realize newfound ecstatic insights in your usual surroundings.

Jes Bertelsen has set up a dream hypothesis in which dreams balance out the psyche's energy fluctuations (that is, when waking life has slipped into an extreme dreaming, life insists on the opposite extreme). This hypothesis actually goes in direct opposition to the monotony Hall found in normal dream series when he used statistical assessments. One can imagine that Bertelsen's hypothesis reflected an actual experience from intensive dream and meditation courses, namely that under those conditions the psyche oscillates between extremes of openness and resistance. The large occurrence of archetypal material, which is to be expected, can contribute to lessening the interest for other aspects of the dream analysis.

The philosophy in the oriental meditations is divided into two mainstreams: the one connected with Taoist philosophy and the other with the yoga tradition. Taoism is a philosophical school that places special emphasis on following self-controlling and independent processes in nature, while the yoga tradition puts the main weight on discipline, exercise, and rigid methods. Jung, and to an even greater degree Mindell, adheres closest to Taoism. Jes Bertelsen writes that he strives for a middle path between Taoism and yoga.

10. Dream and Birth Experience

Dream and birth with the Freudians—Birth and rebirth in Jungian literature—
Otto Rank and the birth trauma—Dream and rebirthing—Conclusion

Dream and birth with the Freudians

Freud thought that "underlying a great number of dreams which frequently are anxiety-filled and often have the passage of confined space or remaining in water as content are fantasies of the intrauterine life, the stay in the womb and the act of birth." In *The Interpretation of Dreams* he gives the following example from a young man: *He was in a deep pit with a window in it like the one in the Semmering Tunnel. At first he saw an empty landscape through the window, but then invented a picture to fit the space, which immediately appeared and filled in the gap. The picture represented a field which was being ploughed up deeply by some implement.* Freud understood the dream to mean that the young man in his imagination used his position in the womb to spy on intercourse between the parents (the field being ploughed).

Freud also interpreted a dream in which a female patient bathed in a moonlit lake as a birth dream. The patient without hesitating construed the birth motif with the words "Isn't it just as though I had been reborn through the treatment."

In the Freudian literature birth symbolism in dreams is usually referred to as "the intrauterine fantasy." What is of interest isn't so much the actual birth experiences the dreams refer to as the psychological consequences the theme can have.

A couple of other dreams about womb life and birth come from Emil Gutheil. A twenty-three-year-old male patient dreams: *I am in the place where I was born. I am sitting in a room which is overheated. I am glad to be in safety, for out of doors there is a snowstorm, and the weather is severe. I think, "To live in solitude like this is wonderful and not without consequences for one's further development."*

Gutheil fastens especially on the expression "the place where I was born" and the contrast between the warm "inside" and the cold "outside," and he sees the dream as "a beautiful picture of the patient's tendency to give up his struggles and to look for protection from storms by enjoying the warmth and security of the mother's womb." He found too that such dreams are connected with respiratory trouble and various anxiety states, and thought that the symptoms were caused by the patient's idea that he is still unborn, in an uncomfortable place that lacks air. This comes to expression in another example:

> *I am crawling through a long, narrow, muddy dark tube which has in it a large number of curves. Whenever I think I am approaching the end, I discover that what I believed to be the exit was in reality another curve. I am uncomfortable and anxious. After much strain, I come to a narrow opening on the upper part of the tube and am free. I feel relieved and breathe freely. I have had this dream repeatedly.*

Calvin Hall reckons that the dream can refer to the fetal state and birth.

BIRTH AND REBIRTH IN JUNGIAN LITERATURE

In the Jungian literature, birth motifs are understood first and foremost symbolically as psychic rebirth.

Erich Neumann in his book *The Great Mother* turns against theories of the biological birth trauma's overwhelming significance. In the language of the unconscious the development of the ego and the self is portrayed as birth: the consciousness, which before was enveloped by an accustomed secure situation, experiences the latter's termination as "rejection by the mother." Every important transition in life therefore implies a symbolic birth trauma. And Neumann doesn't think it is reasonable to reduce this archetypal symbolism to a personal experience.

Jung in numerous works deals with psychic rebirth symbols. In a dissertation on reincarnation he outlines the rebirth theories of various cultures without taking sides as to whether or not reincarnation actually takes place. What interested him were the psychological aspects.

Birth symbolism is widespread. Common in mythology is birth from a tree and birth by water, which is also familiar from baptism as spiritual rebirth. Other birth symbols are described later in this chapter.

OTTO RANK AND THE BIRTH TRAUMA

The person who made the trauma we are exposed to at birth into a therapeutic task in earnest was psychoanalyst Otto Rank. He assigned it paramount importance for man's psychological development. He saw it as a prototype of all anxiety and as a universal explanation for human cultural unfolding.

For Rank it isn't the actual physiological difficulties at birth that cause the trauma, but the fact that you are removed from a more to a less advantageous state. In contrast to conditions in the womb, the child has to cope with irregular provision of nourishment, the mother's absence, temperature fluctuations, loud noise, respiration, defecation, etc.

Freud and later the Czech-American psychiatrist Stanislav Grof ascribed significance for psychic development to the physiological strain at birth itself.

Unfortunately, Rank's book *The Trauma of Birth* doesn't contain dream material and descriptions of symptoms. However, some examples are found in Rank's spiritual heir Esther Menaker. The idea of the all-decisive significance of the birth experience has been taken up by Grof, who is discussed in the next chapter, and by the originator of the rebirthing theory, Leonard Orr.

DREAM AND REBIRTHING

Rebirthing is a form of therapy that regards the birth trauma as the most important factor in the development of the personality. According to this theory, a person's fundamental grasp of life is established during and immediately following birth. This is where the individual's "personal laws" are laid down: his patterns for how he reacts to negative childhood experiences, to adversity, rejection, and so on.

The therapy strives for a living over again of your birth by means of a breathing technique (hyperventilation) that was developed by the American Leonard Orr in the mid-1970s, by means of which it is asserted that you can liberate yourself from the negative "personal laws" and instead live a more positive and energy-filled life. The therapy is clearly regressive, and to an unusual degree one-sidedly experience oriented.

Rebirthing, in the original version, is interested not in the processing of the negative and traumatic contents that might surface, but on the contrary by suggestive techniques that prompt you to let go of them, to let them pass, and to go on to transcendental experiences.

I have not seen dream series reproduced in the literature on rebirthing, but I can give an example from my own practice: a series of three dreams from a forty-year-old man four to seven weeks following a rebirthing experience. The series, compared with the rest of his material, shows that a violent regression took place, displaced in time in relation to the course he participated in, but in a way so we agreed that it is what must have triggered the very strong reaction.

The technique in this case isn't hyperventilation but, among other things, stimulation of body areas affected during birth.

Dream five weeks after rebirthing:

> *A snake, which I am on good terms with, rolls ahead of me like a wheel as I am going to my parents'. When we get there I take the snake—as a friendly gesture toward it—in my hands, but suddenly it becomes hostile, twists loose from my arms, and bites me on the heel. Blood trickles forth from its circular bite marks. I get afraid and ask my parents for help.*

The dream evidences a powerful regression. On the personal level this is seen from the fact that the dreamer becomes like a little child who asks his parents for help. But there is also a wealth of archetypal symbolism that the dreamer wasn't familiar with. The Uroboros, the snake that bites its own tail, is an age-old symbol for the Great Mother, and of the uterine state. He plays with it, but it turns out to be more dangerous than he thinks. The hero who is bitten on the heel by a snake is also well known from mythology. In these myths the snake is in league with the Great Mother and the bite brings about regression (the Egyptian sun god Ra, Philoctetes in Greek mythology).

In a dream seven days later the dreamer is *out sailing with the Queen. The ship capsizes. He manages to reach land alone on an island. There he finds survivors of a catastrophe that has struck the entire world. They are discussing how a new society can be built up.* Here the regression has been expanded to not only a person's but the whole world's destruction. The Queen is a mother figure (the mother of her country). Being swamped can be understood in Freudian terms as birth symbolism. Interpretation of the motif in a Jungian frame of reference can be seen by comparing with Jung's dream series from *Psychology and Alchemy* (see "Dream and alchemy," chapter 2).

Three weeks later he dreams that *he goes down with a boat in a lake near where he lived as a child. But he manages to reach land, and after various entanglements in which he meets a farmer and a stallion he comes out onto a busy road with crowds of people.* The destruction theme is now less pronounced. The feminine figures have been replaced by masculine symbols, and he is on his way back to civilization (consciousness) and activity.

On the outer level the client had felt tired since the rebirthing experience. For two weeks parallel with the dream series it was more than he could manage to go to work, and he completely lost interest in his love partner. He spent most of the time in bed where he "dreamed and dreamed as though I had to get rid of something." After which he got down to work again and resumed his love life.

Naturally there are many ways of reacting to rebirthing, but judging from the case of my client it can be a very powerful technique.

Conclusion

Rank assigned the birth trauma paramount importance as a prototype for all cultural unfolding, and it led him to an independent conception of the nature and function of dreams. He understood dreams as an attempt to live the birth trauma over again and return to the prenatal state. And he thought that dream analyses are the strongest support for the psychological significance of the birth trauma.

Grof and Leonard Orr, as well, make the birth experience a very decisive psychic factor. But as it has been shown, the birth experience in dreams can be understood in numerous ways.

The empirical basis for a connection between dream and birth is modest but is reinforced by Grof's observations, which will be discussed in the next chapter.

My objections to Orr's rebirthing technique are the same as to other experience therapies that do not integrate the powerful experiences in a more long-range psychotherapeutic work. The philosophy behind Orr's rebirthing is in league with the yoga tradition, Hindu philosophy, and reincarnation theories, in which the person himself is responsible for and chooses the life he will be born into because there are certain things it is important for him to learn.

11. DREAM AND CONSCIOUSNESS-EXPANDING TECHNIQUES

Introduction—Categories of LSD experiences—Dream and LSD—Dream series from LSD users—Grof's therapeutic method—Conclusion

INTRODUCTION

In numerous cultures people have used "ecstasy techniques" to achieve altered states of consciousness. Among the many forms are orgies and dances, drums and "high" music, flagellation, isolation or exposure in desolate places, hyperventilation, and trance. Various substances and intoxicants have been used to induce a transcending of the limits of consciousness. The Greeks used wine in their orgies, the Eskimos rotten seal meat, the Indians peyote. Poets have used opium to obtain inspiration, and we have accounts of cosmic experiences from people on coming out of general anesthesia. This led to therapeutic experiments with the anesthetic Ketalar.

The most comprehensive scientific description of the effects of consciousness-expanding substances on the psyche is Stanislav Grof's four-volume work *Realms of the Human Unconscious*. The basis for Grof's research is first and foremost work with LSD-25 (lysergic acid diethylamide), a substance first synthesized by the Swiss biochemists Stoll and Hoffmann in 1938.

LSD is termed a *hallucinogen* (hallucination-inducing substance) and is considered one of the most powerful psychoactive substances known. It induces drastic changes—sensory, emotional, intellectual, and motoric—

in the consciousness. It often produces bizarre artistic, religious, and mystical experiences, and—particularly important—experiences of death, rebirth, and biological birth.

Grof emphasizes that it isn't LSD as such that produces the singular experiences. Rather, LSD is a catalyst for material that already exists in the psyche and that can also be induced by procedures known from shamanistic practices, primitive people's rites of transition, and various healing rituals. Plus, LSD experiences are very much connected with the individual's personality.

CATEGORIES OF LSD EXPERIENCES

Grof distinguishes four categories of LSD experience:

1. abstract and aesthetic
2. psychodynamic (like in ordinary psychotherapy)
3. perinatal (surrounding birth)
4. transpersonal (transcending ordinary ego boundaries)

The *abstract* and *aesthetic* experiences include colorful visions of natural scenery, abstract patterns, and at times fluid and diffuse ideational images, as well as intense experiences of music, painting, and architectural forms. Fascinating sound hallucinations can also be obtained.

The *psychodynamic* experiences comprise material of the sort which turns up in ordinary psychotherapy.

Birth Experiences

Grof is in agreement with the Jungians that birth experiences can be understood as psychological death/rebirth motifs; that is, as symbols for transformation of the personality. Like Rank, he thinks that the separation from the mother at birth is an decisive event in an individual's life. But what for him is momentous are the marks "birth's extreme physiological adversities" leave on the personality.

He has set up his own model for phases of the experiences surrounding birth: the "perinatal experiences."

He divides the *birth experiences* into four "Basal Perinatal Matrices" (BPM I–II–III–IV), which shape later experiences in life: "Each stage of biological birth appears to have a spiritual counterpart." For the undisturbed existence in the womb (BPM I) it is the experience of cosmic unity. The start of the delivery has its counterpart in feelings of "universal engulfment." The contractions of the womb correspond to "no exit" or "hell," and the propulsion through the birth canal parallels the death/rebirth struggle.

Grof grounds the perinatal model in the fact that patients in LSD sessions very often show physical symptoms that can best be interpreted as a derivative of biological birth: muscular tremors, a widely oscillating respiratory rate, along with positions and movements corresponding to the different stages of delivery. In addition, many report visions of or an identification with embryos and fetuses, as well as the feeling of being newly born and behaving like a newborn infant.

Transpersonal experiences are defined as "the feeling of the individual that his consciousness expands beyond the usual ego boundaries and limitations of time and space." His body image doesn't have the usual fixed physical boundaries. He can experience his own identity in a different person, a different form, an animal, a plant, a rock; he can encounter suprahuman spiritual entities, be one himself, transcend temporal limits, have all sorts of archetypal, parapsychological, and mystical experiences.

Jung has described similar phenomena under the designation *experiences* in clients in decisive phases of psychic transformation.

DREAM AND LSD

Grof thinks there is a profound organic connection between dream life and psychedelic (LSD) experiences, and thus that working with dreams should be an integral part of psychedelic therapy. "When LSD patients experientially enter the perinatal area, the quality of their dreams changes and the Freudian approach to interpretation is no longer adequate," he writes in *LSD Psychotherapy*. There the dreams begin to differ from normal dreams in their violent intensity. Themes from the perinatal matrices in dreams are:

BPM I (corresponding to intrauterine life): Visions of "heavenly realms, paradisical atmosphere, beautiful natural sceneries, and oceanic states."

In BPM II (the first clinical stage of delivery with uterine contractions): "Passive experiences of tortures in prisons, concentration camps, gas chambers; frightening claustrophobic experiences in caves, underwater passages, or progressively narrowing corridors, tunnels and pipelines, and hopeless no-exit situations."

BPM III is associated with the third clinical stage of delivery. The fetus experiences "an enormous struggle for survival, with mechanical crushing pressures and frequently a high degree of suffocation" but also a prospect of ending "the unbearable situation." The mother's and the child's interests coincide, and during the conclusion of this stage the child can come into contact with blood, mucus, urine, and feces.

> Various aspects of BPM III generate dreams of titanic warfare or natural catastrophes of enormous proportions; murders, accidents, bloody massacres, rapes, and sado-masochistic orgies; pornographic scenes full of outrageous sexual deviations and perversions; and an atmosphere of decay and unimaginable dirt. Final phases of this matrix are associated with dreams of exciting adventures in military expeditions, hunts, amusement parks, and particularly colorful carnivals.

According to Grof, once the person moves into the transpersonal stage of the LSD process, the dreams decisively change character. "These dreams do not show the distortion and condensation characteristic of those that are biographically determined, and have the quality of past-incarnation memories, ancestral or phylogenetic experiences, encounters with archetypal entities, various types of extra-sensory perception, or out-of-body travels." They are described as being of an experiential nature and intensity quite different than normal dreams. For example, you can dream of having been in a certain city and afterward be convinced that it is a reincarnation experience, that you were actually there.

DREAM SERIES FROM LSD USERS

Considering the great significance Grof ascribes to dreams it seems astonishing that in *LSD Psychotherapy* he devotes only three pages to dream and LSD and has only a couple of dream examples. Nor has it been possible to find investigations of LSD and dream content elsewhere in the body of literature. For concrete examples I must therefore avail myself largely of my own limited material.

In a thirty-one-year-old male client who took a single LSD trip, no dreams were taken down for seven weeks. The first dream following this was about *merging with the cosmos,* after which three out of the next six dreams were of a science fiction–like character with cancellation of normal boundaries of time and space. These four transpersonal dreams were without parallel among approximately six hundred earlier and subsequent dreams.

Especially illustrative is a series of fifty-five dreams over a space of fifteen months from a thirty-five-year-old male client. Ten years prior to entering therapy he had taken close to fifty LSD trips without psychotherapeutic follow-up. He was not taking LSD at the time of therapy and hadn't done so for five years. He was highly educated and socially well adjusted but sought treatment for a painful cleavage in his emotional life. He adored his lovely wife but for two years had been unable to feel sexually attracted to her. He was capable of having brief intense affairs with mistresses but "rapidly burnt out."

Within the first five weeks of therapy he had nine dreams. Apart from the initial dream, all were of a clearly transpersonal and/or perinatal character. Normally dreams of this sort are extremely rare. In these dreams there appeared only a single familiar but not very close person. (According to Calvin Hall's content analyses, dreams are normally populated predominantly with intimates.)

The dreams had the unusually strong emotional intensity Grof describes. Of the subsequent thirty-one dreams, intimate persons appeared in twelve. Half were ordinary dreams of a psychodynamic character, while the rest could be classified according to Grof's system as perinatal or transpersonal. All in all, the dream series departed from what I had otherwise seen. The client himself said that his dreams had radically changed character since he began taking LSD.

A dream recalled from the pretherapy period was unusually beautiful: *[H]e rides across the sky with a boy and vanishes inside a sea of light.* A dream from the therapy's first period had recurred regularly ever since he started taking LSD:

> *He's flying by himself. It gives a very ecstatic feeling. A lot of spectators, the press and TV are there. But the spectators are never anybody he knows. He flies higher than ever, could continue all the way out in the universe, nothing holds him back, on the contrary he accelerates. But suddenly it's too fast, he brakes and turns back.*

The dream fits Grof's transpersonal categories. Jung would call it cosmic, and in esoteric dream theory it is a higher chakra dream. A nearly identical motif of rushing out in space at tremendous speed is also described by Oliver Fox in connection with lucid dreams. Finally, we encountered a related motif in one of Kohut's prepsychotic clients (see "Dream and transference," chapter 1).

Afterward comes a lucid dream and a dream in which *the music from*

Also Sprach Zarathustra *fades in from outer space,* and next *a surrealistic nightmare.* Then a dream *full of ecstatic bliss in which a radiant spaceship comes down to earth and he runs to greet it.* Then again a surrealistic dream: *[H]e sees himself in a mirror and his face becomes grotesquely distorted* (true surrealistic dreams are also very rare and as a rule expressive of extreme anxiety and near psychotic states). Soon afterward he dreams:

> *I run out in some big dunes and play with a person who is unknown to me. Suddenly I realize it is a woman. She's incredibly beautiful. We stand at a distance from each other, we run toward each other in slow motion (like in a romantic film where the two lovers have been separated for a long time). When we meet in an embrace we fuse together in an incredible feeling of bliss and turn to light—a white beautiful shining light.*

A good four months into the therapy comes the following dream: *I try to get out of a very narrow shaft. I feel the pressure intensify, that there isn't room to breathe. I wake up with the same unpleasant feeling. I feel trapped in my own body. I have a feeling of being closed in, buried. It feels very unpleasant (also in the head), as if there suddenly isn't room for everything.* The dream resembles more than any other from my material a perinatal dream from BPM II or III. This is not only on account of the motif with the narrow shaft and the physical symptoms, but also because of the difficulty in breathing and pressure on the head. Death and burial are other typical perinatal symbols. What is most remarkable is that the dream (like most of the others) at the start of the series is completely devoid of personal details.

And as a final example he dreams that *he is a he-lion.* Here it is a question of identification with an animal, which Grof accounts among transpersonal experiences. This motif, too, is very rare in dreams (see "Waking ego and dream ego," chapter 2) (Dieckmann).

None of these dreams in itself evidences the client's having taken LSD. What is overwhelming is the total mass of transpersonal material.

Grof emphasizes the importance of the therapist having an understanding of the material. In this I agree. Archetypal and transpersonal experiences are as a rule very important to the person who has them. A lack of respect for the genuineness and intensity of these experiences can easily destroy confidence and with it the possibility of helping. As elsewhere in these pages, I do not regard this as preventing a view of dreams being based on other frames of reference. If a client, like my thirty-five-year-old LSD user, has a preponderance of transpersonal material idling (dreams repeating themselves for fifteen years without healing his cleavage), as often as not the symbolism can be referred out to the personal sphere.

As in connection with chakra symbols, instead of merely swooning at a person who dreams he is God (see "Lucid dreams," chapter 9), I suggest that we also choose to examine his way of being God and view it in context with his personality in general. An example is dream number eight in the series just mentioned:

> *I'm standing in an apartment. Suddenly I see down in the street that people are panicking—running to all sides. Just then I see that an atomic bomb has exploded. I'm gripped by terror and panic. Should I hide in the cellar or run outside? Both are fatal.* The same night I dream— after having been awake—*that a neutron bomb explodes. I feel the pressure and the heat—I feel totally powerless.*

In Grof's system this is a dream from the transition between BPM III and BPM IV. The pressure, especially, could be reminiscent of the birth experience, and I wouldn't exclude that possibility, but seen therapeutically it is unusable. I outlined a number of other approaches, first the context in the Jungian sense:

The day before the dream (an aspect Grof never includes) the dreamer, for the first time in many months, had allowed himself a "very delectable" sexual experience with a chance female acquaintance. As mentioned under "Dream and touching" (chapter 7), it is sometimes seen that people carrying out sensuality training in which physical tenderness takes precedence over outright sex have dreams about atom bomb explosions. Using Calvin Hall's explanation, model sex can well be symbolized by a bomb, but then it is saying that the dreamer experiences sex connected with violent aggressions.

Of the total series, following this dream there occurred motifs of aggression toward women, the mother included. A Freudian delving into the past showed that there was more than ordinary grounds for aggression toward the woman who had been the first to give him tenderness and bodily contact. Relations with the mother had been extremely poor, characterized by lack of solicitude, feelings of abandonment, demented emotional carryings on by the mother, and anxiety in the boy—experiences that are transferred to other women at close and intimate contact.

In connection with the dream he had stomachaches and severe tension in the solar plexus. In chakra symbolism anxiety is often associated with the solar plexus, and rage with the hara chakra. The dreamer denied having such aggressive feelings, but shortly afterward he dreamed: *A man runs after me with a knife. He wants to stab me.* This is his first encounter with his masculine aggressive shadow; it is associated with a childhood experience in which his emotionally disturbed mother ran after him with a knife. Following this came the dream about meeting with an incredibly beautiful woman and fusing with her to light.

In Grof's view this is a transpersonal dream. In a Jungian frame of understanding it is a meeting with a spiritual anima; that is, an inner complex that is an intensely energy-charged portrayal. In tantric yoga the experience corresponds to the sixth chakra, and that would be impressive indeed. But if the experience of the anima in the man is undifferentiated, it often symbolizes the unconscious, pure and simple. The dream is then saying that the dreamer is enormously fascinated by the unconscious, which in order to take fifty LSD trips must be the case. A neo-Freudian could see the dream as a "reaction formation," as a defense against the aggressions that had surfaced. And it very probably is—together with all the rest.

The therapy lasted fifteen months in all. The frequency of the sessions was lower than I would have wished, but I didn't want to scare him away. The problem was one of close contact. The dreams with increasing frequency took up personal (not transpersonal) material, which we placed in relation to the man's daily life. This direction is diametrically opposite Grof's therapies where the personal material gradually peters out completely.

One day the client could happily report that to his own surprise he had become able to love his wife—also sexually—and I didn't hear from him except for a couple of grateful postcards (therapeutically not entirely satisfactory, but illustrative of his case). What also belongs to the description is that he had been subject to several near-death experiences when he was a child, and that he had meditated.

Grof himself gives a single "brilliant example of a dream whose content reflects perinatal dynamics. In this case the person himself discovered the connection to the birth process":

> *It was a Sunday afternoon and all my family was in the large living room of a house situated on a cliff overlooking the Pacific. Everyone was enjoying themselves in our usual family holiday manner when I noticed that a storm appeared to be gathering force outside. Suddenly, the wind and rain had such power that it began penetrating the windows; at this point my father said in a very significant tone: "It is the fifth wind."*

Then, in a moment that seems magnificent even in retrospect, the entire house began to rotate on its foundations and to fall off the cliff into the Pacific far below. During the few seconds between the time it began its descent and the moment of impact, I realized that all my family and myself were going to die in the cataclysm. At the very moment when I had accepted totally my own death and that of my loved ones, I awoke, just before the house hit the ocean.

"Upon awakening, I was left with an extraordinary exalted feeling, and then I recognized the dream as bearing a deep resemblance to certain sensations I had in recent LSD sessions. In these sessions I appeared to be reliving my birth, and the elements of accepting my death, the end of the world, tremendous elemental forces involved in a cataclysmic explosion."

I am not in disagreement that the dream is unusual and perhaps can be traced back to the transition from BPM II to BPM IV. But the dream's statement, as far as I can see, is that the dream ego is telling itself that he accepts death; in fact that doesn't become a psychic reality. (He doesn't manage to die.) The dream rather is a sign that the experience from the LSD session is already subsiding back into the unconscious through undoing (*Ungeschehenmachen*, as one of Anna Freud's defense mechanisms is called).

I shall conclude this section with one of Grof's own examples of why it is important that the therapist understands transpersonal experiences.

A patient who had twenty-five unsupervised LSD sessions was hospitalized with a psychotic breakdown. The treatment reached an impasse on account of a disagreement with a Freudian therapist about an earlier LSD experience. The patient, under the influence of LSD, had experienced a scene in which he worshiped "the cosmic phallus." The analyst tried to convince him that the vision "obviously indicated a traumatic sight of a grown man's penis at some time or other in his childhood." When the client wouldn't accept this, the therapist interpreted his reaction as resistance.

Many hours were spent in processing the postulated resistance. Grof, who was called in as consultant, saw that the cosmic phallus "appeared in a typical Jungian framework linked together with a number of archetypal experiences, and that it had a clearly religious and mystic character." For example, the worship of the god Shiva's phallus in India. Grof's understanding of this aspect of the symbol won the patient's confidence, and after short-term treatment with Grof he was discharged.

Grof's therapeutic method

While Grof's theoretical point of departure was originally work with LSD, in recent years on account of political and legislational obstacles he has increasingly gone over to using drug-free experiential techniques in which hyperventilation, stimulating music, body work, and group dynamics play an important role.

Two forms of therapy that Grof finds particularly akin to his own method are Perls's gestalt therapy and Janov's primal therapy. Perls because he "places the main weight on full here-and-now experience with all of its bodily, emotional, sensory and ideational characteristics, rather than on recollection and intellectual analyses"; Janov because the crucial element is uninhibited therapeutic discharge of early traumatic experiences, including the birth trauma. Ultimately, Grof finds both of these superficial because they don't recognize archetypal and transpersonal dimensions in the psyche.

Grof thinks Freudian is insufficient. He criticizes a large segment of the existential psychotherapies for being intellectual. He leans on Jung partly because he "was the first to realize that the process of self-discovery is a journey into the unknown, which implies a constant learning process," and partly because the Jungian conceptual apparatus is that which most nearly gives an explanation for archetypal and transpersonal phenomena. (It should be said that Grof's theories would have been inconceivable without Jung.) But he criticizes the Jungians because they don't recognize the value of "deep direct experiential work," or to an adequate degree the perinatal matrices and transpersonal phenomena.

His own procedure is "that you non-specifically activate the unconscious and trust to a spontaneous turning up of the material that reflects the autonomous dynamics in the patient's psyche" and on "the inner wisdom" that the process reflects. The philosophy is that once you experience "the unconcluded gestalts" you are rid of them. By "profound firsthand experiences" Grof means experiences of an intensity that "transcends anything usually considered to be the experiential limit of the individual." As he sees it, these can be obtained only with his powerful techniques.

Conclusion

In the foregoing we have seen how different dream theories and therapeutic methods can be incorporated in a total conception of dreams, in which the interpreter's knowledge, the therapeutic situation, and the creative dialogue between the dreamer and the interpreter determine which interpretations it is most expedient to work with. As we have seen demonstrated, on the basis of an ever-increasing amount of material, dreams have many dimensions.

On a number of points Grof's view is akin to my own conception, at least in theory. He recognizes the validity of many forms of therapy and regards both dreams and LSD experiences as being of a "multi-layered nature." His findings bear out this conception. However, his most important contribution to our present understanding of dreams is the description of the perinatal layers. And as I see it he gives too much weight to perinatal and transpersonal experiences.

The Empirical Basis

None of the themes in psychedelic dreams is entirely unfamiliar to us. They can result from intense meditation, from ecstatic religious practices, in near-death experiences, in powerful states of anxiety and psychoses (see chapter 12), or in decisive phases of transition in life where the psyche is strained to the utmost. Under normal circumstances, however, they rarely break through spontaneously.

And so we see confirmation that in general the psyche, also in dreams, defends the consciousness against certain categories of extreme experience. We must ask ourselves how expedient is it to break down the psychic defense at the rate an LSD therapy or holotropic technique does.

According to Grof, in an LSD therapy you first work through the personal (Freudian) layers and then the perinatal experiences, which leads to the "final experience of ego death and rebirth," after which "transpersonal elements dominate all subsequent LSD sessions of the individual."

A negative side effect of powerfully activating unconscious material is that the unconscious no longer compensates all of the personal and social parts of the individual's life, and that large amounts of nonpersonal material runs idling in the unconscious. As in the case of my client, it is as if the subjects were rocketed out on a strange planet and couldn't come back again. This in contrast to the form of chakra meditation in which you not only strive for "high" experiences but "open" for all of the higher chakras—without simultaneously losing contact with the lower ones.

I do not reject the idea that there might be therapeutic possibilities concealed in LSD and psychedelic techniques. For instance, I think that the thirty-one-year-old man who had a cosmic dream seven weeks after a single LSD trip got an important boost in his development. It would be useful to conduct some long-term dream studies of the phenomenon from people who aren't so one-sidedly enthusiastic as Grof. And as I see it, the experiences that a single LSD trip touch off provide stuff for many, many hours of work without any form of drugs.

To my knowledge there exist no systematic investigations of who comprise the psychedelic clientele.

In my experience, interest in psychedelic substances is greater in men than in women. It could be asked whether this is due to the fact that the idea of a specific "medicine" to be taken and forces you through some well-defined stages where you come out symptom-free on the other side appeals to the conventional male consciousness.

There is something schizoid and compulsory neurotic about some of the illustrations in Grof's books. Even if LSD does burst many psychic limits, you must ask yourself whether the tremendous coercion and at times violent self-torture that an LSD trip can impose on a client has a share in selecting the clientele.

The Philosophical Basis

Grof frequently leans on physicists and the science historian Thomas Kuhn. Kuhn has described how down through history the acceptance of new scientific theories depends not only upon the standard of the research but on the system of dogmas, values, and techniques, the "paradigm," which is current in a given scientific society. This is an important reason, in Grof's opinion, why his work has encountered much resistance.

With his subscribing unconditionally to the healing effects of the independent psychic processes, he is one of the most extreme representatives of the romantic branch of dream interpretation. He acknowledges his affiliation with the Greek Platonic philosophers, who placed weight on the world's form, pattern, and order more than on the material stuff it was made of.

Is there some irony in the fact that Grof the spiritualist throws his soul's salvation into a material substance, LSD?

12. DREAM AND PSYCHOSIS

INTRODUCTION

By *psychosis* is meant a number of serious mental illnesses that are different
from the neuroses. Here we are speaking of more comprehensive disturbances of the perception of reality that can involve complete loss of consciousness and general disorientation. The most important categories of
psychosis are schizophrenia, affective psychoses (such as manic-depressive
psychoses), and paranoia.

Freud traced the psychoses back to disturbances in earliest childhood,
and this conception has on the whole been corroborated by later psychoanalytical observers.

One of the essential problems in psychoses is that the ego's defense
mechanisms are impaired so that the consciousness is flooded by the unconscious contents. Freud thought originally that while the "nuclear complex" in the neurosis is determined by the Oedipus complex, the psychosis
is narcissistic—that is, springing from an earlier conflict in childhood. But
later investigation has shown that in psychosis the contents from both stages
can overlap each other.

Jung was not in disagreement with Freud that the psychoses could be
traced back to earliest childhood. But he didn't think that was enough to
explain "the overwhelming abundance of fantastic symbol formations" one

could see in them. Jung and his successors saw that often there is a preponderance of content from the collective unconscious, and that unusual amounts of archetypal material at the start of a dream analysis can hint at an impending psychosis. One of the reasons Jung began studying mythology was to better understand the symbolism of psychosis.

The literature on the connection between dream and psychosis is not very comprehensive; the reason for this most likely has to do with the general notion that dream therapy is unsuitable for these states. A more modern view is that it isn't dream therapy as such but the way it is applied that determines its usefulness.

DREAM AND SCHIZOPHRENIA

A classification of psychoses based on dream content was carried out by Medard Boss as early as the 1930s, when he analyzed over eight hundred dreams from schizophrenics and organic psychotics and compared them with three thousand dreams from normal individuals.

The examples are illustrative. A man who around twenty years old was well and minded his studies as best he could had the following recurring dream: *I am building a large beautiful house. It has two balconies which are adorned with beautiful flowers. Then there comes a wealthy gentleman and wants to buy the house from me. I don't let him have it before he pays me a million dollars.*

One year following the onset of severe catatonia (schizophrenia with a psychomotor disturbance), when he was improving, he dreamed that *he was building the same house. But this time somebody sneaked into the basement at night and set fire to the house, so he had to flee.* He awoke with great fear. Two years later, when he had once again had an attack of catatonia, he dreamed about *a war in which he was alone against many enemies. He hid in back of the familiar dream house and in a tremendous bloodbath shot all of the enemies.* A year later, when he had gone considerably deeper into psychosis, he dreamed two times in a row: *I am lying with a beautiful woman in her bed. The woman's husband comes in and wants to kill me. But I strangle him and throw him out the window. I do the same to the many policemen who want to capture me. Finally I go down in front of the house and cut the limbs and heads off all the corpses. It incited me tremendously.*

Boss points out how the as yet relatively sound ego in the first dream

clothes the unconscious wishes in a correct form. . . . The beautiful
house is the mother's house. The patient sells it willingly to the father
figure, the great wealthy man, and is content in return with a lot of
money. In the later dreams the confrontation with the other man isn't
nearly as peaceful. He must flee and awakes from the dream in terror,
so dangerous has the fire in the house become for him. In the later
phases he can no longer come to an understanding with his rivals. He
doesn't flee, either, but becomes fearless and aggressive, increasingly
bloodthirsty and destructive.

These dreams illustrate the Freudian view of psychosis, namely that primitive chaotic instinctual contents break through the ego's defense mechanisms. (In 1938, Boss was a Freudian.) In Jungian and gestalt therapy the intruding persons can be seen as sides of the dreamer himself that he will not acknowledge. The assault on them is total self-destruction. An existential interpretation would stress the dreamer's total lack of the ability to relate humanely to others.

A quite different dream style comes from a thirty-eight-year-old paranoid-schizophrenic man. In his psychosis he dreams that *with pomp and magnificence he is admitted to the heavenly hosts as soul brother of Christ.* One year later he sees in a dream that *the Lord himself stood before him with a gleaming sword. He was to touch this sword with his hand, and then he felt how his loins opened and a new son of God was born of him. There stood many angels round about him and sang: Thou art the almighty and mother of God.*

Another twenty-three-year-old schizophrenic man at the onset of the illness dreamed *that he could fly, live in the sea and that he had undreamed-of strength at his disposal. He could with ease wander through the entire world, always coming to marvelously beautiful regions.* Another time in a dream he was *enormously sexually potent. His body grew bigger and bigger until he could play ball with the planet, as if it were a rubber ball.*

These men, before the outbreak of the illness, had dreams in which they were menaced by a bear that wanted to devour them, or about large unknown men who threatened them. But after the anxiety in the dreams ceased, there occurred a flooding of the consciousness with archetypal contents. The first man's dreams are reminiscent of a dream series described in the Swedish mystic Emanuel Swedenborg's dream book, and it is seen that they contain elements from higher chakras.

Jung has described how fantasies and dream images like those of the twenty-three-year-old man can turn up in analysis "once the personal repressions are lifted." The person dreams, for example, that "he is flying through space like a comet, that he is the earth, or the sun, or a star; or else is of immense size, or dwarfishly small . . . is a stranger to himself, confused, mad, etc." Jung describes how these phenomena reveal themselves in the course of the individuation process, but adds that they differ "from the initial stages of mental illness only by the fact that they eventually lead to greater health, while the latter lead to yet greater destruction." The decisive thing here is the ego's ability to and possibility for integrating the archetypal contents.

Boss found a number of dream content characteristics in connection with the onset of schizophrenia. In the first place they are clearly distinguishable from a neurotic's dreams in that they display far more intense destructive tendencies, undisguised sexual perversions, murder, assault, and brutally thoughtless and sadistic behavior. Here it isn't so much the individual content (everybody can dream of extremely violent things) as their quantity that tips the scales.

Other dreams are typical as well. Boss collected from severe schizophrenics twenty-three dreams consisting of images of concrete everyday things, which with terrific speed rushed through "the dream consciousness" with no possibility of retention. One dreamer told, for example, how the following twenty pictures and more had torn through her consciousness "in half a second":

> The gardener raking the gravel; the doctor with a book under his arm; a packet of letters with envelopes; a herd of cows, a fleeing deer; a heap of burning coal; the silhouette of a woods; a milk truck; two buses; a collection of cacti; an empty teacup; a big stack of firewood; sheet music; a plate of bread soup; a policeman; trout in a stream; a lighted floor lamp; an aquarium; a certain cross in a churchyard; a rabbit hutch.

All these things the patient ostensibly has seen in reality the two days preceding the dream.

The dreams were experienced by the patients as very alarming, so much so that they normally didn't tell them. Boss thought that the qualification for being made a party to them at all was that the treatment team had lived together with these patients for several years in a common household, and he saw them as expressing the patients' desperate attempts at pinning down actual reality.

A type of dream that can occur in advance of a psychosis Boss called *endoscopic* (self-observing). Boss found that the ego's ability to divide itself in two and observe itself in dreams was pronounced in schizophrenics, and that the registering instance in the dream possessed much keener powers of observation than the waking consciousness. For instance, a patient who was suffering from chronic severe schizophrenia with hallucinations, and who therefore could only partially manage a regular job, for years had the following dream again and again: *I see a deer-like animal with its belly cut open. It runs through many halls, but time after time comes past me. Each time it comes running past me it has gotten thinner. It makes a tremendous effort and leaps into the air. The last time I see it is only a skeleton, but it still rises up on its hind legs.* The patient "realized that this animal was her own hunted and sick ego."

Frequently the schizophrenic observes his own or the entire world's destruction (*Weltuntergangserlebnis*), in macabre and brutal detail. Boss gives examples of dreams that superficially resemble those of schizophrenics but which have quite a different background; for instance, this dream from a somewhat hysterical, unhappily infatuated girl:

> *I wanted to take my own life. I had a pistol, held the muzzle against my temple, but didn't have the courage to pull the trigger. Then my boyfriend came; I asked him to shoot me. He put his hand around mine on the pistol and slowly squeezed the trigger. After the shot I fell down dead with a blissful feeling in my chest. Even though I was lying dead I could see how my boyfriend put me on a stretcher and placed beautiful flowers all around me.*

The spontaneous flashes of detail in the dream soon put the patient, who knew nothing about psychoanalysis, on the track of erotic recollections and wishes.

Von Franz has explored the connection between dreams and the schizophrenic tendency to split off psychic contents. The splitting off can also take place in neuroses, but there, according to von Franz, the content preserves its normal emotional intensity. In schizophrenics, on the other hand, it disintegrates so the person can't feel what is happening with him or her. In an analysis session she inadvertently wounded a schizophrenic man with a remark that struck at the heart of one of his complexes. He left her in good spirits, but an hour later he got the compulsive idea that a truck driver was going to shoot him, and he was gripped with savage fury. Shortly afterward he dreamed that *somebody had been killed and thrown in a hole in the ground. But soon the body vanished. All that was left was a bit of clothing.* Von Franz regarded the killed man who disappeared as the split-off and disintegrated content. Even after the dream it was impossible for the man to see a connection between his wrath and what had taken place during the session.

In Boss's material there occasionally appear dreams where the ego identifies itself with external, preferably lifeless objects. For example, a schizophrenic man dreamed that *he was a big knife sitting in the wall.* Another patient dreamed that *his soul crept away from the desk at which he sat writing and crept inside a horse's hoof. And the whole person became the horse's hoof.* A third was *a pencil pinched between books which were standing closely on a shelf.* Even though these objects represent the dreamers themselves, they are emotionally indifferent toward them.

I will not give client examples of my own from this sensitive area; I'll merely state my alignment with the conception current with the Jungians, Boss, and the gestalt therapists that these dreams can be interpreted as meaningful expressions of the dreamer's personality.

Still another dream type deals with utterly commonplace events. For example, a woman dreamed that *she was in the hospital. A nurse came and arranged her pillow. She became greatly terrified, woke up shaking with fear and screamed for help.* That something so mundane could be experienced as menacing is bound up with the fact that in the waking state she was totally autistic, that she excluded any contact with the surrounding reality.

Boss thought that to a certain extent it was possible via dreams to distinguish between three types of schizophrenia, which still have an important place in the diagnostic nomenclature: hebephrenic schizophrenia, in which he found powerful sexual contents; catatonic schizophrenia, with aggressive impulses; and paranoid schizophrenia, with predominantly homosexual and narcissistic contents in the dreams.

Statistically based investigations show that it is possible to diagnose schizophrenia exclusively on the basis of manifest dream material. As might be expected, the degree of accuracy is greatest with therapists who are used to working both with dreams and with schizophrenics.

Insomnia is common when psychosis flares up. Improvement is suggested when the dreams become "bland," often dwelling on a single object such as "a wash cloth, a dilapidated house or an empty field." This may, however, be an accurate description of the psychic state following the ravages of an acute psychosis.

A consistent finding in a number of recent investigations that use Calvin Hall's statistical content analyses is that gradually, as the external reality is built up in therapy with schizophrenics, there appear more dreams, and that the better the ego functions the more resources there are in the dreams.

There is a tendency in recent investigations to describe the contents in the dreams of psychotic patients as less bizarre, as simpler and more commonplace than those of normal control groups. This is in contrast to Freud's, Jung's, and Boss's descriptions of either uncontrolled, primitive instinctual impulses, or violent inflations of the consciousness with archetypal contents. An explanation for this could be the present-day widespread use of antipsychotic and anxiety-muting preparations that "put a lid on" the contents the older analysts described.

DREAM AND DEPRESSION

The dreams of depressive patients can appear essentially different from those of schizophrenics. Mentioned in the older literature are "contrast dreams" whose pleasant contents are in stark contrast to the patients' prevailing mood. Recent investigations in dream laboratories and using statistical methods corroborate these observations.

A study by the American psychiatrist Jean B. Miller, though the material is modest, is representative of the general conception of dreams in depressive states. She compared dreams from patients having different varieties of depressive psychoses with dreams from other groups (normal, neurotics, and schizophrenics) and found distinct differences. When the patient was in deep depression the dreams were usually characterized by a pleasant or a bland mood, but when the condition improved they began showing evidence of conflict.

Sixteen deeply depressed patients reported twenty-two dreams, seventeen of which were free of conflicts, threat, or violence from the surroundings and without inner conflict, danger, or worry. Two examples:

> I was by myself with beautiful girls in Venice—in a coffee house. They were dancing there. There was a lot of entertainment. Then suddenly the man from the gondolas came in and said, "Now we are ready to go around the city in a gondola." I had a beautiful girl with me.

I had a pleasant one last night. I gave someone a gift. I can't remember who. Then we were going out in the car. We had to wait to get into the stream of traffic—like on a big thoroughfare. I was happy in it.

When the patients began improving, troubles appeared in nearly all of the dreams.

But while the control group was often subjected to physical harm in the dreams, in the depressives it usually took the form of coercion. For example: *My husband was in a boat fishing and had the outboard motor running. I wanted to get in the boat also but he insisted I stay on the shore and wait while he fished. I decided my fishing license had expired so I wouldn't be able to fish anyway so it was safer I stay on the shore.* Moreover, three out of thirteen dreams dealt with the patient's death compared to zero out of a hundred in the control group. The following brief example is typical: *I dreamed that I was at my own funeral. It was a black coffin and very simple and shut.* This corresponds to the danger of suicide being greatest when depressive patients show the first sign of improvement.

Another study indicated that in a later phase (discharged for at least half a year and without psychopharmaca) the depressive patients had more masochism and more hostility from the surroundings in their dreams than a control group.

DREAMS IN OTHER PSYCHOTIC STATES

In neo-Freudian psychology (Melanie Klein, for example), the depressive is regarded as the defenseless prey of a sadistic superego. In the manic stage the ego, on the other hand, takes revenge on the oppressive superego by throwing itself into all kinds of projects.

The following dream is from a thirty-five-year-old manic-depressive woman at the start of a manic stage: *I was walking along the street. Suddenly I started pouncing on other people's heads, using the heads as soccer and bowling balls. I kicked in their teeth with my shoes. In the dream I was a little surprised at my actions.* But the mania can also be due to the ego being inflated by an archetype, as in the example of the man who dreamed he was the mother of God. It can also be from the higher chakras, cosmic dreams, light experiences, and so forth, which in other cases would act positively.

A number of other typical motifs appear in organic psychoses, dementia, senility, etc. Here I will just mention a dream from a depressive senile arteriosclerotic patient. He *felt in the dream that he was tied by both feet and pulled down in a toilet. Then, enveloped by a huge mass of defecation, he was flushed out through all of the city's sewers.* What is astonishing here is the dream's ability to coldly and clearly reflect not only the man's psychic but also his social situation. Is it that the dreams in psychotic patients often are expressions, superior to the waking consciousness's, of resources still beyond our ability to exploit?

In 1938, Boss could ascertain that patients who after an insulin shock cure had become "completely well" had nearly just as abnormal dreams as before. Even in these psychically impaired persons the dreams were capable of conveying a viewpoint that wasn't debated in public until the "antipsychiatry" of the 1960s: that shock cures and medication might remove symptoms but they did not cure the underlying illness.

BORDERLINE CONDITIONS AND DREAMS

A special category of clients who rather frequently enter psychoanalytical therapy are the so-called borderline personality organization patients. A description of the dreams of this client group is complicated by the fact that the diagnosis covers different states in different authors, and considerations of space prevent a discussion of the diverging conceptions.

This category of clients is characterized as being on the border between psychosis and neurosis: more well than the former and more ill than the latter. They are, according to the English borderline expert Otto F. Kernberg, no more threatened by psychosis than neurotics, but have altogether their own personality structure marked by primitive defense mechanisms and lack of the ability to repress. Often they are very intelligent persons who can't face living on the educational level their gifts entitle them to.

Because they lack the ability to repress, they will, if happy with the therapist, often be able to remember many dreams, up to five or six a night. The dreams do not show the same regular growth processes as normal dreams. One moment you see positive archetypal dreams, which in normal dream psychology appear seldom and which here would signify a decisive development, and the next moment they approximate schizophrenic horrors. The dreams are often very long, but the plot can be oddly labyrinthine so you have the feeling of not being able to move from the spot. They can also have an artificial, unnatural, and surrealistic quality that doesn't appear in normal dreams: the sun is blue, a tree has blossoms and fruit simultaneously, a garden of plastic or candy, and so on. Moreover, there appear rapid trans-formations of the dream ego; for instance, it suddenly becomes other, pos-sibly opposite-sexed dream figures.

The Jungian H. G. Baynes has described an in-depth therapy with two male borderline patients. The one, a thirty-year-old doctor, had the following initial dream:

The scene is on the Mersey. There are many boats, one of which is a battleship. It floats very high in the water, and though it is huge, it looks like a toy ship. It bobs about, turning this way and that, and is in imminent danger of colliding with other boats. At last it makes connec-tion with a towing boat, which drops an anchor. There is some doubt whether the anchor will hold, but it eventually does.

We then go ashore. I have a picture paper in my hand; in it there is a picture of the President, or perhaps the Prime Minister of England, joking with the King. I go up to this man, who is reminiscent of Disraeli, with a flavor of MacDonald. He is continually polishing his eyeglass, which falls to the ground, and I pick it up and polish it for him. This happens several times. Then the eyeglass turns into a microscope slide, which I place on the flat rung of a ladder nearby.

The scene changes. We are going in a carriage to a palace. The palace is modern and surrounded by trees: the whole thing is rather like a Monet painting. As we come up to the front door, I see some exquisite flowers and jump out to smell them, holding them in the cup of my hands. The sensation is exquisite.

We then go indoors, and port and beer are handed around. My wife seems responsible for this, and this stimulates me to say with contempt: "port and beer!"

We then go away and return later, walking. We are late for supper. As we walk down the road, the King passes. He is in a small carriage alone: a racy-looking man. His carriage jogs along. To my delight he seems to recognize us, and waves as he passes.

My wife and I are now in the palace, and Princess Mary is present handing around fruit salad—an inferior diet, I think. There are three women and myself present. I hand fruit salad to two of them and take the third portion myself. The third woman is thus left out. I have dropped a social "brick."

I now go and talk to a lady. While doing so, I put my knee on the end of a bench, which jumps up, and in falling back makes a noise. The conversation ends. A second "brick."

Princess Mary now gives us our places for dinner. When the time comes for us to go in, I find that my shoes are off, and I hastily put them on again. On our way to dinner we go up through an elaborate nursery, without, however, any children in it.

The dining hall is rather like a college hall, and the tables are arranged in an inverted U, the free ends facing the entrance. I walk down the right side and try to sit in a wrong place. Princess Mary puts me right, and I walk around the tables to my correct place on the other (left) side. At the end of the table sits a distinguished-looking man, picking his nose. This might seem disgusting, but he carries it off with aplomb. Next to my place at the table is a broken toothbrush with wire bristles. The bristles loop onto the back of the brush. It is revealed as an "asthma toothbrush."

The question arises as to why I am here, and the answer is that I am a distinguished physician.

I won't go into an interpretation of the dream, but merely point out a few details that could bring to mind a borderline case.

The long involved dream plot that doesn't have any denouement; the surrealistic details: the toylike ship, the monocle that becomes a microscope, the curious asthma toothbrush. The inflated gallery of characters: the prime minister who jokes with the king, his own conviviality with a man who looks like Disraeli, and later the royal personages. His peculiar feelings: contempt and revulsion for the folksy service, beer first and fruit salad afterward, but acceptance of the man picking his nose, and so forth. The elaborate nursery without children. Any of these symbols can appear in normal dreams. What is telling is the total context. Thus, if you haven't seen a lot of dreams you would do well to abstain from diagnosis.

Another example from Baynes's patient number two, a forty-year-old professional illustrator:

I am in a large garden and it is night. The garden is not really a garden, because all the hedges are giant birthday cakes with candles on them. (I do not remember seeing any genuine plants.) I look at the moon and see that it is a crescent, drawn in pink outline on the sky. I think that this is a very pretty idea and I must remember it and use it in a drawing one day. Everything is very dark in spite of the candles.

> *I have on a leather overcoat which is unbuttoned. I flap this at the candles and blow them out one by one till all are extinguished. Then I turn towards an enormously wide marble staircase stretching up to a distant castle, dimly seen in the moonlight. I start running up the steps, and—flapping my coat—I fly. Half whimsically I cry like a bat, and am immediately answered by shrill whistling noises coming from everywhere. To my horror I realize I am a bat and have been accepted as one of them.*

Here we again have the toylike and artificial, which reminds the dreamer of his grandmother's estate where as a child he was surrounded by over-concerned women without real feeling for the boy. The leather overcoat, even though he never liked it, he had taken over from his wife because she didn't think it suited her. And finally the identification with the bat, which is normally associated with vampires and the diabolic. The surrealistic details are by the Jungians designated as a "trickster quality" in the unconscious. It plays jokes that serve no compensatory function.

DREAMWORK AND PSYCHOSIS

Early in his psychiatric career, Jung saw much of what took place in psychoses as processes that attempt to cure the psyche. Investigations of their content showed him that not only do psychoses contain "the tragic destruction" visible on the outside, but that they can have an inside which, after all, is meaningful. In his epoch-making work *Symbols of Transformation* is an analysis of the mythological structures in the fantasies of a schizophrenic American woman.

Jung describes in his memoirs the eighteen-year-old female patient who gave him a first experience of the significance of the content of a psychosis. The young woman had at age fifteen been seduced by her brother and abused by a schoolmate. Afterward she retreated into isolation, became more and more odd, and was finally admitted to a mental hospital with (catatonic) schizophrenia. Slowly, over a period of many weeks, Jung succeeded in getting her to speak. She told him that she had

> *lived on the moon. The moon was inhabited, but at first she had seen only men. They had at once taken her with them and deposited her in a sublunar dwelling where their children and wives were kept. For on the high mountains of the moon there lived a vampire who kidnapped*

and killed the women and children. So she planned to destroy the vam-
pire. But he turned out to be a man of unearthly beauty, who raised her
up and flew off with her.

Jung understood this fantasy in the following way: "As a result of the incest to which she had been subjected as a girl, she felt humiliated in the eyes of the world, but elevated in the realm of fantasy. She had been transported into a mythic realm; for incest is traditionally a prerogative of royalty and divinities. The consequence was complete alienation from the world, a state of psychosis." Jung relates that he succeeded in curing her very quickly, by getting her to realize that if she wanted to be healthy she couldn't go back to the moon.

The Danish Jungian Pia Skogemann has found a similar man-in-the-moon symbolism in the drawings and fantasies of a schizophrenic woman at the turn of the century. Even the conception's content is archetypal: there is in the religious ideas of many diverse peoples a widespread belief that the moon can come down on earth as a man and make women pregnant. This idea is matriarchal, and even though Skogemann isn't blind to the traumatic background in the patient's childhood, she also sees the woman's fantasies and drawings as indicating she had been caught between a matriarchal and a patriarchal worldview.

The neo-Freudian Heinz Kohut used a dream in which a man was about to be fired out into space to diagnose latent psychosis and to form an estimate as to what could prevent the psychosis from breaking out (see "Dream and transference," chapter 1). H. G. Baynes is another eminent example of someone who used dreams in treating psychoses.

Medard Boss used dreams in treating psychotic patients. But like the Jungians Dieckmann and von Franz, he recommended interpretation on a different level than normally, and he emphasized that it was a matter for experts. One of his dream examples is the following:

A friend and I have enlisted in the war against Italy. We were very happy
at first. We were told it wouldn't be a dangerous war. But as we pull
into a station near the Italian border, I see a cripple with only one leg.
All that's left of the other leg is a stump, tightly bound and bleeding
profusely. A train leaves, and the cripple limps after it. He grins at first,
then starts to grow thinner and thinner, as skinny as me, then even
skinnier. Finally I myself am the cripple. I turn into a real skeleton, my
head changing into a grinning skull. Terror grips me. Next the skull

and the train station dissolve into blue mist. I panic and wake up bathed in sweat.

The dream comes from a thirty-year-old schizophrenic Swiss patient who had been out of the hospital for two years. Three months after this dream he had to be rehospitalized because of a new psychotic episode.

The dreamer had no idea that the dream could have to do with the possibility of psychosis. On the contrary, he felt fit. But Boss, from the dream's utter destruction of the patient's universe, understood what was in store. Boss wrote of the dream's theme that "it is common knowledge that the Italian people relate to their fellow men in an emotionally much more open and warmer way than Swiss people." It could therefore be said that the patient was at war with himself, because he had learned to regard any physical sensual relation to others as something hostile, dangerous, and even sinful.

With a neurotic patient Boss would have pointed out his contact difficulties and prompted him to surmount them. But as the patient suffered from schizophrenia, he on the contrary exploited the dream as an aid to avoiding overdemanding interpersonal relationships. He was strongly dissuaded from becoming more deeply involved in a love relationship with a certain woman but was exhorted to be satisfied with a stable friendship with a man.

Boss added: "Only in those rare instances when the analyst is prepared to assume full medical responsibility for the psychotic patient over a period of many years, guiding him through all subsequent eruptions of psychoses, would it be permissible for him to apply the phenomenological approach exactly as he would in the case of a mere neurotic."

Dreamwork with chronic schizophrenics in groups has been carried out by the Jungian psychiatrist Harry S. Wilmer. He treated for over a period of five years a group consisting of chronic schizophrenics and Vietnam veterans with postwar psychic traumas. Patients and personnel met once a week for a Dream Seminar. Wilmer found that the dreams of the Vietnam patients not only dealt with individual problems but also with communal ones, and that in a certain sense they recounted an American epic of the Vietnam War.

One of the inspirations for the Dream Seminar was taken from the exit rituals of the Navaho Indians following warfare, in which retellings of the myth of the war god slowly and systematically readjusted the men who had been in war to a more peaceful, nonaggressive life in society.

The weekly dream seminars were combined with individual analysis and were integrated in the overall program of psychiatric treatment. During the sessions, everyone could comment on the dreams that were presented. The therapists laid stress on the prospective aspects of the dreams and did not allow free association. Gestalt and psychodrama therapeutic techniques were also used in the dreamwork.

Wilmer found this method to be therapeutically valuable; it resulted in patient improvement. One of the aims was to help in the control of insomnia and night fears.

As Freud pointed out, traumatic dreams are frequent after military combat. They are stereotypically repetitive and normally untreatable. Wilmer mentions success in getting traumatic dreams with stereotype content to change to dream series sometimes having a narrative quality.

A thirty-six-year-old Mexican-American Vietnam veteran suffered from both paranoid schizophrenia and post-traumatic disturbances. He had been involved in a massacre in which all of his buddies were killed and he himself killed the enemy with hand grenades. Later he was convinced that his buddies thought he had betrayed them, and he was admitted to the Audie Murphy VA hospital. Every single night for twelve years at the precise moment of the attack he had the following dream:

> *The whole platoon is after me. All the men who were killed in the ravine are running around me. I could see their faces. They caught me and tied my hands behind my back and made me kneel on the ground. Then somebody cut my head off with a big sword. It was my sergeant. My head was rolling down a sandy hill towards the ocean and I was running after it, trying to catch it. I woke up scared and in a sweat. I just couldn't reach my head.*

In the course of the treatment the dream was successfully changed so that it sometimes assumed other forms: *You are in the ravine, Harry [the therapist], your arms are tied and you are calling to me to help you. I sneak in and pull you out, but when I woke up I had tears in my eyes. When it is you, I can cry. Before I always woke up in a cold sweat but never crying.*

I myself join with those analysts who believe that dreams can be used, with the reservations mentioned, to help psychotic and prepsychotic patients. This category of client has great dependency on the therapy and the therapist, and the dreams give valuable information about their performance. Do I seem too active? Too passive? How much can the client take in? And so forth. Here I look especially at the first dream after the last therapy session. This often makes it possible to evaluate the hour. Likewise, the last dream before the present session can tell what can be expected and possible aspects of the work.

As we saw in Boss's example (see "Dream and schizophrenia," above), a psychosis is often heralded far in advance of its outbreak by a dream, which implies that it can be provided against. In some cases, by also investigating what took place the day before an "endoscopic" dream, for example, those factors can be traced that can provoke psychosis and thus help the client to safeguard himself.

First and foremost I put the dreams to pragmatic use, which aims at the immediate adaptation to reality. But if in the course of a few years a good transference with carrying capacity has been established, more profound psychotherapeutic aspects can be applied.

DREAM, PSYCHOPHARMACA, DRUGS, ETC.

There exist a number of studies on the influence of psychopharmaca, consciousness-expanding substances, alcohol, etc. on dream recall and on the duration of REM sleep.

Major and minor tranquilizers on the whole reduce dream recall. REM-sleep time is increased with LSD, opium, and chronic heroin use. Alcohol reduces REM-sleep time. But REM sleep increases to 40 percent of sleep time (as compared with 20 to 25 percent normally) in delirium tremens in alcohol deprived patients.

Barbiturates reduce REM-sleep time, and a psychiatric study found that patients who received barbiturates attempted suicide more often than those who did not.

Beyond what Grof has written, little has been published concerning the connection between dream *content* and psychopharmaca.

CONCLUSION

The accessible material on dream and psychosis corroborates the conception that dreams can be understood on many levels. Jung and his successors stress the compensatory and prospective aspects in dreams, and the Freudian theories about the defense mechanisms' role in dream formation are confirmed dramatically when we see how they cease operating in schizophrenics. In these dreams we also see often undisguised instinctual conflicts being played out. Studies of the dreams of schizophrenics using Calvin Hall's method show at the same time parallels between dream and lifestyle. It is possible to understand schizophrenics' dreams going from most of the frames of reference I have mentioned, but they must be applied in a more gentle manner than normally.

The dreams of depressives show that dreams can powerfully contrast the waking state, though we have no explanation for why this is so. In a way one can regard psychosis as a frame of reference in itself. Studies of dreams and psychoses have not given occasion for any new philosophic or scientific approach.

The *empirical basis* is clearly a different group of dreamers from those we have seen otherwise. This does not alter the fundamental view of dreams, but in a new and unexpected manner underscores the significance of dream activity for mental health.

In the chapter on dream and laboratory experiments I touched on the possibility that dreaming is a process which goes on all the time, and which during the day breaks through as fantasy activity at regular intervals reminiscent of the nocturnal alternation between REM sleep and NREM sleep. Laboratory investigations carried out in the 1960s and 1970s led to the assumption that schizophrenics mix the two forms of thinking, the conscious and the unconscious, together, not only in the waking state but also in dreams.

Rosalind Cartwright found that persons with "high scores" when they were tested for schizophrenia (also when seemingly normal) had NREM dreams which contained more "bizarre hallucinatory fantasy" than normal. On the other hand, dreams in the REM stages were less bizarre the more serious the psychological disturbances appeared in psychological tests.

These investigations indicate that not only do we have a rhythmic cycle of two forms of mental activity—the dreamlike fantasy activity and the rational reality-oriented consciousness—but also that under normal circumstances it is necessary to not mix them together excessively. To be sure, what we are striving for with the dreamwork's creative processes and, for example, meditation is a unity of the two worlds. But it is an ideal that only occasionally is attained. Indeed, in daily life it is important to be able to separate the conscious from the unconscious.

13. DREAM AND SOCIETY

HISTORICAL DREAM LITERATURE

Scarcely any society has been completely uninterested in dreams, and by far most cultures have assigned them a positive meaning.

The oldest known piece of dream literature is a "book of dreams" ascribed to the pharaoh Merikera around the year 2070 B.C. In it dreams are understood in a very simple way, as omens good or ill without personal significance. A number of the symbols are interpreted according to the contrast principle. For instance, good fortune in a dream can be a bad omen.

The Assyrians, as well, had a dream literature. In texts from around 600 B.C. the Assyrians maintained that dreams were due to sorrows and worries, and that the worries would disappear if the dreams were well enough interpreted.

The first interpretations that specifically connect a dream symbol with a waking experience or a future event are presumed to come from India. In old Hindu tradition the object of interest is both the divine and the human aspects of dreams.

The Chinese had elaborate systems of interpretation that combined dream interpretation with astrological data and the book of oracles *I Ching* (see "Other esoteric frames of reference," chapter 9). But the interpretation was also dependent on the dreams' context and thus of important events in the dreamer's life.

In Greece, Plato and Aristotle each had their dream theory. Plato was concerned with the spiritual and divine bases for dreams, while Aristotle was more rationalistic and thought that dreams originated in the body.

Renowned is the dream interpreter Artemidorus of Daldis from the second century B.C. He published a dream analysis in five volumes, the *Oneiocritica*, which was modern in the sense that in order to understand a dream you had to know something about the dreamer: sex, age, background, status, occupation, and other vital social data.

Most of the dream books from the Middle Ages can be traced back to Artemidorus, but they often merely water down his work. Artemidorus's dream interpretation was first published in England in 1644, and in the following century was reprinted twenty-four times.

The attitude of the ancient Jews toward dreams was complex. There was great popular interest, and dream interpretation was influenced by the Near East, where dreams were regarded as messages from many different gods and demons. This polytheistic conception of dreams conflicted with the professed Jewish belief in one God, and the official stance was to discourage interest in dreams.

This duality was transmitted to both Islam and Christianity. Church fathers from the early Christian era like Tertullian, St. Cyril, and St. Cyprian regarded dreams as a potentiality for divine illumination; but they also warned against the dangers of dreams. St. Augustine and St. Ambrose created prayers as an aid to avoiding dreams.

In Greece and Rome an institution existed for so-called *incubation dreams*. Well known is Asclepius, the temple of the god of healing in Epidaurus, to which the ill pilgrimaged. After undergoing various purifying ceremonies, one spent the night in the temple so as to have a dream in which the god of healing revealed himself. On the basis of the dream the local physicians then prescribed a cure for the illness. This practice parallels the idea of initial dreams and is reminiscent of our day's live-in therapy courses, where I have often seen dreams of initial-dream quality.

This tradition was continued in important Christian monasteries and churches. But it was officially condemned, and the condemnation increased. Thomas Aquinas thought that dreams, even when they revealed the truth, were influenced by the devil, and the frequent sexual and aggressive themes in dreams made them suitable as evidence in witch trials. Martin Luther believed that self-knowledge could be obtained in dreams; one could find one's sins and so repent of them. But he found that they were dangerous and prayed that God would not speak to him by this means. Calvin, too, was skeptical of dreams.

The eighteenth century was marked by the Enlightenment and skepticism toward dreams. In the nineteenth century there again came greater openness, and two essentially different currents arose: a romantic spiritual and a rationalistic material. This antithesis became clearly manifested in Jung and Freud but is also recognizable in the later dream theories.

ANTHROPOLOGICAL STUDIES OF DREAMS

Comparative studies of symbolic material across cultural boundaries have absorbed dream theorists since the beginning of psychoanalysis. More comprehensive cross-cultural sociological and anthropological investigations didn't gather momentum until the early 1960s, helped along by Calvin Hall's method.

Carl O'Nell, in the book *Dreams, Culture, and the Individual*, has given a survey of the most important work in this area. O'Nell describes different attitudes toward dreams in so-called primitive cultures. Two Indian tribes from the Colorado River Basin, the Mohave and the Yuma, both assign dreams great significance. The Mohave are interested first and foremost in dreams that validate cultural change, while the Yuma think dreams are concerned with everything that happens in human experience. Common to both of them is that they distinguish between important and ordinary dreams. Important dreams bear on the culture as whole. Dreams can legitimize religious beliefs and give occasion to new ritual dances and songs, and they can confirm shamanistic powers and gifts of healing. "Big dreams" customarily originate with dreaming specialists who are religious practitioners or healers.

For these people dreams are more real than waking reality. Or, put less provocatively: dreams represent a higher and truer reality.

With the Iroquois the great dreams were regarded as messages for the whole tribe. That sort of dream came mostly from chiefs or warriors, but also ordinary tribe members could have them. The latter dreamers were often shown honor and respect but rarely elevated to permanent prestige.

Also the Mae Enga of New Guinea attribute high significance to dreams. For them the dream isn't taking place inside the person, it is the person who is inside the dream. The famous structuralist psychologist Jean Piaget relates that something similar takes place in young children, which corresponds also to mystical and depth-psychological experiences described by, among others, Jung and his successor James Hillman, as well as by the Chinese philosopher Chuang Tse. With the Mae Enga it is a person's status that determines whether his dream can be regarded as significant. Only 5 to 10 individuals out of 350 will have the special status. Such a person is a "big man." The dreams' significance is essentially social and they are used in making decisions of importance for the group. Dreams not easily interpreted are referred to dream experts. Like Freud, these "men of knowledge" try to penetrate behind the manifest dream. They look mainly for aspects of the dreams that are in line with social values and do not hesitate to alter dreams to make them understandable in terms of waking reality.

Many North American Indians cultivated guardian spirit dreams, in which they found a spiritual guide for the rest of their lives. This has been described by anthropologists such as Ruth Benedict and George Devereux, and by Robert Lowe. Among the Crow, a dream that brought the dreamer in contact with the spirit world could be so valuable that it could be sold to persons who hadn't had such an experience. And the Trobriand Islanders of Melanesia, studied by Bronislaw Malinowsky, distinguish between "free dreams," which they don't assign any significance (nor which they have any system of interpretation for), and "official dreams," which are of social importance.

The American anthropologist Roy D'Andrade investigated sixty-three societies for their interest in dreams. He found that dreams had an important role in cultures where young people must learn to survive on their own, because the situation is anxiety-inducing when there is not much external support. Dreams were especially important in societies where young men on marrying had to leave their family's village, and in societies having an unstable economy based on hunting and fishing as opposed to more stable agricultural societies. Dreams gave self-confidence and a feeling of being in control of one's life situation.

D'Andrade found four consistent traits in persons in societies where it was attempted to exert control over supernatural forces:

1. Supernatural figures appear in dreams and give power, aid, rituals, and knowledge.
2. Religious experts (priests and shamans) use their own dreams in their work.

3. Dreams that agree with the cultural pattern are necessary before certain important occupations are conferred.
4. Dreams are induced with special techniques (fasting, drugs, isolation).

THE DREAM LIFE OF THE SENOI

A people that in recent years has aroused attention among those interested in dreams is the Senoi of Malaya. Their special relation to dreams was discovered by the ethnologists Richard Noone and later Kilton Stewart, who is also a psychoanalyst.

Two things in particular make the Senoi of interest to us. The first is that they appear to work more actively with dreams than any other population known. The second is that they are described as a uniquely harmonious people. Dream interpretation is a step in child rearing and is a part of every adult Senoi's all-around education. The highest authority in the Senoi societies (which number about twelve thousand people) are their "dream psychologists," called *tohat*s.

Stewart describes the breakfast table of the Senoi families as a dream clinic in which the fathers and the older brothers listen to and analyze all of the children's dreams. When the family clinic is concluded its male members gather in a council, where the dreams of the older children and all of the male members of the society are reported, discussed, and analyzed.

The Senoi think it is possible to alter dreams in an active and creative way. An important principle is that you must always stand face to face with threatening elements in the dreams and surmount them. If a dreamer surmounts and kills a hostile dream figure, its spirit or being will always turn up as a servant or an ally. If a child tells an anxiety dream, such as of falling, the adult responds enthusiastically: "That's a wonderful dream. Falling dreams are some of the best you can have." If the child replies that he doesn't think so, he is told that he has misunderstood the dream: Everything in a dream has a purpose, and falling is one of the quickest ways of getting in contact with the spirit world. "The falling spirits love you. They are attracting you to their land." It's a matter of relaxing and enjoying the experience, so the fear of falling ends up as joy in being able to fly. The child, when he has a falling dream, will remember what the adult has said and he will be able to alter the dream.

Stewart has "translated" the Senois' dream theory into Western psychological language: As a step in adapting to life, the person creates inner images of the external world. Some of these images are in conflict with ourselves and with each other, and when the hostile images are actually internalized we get in conflict with ourselves and others. In dreams we have the power to see these psychic facts, which have otherwise been disguised in outer forms and charged with fear.

If in a dream we think we are dying, we are in reality merely meeting the powers from "the other world"; that is, our own spiritual powers, who want to unite with us if we will accept them.

Every person should be the supreme ruler in his own dreams and master of his own spiritual world. He can demand and receive help and collaboration from all the powers residing there.

Dreams and their interpretation are closely bound up with social interaction. If you have good relations with your fellowman in the waking state, you will also be able to invoke their aid while you are sleeping.

Pleasant dreams of being able to fly or of sex should be continued, so they reach a point where something beautiful can be passed on to the group when you awaken. If you are flying, for example, you should preferably arrive someplace, meet the beings there, see their art, their dances, and learn what useful knowledge they have (such as a hunting implement). Likewise, sex should be carried through to orgasm, and afterward the song, the dance, the poem should be demanded of the spiritual partner that can convey his or her beauty and knowledge to the group.

If a boy dreams that he is attacked by a friend, his father advises him to tell it to the friend. The friend's father tells *his* child that maybe he has offended the dreamer without wanting to. He should therefore give him a present and be friendly toward him. And so the aggression that is built up around the image of the friend in the dreamer's mind forms the basis for friendly exchanges. If you have good relations with your friends it has a reciprocal effect in the dreams, so your friends will help you in them.

Stewart collected dreams from Senois of all age groups and compared them with dream material from cultures that relate differently to dreams. He found that the dream process developed differently in the various societies. What is exciting in this, apparently the most dream-therapeutic society in the world, is the assertion that there hasn't been a crime of violence or conflict between local communities in two or three hundred years. Stewart writes moreover that psychic and physical illness is practically unknown among the Senoi. However promising this may sound, we ought to give a thought to the Dutch cultural historian Henri Baudet, who has demonstrated how Westerners have always dreamed up a paradise on earth in some exotic culture or other. (See also note at the end of this chapter.)

Inspired by the Senoi, Stewart has founded his own psychotherapeutic institute in the United States. Patricia Garfield, who has also used the method in today's American society, calls it "creative dreaming."

Senoi dreams break the Jungian dogma that dreams are independent entities that cannot be influenced. There are, however, Jungians who have been inspired by Senoi dreamwork.

I have sometimes recommended to clients with violently anxiety laden dreams that they try to alter them. A woman who was so afraid of dogs that in her dreams she exploded in a thousand pieces at the sight of one became able to stand calmly in front of a dog (in dreams) and look it straight in the eye—a happy possibility for her. A year and a half later she ventured touching a dog in the waking state.

Children, in the experience of Garfield, Bertelsen, and myself, are more able to influence their dreams than adults. But as yet very little is known about how that works in our culture.

Other than the Senoi, one of the most dream-minded peoples are the Maya. Out of a population of forty-five thousand individuals nearly ten thousand are claimed to be dream interpreters.

CROSS-CULTURAL STUDIES OF DREAM CONTENT

The comparing of mythological and anthropological material with dream themes absorbed both Freud and Jung. Freud's Oedipus complex and his theory of a primeval patricide had their point of departure in respectively a Greek myth and an anthropological concept, and presupposed that in spite of the boundaries of time and culture it was possible to compare the meaning of the symbolic material.

The dream interpretation of the Jungians, as we have seen, was to an even greater degree based upon mythological and cross-cultural studies of symbols. But it wasn't until the last twenty to thirty years that dreams as such have been compared across cultural boundaries to any great extent. Many of these studies are of a statistical nature and are based on Calvin Hall's methods. They show that universal dream themes exist. But whether they have the same meaning in the different cultures has to be determined in each case. There are also demonstrable differences in manifest dream contents that appear able to shed light on the society's and the culture's influence on the individual.

Age Differences in Men's Dreams

The American psychologist Alan Krohn and professor of psychology David Gutmann studied aging changes in the dreams of male Navaho Indians and compared them with other cultures. So as to exclude culture-specific influences, Gutmann had in advance studied, using psychological tests, the male ego style's age-dependency in the Maya Indians and American urban dwellers. He found three ways by which the male ego endeavored to "master" its life, and investigated this in the Navahos' dreams. Younger men (30–54 years) were active, achievement-oriented, and self-assertive. Older men (55–95 years) were more passive toward the pressure of the surroundings, and regarded the world as complex and unruly. They weren't as interested in leaving their mark on it, but got along through a kind of resigned accommodation. Among the elders in the group, the ego style became more magical and projective.

Seventy Indians aged thirty to ninety years were given psychological tests, and only the first dream from each person was analyzed. Krohn and Gutmann expected that the dreams of younger men would show that they were absorbed by "active mastery" themes such as work and productivity. In contrast to this, older men's dreams should be less centered around active work and either show the dreamer as a "passive, secondary participant in the dream or not even present." Gutmann found much of this corroborated. The younger men had only nine dreams without work and the older men thirty-five dreams without work, even though older men work full-time in the Navaho culture. The younger men had a total of one dream in which the dream ego was entirely absent, while the older men had eleven. And while the younger men had two dreams in which the ego didn't play the central role, the older men had fifteen.

As far as I can see, these statistical studies of aging parallel Jung's development model for men in the second half of life. The passive nonmastery phase would correspond in a positive way to the integration of the feminine in the man, and the later magical outlook to the encounter with the wise old man, or the Self. Gutmann regarded it only negatively as the loss of a masculine mastering ego style, while Jung saw it as a potential for increased receptivity and a more religious outlook. As Gutmann's investigational apparatus had no adjustment for these things, he omitted questions that could have turned out to the older men's benefit. Moreover, the older men had more dreams and were better able to see a correspondence between dream and waking lifestyle than the younger men (corresponding to a more flexible and creative attitude to life?). And contrary to expectations, they had just as much control over dream events and were as objective as the younger men.

Gender Role Patterns in Dreams

One of the subjects that has interested cross-cultural dream investigators most is gender role patterns. Are there specific dream patterns for the two sexes that recur in all or most cultures and reflect differences in the gender role pattern in dreams?

I mentioned in chapter 3 a number of differences in American men's and women's dreams investigated by Calvin Hall and his colleagues. In men's dreams there appear two men for every woman, while women have about equally many men as women in their dreams. The men's dream ego was involved in a greater number of aggressive actions with men than with women, while women apportioned their aggressions equally between both sexes. Moreover, the male dream ego had a greater number of friendly contacts with women than with men, while women had equally many friendly contacts with men and women. The universal validity of these phenomena was corroborated through analysis of 3,874 dreams from Hopi Indians and Australian Aborigines, and similar results were obtained with smaller material from a Bantu people in Africa.

A pioneer cross-cultural undertaking was carried out by Kenneth Colby of Stanford University. Colby had access to an anthropological collection of 1,843 dreams from men and women in "primitive" cultures. In the collection, seventy-five different tribes spread over the entire globe were represented: Indian, Australian, African, Arab, Melanesian, and so forth.

Using a statistical technique, Colby selected from the anthropological material 549 dreams from 366 men and 183 women. All of the dreams were examined for the occurrence of nineteen different "qualities." For the men there was found a clear preponderance of the qualities *wife, weapons, sexual intercourse, death, animals.* For the women it was *husband, mother, clothes, female person.* One problem in such investigations is that in simplifying the categories so as to make practicable the processing of a large material the more diffuse they risk becoming.

The American anthropologist Richard M. Griffith, together with the Japanese Miyagi and Tago, carried out a cross-cultural investigation of "typical dreams" (a concept that originated with Freud). Griffith and his colleagues thought dreams that appear with the same frequency in different cultures refer to more universal human states which are less apt to be influenced by local differences of mentality. They compared the frequency of thirty-four typical dream themes in 134 male and 116 female college students from Kentucky with the frequency in 132 male and 91 female college students from Tokyo. The investigation was in the form of a questionnaire with the wording: "Have you ever dreamed about . . . ?" The Americans had on an average dreamed 14.96 of the 34 themes enumerated and the Japanese 14.93, evenly distributed between men and women.

There were great differences among individuals in the two cultures. Some had had all thirty-four dreams, while others had had none of them at all. There were also cultural differences. The Americans clearly had the most dreams having themes of "coming late," "being locked in," "the death of loved ones," "finding money," "being unsuitably dressed," "of nudity," "of insane persons." The Japanese had a predominance of "being attacked or pursued," "trying something again and again," "school/teachers/studies," "fire," "flying," "violent wild animals."

Men in both cultures dreamed considerably more about sex than did women. On the other hand, both American and Japanese women dreamed more about looking at themselves in the mirror. To the question "Have you ever killed somebody in your dreams?" 38 percent of the American men replied yes, but only 11 percent of the women. In contrast 39 percent of the Japanese women had killed in their dreams, but only 20 percent of the men.

On the one hand these differences give food for reflection and indicate that dreams can teach us much about universal versus culturally determined human traits. But as most writers agree, we can't be positive that because certain themes are universal the *meaning* is "universal." A weighty problem of method is also that only to a certain extent are typical dreams similar. When, for example, Marie-Louise von Franz relates that she has analyzed sixty thousand dreams and never found two alike, what it means is that if you go deeply enough into the details then the conditions for typicality will be different.

If any psychological conclusions were to be drawn from the above mentioned investigations they would have to be far more specific. When women dream of looking at themselves in the mirror more than men it is very much in keeping with the mirror of Venus as a symbol of femininity. In terms of symbolism the mirror in dreams has several meanings. On one hand there is vanity, and on the other the ability of self-reflection. Whether it is the one or the other depends on the circumstances. And what does it mean that Japanese women are so murderous in dreams? Is their aggression directed outward, or is it a matter of self-repression? And are American men better permitted to live their aggressiveness out—like the "robust" Gene from Calvin Hall's example (chapter 3)—than Japanese men?

Other Cultural Similarities and Differences

A study comparing the dreams of Chinese with Americans and with Turkish students concluded that sociological analyses of dream contents can be used to characterize different cultures. When Americans had animals in dreams, they were usually tame, while the Chinese had mostly wild and unpleasant animals. The Turks were more egocentric, self-assured, and heroic in their dreams than the Chinese. The Turks often dreamed of sexual intercourse, while the Chinese dreamed of philandering. In sexual dreams the Turks' open and tangible manner contrasted with the romantic, frustrating, and yearning attitude of the Chinese.

An investigation of the connection between dreams and the local outlook on life was carried out in the village of Tzintzuntzan in Mexico. The anthropologist G. M. Foster, who had studied the Tzintzuntzeños for a period of twenty years, found that they accepted life as it was and rejoiced at the small things, but that they were prejudiced, timorous, and conformist. They experienced the world as hostile, and their little self-confidence made them passive.

Foster analyzed the central themes in 334 dreams. Every third dream dealt with threatening situations, every tenth dealt with failure, and in every tenth the dreamer was alone and abandoned, and so on. The typical overtone in the dreams was fear and disappointment, and in 80 percent of all the dreams that dealt with change it was for the worse. He concluded that the dreams clearly reflected the villagers' character, thoughts, and outlook.

A group of researchers from the University of Tel-Aviv, using questionnaires, investigated the dreams of 409 Arab and 216 Israeli high-school students. The researchers found that the Israeli's dreams revealed structured personalities that reacted with guilt and anxiety when they didn't live up to internalized norms. The Arab students' dreams generally didn't show fear, which indicated that there were no internalized conflicts. Men from both groups showed strong competitive tendencies but did not realize them to an equally great degree. Israeli girls seemed afraid to live up to the society's demands, while "Arab girls showed masculine traits and appeared to be involved in rather hostile warfare between the sexes."

A recent object of research is cultural subgroups. As an example, the American psychiatrist Ronald Farrell showed in statistical content analyses how dreams from 148 male homosexuals deviated with good statistical certainty from the rest of the male population in the area. They had more sexual interplay, more homosexual themes, and more often took place indoors. Using social-psychological analysis techniques, Farrell attempted to determine the share of social influence in the divergent dream contents of homosexuals. Here he found that the stereotype social reactions the homosexuals were met with forced them further into a homosexual role.

Another comparative investigation of subcultures in a society showed that housewives (in Canada) "had more open hostility in dreams" than women who worked outside the home.

DREAMS UNDER TOTALITARIAN REGIMES

The best, but far from perfect, testimony to the connection between dream content and totalitarian regimes is presumably Charlotte Beradt's book *The Third Reich of Dreams*. During the period from Hitler's coming to power in 1933 until 1939 when she had to leave Germany, Charlotte Beradt recorded the dreams of nearly three hundred persons. They were people in whom she trusted so much that she could safely ask them about dreams. By far, most did not actively oppose the regime, and most were not in psychotherapy.

Herr S., an upright man and owner of a factory, three days after Hitler seized power dreamed that *Goebbels was visiting my factory. He had all the workers line up in two rows facing each other. I had to stand in the middle and raise my arm in the Nazi salute.* In the dream this was experienced as an extreme humiliation, and Herr S. struggled for half an hour before the arm would go up. When he finally managed to get his arm up, Goebbels said, "I don't want your salute," and limped out on his clubfoot. Herr S. had this nightmare in many variations. One time, while struggling to lift his arm, *his back—his backbone—breaks.*

Beradt was struck by the fact that dreams from 1933, immediately after Hitler's power takeover, didn't depart essentially from dreams from 1939.

In 1934 a forty-five-year-old doctor dreamed that he lay down on the sofa in his apartment to read a book which for him represented the embodiment of German culture, when *suddenly the walls of my room and then my apartment disappeared. I looked around and discovered to my horror that as far as the eye could see no apartment had any walls any more. Then I heard a* loudspeaker boom, *"According to the decree of the 17th of this month on the Abolition of Walls."*

A middle-aged housewife dreamed that her Dutch blue tile stove divulged to one of Goebbels's Storm Troopers everything negative she had said and thought about the regime, whereupon she was led away tied with her dog's leash. Others dreamed that cushions and lamps began informing against them, and the cherubs in the ceiling were keeping an eye on the bed.

Beradt points out that these dreams were from 1933 and that the systematic installation of listening devices neither took place in reality nor in fiction at that point. She took the dreams as expressing that the regime, by imperceptible techniques, tyrannized people into installing microphones themselves—psychically.

The dreams were often touched off by an everyday event. The man who dreamed that the walls vanished had been visited by the block warden, who wanted to know why he hadn't hung out the Nazi flag. And the woman with the blue tile stove had spoken with her dentist about dangerous rumors.

A man told: *I dreamt that I no longer dream about anything but rectangles, triangles, and octagons, all of which somehow look like Christmas cookies— you see, it was forbidden to dream.* Beradt commented, "Here is a person who decides to avoid risk altogether by dreaming nothing but abstract forms." She noted half a dozen dreams of that kind. I myself have never met with this in clients or in the literature.

A woman: *[I] dreamt I was talking in my sleep and to be on the safe side was speaking Russian . . . so I'd not even understand myself.*

The Nazi propaganda recurred in many dream elements but could also turn up in a dream's main theme. A man who was very sensitive to noise dreamed his radio was blaring over and over *"In the name of the Führer, in the name of the Führer."* And a young woman dreamed that she saw the slogan PUBLIC INTEREST COMES BEFORE SELF-INTEREST printed in endless repetition on a fluttering banner.

Beradt found many dreams that she thought reflected the childish wish to "belong" in people who were against the regime. An office worker dreamed: *Goering himself came to inspect my office and gave me a satisfied nod. This unfortunately pleased me enormously, even though I was thinking what a fat swine he is.* Another man dreamed that *Goering appeared in a brown leather jerkin, shooting a crossbow, which made me laugh out loud. A little later the dreamer was dressed exactly like Goering and appointed his personal archer.*

Beradt recorded dozens of dreams in which the main character is a friend or counselor of Hitler, Goering, or Goebbels, as well as women who had erotic contact with Hitler and Goering even though they were opposed to them. An even stronger denial of own values could be seen in dreams from Jews who succumbed to the brutal intimidation on the part of the regime following the introduction of tightened race laws. The dreams might reveal violent hatred or death wishes directed at relations or friends with whom one was otherwise on good terms, but who placed one in jeopardy because they were Jews. And there might be hatred of one's own complexion or the shape of one's nose. Even more humiliating but not atypical, a Jewish lawyer went in a dream to complain to a Nazi Minister: *The guards grabbed me and threw me to the floor. Lying there, I said, "I even kiss the ground on which you throw me."* And another Jewish lawyer dreamed that *I sat down on the trash can and hung a sign around my neck like the ones blind beggars sometimes wear—also like those the government makes "race violators" wear. It read,* I MAKE ROOM FOR TRASH IF NEED BE.

As a common denominator for the Third Reich dreams, Beradt found that they reflected the systematic destruction of the individual's personality. They portrayed or anticipated the methods of the totalitarian system—playing on insecurity, on universal suspicion, racism, public humiliation—and they described the regime's sinister methods of propaganda, espionage, and surveillance even before they were implemented. But that is not the entire explanation for them.

A more psychological analysis is given by the highly regarded classical Freudian Bruno Bettelheim. Bettelheim generally considered dreams as a possibility for recreating the emotional balance that has been lost during the day. But the anxiety that the Nazis implanted killed the possibility for obtaining emotional release, and also got the dreamers to experience even at night that opposition was impossible. Bettelheim compared these person's dreams with those of prisoners in concentration camps and relates that the latter hardly ever dreamed about the dangers stalking them or being persecuted by the Nazis. He thought it lay in the fact that there was no more struggle in the unconscious between the wish to be oneself and the wish to submit to the Nazis. "Most of their dreams were of the good times they had had or were going to have"; or they were "dreams of escape or revenge."

Another basis for comparison that both Beradt and Bettelheim used was people who had resisted actively. Bettelheim writes, "These were typically 'normal' dreams: that is, dreams of anxiety (about the tortures one suffered at the hands of the SS), dreams of victory and revenge (how one defeated the SS). Hardly any of them were about forcing oneself to obey the enemy by suppressing one's will."

Bettelheim interpreted the dream about the factory owner who broke his back as a typical collaborator's dream. He determined it was the man's moral backbone, his position, and his conviction that was broken down, because he collaborated with a regime which in his heart he disapproved of. "Had the man taken the inner position that he did not want to compromise with the Third Reich, he could have dreamt that he called his devoted workers together and with their help threw Goebbels out of the factory."

The dreams from resistance fighters that Beradt describes point in the same direction: "The stronger an individual's moral fiber and political backbone, the less absurd and more positive were his dreams."

The weak of fortitude dreamed that they couldn't formulate their protests or get a word out. The wife of a resistance fighter who had eluded the Nazis frequently had anxiety dreams in which he was captured. But she could still scream *"All enemies have to die!"* or kick in the door to her husband's cell. And while the collaborators dreamed "What can one possibly do?" a woman in the resistance who dreamed she had to cross a border guarded by the Nazis told herself: *"You've just got to want to, and although he (the passport official) raised an eyebrow, I got by."*

These people's dreams were full of fear and violence, but, as Beradt writes, they weren't reduced to "nonpersons."

Sophie Scholl, student and resistance fighter, the night before her execution had the following dream that she told to her cellmate:

> It was a sunny day, and I was carrying a little child dressed in a long, white gown to be baptized. The path to the church led up a steep hill. But I was holding the child safely and securely in my arms. All of a sudden I found myself at the brink of a crevasse. I had just enough time to set the child down on the other side before I plunged into the abyss.

While Beradt thought that many of these dreams were purely political, Bettelheim's main view was that they reflected inner conflicts, especially unresolved childhood conflicts, which were not created by the regime but were "extremely agitated by it."

Some of the dreams Beradt describes adhere closely to what I have outlined in chapter 12. The surrealistic ideas of talking and listening stoves, cushions, and Easter eggs approach the borderline psychotic. Walls that disappear as the only and central motif point toward paranoid schizophrenia. The utterly debased lawyer sitting on a garbage can is reminiscent of the depressive senile man who is flushed down a toilet (see "Dreams in other psychotic states," chapter 12). In more general terms it concerns the disorientation, depersonalization, and loss of identity and context that Beradt speaks of.

Bettelheim understood that the concentration camp prisoners' good dreams were assuring them that the nightmare of the camps wasn't permanent, and that dreams of escape and revenge were based on the unconscious feeling that resistance even in fantasy helped one to survive. It sounds almost like a compensatory function.

As regards the good dreams there is, however, the possibility that it is a parallel to the "bland dreams" from persons who are so deeply depressive that they don't even have the surplus for thoughts of putting an end to their misery (see "Dream and schizophrenia," chapter 12).

In connection with the dreams of schizophrenics, a study indicated that "a strong ego in waking life" can lead to a "strongly coherent dream with many resources." Something similar seems to be valid for dreamers under totalitarian regimes.

Beradt didn't see it as her task to describe the many dreams that were told to her about being shot, pursued, or tortured. These dreams could have occurred during any war whatever and weren't specific to the Hitler regime.

Anthropologist Kenneth Johnson investigated dreams from students at a university in Uganda under the tyrant Idi Amin, who was extremely hostile toward intellectuals. As far as I can judge from the examples and statistical material it is a question of more "normal" dreams of anxiety, persecution, executions, and so forth, that very clearly reflect the actual political situation but which do not have the character of "the Third Reich of dreams." I think it has to do with the fact that the Amin regime was nowhere near as regimented and effective in its propaganda as the Nazis.

Shortly before the assassination of Martin Luther King Jr., Paul Robbins and Roland Tanck from George Washington University's department of psychiatry were in the process of investigating aggressive content in dreams in forty-eight female students. The assassination resulted in several days' civil disorder in the city, including widespread fires, looting, arrests, and the deployment of twelve thousand soldiers. The study showed with good statistical certainty less aggression in the dreams during the disturbances than prior to them. Could the reason for this be that the disturbances forced the female students into a more collected inner attitude?

CONCLUSION

The existing studies of dream and society provide us with a survey of different cultures' view of the nature of dreams. The Maya Indians assign dreams greater value than waking experiences, as revelations, while the Negritas of the Philippines assigned the two realities equally great value (dream and waking exist on different levels, but they are mutually connected). In our culture dreams are generally regarded as less real than waking consciousness.

Each of these three attitudes can be encountered in different cultures, and they correspond to their respective foremost dream theorists: Jung, Hall, and Freud. Thus we find support for the assumption that all three theoretical orientations are each of limited validity.

The Nature of Dreams

The distinction between "great" dreams, which have significance for society, and "small" dreams that pertain at most to the individual, appears to be known in most primitive cultures and in the historic material. The Jungian Kluger has seen it as evidencing that the distinction between archetypal dreams and everyday dreams, which he found statistically corroborated, is universally widespread.

The cross-cultural studies corroborate that there exist universal symbols and dream themes; but they also point out that in every single case they must be evaluated on the basis of their personal and cultural context.

Of particular interest to investigators has been how gender differences across cultural boundaries are reflected in dreams. Age differences as well have been the object of interest. Besides the studies of men's aging changes in dreams it can be mentioned that European and Chinese children began to regard their dreams as inner fictional events at about the same age, and that children in all the cultures investigated dreams more of animals than of adults.

It would seem that you can take any reasonably well-defined social group whatever and find connections between dream and lifestyle for the group as a whole. Not only do the informative aspects of symbols appear, but also repressions (the lack of sex and aggression in the Tzintzuntzaños), concealments, and omissions (the dreams of the Third Reich). This indicates that dreams not only reflect psychological but also social factors. The manner in which they do it appears to be complex.

The Dream's Social Function

Both the connection between the social group and the dream, and the fact that "great dreams" in many cultures have been interpreted as being statements concerning the whole group's welfare, would indicate that dreams have a function for the society. Dream and creativity are closely related, and if with Bettelheim's words the tyrant succeeds in "murdering sleep" and infusing dreams with fear and defense mechanisms, the society is sick in earnest.

Rosalind Cartwright in her laboratory investigations found a parallel to Roy D'Andrade's studies of cultures that are interested very much in dreams. This interest appears to be connected with "inner tension, with anxiety and a feeling of having the responsibility for working this through." Her guess was that this could explain the increased interest in dreams among youth in the Western world, just as loosened family ties and economic insecurity since the 1960s could make the youth eager to find new resources.

The Dream's Interpretation

It is a common conception that dreams do not take much of a position on current political events. They often seem like "the day's residues," which— the way Freud assumed—are incorporated in themes with a more personal significance. All in all, our material indicates that dreams, even under severe external pressure, connect social and political events with inner psychic attitudes.

On the other hand, the interest of cultures in widely dissimilar sides of the phenomenon dreams forces us to probe whether the interpreter's social horizon doesn't influence whatever he is capable of seeing in dreams. In one of his most important essays on dreams, Jung interprets the following dream from a young man: *I was standing in a strange garden and picked an apple from a tree. I looked about cautiously, to make sure that no one saw me.* The evening before he had secured a rendezvous with a servant girl but hadn't yet been to bed with her, and his associations referred mainly to a guilty conscience on account of the sexual wishes. He happened to think of how his father had punished him severely when he had spied on the girls during bathing—the Christian myth of the Fall turned up in his thoughts, and other associations referred to viewing the erotic experience as an offense.

Jung thought that the unconscious's aim with the dream was to "instruct" the dreamer that he should desist from his erotic venture on grounds of conscience. The question as to whether this dream was meaningful or not depended on whether one accepted "the standpoint of morality, handed down through the ages." Jung's argument for the moral viewpoint was that primitive people also have severe sexual laws.

Personally, I think the interpretation is too narrow. In phenomenological terms, something the dream shows is that the young man can't bring the two dream elements—enjoyment and the dream ego—together without having a guilty conscience. This guilty conscience is associated with a severe paternal authority and Old Testament sexual morals that have been considerably changed since Jung, without the world going to pieces. It must be assumed that if this state of affairs is not processed, then the constellation sexual enjoyment = guilt might be displaced onto a neglected wife-to-be.

The interpretation's weakness is that here Jung takes sides with the Lord God of the Old Testament instead of discovering the profusion of information the dream contains. But doesn't the young man's rash desire constitute criminal folly, in that society, toward the servant girl? To be sure. She could get pregnant and be fired. What, then, if he actually gave in to his feelings? Could it be excluded that he fell in love? That he married her? Began to understand her position and brought that understanding into his own class?

One of Freud's male clients dreamed that he slipped inside a narrow inclined passage situated between two imposing palaces. Freud associated from this image "the two stately buttocks of the female body. The narrow passage rising in an incline stood, of course, for the vagina." And so the dream image represented "an attempt at *coitus a tergo*" (intercourse from the rear). And sure enough, on the previous day "a girl had come to live in the dreamer's household" who had "given him the impression that she would raise no great objections to an approach of that kind." The dreamer was too "considerate" to subject his wife to such crude desires.

Would it be too bold to suppose that the representation of erotic servant girls as respectively apples and palaces testifies to an objectifying conception of lower social strata? Is the conclusion then that the social dilemma was so repressed that servant girls could at that time only appear in dreams via the associative material?

The Empirical Basis

The cross-cultural studies have enriched our empirical material with dreamers from the entire world, and a portion of this appears to buttress our earlier findings. But comparing the material is not without problems.

Most cross-cultural dream studies have been undertaken by anthropologists, and they have generally avoided the psychoanalytical approach. The Finnish anthropologists Kalle Achte and Taina Schahir think that Freud's somewhat too literal application of his theories on cross-cultural material without regard to the distinctive character of the cultures has been found repellent. Meanwhile there is an emerging realization of the value of psychoanalytical theories, provided they respect the anthropological facts. The problems of method have been discussed by most of the anthropologists mentioned in this chapter.

A source of error in the anthropological questionnaire method is that it removes separate dream elements from their context, that the questions are leading, and that the information in order to be processed statistically must be simplified to a degree that can make it rather inane. The question of whether you can transpose concepts from a complex culture to a primitive one has been countered by Krohn and Gutmann, among others. Their assertion was that "if the dream variables behave . . . as predicted by theory, then it does not matter if that theory is consistent with the conceptions of the culture in which it is tested, or foreign to them. Given a positive result, then both the theory itself and the practice of applying it beyond its native heath will have received support."

Generally, the quality of these investigations depends upon the ability of the investigators to enter into the philosophy and view of life of other cultures.

NOTE: Since *The Dimensions of Dreams* was first published, an overlooked book has come to my notice: *The Mystique of Dreams: A Search for Utopia through Senoi Dream Theory* (Berkeley, 1985). In it the American dream investigator Bill Domhoff gives the life and dreams of the Senoi renewed scrutiny. He finds the sources unreliable and the life of the Senoi much less rosy than described. In a concluding chapter on the efficacy of Senoi dream theory he nevertheless writes:

> The fact that Stewart's theories of dream sharing and dream control are not practiced by the Senoi or that they were embraced rather uncritically by an eager new generation of ever-hopeful Americans does not invalidate his ideas. It may be that sharing dreams is beneficial for individuals, groups, or societies. It may be that Stewart's principles of dream control are useful in ridding dream life of the aggression and

negative feelings that predominate over friendliness and positive feelings, as has been found in dreams from all over the world that have been studied systematically by Hall and others.

Domhoff also presents scattered documentation that "dream sharing" can increase creativity and reduce tensions in small groups, such as schoolchildren in small classes. As for the effects of dream control, he sets up criteria for experimental testing of Stewart's theories.

14. OTHER DIRECTIONS AND METHODS

Introduction—Dream and groups—Dream and picture therapy

INTRODUCTION

Hundreds of new forms of therapy have been developed in recent decades. However, many of these are not particularly epoch-making, specializing in aspects of already known therapies, combining two or three techniques under a new name, or being simply redundant. In this chapter I will be dealing with the main currents.

There is also a considerable overlapping of old and new theories of dream interpretation. The Italians Ernesto Rossi and Roberto Assagioli, in addition to Ann Faraday, all stand for creative and synthesizing conceptions of dreams, and even though they are splendid dream theorists their viewpoints are on the whole covered by the foregoing.

A prominent neo-Freudian psychoanalyst like Melanie Klein found that dreams continue waking thoughts that, once set in motion, press to be completed in dreams. Here we recognize Freud's assumption that the previous day's events are incorporated in dreams, Calvin Hall's and Alfred Adler's understanding of the connection between dream and waking lifestyle, and Perls's idea that dreams finish off situations that hadn't been concluded in the waking state.

Melanie Klein, going from Freud's and his daughter Anna Freud's theories of defense mechanisms, developed an *object-relation theory* that here forms a very significant psychoanalytical school. The crux of Klein's theories is that children project their own emotional states onto external objects (persons) and especially the mother. They come to partly confuse their experience of others with their own feelings. But these experiences are then assimilated again (introjected) as inner "objects" that control the child's behavior and experience. This approach is reminiscent of Jung's theory of complexes. An example of Klein's frame of reference in relation to dreams will be given in the section on dream and groups.

A school within cognition theory and psychology that has concerned itself with dreams are the French structuralists. Of these, Jean Piaget has aligned with Jung's conception that there is in man a universal predilection for forming symbols, but he has mostly treated symbols as a step in children's intellectual development. Another, Freud-inspired structuralist is Jacques Lacan, who appears to regard dreams as forms of experience that are fundamentally untranslatable to normal language. A similar conception is met with in Charles Rycroft, a former Freudian. Jung expressed this by saying that the dream is "the essentially unknown."

The German philosophical movement called the Frankfurt school has undertaken critical studies of the scientific premises of dream interpretation. With the removing of false ideologies as its ideal, the movement has concerned itself with premises, religious ideas, and prejudices that determine what science regards as being true. According to the Frankfurt school, the first (*hermeneutic*) phase of the research process consists in bursting the frameworks of these "preunderstandings." This parallels my criticism of biased (hypostatizing) dream interpretations. In the second (*quasi-naturalistic*) phase, new congruities are looked for and theories set up, the way so many dream theorists have done on the basis of clinical experience. In the third and final (*naturalistic*) phase, the work is with "object cognated" data; Calvin Hall, for example, has tried with his statistical content analyses.

In the following I will mention two new aspects of working with dreams that are of practical importance. They concern group work with dreams, and dreams and painting therapy. These areas require practical skill that could fill other books, but their significance for understanding the phenomenon dreams as such has been largely covered in the preceding section.

DREAM AND GROUPS

Dream and groups has been touched on in the section on gestalt therapy and psychodrama, as well as in connection with the Senoi of Malaya. But there are other aspects. Dreams have been used in psychoanalytic group therapies in which the individual's dreams are interpreted. Here, just as with Perls, the individual's development is taken up in group context. Another angle of approach is what dreams can say about group processes; that is, the interplay between members in a running therapy group.

Psychiatrist David Zimmermann, who leads a "Melanie Klein department" at a Brazilian hospital, has given examples of such group processes— which simultaneously can be a sampling of a Melanie Klein frame of reference. A woman group member dreamed:

> In the middle of a room there was a naked model, and everybody was painting at easels. I don't know why, but the model was myself. The model's breasts were enormous, like those on the latest Miss Universe. According to the newspapers she had them enlarged, which possibly should have disqualified the girl. In the next scene of the dream the people who had been painting were sucking the model's body.

In Melanie Klein's system the expression "the good breast" is used about the good or idealized image of the mother, and "the bad breast" stands for a negative experience of the mother. For a Kleinian, the model naturally represents "the good breast," and the image can be further transferred to the therapist. According to Zimmermann, the model therefore symbolized simultaneously patient and therapist. That the clients are painting the model is construed as meaning that psychically they are "assimilating" (introjecting) her. As the breasts are artificially enlarged, the "introjecting object" in reality gets nothing, and the participants fall on the girl in a vampirelike attempt to "destroy the object" (the mother). (The aggressive and destructive feelings toward the mother are also important factors in Kleinian theory.)

In the next group session another woman dreamed that *the group was in the middle of a session. The analyst started serving them very appetizing plates of food.* As this dream was told in the group, everyone got in a jolly mood, talking and laughing all at once. This made a participant recall Sunday dinners where Mother served such wonderful food that everybody chattered and nobody heard what the others said. The only thing that mattered was Mother's good food. Another thought of Gauguin's picture of a native woman carrying a dish of fruit close to her breasts, and so forth.

The dream and the associations were seen as an expression for the group's collective wish to relate to Zimmermann as to "a mother with buxom breasts that give them plenty of nourishment." Zimmermann would not assume that role, and the reactions to this were reflected in dreams in the subsequent session.

Even though Zimmermann appears to overinterpret so as to make everything fit into Klein's theories, and although it is possible to imagine different supplementary interpretations, there can hardly be any doubt that the two dreams deal with group processes.

Observations of the above mentioned sort have prompted some theorists to distinguish between "group dreams" and dreams that deal with the individual in the group. There is discussion as to whether dreams in a group therapy are different from dreams in individual therapy. Klein-Lipschutz thought that dreams in group therapy had something direct and childish about them, and were less "distorted" because the transference in a group therapy is less terrifying than in individual therapy. To be sure, it is also my own experience that dreams in a group therapy frequently are simpler. But this can be due to the fact that there is less time for the individual, who rather quickly learns to relate concise and intelligible dreams.

Unlike Klein-Lipschutz, classical Jungians have rejected group therapy on the grounds that it would be impossible to open for deeply personal material. Whitmont, a neo-Jungian, found that in people with a strongly intellectual defense it would be well to begin with group analysis, while persons with a feeble ego ought to have it strengthened in an individual therapy, as otherwise it would be difficult for them to preserve their integrity in the "more irrational" group process.

It is a recognized working principle that group therapists select from a dream what they find best suited to include in a session. This can be a sound practical consideration, but it also has its elements of peril. Group therapist Benjamin Fielding regarded abstractions and symbolism in dreams as a way of keeping threatening conflicts away from the consciousness, and thought that it cuts the client off from realistic interplay with others. He even developed methods for eliminating such themes. In that way the most important part of what the great dream theorists have given us the means to understand is cut away.

On the basis of the relatively modest literature on dream and groups there doesn't seem to be any reason to assume that the dream theories must be changed on any important points. Here I will simply summarize a few practical working forms which I haven't mentioned previously.

Montague Ullman, who puts less weight on expert knowledge than the Freudians and Jungians, has given a practical line of approach for dream groups. The work with the dream has three phases:

Phase I: A group member tells a dream. The others listen, can take notes, and afterward can ask questions if there is something in the dream they have missed out on. But there is no interpreting.

Phase II: The group members give expression to the most important feelings they have had while the dream was being told. Then they tell how they would construe the dream images if they themselves had dreamed them.

For example, to climb up on a hilltop: "I have a view in two directions, both ahead and back," or "I realize that what I left behind me isn't so bad." In this phase the dreamer listens, can take notes. Ullman deliberately avoids confrontation, confident that the dreamer herself will sort out what she has use for without having to defend herself. "Good" comments give the dreamer good ideas. "Wrong" comments help her decide what an image does not mean.

Phase III: Here the dreamer is again in the foreground. It is she who now must find her interpretation. The group leader helps by organizing the material. The other participants may raise questions that can put the dreamer on the right track. But in the final instance it is her own interpretation that counts.

What is new in Ullman's method is Phase II, and I think there is good sense in it, especially if the group leader isn't an "expert." It has the effect that, besides the inspiration the participants give, their projections come out in the open without their having the possibility of pressing the dreamer with them.

Ullman's view of dreams is considerably simpler than most of the other theories we have seen. Dreams are regarded as "expressions for feelings," and "feelings don't lie." "The therapeutic importance of dreams is naturally that they tell the truth." When we move from "the field of honesty" (dreams) to the waking state, we begin, without beating around the bush, balancing off what the dream told with "the social self-image we wish to preserve." And here is where the group comes into the picture. Often the group will have a leader, but Ullman stresses that "no one can be an expert in others' dreams." Symbols, in Ullman's theory, are entirely personal; only the dreamer can say what they really mean. And "when a dream is remembered the dreamer is ready to be confronted with the message it contains."

Here Ullman disregards the established knowledge about defense mechanisms, about the ego's ability to integrate, and about research into archetypal symbols.

When I myself am working with dreams in continuing groups, in order to get the greatest creative benefit from the dreams I am open for using the frames of reference and techniques mentioned until now. It might be analysis, psychodrama, gestalt, drawing, meditation, and so forth—whatever the situation calls for.

Here I will describe a special use of transference that is possible in a group. Say a woman brings a dream in that some men seem threatening while the women in the dream are sympathetic and understanding; she is likely to have more difficulty accepting comments from men in this situation. Being a male therapist, I would then, by tone and questions, try to get female participants to comment on the dream while keeping myself out. The male comments I would treat as "acting in" (see "Dream and psychodrama," chapter 5). If on the other hand the men, or a person who in particular could symbolize the analyst, are positive in the dream, I would step in more actively. I often keep in the background for a while, let the others comment, yet am closely attentive to—both in body language and verbal exchanges—what the dreamer can take in and not take in and from whom.

In addition, what is the nature of the commentors' engagement? How is their body language? Are they very emotional and persistent in their attempts to convince the dreamer of this or that explication? If they are, do they have countertransference and thus get material for understanding their own problems and dreams? In that way I don't slip so easily into countertransference problems and avoid a resistance that can delay the integration processes. It is particularly important, because the therapist's word has much greater authority than that of any of the other participants'.

With dreams where it is hard to get the dreamer to accept an interpretation or the material appears inflammable, it can be a good idea to apply Ullman's technique, as the comments will seem more noncommittal and innocuous. Another gentle technique is "sharing"; that is, after the dream has been worked through, the group participants tell about similar experiences they themselves have had and that they feel are related.

Two further examples of transference work in groups are given in chapter 7.

Besides the more direct here-and-now experience, I also ask for a written version of the dream that has been presented, so that in the classical Jungian manner I can form an idea of the way the processes are advancing.

One of the advantages of working with analysis in groups, which the neo-Jungian Edward C. Whitmont emphasizes, is that "One's groupmates can trigger complexes [by "acting in"] and can catch a broader spectrum of affects than the analyst can alone." And whereas in individual therapy it can sometimes be hard to get people to describe the everyday situations where their complexes hamper their personal relations, this is often openly and visibly lived out in relation to other group members. There is great sympathy in a group for the individual's drawbacks, because in it nobody (except the analyst) can play holier-than-thou. Also noted is that the therapist can more easily be pinned down on countertransferences and over-interpretations. My experience here, however, is that if a group therapist wishes (unconsciously, naturally) to manipulate, he has just as many strings to play on as an individual therapist. It depends which context he is most competent in.

Of the disadvantages remaining for me to mention on my own account is that seldom is there enough time for the individual, and that many people have more difficulty opening themselves in a group than in individual therapy.

Like Ullman, I believe that you can create dream groups without psychological experts; on the other hand I also think that it is well to utilize the existing expert knowledge about dreams. In my opinion it much facilitates the interpretation to have a neutral leader who doesn't bring in his own material. In our part of the world, knowledge about dreams is ever further from being a common heritage, but group work can be a step in the right direction.

<h2 align="center">DREAM AND PICTURE THERAPY</h2>

As a final supplementary method for working with dreams, I will mention *picture therapy*. Picture therapy is in itself an area with a comprehensive literature, and many different ways of working that can call for independent presentation. But just like group therapies, experiences with picture therapy don't fundamentally alter the theories on the interpretation of dreams. And so I will be brief.

To Paint a Dream

If you are going to paint or draw a dream, it will often be difficult to include all of the elements. The dream must be transferred to a different medium, an elapse of time must be transposed to a flat expanse. Difficulties of naturalistic representation can make simplification necessary; colors, style, and technique must be chosen, and so forth. In this creative process the unconscious is allowed to express itself anew. This gives an enrichment of the associative material, reinforces the dream experience, and can draw forth important factors or expand on the dream's theme.

Jung was fond of recommending to his patients that they paint their dreams. The Jungian Jolande Jacoby has provided a method that interprets the painting's elements on the basis of their location according to rules of graphology. She has also placed the person's appearance in relation to classical physiognomy. The Freudian and Jungian sciences of symbolic meanings, and color symbolism especially, are extremely useful tools. Jung thought that pictures were just as worthy expressions of the unconscious as dreams, and he has interpreted the course of the individuation process on the basis of picture series. Representing the same school, Aniela Jaffé has examined the symbols in art, and S. Bach has described the pictures of the severely mentally ill.

The Danish psychologist Hanne Hostrup Larsen has taken her point of departure in Victor Lowenfeld's studies of drawing development in children, and placed them in relation to Freud's and Erikson's psychosexual and psychosocial development stages. The writer has developed a technique that combines working with dreams, pictures, feelings, bodily sensations, and thought associations.

Here I will give some practical examples of the connection between dreams and pictures.

A fifty-three-year-old woman in a dream therapy group had an initial dream whose content can be summarized as follows:

> She ascends by a golden gleaming spiral stair (possibly of brass) together with her husband's former boss. She is thinking about whether he wants to have intercourse with her. On the way she is afraid of falling, but is happy to see that there is a banister. When she has come all the way up and in through the door she sees workmen busy. They ask who she is, and she tells them they can phone her husband (who has gone into partnership with the old boss) and get her appearance corroborated.

As it is an initial dream, we must assign it special significance, and this is confirmed by its archetypal character: it is a feminine counterpart to Wolfgang Pauli's vision of a woman on a stair. While with Pauli it was the anima that appeared as psychopomp, here it is an animus figure (the boss) who guides upward toward spiritual development. In the dream, personal elements appear, but the picture underscores precisely the impersonal in the figures. No floor has been drawn, and so the persons can fly—like angels. Blue and white colors on the workmen and on the dreamer are spiritual colors. All in all, the drawing emphasizes the archetypal and developmental in the dream, withdrawing it from the personal and sexual spheres. The main stress is thus on the woman's spiritual seeking. The dream could be regarded from various other angles, but this is sufficient here.

Another example is a woman who had a long dream in which *her analyst [me] was supposed to help her vanquish an evil witch.* Among the things we explored was the significance for her of the dream element "the witch." During the session we succeeded in placing the image of the witch in connection with various emotional states that I asked her to observe in the coming days and paint. The resulting pictures showed that the dreamer attempted to curb the feelings the witch in the dream represented. Besides depicting inner states, the pictures also corresponded to modes of behavior (to look anguished, anxious, angry, or cold) with which the dreamer could manipulate her surroundings and score neurotic gains. The pictorial representation made the dream problem graphic for the woman, and at the same time gave the analyst an unusually clear picture of the nature of the feelings she needed help with.

Finally, this example of how through combining picture therapy with bodywork it is possible to increase the ego's ability to integrate a dream content. A woman in her late thirties dreams that *she is in bed with a former lover. At one point she is afraid of AIDS, but surmounts her fear. And they enjoy themselves together.*

I asked the dreamer to draw the dream with crayon, but even though she was used to drawing during the sessions, she had difficulty getting started. The unpleasant feelings showed up as abdominal pains, among other things, so I asked her to draw her bodily sensations.

First she drew brown, then green colors radiating out from the center of the picture surface, then some red nearly heart-shaped dots. This color she began smudging out, only to come to a standstill. I could see by her body that she wasn't really engrossed in the drawing, and on giving it a closer look she thought it was too pretty. Nor did it resolve any of the abdominal tension.

I asked her to then draw the feelings that were left, and with great energy she executed two drawings with vivid red, orange, and yellow radiating from the center. The feelings that had been located especially around the solar plexus moved to the heart region and the hara chakra but were now much lighter and airier. From this point she was able to draw herself and a man nude together. In a series of thirty pictures this was the first revelation of a reconciliation of the masculine and feminine in her.

15. Multidimensional Dream Interpretation

The multidimensional nature of dreams—The multidimensional function of dreams—Multidimensional dream interpretation—Multidimensional association—An example—Theoretical and methodological considerations—The dimensions of dreams and a new world picture

THE MULTIDIMENSIONAL NATURE OF DREAMS

In the foregoing chapters I have described, analyzed, and compared theoretical and empirical material from the most important methods in historical and scientific dream investigation. I have in this process tried to be as open as possible to the insights of the various schools, and although I prefer to present their own examples, I have all the way through tested the methods in my own practice. This has required a constant confrontation with my own biases and a sharpened awareness of my preconceptions.

The knowledge about dreams has been developed through a tacking procedure or dialectic between my interpretation of the principles of each school and a more global understanding of dreams. My synthesis concerning the nature, function, and interpretation of dreams is not intended to be complete. Rather, it should be open enough to integrate new knowledge. This way of developing knowledge is in accordance with modern *hermeneutics* (the art of interpretation). The description of the various traditions can never be totally from their own point of view. It inevitably includes the new and broader horizon and is therefore to some extent a new understanding. Some of the methods have defined themselves as schools, while others have been lumped together upon examination of techniques and theoretical premises.

The first two categories include Freud's and then Jung's psychological dream theories. The third grouping, in chapter 3, while not clearly a school can nevertheless be regarded as embracing those who see dreams as being closely bound to waking lifestyle. None of these latter methods is a great theoretical system builder, but they do establish that some dreams perform cognitional work that is of practical use in the everyday here and now. To be sure, Freud and Jung also laid stress on the relationship of dreams to the immediate life situation, but it was given less significance than other aspects. As in so many areas, it is a question of overlapping methodological viewpoints.

Going further, meanwhile, a philosophically existential attitude was found to define a fourth direction whose method is claimed to be phenomenological, while clustered about a fifth are psychotherapies that lay weight on experiential procedural methods and take philosophy and theory more lightly. Gradually, as more methods were developed, there appeared a many-faceted picture of the body of dream investigation, which in spite of differences in concept showed more agreements than expected.

As each new direction examined appears to give off observations and theoretical considerations not contained in the foregoing ones, our horizon is constantly expanded with positions from which to see the latter in new perspectives. Conversely, the pioneer work of the earlier dream theorists can help us identify and cull the sports from among the newer theorizations.

Thus the first goal of *The Dimensions of Dreams* has been to survey the existing mass of material on dream investigation. The next is to inquire whether it is possible in a meaningful way to combine the various interpretational and working techniques that until now have led more or less separate existences. This possibility was demonstrated chapter by chapter with examples.

The fact is that the great dream theorists, when working in practice, are often obliged to overstep their own bounds. This is seen in their own works. And if we turn to the practical therapeutic situation, which is far less censored than the publicized accounts, I think there will be much agreement that the flexibility with regard to theory and method is many times greater.

The ideal must be a theory that can contain as many of the known data as possible and indicate guidelines for application and verification/refutation procedures that approximate the reality encountered in practice. What is desirable, then, is a new theory of the nature, function, and interpretation of dreams. But for now let us sum up what we found concerning the nature of dreams.

First of all, what is a dream?

Modern laboratory research has documented that dreams are a real phenomenon. That is to say, while we are asleep we have mental activity whose individual sequences correspond roughly to the elapse of time described in the waking state. Dreams are usually associated with a well-defined physiological state called REM sleep, but they can also appear outside it. This has given rise to the hypothesis that we are dreaming all the time, but in the waking state we have so much "noise" in our consciousness that it drowns out the dream.

A simple definition of a dream is given by Calvin Hall: "A dream is what a person describes when asked to relate a dream with the exclusion of comments and interpretations." This definition has shown its usefulness in certain scientific settings, and it demonstrates that it isn't necessary to know the dream phenomenon in its entirety in order to work with it in practice. But this is too narrow for the phenomenon I have described in the preceding chapters. The laboratory investigations establish that what we relate as a dream often is only the end of a sequence that can have lasted from a few minutes up to an hour. And so what we call the dream is a fragment taken out of a context.

In a number of methods the interpretation is inseparably bound up with the material enveloping the dream. Freud's conception of a latent dream behind a manifest facade in reality defines the dream as a combination of the associations understandable using his frame of reference. Jung in practice has his grasp of the context be determining for what the dream basically deals with, and his experience of the dream is inextricable from a sometimes profound symbolic understanding. We have also seen that experiential work like free association, active imagination, gestalt, psychodrama, bodywork, meditation, and picturework can draw out material that fits in with the dream's context and makes both Freud's association method and Jung's symbol amplification seem in some respects superficial, in others deeply penetrating.

So a dream, for most investigators, is not a clearly defined phenomenon but a combination of some clinical data and a method for working with them. Data gathering is value and/or theory laden, which is fully legitimate if in reflecting on one's premises this is acknowledged.

As for the five mainstream schools of dream interpretation, we concluded that the dream is compounded in a more complex way than any of the individual theories have so far described. A complete theory of the nature of dreams cannot be contained in the Freudians' more or less reductive system of reference, nor in the classical Jungian system where it refers to a developmental tendency or gives a didactic hint, nor in Hall's "cognitive" understanding, Adler's emotions theory, Fromm's notion that the dream speaks for itself, or Medard Boss's normative existentialism, which doesn't include associative material. Neither is Perls, for whom the dream concludes a gestalt when the five layers of the personality have been worked through, adequate for our understanding.

With Perls and with phenomenological dream understanding, we see that it is no use pretending you don't have a theory when, knowingly or not, you automatically interpret the material put forth and use this as the basis for the method used to explore the dream material.

When after examining dream interpretation new areas were involved, it turns out that the dream interpreters largely concern themselves with other layers in the material than their predecessors, and that the new discoveries don't necessarily lead to the invalidation of older findings. But although we found a wealth of frames of reference for dreams, and a tendency among younger theorists to combine them, none of them is entirely satisfactory.

In connection with dream and the body, I pointed out that at the moment a person registers a body sensation he has body consciousness. But if the body's signal is unable to be integrated in an existing interpretation of the world, it subsides in meaninglessness back into the unconscious. In the infancy of psychoanalysis a body signal had to be so strong that it produced a physical illness before it could be given a place in the psychoanalyst's— and with him the dreamer's—consciousness and self-understanding. Today a far greater spectrum of bodily expressions can be accounted for in the consciousness. This has brought us to a deepened understanding of the relationship between dream and the body.

Parapsychological material is accepted by many researchers as a part of the associative material. And here I suggested that besides the day's residues, dreams exploit not only the individual's ontogenic and phylogenetic past for building materials, but also the future. In dealing with the esoteric we were introduced to aspects of dream phenomenology that had been overlooked or declared nonexistent but which turned out to be includable in a synthesis with elements of many of the earlier theories. Old theories that birth experiences are reflected in dreams were corroborated with rebirthing and consciousness-expanding techniques. Both here and in the esoteric section it became clear that the way in which the consciousness works with dream and development has an influence on the array of dream experiences.

It must be remembered that uniting the dream theories is the fact that nearly all those who have been involved for any length of time with the collection and interpretation of dreams maintain that they throw light on fundamental psychic problems.

Theories that defense mechanisms have some significance for dream formation are supported by nearly incontrovertible evidence. On the other hand there exist innumerable documented examples that dreams are creative, prospective, and have a problem-solving tendency.

The dream ego's great continuousness with the waking ego also appears to be substantiated. On the other hand, dreams have content that isn't necessarily similar to the consciousness.

There is universal agreement concerning the high emotional intensity of dreams, and both LSD experiments and studies of psychoses indicate that normally dreams defend the consciousness against violent instinctual impulses and high-intensity archetypal symbols. Even though Freud's theory that dreams are sleep preserving doesn't hold, a compromise still seems to exist between a release of tension and a series of defense mechanisms that safeguard the ego.

As early as Jung's theory of the collective unconscious it was asserted that universal dream motifs exist, and that the culture puts its mark on dreams. Studies of dream and society show that not only individuals but an entire society can exclude certain themes from their dreams and cultivate others of more interest.

We have also seen that dreams preserve their expressive ability both under extreme social conditions and in psychotic states. Studies of dream and psychosis pointed to the necessity for mental health of having two separate experiential modes, the dreamlike and the more logically rational.

The Principle of Multidimensionality

On the basis of the above it will be agreed that the dream experience is more intense, analogous, emotionally charged, dramatic, full of images, and totality oriented than the waking experience. Moreover the material presents us with the realization that the dream can be meaningfully processed going from more theoretical and methodological angles of approach than a normally focused product of waking consciousness. It confronts us with the recurring experience that the dream contains significant and psychodynamically intense material that seems to give off more information about the personality's dynamism than our ordinary everyday thoughts.

Our analyses show us, in not always palpable ways, that the dream material is organized according to certain laws, and that the dream thus doesn't merely represent a disorganized confluence of primary process matter. The multiplicity of interpretational intakes naturally parallels, in other areas too, the obtaining of differing results with different kinds of measuring apparatus. This is obviously so, but it doesn't explain why in psychodynamic psychotherapy dreams are preferred to using a consciously formulated statement that, after all, could be analyzed with the same methods.

No, there is a fundamental difference that must be included. It is as if dreams' dynamism and meaning is "folded into" the dream narrative we are first presented with, and as if it first unfolds through the creative process of dream interpretation. As dream theorists from Freud onward have experienced, this unfolding is most voluminous in ratio to the presented material.

True, all of the interpreters we have dealt with regard the symbol as a complex entity, although their understanding of this complexity isn't altogether congruent. While Freud regarded the symbol as an "overdetermined" disguise and Jung saw it as an energy transformer, Hall asserted that it was a compressed stenographic language. In using the experiential therapies, Jung's energetic viewpoint was demonstrated in unexpected ways. The expressive work showed that dream symbols can release tremendous emotional energy and unfold entire dramas from the person's inner world in the here and now. In Stanislav Grof and Jes Bertelsen we encountered an increased understanding of the "multilayered nature" of dreams and symbols, along with an idea of the greater information density in the symbol, which can be perceived from several angles.

My proposal for an integration of these viewpoints is that the dreams and their symbols present us with an information set that both in terms of cognition/intelligence and emotion/energy is highly compressed, and that certain properties of the state of consciousness in which the dream process takes place make this possible.

The individual symbol or element in the dream is, according to most investigators, encumbered with clusters of connotations of varying intensity. My hypothesis is that in the dream a symbol's many connotations are used intelligently, deliberately, and, if you will, purposefully. If, for instance, a steeple and a penis associate to each other—to use a famous dispute between Freud and Jung—it isn't necessarily a question of whether the steeple symbolizes a penis (Freudian) or whether a penis can symbolize a steeple (Jungian). Rather, the associations to the dreams may show that the two phenomena are connected in the dreamer's psyche, and we might in the therapeutic process—be it analytic, expressively, bodily, or imaginatively—get information as to the energy charge in each of these connotations. Thus different interpretations can cohere in a state of tension whose strength can only be determined by a psychic process.

But how is it possible for the psyche to keep house with such complex patterns of information and creativity?

Recent years' investigationof artificial intelligence and comparisons with human brain activity provide some interesting analogies. The brain consists of hundreds of millions of processing units, and each of them has thousands of connections to other units. In contrast to the old-fashioned serial computer, which works with inferences as in logic, it is more likely that the brain performs its complex perception and thought operations parallel. In other words, it processes a mass of information simultaneously, and instead of using logical rules has various restrictions as to what constitutes a sensible solution that can trigger a decision. Here it is the strength or weakness between the individual connections that determines the result. Correspondingly, I think that the dream's effect on the mind depends on the distribution of energy in symbols and patterns.

In the classical theories the ego and the consciousness are a relatively static system, in contrast to the violent dynamic forces of the unconscious. But the consciousness could just as well be understood as a dynamic system, maintaining itself by a constant addition of tasks and collapsing when those tasks are withheld—as in sleep, when all the emancipated energy makes possible a profusion of other mental activity.

Recent studies have shown that the brain can perform hundreds of billions of operations a second (Campbell, 1990). And a well-founded axiom of depth psychology has been that energy can be displaced among various psychic contents and moved from the body to the psyche and back again. It has been proved that even though normal thought activity, the entire sensory system, and the motor system are disengaged during REM sleep, the brain is still physiologically fully active at all levels. Proceeding from an ordinary knowledge of biology, it is hard to imagine that such activity would not take place under suitable forms. It is my suggestion, therefore, that the surplus information-processing capacity is synthesized in cumulative introspective processes that generate the complex patterns characteristic of dreams. These are an important part of the psychic processes' total ecology.

To use another image, seen from the viewpoint of the waking consciousness, it is as though the world where dreams take place is a universe having many dimensions being experienced from a universe having fewer dimensions. In another connection, the American nuclear physicist and philosopher David Bohm has tried to give "an intuitive sense" of what is meant by this. He uses a setup that I will improvise on in order to illustrate the *multidimensional dream theory*.

Imagine an aquarium with fish that are being regarded by two TV cameras. The two screens show different pictures but refer to the same event. We can say that the two TV pictures represent two different views or conceptions, two frames of reference seeing the same phenomenon from different positions. They will overlap, but seen from the two-dimensional universe there will be definite differences. Meanwhile, by rising to a higher spatial dimension—here three dimensions—we obtain a more complete picture. It then appears that neither of the two TV cameras is recording the entire truth, but that each by itself gives important information about what is taking place.

Let us imagine that in some sense or other dreams exist in a multidimensional experiential universe. We then have a model for explaining the contradictions that in the light of our investigation seem excessive, and why it gives meaning to apply several frames of reference to the same dream. This isn't to claim that the dream's multidimensional experiential form is intrinsically more valuable than a waking experience. The advantage of the two TV cameras is that they can analyze part aspects more thoroughly, that they can zoom in, freeze the picture, or do an instant replay—all parallels to the way in which the waking consciousness regards dreams.

There can be good reasons for studying the fish from in front. But it is unreasonable to denounce he who views them from the side as being unscientific or somehow ignorant.

THE MULTIDIMENSIONAL FUNCTION OF DREAMS

In scientific theory the concept of function is associated with causal relations between two or more entities. Very simply, the concept "the function of dreams" can be translated to: "dreams have the effect that . . . ," and their effect might be that you sleep better, that you become more whole, etc. Freud set the tone by defining function as the "reason why we should dream" (see "The nature and function of dreams in Freud," chapter 1). With this he established a utilitarian outlook and besides conceived the function of dreams as something positive. Adler and Jung developed their compensation concepts on the basis of physiology and likewise understood their practical function. This pragmatic and rather uncomplicated view has since been assumed by the majority. It's as if you are saying, "I can use dreams for this purpose, ergo dreams have the function of serving this purpose."

That dreams are useful in one or several ways has been supported by the fact that you dream two hours each night, and it is biologically improbable that a species possesses such a time-consuming activity without it having an expedient function. Here I will enumerate a number of the supposed functions of dreams that, while none of them can claim a monopoly, are all based on methodically gathered data and logical discussion.

Dreams function as a safety valve and, as mentioned earlier, defend the consciousness against unconscious material (Freud). They are compensatory (Jung), and they build up the ego and process and solve emotional problems (the neo-Freudians, Adler, Fromm). Dreams can adjust the person to important life transitions such as mid-life crisis (Jung) and death (Jung, von Franz). Early ego development (Neumann) and the consolidation of masculine and feminine sexual identity (Vedfelt, Skogemann) can also be anticipated in dreams. Dreams thereby schedule the individual for inner transformations (Jung) and social life tasks. They furnish the dreamer with a creative ego (Dieckmann) and finish off unconcluded situations (Perls). Dreams even in the fetal stage serve as mental training and preliminary exercise; they preprogram instinctive and archetypal patterns (Jouvet, Jung, Watson), they share in maintaining the body image and sense of movement (Lerner), and they supply us with information about bodily processes and physical illness.

Laboratory research has for the most part regarded the function of dreams as adaptation to the surroundings: they consolidate ego functions like learning, mastery of situations, and problem solving. This research has made it even more probable that dreams have important functions regardless of whether we recall them or not, which is also implied in Freud's safety-valve function, Jung's autonomous processes, Adler's conception of dreams, and Perls's theories.

Dreams moreover promote psychological and intellectual development, both in the Western sense as individuation (Jung) and in combination with Eastern meditation systems (Bertelsen).

Other functions are to reexperience the birth trauma (Rank), as a necessity for human survival (Snyder), and for a social vigilance (Ullman). Dreams reflect both repressions and development potentials in a society and have been used for both socially constructive and socially renewing activities. A few dream theorists as a matter of principle do not ascribe any function to dreams but nevertheless think they can be used to improve our self-knowledge (Hillman) or our interplay with our surroundings (Boss).

Seen in relation to the earlier more or less "monofunctional" dream theories, a synthesis of the above possible functions is naturally a big mouthful. On the other hand, it might be asked what is to hinder dreams—just like the waking state—from handling many functions, and why so complex a system as the waking consciousness shouldn't have a just as complex counterpart.

The most controversial subjects are the parapsychological observations that ascribe to dreams communication functions across boundaries of time and space, and prediction of concrete future events. For those who would exclude the occurrence of any such thing we have left open the possibility of regarding these phenomena as associative empirical data relative to the dreams.

The idea of most psychotherapeutic dreamwork techniques is to reinforce the positive functions assigned to dreams so that the waking consciousness can make use of them.

A weakness of the function theories is that they are not so much derived from the dreams themselves as from the investigators' systems of interpretation. However, the concept of function has made it possible to summarize and pass on a number of important findings in dreamwork, making it reasonable to uphold it. Still, in the future it would be important to obtain a clearer distinction between the conception of dreams' usefulness for us as psychotherapists and ordinary dreamers and their more autonomous functions in the ecology of the human organism. In this case we could abandon oversimplified notions about function that don't harmonize with the complexity of the phenomenon. Instead, the function of dreams could be pluralized and incorporated in a multidimensional understanding.

MULTIDIMENSIONAL DREAM INTERPRETATION

The word *interpretation* has been used in connection with dreams principally in an intellectual and explanatory sense. But let us, at least tentatively, expand it to cover any meaningful further processing of dreams, be it explanatory, dramatized, painted, bodily, or whatever expression that makes it possible to unfold what we can regard as "enfolded" aspects of the dream. Interpretation can then be understood in a creative and artistic sense—

which doesn't prevent us from subjecting an interpretation to scientific scrutiny.

Dreams can be understood and processed on many levels and proceeding from many different experiences of reality. The simplest but not necessarily the poorest way is to let their special kind of experiencing into waking life by being attentive to them, thinking about them, improvising on them, painting them, and so on, without referring to any systematic method. We have seen with the Jungians, and in connection with later psychological studies, that simple mindfulness of dreams can develop personality. (A more questionable way is to bring the creativity of dreams into daily life through REM-sleep deprivation in uncreative persons; see "The psychological significance of the amount of dreaming," chapter 6.)

Sharing dreams with others—simply telling them—can have a helpful effect. It can take place in groups, but it would be advisable to use a method that avoids as much as possible getting stuck in transferences and countertransferences. This can be under a therapist's guidance or with a neutral group leader, such as Montague Ullman suggests. Another method is for an expert from a single frame of reference to help in processing the dream material. As we have seen, this can be effective and contribute to development and self-insight in the dreamer.

But if the system of reference is narrow, we can't exclude the criticism that has been aimed at psychoanalysis: that the main worth of interpretation is to furnish the dreamer with "a frame of reference from which he feels he is able to control what is happening with him." Viewed positively, one of its strengths is that the expert has a wide-ranging training and clinical tradition, and experience of the lines he must draw for his intervention in the dreamer's psyche under the given conditions. Dreamwork without thorough training can, on the contrary, be problematic if someone sets himself up as an expert and gets a dreamer to believe it. A transference is established which can get the dreamer to let go of more of himself than the interpreter can handle. It becomes more complicated if, as our examples have demonstrated, we let the different methods of interpretation enter into creative syntheses. In the long run I believe it will be discovered, as the necessary skills are acquired, that such a method is more naturally in keeping with the mercurial nature of dreams and associations, and that ambiguousness can be turned to advantage and provide a flexibility that is important in the therapeutic situation.

Creative syntheses can be understood in two ways. In the first the various

methods of interpretation are regarded as different fishing tackle that gives
different catches. In the second we will further develop the assumption that
the particular interpretation and working methods are different perspectives
from which we can discern a multidimensional universe of experience.

MULTIDIMENSIONAL ASSOCIATION

Associations to the dreams allow us to contact the layers of the personality,
which are not accessible in the normal conscious waking state but are assumed to be bring us closer to the meaning of the dreams.

In classical psychoanalysis, if you ask a dreamer to give associations he
will report associations of ideas, but often they will be related by rote and
without emotional involvement. This can be because the ego automatically
continues doing what it has been asked to do, while the flow of psychic
energy set in motion in working with dreams goes elsewhere. This will often
be shown when the body begins sending signals (see "Dream and body
language," chapter 7). Or, when an image replaces a thought, it can be
followed up in a series of fantasy images as in active imagination. But again
it will be apparent that the efforts lack involvement, because the energy
jumps from image formation to bodily sensation to an outer sensing or to an
association of ideas.

One way image and bodily sensation can be connected is by having the
dreamer express what he associates with colors on paper. Perhaps the image
gives rise to a bodily sensation, and the bodily sensation to a new drawing
or a chain of thought. ("Dream and picture therapy," chapter 14, gives an
example of the progression: dream—bodily sensation—image—feeling—
thought.) Added to this can be any form of experience work, body therapy,
meditation, or consciousness-expanding techniques.

Such associations are not produced at random, but they follow laws other
than rational thinking. In my book *Consciousness* I have described how body
signals, imagery, feelings, etc. can be understood as different ways of processing information. And in a work in preparation I am outlining a theory
that accounts for the relation between dream, associations, and personality.
This is outside the scope of the present book, though.

Important here is that associations can have varying depth and thus relate
to various strata of the multilayered material that belongs to the dream.

Transference is significant to associations too. In classical psychoanalysis
the therapeutic situation was comparatively neutral. But as seen in Perls,
the therapist's intervention can have a decisive influence on the chain of

associations. The same applies to touching. Even the therapist's physical proximity to the client is important for what thoughts she can permit to come to expression in a given situation.

An interpretation that observes the dream's emotional energy and is not merely intellectual will benefit by being able to jump from one experiential dimension to the other—this we would call a multidimensional association method. Such a method doesn't disclose any definitive interpretation of the dream. What our investigations have made clear is that, consciously or unconsciously, the interpreter is proceeding from some frames of reference. What happens in working with the dream is that the dreamer and/or the interpreter, on the basis of their backgrounds, form ideas about which path to pursue. These ideas become a guideline for the exploration of the material.

An extreme is Calvin Hall's dream series analyses, in which the dreamer's contribution is written material that is analyzed without his further help. Another extreme is in experience work or free association, where the dreamer's experience occupies the foreground with the least possible comment.

The interpreter's sense of what direction exploration of the material is to take can be conveyed in many ways: through symbol translation or referring to frames of reference; through feedback, active listening, empathy, telepathy, or even the appearance and spontaneous body attitudes of the dreamer; plus through the transference the latter has to him.

In practice a multidimensional association not only brings out material for understanding the dream, it also sets off a dynamic process. An important advance would therefore be to develop and discuss rules for a multidimensional association method.

AN EXAMPLE

Earlier we saw examples of interpretation combining different methods. Now I will give a hypothetical example of a dream with suggestions for some of the possibilities that might be explored, all according to what the situation called for.

A fifty-year-old woman had the following dream:

> I am lying sleeping in my newly renovated house. I am awakened by a terrible storm. The house is being destroyed. The new floor bulges from the marsh of water underneath. All at once a plane lands and out come

three men in white suits. They sit down in my kitchen as though nothing had happened, they take the food in my refrigerator as I stand speech-lessly looking on. None of them comes to my aid. Outside it appears that the house is all the way down by the sea. The ground is marshy and all soft from the storm. I walk out in the sea and it's unpleasant. Somebody says that it's polluted.

The woman had tension and pain across the small of the back for a period, but around the time of the dream it loosened up.

Let's begin by viewing the dream from a Freudian angle. The theory entitles us to certain expectations. The storm and rain that swamps the ground, the men who intrude into the house, and their helping themselves from the refrigerator could be sexual symbolism, possibly disguising a sexual wish for the father. That contact with the men is so sporadic, and the sexual motives spread throughout the dream, could reflect the dreamer's experience of how the father related to the mother or to herself. Moreover, in this food problem we can see a reference to the oral stage. The soft mud, on the other hand, can refer to an anal problem. Using our knowledge of psychosexual and psychosocial development stages we can investigate the possible causes of the conflict in her early childhood. Regarding transference, we must ask whether the woman relates to a male therapist like she relates to the men in the dream; that is, if is it hard for her to believe that they will get involved and help her.

What is decisive, however, is that we divide the dream up into elements and have the dreamer freely associate from them. Which interpretation we arrive at depends on the sequence of the associations. But our supplemen-tary questions, feedback, or even silence is determined by our knowledge.

A Jungian interpretation starts by establishing a context. Besides asso-ciations, which don't go as far as Freud's, it examines what took place the day before, then looks at the dream as a step in a series, amplifies the separate dream elements with mythological parallels, and surveys the dream's dramatic structure. The dream's starting situation is that the woman is sleeping in her newly renovated house. Its main conflict is the storm that threatens to destroy the house. The problem culminates when the men crowd inside her house and instead of helping her, help themselves to food from her refrigerator. The solution is vague: she walks out in the sea but is warned that it is polluted.

The dreamer apparently doesn't have real contact with her masculine side and what it symbolizes of constructive initiative, dynamism, spirituality, and so on. The solution she chooses in the dream isn't good. The opening indicates that she must salvage the development of her consciousness through contact with her animus, but she walks out in the sea, the unconscious.

In Neumann's stages for development of the feminine consciousness, the dream corresponds to "intrusion by the masculine." The ground and the refrigerator are mother symbols. Again we can go back to childhood, explore her experience of the relation to the mother, and examine how the stage in question went off for her. And we can look at how it is active in her now.

The flooding motif, the masculine intrusion, and the raging elements all give the dream an archetypal character. It is therefore a particularly important dream.

We will look at what connection it has to the previous day's events but will place special weight on its development aspect. The masculine storm's raging over the two feminine elements, the water and the earth, can be regarded as fertilization symbolism. But as it concerns impersonal elements it must be a question of processes that are beyond the ego's and the consciousness's control. The three men are human beings and represent contents closer to consciousness. Fertilization from masculine to feminine is therefore more intense in the unconscious than the consciousness. On a deeper unconscious level a fertilization actually occurs that can herald "the meeting with the man" on the conscious level. We have only to expect that some time passes before it can be integrated.

The newly renovated house presumably symbolizes the positive result of the woman's working with personality development. It is evidence of a progression. The refuge in the sea—the collective unconscious—is a regression, however, a step backward. Perhaps the preceding and subsequent dreams will give us more detailed information about which areas of life in particular are touched on, as well as constructive ideas for how the conflict can be solved. We can also, with active imagination, let the dreamer imagine herself into the dream again and try to create a more satisfactory solution. The water she walks out in is, moreover, polluted. Perhaps we will advise her to go back and solve the conflict in the house, which symbolically can be conceived as a condition for the pollution.

From the dream ego's behavior our guess is that a favorite defense mechanism is to avoid conflicts. In the continuing dream therapy we will see these interpretations invalidated or substantiated by the Jungian methods while keeping a running check on the progress. We will also have a look at how the dream reflects the woman's lifestyle. To get reliable information it will be necessary to examine a dream series and eventually make content analyses of the elements in accordance with Hall's instructions. But let's say that the dream is typical for the woman. Then she is living a stormy life. Her relations to men is depicted in the way she lets them dine from her refrigerator. She demands nothing in return. If the men's invasion of the refrigerator is a sexual symbol, Calvin Hall would ask why she doesn't choose a sword in a scabbard or ordinary sexual intercourse. It must have more meanings. Frigidity? (If the icebox contains other than cold cuts.) Does she experience her own sexuality as something stationary that must be opened up?

A phenomenological consideration avoids the frames of reference I have mentioned till now. With Medard Boss we are interested in renovatedness, storminess, refrigeratorness, and pollution as existential phenomena. We could carry out a reframing of the content and say: "It's so good that renewal plays such a large role in your dreams, but doesn't it make you worry that you don't ask for help when you need it? I also think it is very positive that you have something to give others. The refrigerator is a very practical arrangement, because it permits keeping food fresh until it is to be used— and so you have a tool for administering your own resources. So why don't you let the men give something before they get?"

We can also merely keep this strategy in mind and settle for backing such thoughts and feelings up if they appear in working with the dream.

If we tackle it more experientially, we can explore the dream elements' significance for the dreamer by having her act them either gestalt therapeutically or in a psychodrama: What is it like being a floor bulging from water? Have her feel the power there is in being a storm, the men, or the refrigerator, in order to make it possible for her to get in contact with these sides of herself.

If we work creatively we will meet with surprises, so the separate elements reveal entirely different levels of meaning or lead us to traumatic experiences that otherwise would remain undisclosed.

An experience-oriented method wouldn't be so concerned with whether the dream's "solution" is good or poor: it indicates a universal human situation, and how the dreamer copes with it is her here-and-now responsibility. From a Jungian viewpoint the dream's conclusion points at a regression (seeking refuge in the sea, the unconscious), which makes it difficult to use the developmental progress (the newly renovated house) to the ego's advantage. We now turn this to an advantage in that we let the dreamer experience the full consequence of the urge to regression. We go along with the resistance, confront her with all the evasions, and work through the "neurotic strata" so she gets in contact with the vital layer. If it goes well, an uncompleted gestalt will be finished off, and the emotional release will make it possible for her to regard the dream and its correlation with her life more clearly.

During this work we can consider bodily sensations and body language, amplification of the pains across the small of the back or other symptoms, plus a combination with picture therapy. Further, we can combine it with one or another specific body therapy.

As the dream is so archetypal it can be relevant to look at its relationship to chakra symbolism. The elements air, water, and earth are represented here, and the dissolving of the ground could correspond to the dissolving of the blockage in the lower part of the body, which actually took place in the case of the woman. If there is to be meditative work, the element air corresponds to the heart chakra, the element water to the hara chakra, and the element earth to the root chakra. We can, moreover, locate the dream in the volcanic birth matrix, which Grof has described, and possibly work through it in a rebirthing seance. We do not content ourselves with experience work alone, but regard it as a potential part of multidimensional associating, and we see to it that the results are incorporated into a more insightful understanding of the dream that connects them with concrete events in the dreamer's daily life. Which methods we choose will depend on defense mechanisms and on the ego's ability to integrate at the given time, together with what we have worked with in her earlier.

Practical, external circumstances around the dreamwork play a role: How much time is there? Is it group or individual? How often do we meet? What are her possibilities for working further? What is the therapist good at? And so forth.

If the dream is typical for her we will be able to get much information for diagnosing the woman's personality. We obtain insight into her past and an idea of her future prospects. But the dream isn't a perfectly objective and well-defined quantity. There is no absolute context. On the contrary, multidimensional input turns it into an extensive project for self-exploration.

Naturally we can't present the dreamer with all of these suggestions at once. In practice we must at one point close off the interpretation and choose an aspect to work with. But the method will—and this is important—avoid stereotype interpretations.

In the ideal dreamwork, the interpreter's system of references is the most comprehensive possible and his mind is cleansed of unresolved feelings and dogmatic attitudes. He allows himself to imagine what expansion of consciousness will be most profitable for the dreamer, and acknowledges that he has such ideas. But he is also prepared at any time to switch conceptions and follow the process in other directions. In that way the dreamer's self-understanding, her work, and her associations enter into a creative dialogue with the interpreter's resources. Each dream interpretation then becomes a creative act in which dreamer and interpreter work jointly. Both parties venture to let their wealth of ideas come to expression, both take risks and make choices, and both are responsible for the direction the work takes. But as they are open for the responsibility they now assume, it isn't hard, if the old one didn't lead to change, to take responsibility for a new interpretation.

And so to interpret becomes a creative unfolding of the dream's implicit dynamism and meaning.

THEORETICAL AND METHODOLOGICAL CONSIDERATIONS

It isn't hard to demonstrate that the great pioneers of modern dream interpretation constructed their theories very much as creative syntheses of already existing knowledge. This has been obscured by polemic and the urge to highlight one's own method at the expense of competitors. The empirical material was largely their clients', which makes their contributions correspondingly modest. Meanwhile, the experience of later generations not only contributed to substantiating a number of basic assumptions within the individual schools, but has more and more begun bridging the old gaps.

The total dream material has not been evaluated from standardized premises but from a broad spectrum of the methods and ideals of scientific theory. Psychoanalytical observations are regarded as a combination of clinical science and hermeneutics, but methods from comparative religious history and phenomenology have also been used. Characteristic of most dream theories is that they practically take it for granted that dream activity is controlled by a few simple principles. This applies to both the dream process's psychological "mechanisms" as well as to their function.

With Freud, Jung, and most of their successors, the dreams themselves have been used to create a psychological theory, and then when the theory is established the dreams become a means of substantiating it. At the same time, data which didn't fit the pattern was sifted out. This is plain from a number of our interpretation examples (Freud, Vanggaard, Jung, Hall, and others).

It is striking that the theoretical models have often been transposed from altogether different scientific areas like physics, physiology, gestalt psychology, etc., but that possible mismatches haven't also been taken into account. Besides, in attempting to cover the phenomena they describe the models have been stretched thin. Something else that appears from our inquiry is that variations in philosophical background can lead to openness toward different aspects of the dreams, so you see different patterns in the material while substantiating the observations through altered input conditions.

The starting point for my own observations has been multitheoretical. That is, I acknowledged that there can be more than one good theory and that theories can have different areas of validity and application. To be sure, this attitude presupposes a thorough familiarity with what separates the theories and where they can supplement each other, as well as a knowledge of what different theorists read into related subjects. This as opposed to eclecticism, which is an uncritical rehashing of mutually conflicting theories.

To be desired is a theoretical metalanguage, which in a neutral and responsible way can embrace all of the phenomena that have been seriously described during nearly a century of modern dream investigation. But one doesn't exist, and I will maintain that it is possible to conduct fruitful investigation anyway.

Within other areas of inquiry, such as physics, there has also been a lack of "a combined theory." But researchers have "instead made progress by finding part theories which describe a limited assortment of events, and by ignoring other effects or approximating them," to quote Stephen Hawking, one of the leading astrophysicists of our time.

A combined theory naturally has many advantages, both because it is a simpler tool and because it can more easily be made the object of discussion and criticism. But just as the stars and planets are still in motion regardless of a missing unity in physics, so too does dream life go on. Dreams are being worked with in and outside of therapies and often with fruitful results. In the present mishmash of theories it is my hope that *The Dimensions of Dreams* will be a practical tool for the working therapist and important to the ongoing theoretical debate.

A unifying theory would require a new Archimedian point from which the old theories and their empirical material could be regarded. It would doubtless require more complex and dynamic models for the dream processes's mental activity, and for consciousness in general. It would also call for at least an outline of a unified theory of personality, as well as a more specified method of multidimensional associations. We would need rules for a combined method of therapy and observation that revise and expand psychoanalytic technique to include a variety of the approaches described. In the end this might lead to a new theory of knowledge. Here I think that the development in scientific theory we have witnessed in recent decades will prove to be of use.

A recurring image in these pages is that dreams are like a multidimensional universe that contains an enfolded meaning and dynamics which can be unfolded in the creative process of dream interpretation. The writing of *The Dimensions of Dreams* has provided stuff for a theory whose point of departure is that image.

I have in my book *Consciousness* created a new comprehensive "cybernetic" theory of the multilayered consciousness, using system and information theories as the theoretical framework. In these are also laid the foundations of a multidimensional theory of association.

A book on theory of personality by the author is currently being prepared.

THE DIMENSIONS OF DREAMS AND A NEW WORLD PICTURE

In recent years there has been much discussion of a new paradigm—that is to say, a new outlook and mode of thinking in science, art, and ordinary life. In the traditional scientific world picture, the universe is a senseless motor and living organisms are regarded as closed systems that, in keeping with the laws of thermodynamics, progress from order to disorder until all processes die out. This model for understanding, meanwhile, has obscured an understanding of the emergence of new structures and functions that occur everywhere in nature, and that have resulted in the evolution of ever higher forms of life, interwoven in immensely complex and finely balanced ecological patterns.

Mechanistic functions are based on linear chains of cause and effect. But such models fall short of explaining the ever more complex structures discovered in modern research the deeper it penetrates the mysteries of nature. The new sciences—inspired by system philosophy—are finding that living organisms are better understood as complex and layered structures, with cross-connected communication paths and such qualities as self-organization, self-renewal, and the creative potential to develop toward higher levels.

Parallel with the understanding of the creativity and complexity in nature, a new conception of the mind has begun to assert itself. Formerly *mental, psychic*, or *spiritual* processes were regarded as reserved for human beings. But long before any human consciousness became capable of reflecting on itself and the world, nature had been through a process of creation far more complex than anything the best human means can approximate. Biologists now speak of cognition as a basic characteristic of life, and declare that "mind" is part and parcel of all organisms, knowing, deciding, remembering, and communicating. Leading physicists are working with concepts like meaning, information, and implicit order at the subatomic level. It is possible to imagine such an interpretation including communication between cells, tissues, organs, and psychic structures on numerous levels, and the mind—which can't be placed unequivocally in a particular physical or psychic location—functioning in psychosomatic unities.

There is a remarkable similarity between this view of nature and the structures and processes we read in dreams. The polysemous, multidimensional, and intensely meaningful patterns formed by dreams and their associative networks appear to reflect complex, layered, and cross-connected psychosomatic unities. They display spontaneous creativity related not only to the conscious ego's narrow objectives but to the total ecology of the human organism. Dream investigation and the new sciences will undoubtedly be able to learn much from each other, and the functional mode of the dreaming consciousness will be able to shed new light on the nature of consciousness in general.

Scientific history is full of examples of how innovative thinking like the above is dependent on the overall development in the sciences, as well as being contingent on the mental climate as a whole. In our culture the collapse of the old world picture is connected with the philosophical laying to rest of positivism, with the longing for coherence in a split world and with the acknowledgment of the ecological *Götterdämmerung* that can be a consequence of the mechanistic view of nature.

While previously life and evolution were understood in terms of the Hobbesian "every man against every man," now attention is increasingly focused on nature's capacity for synthesis and ecological collaboration. As opposed to the fragmented world picture of traditional science there is a widespread effort to establish a holistic view of the world as one vast living organism with interplay on all levels, from inorganic matter over biological structures to the human psyche and society, to the biosphere and the entire cosmos.

In accounting for new discoveries, this century's many movements in dream analysis tend to overemphasize differences and oppose syntheses. They split up into mutually contending schools and so contribute to a fragmenting of life that all of them, when all is said and done, are a protest against. *The Dimensions of Dreams*, with its integrating approach and method, will here make its contribution to the new world picture—the contours of which we can still only glimpse.

NOTES

1. FREUD AND THE NEO-FREUDIANS

p. 1 *Freud claimed* Thomas French and Erika Fromm, *Dream Interpretation: A New Approach* (New York, London: Basic Books, 1964), 118–20.

p. 1 *interpretation . . . is not enough* Sigmund Freud, *Beyond the Pleasure Principle* (1922), 29–30.

p. 1 *neurotic symptoms to dreams* Sigmund Freud, *The Interpretation of Dreams* (London: Hogarth Press, 1981), 101–2.

p. 1 *"unveiled the mystery of dreams"* Erik H. Erikson, "The Dream Specimen of Psychoanalysis," *Journal of the American Psychoanalytic Association* 2 (1954): 7.

p. 2 *his most important work* Ernest Jones, *The Life and Works of Sigmund Freud* (New York: Basic Books, 1984), 299; Sigmund Freud, "Revision of the Theory of Dreams," in *New Introductory Lectures on Psychoanalysis*, Standard Edition, vol. XXII (London: Hogarth Press, 1964).

p. 2 *Freud constantly revised his concepts* Sigmund Freud, *A Metapsychological Supplement to the Theory of Dreams*, Standard Edition, vol. XIV (London: Hogarth Press, 1957), 219; Sigmund Freud, *The Ego and the Id*, Standard Edition, vol. XIX (London: Hogarth Press, 1961); Freud, "Theory of Dreams."

p. 2 *one can symbolize another* Charles Rycroft, *A Critical Dictionary of Psychoanalysis* (New York: Penguin Books, 1979), 66.

p. 2 *corresponding to the unconscious* Charles Brenner, *An Elementary Textbook of Psychoanalysis* (New York: Doubleday, 1974); Ole Andkjær Olsen, et al, *Metapsykologi II. Indledning til Metapsykologisk supplement til drømmelæren* (Metapsychology I. Introduction to the metapsychological supplement to the theory of dreams) (Copenhagen: Hans Reitzels Forlag, 1983).

p. 3 *conscious thought processes* Freud, *Interpretation of Dreams*, 76.

p. 3 *to preserve sleep* Humberto Nagera, *Basic Psychoanalytic Concepts on the Theory of Dreams* (London: Marcsfield Reprints, 1981), 15–18.

p. 3 *free association* Freud, *Interpretation of Dreams*, 101–2.

p. 4   *parents are involved in it*   Ibid., 584–85.

p. 4   *distinction on the official*   Ibid., 137–38, 145.

p. 5   *psychically significant sources*   Nagera, *Basic Psychoanalytic Concepts*, 19–22.

p. 5   *in disguised form*   Freud, *Interpretation of Dreams*, 183–85.

p. 6   *at the time*   Ibid., 189.

p. 6   *very early in childhood*   Ibid., 203.

p. 6   *copious material for dreams*   Ibid., 183–85.

p. 6   *most important*   Nagera, *Basic Psychoanalytic Concepts*, 15–18.

p. 7   *the dream's meaning*   Freud, *Interpretation of Dreams*, 282.

p. 7   *smooth facade*   Nagera, *Basic Psychoanalytic Concepts*, 62–68.

p. 7   *". . . future tense"*   Freud, *Interpretation of Dreams*, 97–98.

p. 8   *through interpretation*   Ibid., 100.

p. 8   *language of dreams becomes*   Nagera, *Basic Psychoanalytic Concepts*, 77.

p. 8   *solutions were uncommon*   Samuel D. Lipton, "Freud's Position on Problem Solving in Dreams," *British Institute of Medical Psychology* 40 (1967): 147–49.

p. 9   *placed over there*   Freud, *Interpretation of Dreams*, 465.

p. 9   *positive notions*   Ibid., 468–70.

p. 10   *he must die*   Ibid., 472.

p. 10   *his theoretical system*   Nagera, *Basic Psychoanalytic Concepts*, 103.

p. 11   *true wish motif*   Freud, *Interpretation of Dreams*, 155–57.

p. 11   *preconscious forces in the psyche*   Ibid., 473.

p. 11   *wakes up with renewed terror*   Freud, *Pleasure Principle*, 25–26.

p. 12   *". . . wish fulfillment"*   Nagera, *Basic Psychoanalytic Concepts*.

p. 12   *generally not recommended*   Ibid., 96.

p. 12   *second place to free association*   Ibid.

p. 12   *Fräulein Weiss*   Freud, *Interpretation of Dreams*, 411–12.

p. 13   *knowledge of the theory*   Erikson, "Dream Specimen," 6.

p. 13   *compared dreams to the creative process*   Ibid.; Richard M. Jones, *Egosynthesis in Dreams* (Cambridge, Mass.: Shenkman, 1962); Ernest Kris, "On Preconscious Mental Processes," in *Psychoanalytic Explorations in Art* (International University Press, 1962), 303–18.

p. 13   *meaningful statement in itself*   Erikson, "Dream Specimen"; Robert I. Langs, "Manifest Dreams in Adolescents: A Controlled Pilot Study," *The Journal of Nervous and Mental Disease* 145, no. 1 (1987): 43–52; Robert I. Langs, "Day Residues, Recall Residues, and the Dreams,"

Journal of the American Psychoanalytic Association 19 (1971): 499–523; L. J. Saul, "Utilization of Early Current Dreams in Formulating Psychoanalytic Cases," *Psychoanal. Quarterly* 9 (1940): 453–69; Hermann Schultz, *Zur diagnostischen und prognostischen Bedeutung des Initialtraumes in der Psychotherapie* (On the diagnostic and prognostic significance of initial dreams in psychotherapy) (diss., Universität Ulm, 1969), 93.

p. 13 *during the different development stages*   Rycroft, *Dictionary of Psychoanalysis*, 28.

p. 13 *furthered by the neo-Freudians*   Brenner, *Textbook of Psychoanalysis*, 152.

p. 13 *common defense mechanisms*   Anna Freud, *The Ego and the Mechanisms of Defense* (New York: International University Press, 1968).

p. 13 *especially in pathological narcissists*   Otto F. Kernberg, *Borderline Conditions and Pathological Narcissism* (New York: Jason Aronson Inc., 1981), 25–34.

p. 13 *integrated into consciousness*   Rycroft, *Dictionary of Psychoanalysis*, 28.

p. 14 *camouflaged form*   Brenner, *Textbook of Psychoanalysis*, 155.

p. 14 *the dream appears diffuse*   Ibid., 162.

p. 15 *Her anxiety subsides*   Bela Mittelmann, "Ego Functions and Dreams," *Psychological Quarterly* 18 (1949): 439–40.

p. 15 *frightening element in the dream*   R. Whitman, "Remembering and Forgetting Dreams in Psychoanalysis," *Journal of the American Psychiatric Association* 11 (1963): 752–74.

p. 15 *for that reason*   Emil A. Gutheil, *The Handbook of Dream Analysis* (New York: Liveright, 1971), 381.

p. 16 *regression for its own purposes*   Kris, "Mental Processes," 303–18.

p. 16 *integrate the dream contents*   S. A. Arlow and C. Brenner, *Psychoanalytic Concepts and the Structural Theory* (New York: International University Press, 1964).

p. 16 *unsure of himself*   Mittelmann, "Ego Functions," 434–47.

p. 17 *relevant associations*   Ibid., 436.

p. 17 *he in fact did not feel*   Ibid., 438.

p. 17 *narcissistic neuroses cases*   Mats Alveson, "Narcissisme i socialpsykologisk belysning" (Narcissism in the light of social psychology), *Nordisk Psykologi* 35, no. 2 (1983): 100–124.

p. 17 *Freud worked with most often*   Kernberg, *Borderline Conditions*.

p. 17 *"froze" with anxiety*   M. Masud R. Khan, "Dream Psychology and the Evolution of the Psychoanalytic Situation," *International Journal of Psychoanalysis* 43 (1962): 27–28.

p. 18 *transference*   Freud, *Pleasure Principle*, 29–30.

p. 18 *Wilhelm Fliess*   Khan, "Psychoanalytic Situation," 22–26.

p. 18 *physically exposed on the beach*   Schultz, *Initialtraumes*, 93.

p. 18 *narcissistic transference*   Heinz Kohut, *The Analysis of the Self* (New York: International University Press, 1983), 4–5.

p. 19 *he, too, could be afraid*   Patrick Casement, *On Learning from the Patient* (London: Tavistock, 1987), 86–87.

p. 19 *"neurosis structure"*   Saul, "Early Current Dreams."

p. 19 *results were encouraging*   Robert I. Langs, "Manifest Dreams from Three Clinical Groups," *Archive of General Psychiatry* 14 (1966): 634–43.

p. 19 *plastic clarity*   Schultz, *Initialtraumes*, 43.

p. 20 *"swallow everything raw"*   Calvin S. Hall, *A Primer of Freud's Psychology* (New York: The New American Library, 1954), 102–13.

p. 21 *tasty and rare treat*   Hans Dieckmann, *On the Methodology of Dream Interpretation*, in *Methods of Treatment in Analytical Psychology* (Stuttgart: Bonz, 1980), 48–59; "Integration Process of the Ego Complex in Dreams," *Journal of Analytical Psychology*, vol. 10, no. 1 (1962): 55.

p. 21 *wastefulness*   Hall, *Freud's Psychology.*

p. 21 *important and positive*   Erling Jacobsen, *Neuroserne og samfundet* (The neuroses and society) (Copenhagen: Hans Reitzels Forlag, 1973).

p. 21 *blame . . . on the mother*   Hall, *Freud's Psychology.*

p. 22 *dressed like a woman*   Calvin S. Hall and R. van de Castle, "An Empirical Investigation of the Castration Complex in Dreams," *Journal of Personality* 33 (1965): 20–29.

p. 22 *Freud's theories*   Otto Fenichel, *The Psychoanalytical Theory of Neurosis* (London: Routledge and Kegan Paul, 1977), 33–116.

p. 22 *Calvin S. Hall*   Hall, *Freud's Psychology.*

p. 23 *Integrity versus disgust*   Erik H. Erikson, *Barnet og samfundet* (The child and society) (Copenhagen: Hans Reitzels Forlag, 1983), 258–59.

p. 23 *inspired by C. G. Jung*   Henri F. Ellenberger, *The Discovery of the Unconscious* (New York: Basic Books, 1970), 732.

p. 23 *needs of his surroundings*   Erikson, "Dream Specimen," 35.

p. 24 *had not been clean*   Freud, *Interpretation of Dreams*, 107.

p. 25 *younger generation* Erikson, "Dream Specimen," 36.

p. 26 *religious symbolism of other peoples* Erikson, "Dream Specimen." 7.

p. 26 *Vanggaard's own modus operandi* Thorkild Vanggaard, *Angst: En psykoanalyses forløb* (Angst: The course of a psychoanalysis) (Copenhagen: Gyldendal, 1987), 9.

p. 27 *also be the father* Ibid., 22–24.

p. 28 *dealing with institutions* Ibid., 61–63.

p. 28 *came to feel anxiety afterward* Ibid., 94–95.

p. 29 *the situation with O* Ibid., 96–97.

p. 29 *that produced the anxiety* Ibid., 133–34.

p. 29 *"not determining for . . . correctness"* Esben Hougrd, "Psykoterapi som non–specifik behandling" (Psychotherapy as nonspecific treatment), *Psykologisk skriftserie Aarhus* 8, no. 6 (1983): 43.

p. 29 *thinking about anything* Paul Sloane, *Psychoanalytic Understanding of Dreams* (New York, London: Jason Aronson, 1976), 18–20.

p. 29 *understanding and intuition* French and Fromm, *Dream Interpretation*, 118–20.

p. 30 *regard it objectively* Sloane, *Psychoanalytic Understanding*, 21.

p. 30 *premature closure of the interpretation* K. B. Madsen, *Sammenlignende videnskabsteori for psykologer og pædagoger* (Comparative scientific theory for psychologists and educators) (Copenhagen: Lærerforeningens materialeudvalg, 1980), 70.

p. 31 *psychological rebirth motif* Freud, *Interpretation of Dreams*, 400.

p. 31 *flying expresses longing* Ibid., 394.

p. 31 *". . . something dreadful"* Vanggaard, *Angst*, 33.

p. 31 *never have done this in reality* Ibid., 81–82.

p. 31 *nomination to a professorship* Ibid., 83–84.

p. 32 *relationship with her* Ibid., 136.

p. 32 *hypostatization* Wilhelm Laiblin, *Märchenforschung und Tiefenpsychologie* (Folktale study and depth psychology) (Darmstadt, 1969).

p. 33 *dreams can have several meanings* French and Fromm, *Dream Interpretation*, 205.

p. 33 *dreams have a "cognitive" structure* French and Fromm, *Dream Interpretation*.

p. 33 *separate and instructive ways* Erikson, "Dream Specimen," 55.

p. 33 *synthesizing* Jones, *Egosynthesis*.

p. 33 *"father dominated"* Harry S. Guntrip, *Psychoanalytic Theory, Therapy, and the Self* (New York: Basic Books, 1971).p. 33 *"Shame on you!" in general* Erikson, "Dream Specimen," 36.

p. 34   "... *analyzed over a thousand dreams*"   Freud, *Interpretation of Dreams*, 104–5.

p. 35   *in the section ... above*   Khan, "Psychoanalytic Situation," 27–28.

p. 35   *interpretation of the transference*   Guntrip, *Psychoanalytic Theory*.

p. 35   *statistical test methods*   Madsen, *Sammenlignende videnskabsteori*.

p. 36   "*fictitious theory*"   Olsen et al, *Metapsykologi II*, Redaktionel in-dledning (editorial preface), vol. 2, 13.

p. 36   "... *could be studied exactly*"   Ellenberger, *Discovery of the Unconscious*, 15.

p. 36   *religion as illusion*   Ibid., 534–46.

p. 36   *special symbolic language*   Carl O'Nell, *Dreams, Culture and the Individual* (Los Angeles: Chandler and Sharp, 1976), 37.

p. 36   *and so on*   Freud, *Interpretation of Dreams*, 86.

p. 36   *science of interpreting texts*   Madsen, *Sammenlignende videnskabsteori*.

p. 36   *society and the culture*   Erikson, *Barnet og samfundet*; John E. Gedo, *Portraits of the Artist* (New York: The Guilford Press, 1983); Guntrip, *Psychoanalytic Theory*.

2. Jung and the neo-Jungians

p. 37   *dreams as their subject proper*   C. G. Jung, *The Practical Use of Dream Analysis* (1934), in *Collected Works* I–XX (London: Routledge and Kegan Paul, 1960–80), 136–63; C. G. Jung, *General Aspects of Dream Psychology* (1948), in *Collected Works* VIII, 237–80; C. G. Jung, *On the Nature of Dreams* (1948), in *Collected Works* VIII, 281–300; C. G. Jung, *Symbols and the Interpretation of Dreams* (1961), in *Collected Works* XVIII, 185–266.

p. 37   *later published*   C. G. Jung, *Seminar on dream analysis* (1928–30), ed. William McGuire (Princeton: Bollingen Series XCIX, 1984); C. G. Jung, *The Visions Seminars* I (1930–32) (Zurich: Spring Publications, 1976); C. G. Jung, *The Visions Seminars* II (1932–34) (Zurich: Spring Publications, 1976); C. G. Jung, "Kinderträume" (Childhood dreams) I and II (1938–39), edited stenogram (Zurich: Eidgenossische Hochschule).

p. 37   *thrown out in passing*   M. Fordham, *The Empirical Foundation of C.G. Jung's Work*, in *The Library of Analytical Psychology*, vol. I (London: W. Heineman, 1973), 12.

p. 38   *experiences and sum of knowledge*   Jolande Jacoby, *Die Psychologie von C. G. Jung* (The psychology of C. G. Jung) (Zurich: Rascher Verlag, 1959).

p. 38   *sum of knowledge*   A. N. Amman, *Aktive Imagination* (Active imagination) (Olten: Walter Verlag, 1978).

p. 38   *. . . artificial intervention*   Jacoby, *Psychologie von C. G. Jung*, 128.

p. 39   *"universal human being in us"*   Mary Ann Mattoon, *Applied Dream Analysis* (London: John Wiley and Sons, 1978), 121.

p. 39   *what do you think of me?*   Ibid., 103.

p. 39   *collective unconscious*   Ibid., 135.

p. 40   *she was silver*   C. G. Jung, *Modern Psychology* I–II (Zurich: Eidgenossische Technische Hochschule, 1959), 203–4.

p. 40   *something wrong with*   Mattoon, *Dream Analysis*, 134.

p. 40   *it "hit home," Jung writes*   Jung, *Symbols*, 469.

p. 40   *a problem in himself*   Mattoon, *Dream Analysis*, 101.

p. 41   *die away*   C. G. Jung, *Memories, Dreams, Reflections* (London: Fontana Paperbacks, 1983), 186–87.

p. 41   *something relatively unfamiliar*   Jacoby, *Psychologie von C. G. Jung*, 117.

p. 41   *spirit and imagination*   Jung, "Kinderträume," I.27.

p. 41   *isn't understood intellectually*   Jacoby, *Psychologie von C.G. Jung*, 114–15.

p. 41   *get up every morning*   Jung, *Symbolic Life*, 274.

p. 41   *"symbolical attitude"*   Gerhard Adler, *The Living Symbol* (New York: Pantheon Books, 1961), 9–10.

p. 42   *higher cosmic order*   Jung, *Symbols*, 185–266.

p. 42   *a curative effect*   C. G. Jung et al., "Approaching the Unconscious: The Importance of Dreams," in *Man and His Symbols* (London: Aldus Books, 1964), 95.

p. 42   *a "transcendent" function*   Adler, *Living Symbol*, 9–10.

p. 42   *in the physical world*   Jung, "Importance of Dreams," 93.

p. 43   *when she was eleven*   Jung, *Symbols*, 525–35.

p. 43   *anima or animus*   Ibid., 543.

p. 44   *creative processes in the unconscious*   M.-L. von Franz, *Träume* (Dreams) (Zurich: Daimon, 1985), 13.

p. 44   *no connection . . . can be found*   Jung, "Kinderträume," I.5–6.

p. 44   *impression from the previous day*   von Franz, *Träume*, 25.

p. 45   *healthy until his death*   C. A. Meyer, *Die Bedeutung des Traumes* (The meaning of dreams) (Olten: Walter Verlag, 1972), 22–23.

p. 46   *psychosis or severe neurosis*   Jung, "Kinderträume," I.6–7.

p. 46   *a large, waiting crowd*   Jung, *Memories, Dreams, Reflections*, 200.

p. 46   *perspiring with excitement*   Jung, "Kinderträume," I.6–7.

p. 47   *". . . as much to learn as the dreamer"*   Jung, *The Archetypes and the Collective Unconscious*, in *Collected Works* IX–I, par. 54.

p. 47   *closing phase of the narrative*   Jung, "Kinderträume," I.31.

p. 47   *how they end*   Jacoby, *Psychologie von C. G. Jung*, 102–3.

p. 48   *". . . combination of probabilities"*   Jung, *Dream Psychology*, par. 237–80.

p. 48   *i.e., amplification*   Jung, "Kinderträume," II.2.

p. 49   *in a constructive way*   Ibid.

p. 49   *ones that do not*   M.-L. von Franz, *Redemption Motifs in Fairy Tales* (Toronto: Inner City Books, 1980), 29.

p. 49   *personal, cultural, and archetypal*   James A. Hall, *Jungian Dream Interpretation* (Toronto: Inner City Books, 1983), 34.

p. 49   *associated with it*   Jung, "Kinderträume" II.2.

p. 49   *life, passion, strong feelings*   Sven Tito Achen, *Symboler omkring os* (Symbols around us) (Copenhagen: Gad, 1975), 23.

p. 50   *elevated above the axis*   Aniela Jaffé, *Symbolism in the Visual Arts*, in *Man and His Symbols*, 243.

p. 50   *special meaning for Christians*   Jung, "Importance of Dreams," 96.

p. 50   *no personal associations*   Jung, "Kinderträume," I.6–7.

p. 51   *and so on*   C. Salles, "Symbols of Transformation in a Dream," *Journal of Analytical Psychology* 30 (1985): 347–52.

p. 51   *indexes of symbolic meanings*   Ad de Vries, *Dictionary of Symbols and Imagery* (London: North Holland Publishing Co., 1974); J. E. Cirlot, *A Dictionary of Symbols* (London: Routledge and Kegan Paul, 1967); Tom Chetwynd, *Dictionary of Symbols* (London: Granada Publishing Co., 1982).

p. 52   *distorted or otherwise altered*   Jung, *Seminar on Dream Analysis*, 29–30.

p. 52   *". . . statement becomes untrue"*   Jung, *Symbols*, par. 426–29.

p. 52   *complications*   Victor W. Eisenstein, "Dreams Following Intercourse," *Pschoanal. Quarterly* 18 (1949): 154–72.

p. 53   *the physical world*   Andrew Samuels et al., *A Critical Dictionary of Jungian Analysis* (New York: Routledge and Kegan Paul, 1986), 85.

p. 53   *getting to the interior level*   Hans Dieckmann, *On the Methodology of Dream Interpretation*, in *Methods of Treatment in Analytical Psychology* (Stuttgart: Bonz, 1980).

p. 53 *lightning and thunder* Jung, "Kinderträume," II.5.

p. 53 *it "clicks"* Ibid., II.2.

p. 53 *". . . the patient's consent"* Jacoby, *Psychologie von C. G. Jung*, 92.

p. 54 *puberty, mid-life, and death* Jung, "Kinderträume," I.1.

p. 54 *foretell a person's fate* Ibid.

p. 54 *long since forgotten* Ibid.

p. 55 *noneveryday-oriented side* Ibid., II.31–2.

p. 55 *try to emancipate* Ibid., II.41.

p. 55 *at any rate was reduced* Ibid., II.97–101.

p. 56 *exuberant joy in living* M.-L. von Franz, *Jung, His Myth in Our Time* (Boston: Putnam, 1975), 17–19.

p. 57 *these observations* Hermann Schultz, *Zur diagnostischen und prognostischen Bedeutung des Initialtraumes . . .* (On the diagnostic and prognostic significance of initial dreams . . .) (Ph.D. diss., Universität Ulm, 1969), 12–15.

p. 57 *ongoing series* Ibid.

p. 58 *new prognostic aspects* Ibid., 110–11.

p. 58 *transference reaction* T. D. Harris, "Dreams About the Analyst," *International Journal of Psychoanalysis* 43 (1961): 151–58.

p. 59 *work with dreams* C. G. Jung, *The Relations Between the Ego and the Unconscious*, in *Collected Works* VII, par. 254.

p. 60 *an entire culture's shadow* Ole Vedfelt, *Det kvindelige i manden* (The feminine in the man) (Copenhagen: Gyldendal, 1985), 33.

p. 61 *". . . in a masculine way"* Jacoby, *Psychologie von C. G. Jung*, 135–37.

p. 61 *sentimental* M.-L. von Franz, *The Process of Individuation*, in *Man and His Symbols*, 177–78.

p. 61 *deeper layers in the unconscious* von Franz, *Process of Individuation*, 189–91.

p. 62 *in his present life* Jung, *Seminar on Dream Analysis*, 7–8.

p. 62 *potentialities in the personality* Mary Howells, in Jung, *Seminar on Dream Analysis*, 567–73.

p. 63 *". . . lead him to this realization"* von Franz, *Process of Individuation*, 183–85.

p. 63 *creative and meaningful activity* Ibid., 193.

p. 64 *expression of the highest wisdom* Ibid., 183–85; Jung, *Visions Seminars* I, 172.

p. 64 *such as a Gandhi* von Franz, *Process of Individuation*, 194.

p. 64 *existence of such a process* Kenneth Lamberth, "A Critical Commentary to C. G. Jung's Seminar on Dream Analysis," *Journal of Analytical Psychology.*

p. 65 *anima problems* Jung, *Seminar on Dream Analysis.*

p. 65 *dreams and fantasies* Jung, *The Visions Seminars* I and II.

p. 65 *texts of the old alchemists* M.-L. von Franz, *Alchemy* (Toronto: Inner City Books, 1980), 14–15.

p. 65 *role in their work* C. G. Jung, *Psychology and Alchemy,* in *Collected Works* XII, par. 274.

p. 65 *psychic symbols* von Franz, *Alchemy,* 14–15.

p. 65 *spiritual development* Jung, *Psychology and Alchemy,* 255ff.

p. 66 *individuation process* Ibid., 242ff.

p. 66 *into the consciousness* Ibid., 44–45.

p. 66 *following dream series* Ibid., 242ff.

p. 66 *material worth mentioning* Ibid., 44–45.

p. 67 *". . . of its own accord"* Ibid., 50.

p. 67 *without any result being produced* Ibid., 87.

p. 68 *related symbols in alchemy* Ibid., 47–89.

p. 69 *and so on* C. G. Jung, *Psychology and Religion,* in *Collected Works* II, par. 75–77.

p. 69 *each gave* Jung, *Psychology and Alchemy,* 222.

p. 70 *". . . quaternity, etc."* Jung, *Psychology and Religion,* par. 75–77.

p. 70 *closer to dreams* von Franz, *Alchemy,* 14–15.

p. 70 *water in the unconscious* Jung, *Psychology and Alchemy,* 47–89.

p. 72 *until the next session* M.-L. von Franz, *Problems of the Feminine in Fairy Tales* (Zurich: Spring Publications, 1972).

p. 72 *inexhaustible of meaning* von Franz, *Träume,* 12.

p. 72 *interpret them themselves* Jung, *Dream Analysis,* 322.

p. 72 *set off a process* Amman, *Aktive Imagination,* 15.

p. 73 *M.-L. von Franz* M.-L. von Franz, *On Active Imagination in Methods of Treatment in Analytical Psychology,* ed. I. F. Baker (Zurich: Bonz, 1980).

p. 73 *Barbara Hannah* Barbara Hannah, "Regression und Erneuerung im Alter" in *Psychoterapeutische Probleme* (Regression and age restoration Psychotherapeutische Probleme) (Zurich: Rascher, 1964).

p. 73 *Jane Dallet* Jane Dallet, "Active Imagination in Practice," in Murray Stein's *Jungian Analysis* (London: Shambhala, 1984), 173–92.

p. 73 *situations that arise* Amman, *Aktive Imagination,* 9–10.

p. 73 *his outward success* Ibid., 9–13.

p. 74 *unopened doors* Ibid., 23–24.

p. 74 *the ethical aspect*   Ibid., 23–27.

p. 74 *active imaginings*   Jung, *Modern Psychology* I–II, 203–4.

p. 74 *black magic*   Amman, *Aktive Imagination*, 29–31.

p. 75 *setting new bounds*   Andrew Samuels, "The Emergence of Schools in Analytical Psychology," *Journal of Analytical Psychology* 28 (1982): 351–52.

p. 75 *". . . reality we perceive directly"*   Ibid., 353.

p. 75 *". . . not the dream"*   Andrew Samuels, *Jung and the Post-Jungians* (London: Routledge and Kegan Paul, 1985), 236.

p. 76 *C. A. Meyer*   Meyer, *Bedeutung des Traumes*.

p. 76 *James A. Hall*   James A. Hall, *Clinical Uses of Dreams* (New York: Grune and Stratton, 1977), 123.

p. 76 *Mary Ann Mattoon*   Mattoon, *Applied Dream Analysis*.

p. 76 *". . . what he will later become"*   Jung, "Kinderträume," I.21.

p. 76 *nearly fifty years*   Sheila Moon, *Dreams of a Woman* (Boston: Sigo Press, 1983).

p. 77 *extremely split*   Ibid., 9–10.

p. 77 *male-dominated society's terms*   Ibid., 6–8.

p. 77 *cautious girl*   Ibid.

p. 78 *individuation process*   Jung, *Psychology and Alchemy*, 67.

p. 78 *". . . tried to destroy me"*   Moon, *Dreams of a Woman*, 13.

p. 78 *young man to the floor*   Ibid., 27.

p. 78 *". . . all friends"*   Ibid., 26.

p. 78 *". . . my right hand"*   Ibid., 26–28.

p. 79 *recommends that she commit suicide*   Ibid., 31.

p. 79 *sharp and in clear black*   Ibid., 79.

p. 79 *"the night's son"*   E. Neumann, "The Moon and Matriarchal Consciousness," in *Fathers and Mothers* (Zurich: Spring Publications, 1973).

p. 79 *"matriarchal consciousness"*   Moon, *Dreams of a Woman*, 27.

p. 79 *any other time in her life*   Ibid., 56–66.

p. 79 *some problems*   Ibid., 99.

p. 80 *psychic transformation*   Ibid., 106.

p. 80 *as is our love*   Ibid., 115.

p. 80 *". . . in a creative sense"*   Ibid.

p. 81 *conscious and the unconscious*   Ibid., 110.

p. 81 *Book of the Zohar*   Ibid., 118.

p. 81 *something to the world*   Ibid., 207.

p. 81 *common destiny*   Jung, *Symbolic Life*, par. 274.

p. 82 *helps give them meaning* M.-L. von Franz, *Jung, His Myth in Our Time* (Boston: Putnam, 1975).

p. 82 *". . . gave life a new direction"* Jung, *Relations*, par. 254.

p. 82 *Paul D. Huss* Amman, *Aktive Imagination.*

p. 82 *therapy of some sort* John R. Johnson, "Vocation, Dreams and the Self" (diploma diss., C. G. Jung Institute, Zurich, 1977), 26.

p. 82 *inner need and social role* Ibid., 127.

p. 82 *the person in question* Ibid., 117.

p. 83 *Isaiah's vocation* Ibid., 35–38.

p. 84 *harbinger to the iniquitous* *Bible*, 6 Isaiah.

p. 84 *very sad* Johnson, "Vocation, Dreams and the Self," 123.

p. 84 *psychosis, fanaticism, and abuse* Ibid., 8.

p. 84 *initiate others in them* Mircea Eliade, *Shamanism* (Princeton: Princeton University Press, 1964), 4.

p. 85 *". . . one of the elected"* Jes Bertelsen, *Genfødslens psykologi* (The psychology of rebirth) (Copenhagen: Borgen, 1979), 18.

p. 85 *we have no children* Eliade, *Shamanism*, 72.

p. 86 *I wake up* Helle Lassen, "Symbolikken hos Chagall" (The symbolism in Chagall), *Louisiana Revy* 23, no. 2 (1983): 34–35.

p. 86 *Kübler-Ross* E. Kübler-Ross, *Reif werden zum Tode* (Become ripe for death) (Stuttgart: Kreuz, 1975).

p. 87 *Raymond Moody* Raymond Moody, *Life After Life* (Georgia: Mockingbird Books, 1975).

p. 87 *Stanislav Grof* S. Grof and J. Halifax, *The Human Encounter with Death* (New York: E. P. Dutton, 1977).

p. 87 *profound transformation processes* M.-L. von Franz, *On Dreams and Death* (Boston and London: Shambhala, 1986), xi.

p. 87 *Jane Wheelwright* Jane Wheelwright, *Death of a Woman* (New York: Putnam, 1981).

p. 87 *Barbara Hannah* Barbara Hannah, *Encounters with the Soul* (Boston: Sigo Press, 1977).

p. 87 *Edvard Edinger* E. Edinger, *Ego and Archetype* (New York: Putnam, 1972).

p. 87 *life after death* von Franz, *On Dreams and Death*, 105.

p. 87 *Egyptian death rituals* Ibid., xiii.

p. 87 *the wishful ego* Ibid., xi.

p. 87 *died soon afterward* Ibid., 30.

p. 87 *through meditation* Ibid., xvi.

p. 88 *Egyptian death rituals* Ibid., 19.

p. 88 *objective level* Ibid., xv.

p. 88 *". . . beyond life and death"* Ibid., 10–13.

p. 88 *became trees again* Ibid., 25.

p. 89 *intermediary for the beyond* Ibid., 46–47.

p. 89 *". . . I will soon lose my patience"* Ibid., 51.

p. 90 *brightly shining diamond* Ibid., 59.

p. 90 *reincarnation* Ibid., 4–5.

p. 90 *mummification rituals* Ibid., 17.

p. 90 *". . . dangerous barrier"* Ibid., 105.

p. 90 *life that remains to be lived* Kübler-Ross, *Reif werden zum Tode*; Moody, *Life After Life*; Grof and Halifax, *Human Encounter with Death*; von Franz, *On Dreams and Death*.

p. 90 *organic chemistry* Hans Dieckmann, *Träume als Sprache der Seele* (Dreams as the language of the soul) (Stuttgart: Bonz, 1984), 113ff.

p. 91 *autonomous complexes* Ibid.

p. 91 *the creative process* M.-L. von Franz, *Creation Myth* (Zurich: Spring Publications, 1972), 173.

p. 91 *complicated material together* Ibid.

p. 92 *developments in Germany* Samuels, "Emergence of Schools," 345–62.

p. 92 *". . . objects in the external world"* Fordham, *C. G. Jung's Work*, 20.

p. 92 *archetypal basis* Erich Neumann, *The Child* (New York: Putnam, 1973).

p. 92 *ethnological symbolism* Erich Neumann, "Zur Psychologie des Weiblichen" (On the psychology of the feminine), *Umkreisung der Mitte* II (1953): 9.

p. 93 *a kind of mother* Pia Skogemann, *Kvindelighed i vækst* (Growing femininity) (Copenhagen: Borgen, 1984), 18–20.

p. 93 *doesn't much interest her* Ibid., 32.

p. 93 *". . . impersonal masculine form"* Ibid., 33.

p. 93 *not awakened* Ibid., 18–20.

p. 94 *". . . spirit has been activated"* Ibid., 65.

p. 94 *male society's terms* Ibid., 35.

p. 94 *". . . phases in psychological development"* Ibid., 41–42.

p. 95 *captivity in the matriarchy* Vedfelt, *Det kvindelige i manden*, 34–35.

p. 95 *an unpleasant wait* Ibid., 39.

p. 96 *". . . matriarchy to patriarchy"* Ibid., 141–48.

p. 96 *the film 2001* Ibid., 84.

p. 96 *and a sea floor* Ibid., 153.

p. 97 *toward me*   Ibid., 169.

p. 97 *revolver in my pocket*   Ibid., 47.

p. 97 *the feeling of ego*   Hans Dieckmann, "Integration Process of the Ego Complex in Dreams," *Journal of Analytical Psychology*, vol. 10, no. 1 (1962): 51.

p. 98 *". . . even in the dream ego"*   Hans Dieckmann, "On the Methodology of Dream Interpretation," in *Methods of Treatment in Analytical Psychology* (Stuttgart: Bonz, 1980), 49.

p. 98 *identify himself*   Ibid.

p. 98 *unconscious content*   Ibid., 48–51.

p. 98 *solved by flight*   Ibid., 49.

p. 98 *went off with the girls*   Dieckmann, "Ego Complex," 53.

p. 98 *went on fighting*   Ibid.

p. 99 *waking ego*   Ibid., 55.

p. 99 *". . . breaking off of the analysis"*   Dieckmann, *Methodology*, 53.

p. 99 *their own objectives*   James Hillman, *The Dream and the Underworld* (New York: Harper and Row, 1979), 1.

p. 99 *see through its "reality"*   Hillman, *Underworld*, 95.

p. 100 *dynamic attributes*   Yehezkiel Kluger, "Archetypal Dreams and 'Everyday' Dreams," *Israel's Annals of Psychiatry and Related Disciplines* 13 (1955): 6.

p. 100 *activated during analysis*   Ibid., 22.

p. 100 *Book of Revelation*   Ibid., 23–25.

p. 101 *rational to nonrational*   Ibid.

p. 101 *dreams of analysands were archetypal*   Ibid., 31–32.

p. 101 *through meditation*   P. A. Faber et al., "Induced Waking Fantasy: Its Effects upon the Archetypal Content of Nocturnal Dreams," *International Analytical Psychology* (1983): 141–64.

p. 101 *waking fantasy*   Ibid., 149–50.

p. 102 *disclosed to the subjects*   Ibid.

p. 102 *18 percent*   Ibid., 152.

p. 102 *quantity of archetypal dreams*   P. A. Faber et al., "Meditation and Archetypal Content of Nocturnal Dreams," *Journal of Analytical Psychology* 23 (1978): 1–22.

p. 103 *preconceived theory*   Jung, *Collective Unconscious*, par. 54.

p. 103 *fifty years later*   von Franz, *Träume*, 38.

p. 103 *one-sidedly intellectual*   Samuels, *Post-Jungians*, 236.

p. 103 *dreamer's interpretation*   Dieckmann, *Sprache der Seele*, 113ff.

p. 103 *into their therapy* Sylvia Brinton–Perera, *Descent to the Goddess* (Toronto: Inner City Books, 1981); Edward Whitmont, "Recent Influences on the Practice of Jungian Analysis," in *Jungian Analysis*, 335–36.

p. 104 *corrections of the consciousness* Jung, *Symbols*, 507.

p. 104 *textbook on dream analysis* Hall, *Clinical Uses of Dreams*, 123.

p. 104 *relation to the unconscious* Meyer, *Bedeutung des Traumes*, 141.

p. 105 *". . . love scene with this person"* von Franz, *Träume*, 14–15.

p. 105 *hauling the boss . . . in a dream* Eigil Nyborg, "Drømte mig en drøm" (I dreamed a dream), *Hug* 9, vol. 23, no. 45 (1986): 23.

p. 105 *swollen self-regard* Jung, *Symbols*, 507.

p. 105 *overly aggressive* Stubbe Teglbjerg, *Lev dine drømme* (Copenhagen: Klitrose, 1984).

p. 105 *". . . youthful attitude for his age"* Eigil Nyborg, *Drømmenes vej til selvet* (Dreams' way to the self) (Copenhagen: Tiderne Skifter, 1986), 11.

p. 105 *". . . psychological automatic control"* Jung, *General Aspects*.

p. 106 *". . . in reality"* Dieckmann, *Methodology*, 53.

p. 107 *". . . constantly more meaningless"* Jung, *On the Nature of Dreams*, par. 281–300.

p. 107 *". . . supposed to do"* Mattoon, *Applied Dream Analysis*.

p. 107 *responsibility on the dreams* M.-L. von Franz, *Shadow and Evil in Fairy Tales* (Zurich: Spring Publications, 1974).

p. 108 *overlaid and distorted* Jung, *Symbols*, 42.

p. 109 *". . . in a creative sense"* Moon, *Dreams of a Woman*, 115.

p. 110 *the wish can be realized* Dieckmann, *Sprache der Seele*, 113ff.

p. 110 *other organs* C. G. Jung, *Psychological Types*, in *Collected Works* V, par. 163–65.

p. 110 *". . . earthly ego"* von Franz, *Träume*, 33.

p. 111 *". . . cure will work"* Freud, *Interpretation of Dreams*, 306–7.

p. 112 *returned to the United States* Murray, "Postscript," 517–21.

p. 112 *thrown away* Jung, *Visions Seminars* II, 436.

p. 112 *". . . getting to the basics"* Jung, *Visions Seminars* I, 3.

p. 113 *cover figure for himself* Ibid., 7.

p. 113 *Christina cared for the lamb* Ibid., 19.

p. 113 *her own religious path* Ibid., 19–28.

p. 113 *"It is the book of illumination"* Jung, *Visions Seminars* II, 271.

p. 113 *these strange steps* Ibid., 383.

p. 114 *about the archetypes* Ibid., 475.

p. 114   *unusually developed personality*   Murray, "Postscript," 517–21.

p. 114   *Pia Skogemann*   Pia Skogemann, *Religion og symbol* (Religion and symbol) (Copenhagen: Borgen, 1988), 54–56.

p. 115   *without contradiction*   Erikson, *Dream Specimen*, 48–49.

p. 115   *no place in Freud's universe*   Ole Vedfelt, "Interview med Ole Vedfelt" (Interview with Ole Vedfelt), in *Hvad er psykoanalyse?* (What is psychoanalysis?), ed. Elna Bering (Copenhagen: Rosinante, 1988).

p. 115   *eighty thousand dreams*   C. Hall and V. Nordby, *C. G. Jungs psykologi* (The psychology of C. G. Jung) (Copenhagen: Hans Reitzels Forlag, 1976).

p. 116   *upper social strata*   Fordham, *C. G. Jung's Work*, 19.

p. 116   *". . . twenty-five years"*   M.-L. von Franz, *On Divination* (Toronto: Inner City Books, 1980), 42.

p. 116   *psychic equilibrium*   Hans Dieckmann, "Über einige Beziehungen zwischen Traumserie und Verhaltungsanderungen" (On some connections between dream series and behavioral changes), *Zeitschrift für Psychosomatisches Medizin* 8 (1962): 281.

p. 117   *investigation of the personal level*   Liliane Freyh–Rohn, *From Freud to Jung* (New York: Putnam, 1974), 126–30.

p. 117   *universally accepted*   Jean Piaget, *Play, Dreams and Imitation in Childhood* (New York: W. W. Norton, 1962), 196.

p. 117   *modern branches of science*   Pia Skogemann, *Arketyper* (Archetypes) (Copenhagen: Lindhardt og Ringhof, 1976).

p. 118   *the object being observed*   Leopold Stein, *Analytical Psychology: A Modern Science*, in *Library of Analytical Psychology*, 3.

p. 118   *scientific cognitional process*   Abraham Maslow, *Motivation and Personality* (New York: Harper and Row, 1970).

p. 119   *stimulate development of the personality*   Henri Ellenberger, *The Discovery of the Unconscious* (New York: Basic Books, 1970).

p. 119   *form, pattern, and order*   S. Grof, *Beyond the Brain* (Albany: State University of New York Press, 1985).

p. 120   *". . . inner development"*   Jung, *Memories, Dreams, Reflections*, 10.

3. DREAMS AND WAKING LIFESTYLE

p. 121   *safety valve for primitive drives*   Louis Breger, "Function of Dreams," *Journal of Abnormal Psychology* 72, no. 5 (1967): 1.

p. 121   *future-directed*   Alfred Adler, "Dreams Reveal the Life Style," in *The New World of Dreams*, ed. Ralph Woods and Herbert Greenhouse (New York: MacMillan Publishing Co. Inc., 1974), 213–16.

p. 121 *". . . must not be reduced"* Alfred Adler, "On the Interpretation of Dreams," *International Journal of Individual Psychology* 2 (1936): 13–16, 225.

p. 122 *when he is asleep* Ibid.

p. 122 *opposed to the sister* Breger, "Function of Dreams," 1.

p. 122 *Freud's or Jung's* David Foulkes, "How Is the Dream Formed? Another Look at Freud and Adler," in *The New World of* Dreams, 303–13.

p. 122 *". . . moral capacity"* Erich Fromm, *Det glemte sprog* (The forgotten language) (København: Hans Reitzels Forlag, 1967), 48.

p. 122 *psychological makeup, and so forth* Calvin Hall and Vernon Nordby, *The Individual and His Dreams* (New York: New American Library, 1972), 9.

p. 123 *he had to try a new one* Calvin Hall, *The Meaning of Dreams* (New York: McGraw-Hill Book Co., 1966), 72.

p. 123 *we kissed each other* Ibid., 37–38.

p. 124 *prefer a practical career* Ibid.

p. 124 *means of dreams* Calvin Hall, "Diagnosing Personality by the Analysis of Dreams," *Journal of Abnormal and Social Psychology* 42 (1947): 68–79.

p. 124 *increased its effectiveness* Hall and Nordby, *Individual and His Dreams*, 56–57.

p. 125 *first several hundred dreams* Ibid., 21.

p. 125 *generalizability* Calvin Hall, and Robert van de Castle, *The Content Analysis of Dreams* (New York: Appleton Century Crofts, 1966), 2.

p. 125 *". . . comments and interpretations"* Ibid., 18.

p. 126 *the dream experience itself* Ibid., 19.

p. 126 *as in women's dreams* Calvin Hall and Robert van de Castle, "An Empirical Investigation of the Castration Complex in Dreams," *Journal of Personality* 33 (1965): 20–29.

p. 126 *superego . . . in women and in men* Calvin Hall, "A Modest Confirmation of Freud's Theory of the Distinction Between the Superego of Men and Women," *Journal of Abnormal and Social Psychology* 69, no. 4 (1969); 440–42.

p. 126 *comparison with his own* Kluger, "Archetypal Dreams," 6–47.

p. 126 *two sets of dreams* Hall and Nordby, *Individual and His Dreams*, 84.

p. 127 *fellatio on his father* Ibid., 23.

p. 127 *all her life* Ibid., 83.

p. 128 *she feels she may be* Ibid., 42–44.

p. 128   *first and foremost anxiety*   Ibid., 9.

p. 128   *radical changes in the surroundings*   Ibid., 109.

p. 128   *settings, characters, actions, emotions*   Hall, *Meaning of Dreams*, 21.

p. 128   *everyday routines*   Ibid., 22.

p. 129   *person is very isolated*   Ibid., 28–33.

p. 129   *carrying dishes*   Ibid., 35.

p. 129   *one woman for every man*   Calvin Hall and Bill Domhoff, "A Ubiquitous Sex Difference in Dreams," *Journal of Abnormal Social Psychology* 62 (1963): 278–80.

p. 129   *present at the age of six*   Patricia Garfield, *Your Child's Dreams* (New York: Ballantine Books, 1984), 39.

p. 129   *between the two sexes*   Hall and Domhoff, "Ubiquitous Sex Difference," 278–80.

p. 129   *between men and women*   Calvin Hall and Bill Domhoff, "Aggressions in Dreams," *International Journal of Psychiatry* 9 (1963): 259–67.

p. 129   *women make no such distinctions*   Calvin Hall and Bill Domhoff, "Friendliness in Dreams," *Journal of Social Psychology* 62 (1964): 309–14.

p. 130   *throughout life*   Hall and Domhoff, "Ubiquitous Sex Difference," 278–80.

p. 130   *Men are more often sexual*   Hall and van de Castle, *Content Analysis of Dreams*, 181.

p. 130   *a banker, a clerk, a butcher*   Hall, *Meaning of Dreams*, 28–33.

p. 130   *steered and controlled*   Garfield, *Your Child's Dreams*, 39–41.

p. 130   *survey of 247 dreams*   Ibid., 390.

p. 131   *ego's intellectual system*   Calvin Hall, "A Cognitive Theory of Dream Symbolism," *The Journal of General Psychology* 48 (1953): 169–86.

p. 131   *mechanical conception of sex*   Hall, *Meaning of Dreams*, 14.

p. 131   *I had an ejaculation*   Ibid., 51.

p. 132   *incest the next night*   Ibid., 94–95.

p. 133   *". . . scientific manner"*   Ibid., 85–89.

p. 134   *checking their own interpretations*   Hall and Nordby, *Individual and His Dreams*, 156–91.

p. 134   *checking for countertransference*   Ibid., 160.

p. 134   *"style of representation"*   Erikson, *Dream Specimen*, 143.

p. 135   *useful guidelines*   Hall and Nordby, *Individual and His Dreams*, 145.

p. 135   *most useful*   Ibid., 23.

p. 135   *Hall and Fromm . . . Adler*; Leo Gold, "Adler's Theory of Dreams," in

Handbook of Dreams, ed. Benjamin B. Wolman (New York: Van Nostrand Reinhold Co., 1979), 328.

p. 135   *what the symbol means*   Montague Ullman, *Forstå dine drømme* (Understand your dreams), 15.

p. 135   *individual dreamer*   Hall and Nordby, *Individual and His Dreams*, 64–65.

p. 135   *several possible meanings simultaneously*   Fromm, *Det glemte sprog.*

p. 135   *several levels at the same time*   Gold, "Adler's Theory of Dreams."

p. 135   *adheres closely to this idea*   Fromm, *Det glemte sprog*, 141.

p. 135   *fundamental theory*   Montague Ullman, "Dreaming Life Style and Physiology: A Comment on Adler's View of the Dream," *Journal of Individual Psychology* 18 (1962): 18–25.

p. 136   *excludes from his life*   Gold, "Adler's Theory of Dreams," 332.

p. 136   *sleeping state*   Hall and Domhoff, "Ubiquitous Sex Difference," 278–80; Hall, *Meaning of Dreams*, 232–34.

p. 136   *satisfactory relations*   Hall, *Meaning of Dreams*, 31.

p. 136   *". . . causes and contexts"*   Ullman, *Forstå dine drømme*, 15.

p. 136   *life versus death*   Hall, *Meaning of Dreams.*

p. 137   *"esoteric or mysterious in dreams"*   Ibid., 85.

p. 138   *man's desire for rejuvenation*   Ibid., 195–99.

p. 138   *artistic inspiration*   Gold, "Adler's Theory of Dreams," 309.

p. 139   *significance for any dream*   Fromm, *Det glemte sprog*, 119; Ullman, *Forstå dine drømme*, 58; Foulkes, "Freud and Adler," 307.

p. 139   *Alphonse Maeder*   Alphonse Maeder, "Über die Funktion des Träumes," *Jahrbuch für psychoanalytische und psychopatologische Forschungen* 5 (1913): 647–86.

p. 139   *Melanie Klein*   Jane Dallet, "Theories of Dream Function," *Psychological Bulletin* 79, no. 6 (1973): 408–16.

p. 139   *fifty thousand dreams*   Hall and Nordby, *Individual and His Dreams*, 9.

p. 139   *not in therapy*   Hall, *Meaning of Dreams*, 232–34.

p. 139   *societies, cultures, and subcultures*   Hall and Nordby, *Individual and His Dreams*, 9.

p. 140   *men's dream egos . . . than women's*   Hall and van de Castle, *Content Analysis of Dreams*, 181.

p. 140   *Erik Schultz*   Erik Schultz, *Drømmeforståelse og drømmeteorier* (Dream understanding and dream theories) (Ph.D. diss., University of Copenhagen, 1977), 52–53.

p. 140   *Aristotle's dream theory*   Hall and Nordby, *Individual and His Dreams*, 145.

4. EXISTENTIAL AND PHENOMENOLOGICAL DREAM INTERPRETATION

p. 141 *apparently separate worlds* Arne Næss, *Moderne filosoffer* (Modern philosophers) (Copenhagen: Vintens Forlag, 1965), 156.

p. 141 *all theoretical abstractions* Arne Næss, *Filosofiens historie* (The history of philosophy) III (Copenhagen: Vintens Forlag, 1963), 119.

p. 141 *what they would find* Hall, *Individual and His Dreams*, 11.

p. 142 *worked with the method* Susan Knapp, "Dreaming: Horney, Kelmann and Shainberg," in *Handbook of Dreams*, ed. Benjamin B. Wolman (New York: Van Nostrand Reinhold Co., 1979), 342–60.

p. 142 *Rollo May* Leopold Caligor and Rollo May, *Dreams and Symbols* (New York: Basic Books, 1968).

p. 142 *his Dasein* Næss, *Moderne filosoffer*, 9–156, 181–209.

p. 142 *present in the world* Walter James Lowe, "On Using Heidegger," in *On Dreaming*, ed. Charles E. Scott (Chico: Scholar Press, 1977), 36–37.

p. 143 *". . . aim of his Dasein"* Ibid., 57.

p. 143 *". . . something else than what it is"* Paul J. Stern, foreword to Medard Boss's *I Dreamt Last Night* (New York: Gardner Press Inc., 1977), xiii.

p. 143 *". . . experience itself"* Medard Boss, *I Dreamt Last Night* (New York: Gardner Press Inc., 1977), 3.

p. 143 *it is possible to understand* Ibid., 22–24.

p. 143 *world and life* Eugene T. Gendlin, "Phenomenological Concept vs. Phenomenological Method," in *On Dreaming*, 59.

p. 143 *anything of the sort* Stern, foreword to *I Dreamt Last Night*, xii.

p. 144 *something to be longed for* Boss, *I Dreamt Last Night*, 147ff.

p. 145 *creatures who deserved to die* Ibid., 50–52.

p. 145 *". . . terrible chaos"* Ibid., 77.

p. 146 *analyses to the dreamer* Ibid., 74–75.

p. 146 *". . . erotic presence of women?"* Ibid., 79–80.

p. 147 *which word was involved* Ibid., 59–62.

p. 147 *influenced her to this* Ibid.

p. 147 *method called* reframing Bandler and Grinder, *Reframing* (Moab, Utah: Real People Press, 1982).

p. 148 *a typical neurotic trait* Knapp, "Dreaming," 351–52.

p. 148 *carry on a dialogue* Gendlin, "Phenomenological Concept," 61.

p. 149 *appearing in his dreams* Stern, foreword to *I Dreamt Last Night*, xiii; Medard Boss, *The Analysis of Dreams* (New York: Philosophical Library, 1975).

p. 149   *broken through*   Boss, *I Dreamt Last Night*, 128–29.

p. 149   *woman   friend's   genitals*   Sigmund   Freud,   "Revision   af drømmelæren" (Revision of the theory of dreams), in *Nye forelæsninger til indføring i psykoanalysen* (New introductory lectures in psychoanalysis) (Copenhagen: Hans Reitzel, 1973), 21.

p. 150   *". . . desirous lover"*   Stern, foreword to *I Dreamt Last Night*, xi.

p. 150   *in the dreamer's waking life*   Boss, *I Dreamt Last Night*, 214.

p. 150   *in the waking state*   Ibid., 192.

p. 150   *as yet unrealized potentialities*   Boss, "The Dreamer Lives in a Real World," in *The New World of Dreams*, eds. Ralph Woods and Herbert Greenhouse (New York: MacMillan Publishing Co. Inc.), 223–25.

p. 151   *"something unshapely"*   Stern, foreword to *I Dreamt Last Night*, xiii.

p. 152   *". . . let the person taste"*   Fromm, *Det glemte sprog*, 17.

p. 153   *". . . vegetable kingdom"*   Boss, *I Dreamt Last Night*, 79–80.

p. 153   *". . . whenever it is allowed to"*   Ibid., 50–52.

p. 153   *"the old wise man"*   Gendlin, "Phenomenological Concept," 61.

p. 154   *". . . constituting an emergency, etc."*   Ibid., 60.

p. 154   *nearly one hundred thousand dreams*   Boss, *I Dreamt Last Night*.

p. 155   *". . . too simple"*   Christine Downing, "Poetically Dwells Man on This Earth," in *On Dreaming*, 86, 87, 99.

5. EXPERIENTIAL DREAMWORK

p. 157   *humanistic psychology*   Ville Laursen, *Fritz Perls* (Copenhagen: Forum, 1980), 23–24.

p. 157   *new therapeutic method*   Fritz Perls, Ralph Hefferline, and Paul Goodmann, *Gestalt Therapy* 1 & 2 (New York: Julian Press, 1951).

p. 158   *self-regulation can resume*   Laursen, *Fritz Perls*, 23–24; Fritz Perls, *Gestalt Therapy Verbatim* (New York: Bantam Books, 1971) 5, 15.

p. 158   *emotional discharges*   Laursen, *Fritz Perls*, 36.

p. 158   *to be responsible*   Perls, *Gestalt Therapy Verbatim*, 60–61.

p. 159   *self-regulation*   Ibid., 54–56.

p. 159   *"avoidance"*   Ibid., 41–42.

p. 159   *self-impoverishment*   Ibid., 55, 72.

p. 159   *manner of avoiding*   Ibid., 41–42.

p. 159   *". . . make you feel uncomfortable"*   Ibid., 51.

p. 159   *he wanted to have dialogue*   Ibid., 81.

p. 159   *all of the roles himself*   Erving and Miriam Polster, *Gestalt Therapy Integrated* (New York: Vintage Books, 1974), 316.

p. 159   *should relate to his life*   Perls, *Gestalt Therapy Verbatim*, 152–53.

p. 160   *accomplished through role-playing*   Ibid., 72.

p. 160   *to be shit on*   Polster, *Gestalt Therapy Integrated*, 265–67.

p. 160   *interpretations, analyses, and explanations*   Perls, *Gestalt Therapy Verbatim*, 31.

p. 160   *". . . to the hesitations"*   Ibid., 57.

p. 160   *everything you see and sense in her*   Ibid., 160–67.

p. 160   *this example*   Polster, *Gestalt Therapy Integrated*, 272–74.

p. 166   *stimulation can arise*   Ibid., 271.

p. 167   *personal mobility*   Ibid., 272.

p. 168   *Dean and Doreen Elefthery*   Ellinor Barz, *Psykodrama* (Psychodrama) (with special reference to Jung's theories. O.V.) (diploma diss., C. G. Jung Institute, Zurich, 1985).

p. 168   *techniques that Perls also uses*   Eva Røine, *Psykodrama* (Psychodrama) (Oslo: Aschehoug, 1978).

p. 169   *activate the* recollection   Ibid., 145.

p. 169   *Eva Røine*   Ibid., 146–47.

p. 171   *king of fools*   Ibid.

p. 171   *on the subjective level*   Barz, *Psykodrama*.

p. 171   *can derive benefit*   Røine, *Psykodrama*, 87.

p. 172   *". . . troublesome life experiences"*   Polster, *Gestalt Therapy Integrated*, 312.

p. 172   *". . . unassimilated and unused"*   Perls, *Gestalt Therapy Verbatim*, 55.

p. 172   *Moreno's view of dreams*   Røine, *Psykodrama*, 21.

p. 173   *freeing herself from them*   Whitmont, "Jungian Analysis," 346.

p. 173   *understanding level*   Ibid., 345.

p. 174   *full and gleaming*   Polster, *Gestalt Therapy Integrated*, 268–69.

p. 174   *". . . nothing will change"*   Perls, *Gestalt Therapy Verbatim*, 55.

p. 174   *blameless persons*   Ole Vedfelt, interview in Elna Bering's *Hvad er psykoanalyse?* (What is psychoanalysis?) (Copenhagen: Rosinante, 1988).

p. 175   *a mother complex*   Ole Vedfelt, *Det kvindelige i manden* (The feminine in the man) (Copenhagen: Gyldendal, 1985), 175.

p. 176   *"never, never interpret"*   Polster, *Gestalt Therapy Integrated*, 266.

p. 177   *so forth and so on*   Perls, *Gestalt Therapy Verbatim*, 90, 93.

p. 177   *the way we comprehend life*   Villy Sørensen, *Digtere og demoner* (Poets and demons) (Copenhagen: Gyldendal, 1979), 139.

p. 177   *except the analysand himself*   Perls, *Gestalt Therapy Verbatim*, 75.

p. 177   *more insistent than all the others*   Laursen, *Fritz Perls*.

p. 178   *primitive "action"*   Milton Berger, introduction to Polster's *Gestalt Therapy Integrated*, ix–xii.

p. 178   *popular psychotherapy*   Polster, *Gestalt Therapy Integrated*, 314.

p. 179   *". . . person who makes the discovery"*   Maslow, *Motivation and Personality*, 1.

p. 179   *attitudes of the researchers*   Ibid., 3–4.

6. LABORATORY RESEARCH WITH SLEEP AND DREAMS

p. 182   *REM (Rapid Eye Movement) sleep*   Calvin Trillin, "The Discovery of Rapid Eye Movements," in Ralph Woods and Herbert Greenhouse's *The New World of Dreams* (New York: MacMillan Publishing Co., 1974), 274–78.

p. 182   *partial erections during REM sleep*   Herbert Greenhouse, "Penile Erections During Dreams,"in *New World of Dreams*, 296–302.

p. 183   *closing out other sounds*   Rosalind Cartwright, *Night Life* (Englewood Cliffs, NJ: Prentice–Hall Inc., 1977), 38.

p. 183   *premature infant's*   Dreyfuss–Brisac, "The EEG of the Premature Infant and the Fall Term Newborn," in *Neurological and Electroencephalogic Correlative Studies of Infancy*, eds. Kelloway and Petersen (New York: Grune and Stratton, 1969).

p. 183   *dreams are in color*   Cartwright, *Night Life*, 10.

p. 183   *thirty to forty minutes*   Ibid., 11.

p. 183   *person's daily routines*   David Foulkes, "You Think All Night Long," in *New World of Dreams*, 298–319.

p. 183   *ten minutes into the dream*   David Foulkes, "How Is the Dream Formed?" in *New World of Dreams*, 309–10.

p. 184   *around 150 million years*   Allison Truett and Henry van Twyver, "The Sleep and Dreams of Animals," in *New World of Dreams*, 342–55.

p. 185   *physical training class*   Hall, *Meaning of Dreams*, 6–7.

p. 185   *corresponding dream sequences*   W. Dement and E. Wolpert, "The Relation of Eye Movements, Body Mortality, and External Stimuli to Dream Content," *Journal of Experimental Psychology* 55 (1958): 543.

p. 185   *recall after awakening*   A. Arkin, J. Hastey, and M. Reiser, "Post–Hypnotically Stimulated Sleeptalking," *Journal of Nervous and Mental Disease* 142 (1953): 273.

p. 186   *reactions to the unpleasant ones*   P. Verdone, "Temporal Reference of Manifest Dream Content," *Perceptual and Motor Skills* 20 (1965): 1253; Milton Kramer et al., "Patterns of Dreaming: The Interrelationship of the Dreams of a Night," *Journal of Nervous Mental Disease* 139 (1964): 426–39.

p. 187   *problem-solving tendency*   Cartwright, *Night Life*, 30–31.

p. 187   *educational institution*   Ibid., 21.

p. 187   *washes the inside of his ear*   Ibid., 22.

p. 188   *he could never win*   Ibid., 18–24.

p. 188   *paper which he unrolled*   Ibid., 24.

p. 189   *drunk and very nasty*   Ibid., 25.

p. 190   *". . . loses control"*   Ibid., 26–27.

p. 190   *concerned with contemplating solutions*   Ibid., 28–31.

p. 190   *". . . not much help"*   Ibid., 55.

p. 191   *as many believe*   Ernest Hartmann, *The Functions of Sleep* (New Haven: Yale University Press, 1973), 68.

p. 191   *more creative than normal*   Cartwright, *Night Life*, 51–53.

p. 191   *seven weeks of REM deprivation*   G. Vogel et al., "Sleep Reduction Effects on Depressive Syndromes," *Archives of General Psychiatry* 18 (1968): 287.

p. 191   *biological need for REM sleep*   W. Dement, "The Effect of Dream Deprivation," *Science* 131 (1960): 1705–7.

p. 191   *more evenly balanced personalities*   Cartwright, *Night Life*, 40–41.

p. 191   *creative persons*   E. Hartmann, "Psychological Differences Between Long and Short Sleepers," *Archives of General Psychiatry* 26 (1966): 463.

p. 192   *low sleep requirement*   Hartmann, *Functions of Sleep*, 68.

p. 192   *sleep late on weekends*   Cartwright, *Night Life*, 40–41.

p. 192   *better on the social level*   Harry Fiss, "Current Dream Research: A Psychobiological Perspective," in Benjamin Wolmann's (ed.) *Handbook of Dreams* (New York: Van Nostrand, 1979), 60.

p. 192   *brain structures become involved*   Ibid., 20–75.

p. 193   *waking state*   Robert McCarley and Allan Hobson, "The Form of Dreams and the Biology of Sleep," in *Handbook of Dreams*, 76–130.

p. 193   *"sentinel" function*   Frederich Snyder, "Towards an Evolutionary Theory of Dreaming," *American Journal of Psychiatry* 2 (1966): 123, 121–42.

p. 193   *". . . even a certain amnesia"*   Lyall Watson, *Livstidevandet* (Life tide, 1979) (Copenhagen: Gyldendals Bogklub, 1980), 224.

p. 194   *complex tasks are handled*   P. Roffwarg, *Ontogenetic Development Science* 152 (1966): 604–19.

p. 194 *". . . habitual defense reactions"* J. Tolaas and M. Ullman, "Extra-sensory Communication and Dreams," in *Handbook of Dreams*, 192–93.

p. 194 *new learning processes* Fiss, "Current Dream Research," 36.

p. 194 *"the adaptation hypothesis for REM sleep"* Ibid., 38.

p. 194 *functions with dreams* Francis Crick and Graeme Michison, "The Function of Dream Sleep," *Nature* 304 (1983): 111–14.

p. 195 *". . . several times"* Søren Brunak and Benny Lautrop, "Drømmesøvn: Naturvidenskabeligt set" (Dream sleep: In the light of science), *Hug* 45 (1986): 59–60.

p. 195 *far inferior to it* Ibid., 59.

p. 196 *". . . brain's functioning"* Ibid., 54.

p. 196 *trials and loads of the day* Fiss, "Current Dream Research," 60.

p. 196 *". . . indicate his problems"* Foulkes, "How Is the Dream Formed? 312.

p. 196 *NREM thoughts* Ibid., 309.

p. 196 *dangerousness of the unconscious content* David R. Hawkins, "A Review of Psychoanalytic Dream Theory in the Light of Recent Psychophysiological Studies of Sleep and Dreaming," *British Journal of Medical Psychology* 39 (1966): 93–94.

p. 197 *when we are dreaming* McCarley and Hobson, "The Form of Dreams," 76, 124–25.

p. 197 *higher cerebral regions* Kluger, "Archetypal Dreams," 21; McCarley and Hobson, "The Form of Dreams," 112.

p. 197 *evolutionary history* Kluger, "Archetypal Dreams," 21.

p. 197 *inherited psychic structures* Ibid.

p. 197 *generated from within* Cartwright, *Night Life*, 18–24.

p. 197 *alarming and distorted dreams are* David Foulkes, "The Dreamlike Fantasy Scale," sleep study abstracts, *Psychophysiology* 7: 335–36; Foulkes, "How Is the Dream Formed?" 309–10.

p. 198 *told to a therapist* Bill Domhoff, "Home Dreams Versus Laboratory Dreams," in *Dream Psychology and the New Biology of Dreaming*, ed. M. Kramer (Springfield, 1969).

p. 198 *not especially profound* Jane Dallet, "Theories of Dream Function," *Psychological Bulletin* 79, no. 6 (1973): 408.

p. 198 *American psychology is based on* Ibid., 415.

p. 199 *". . . low level all the time"* C. G. Jung, *Analytical Psychology, Its Theory and Practice* (New York: Pantheon Books, 1968), 68.

p. 199 *dream an appropriate amount*   Cartwright, *Night Life*, 51–53.

p. 199 *fantasticality of psychic contents*   Foulkes, "Dreamlike Fantasy Scale," 335–36.

p. 199 *dreamlike . . . nature*   D. Foulkes and S. Fleischer, "Mental Activity in Relaxed Wakefulness," *Journal of Abnormal Psychology* 84: 72.

p. 199 *occur in the waking state*   D. Kripke and F. Sonnenschein, "A Biological Rhythm in Waking Fantasy," in *The Stream of Consciousness*, eds. J. Pope and K. J. Singer (New York: Plenum Press, 1978), 322.

7. DREAM AND THE BODY

p. 201 *or in the literature*   Mental Health Abstracts Database, key words: dream, body; Broeners; Reich; Lowen (Copenhagen: Det Kongelig Bibliotek, 1986).

p. 201 *repressed hostility in dreams*   L. Saul and E. Sheppard, "An Attempt to Quantify Emotional Forces," *Journal of the American Psychoanalytic Association* 4 (1956): 486–502.

p. 201 *between menstrual periods*   Ethel Swanson and David Foulkes, "Dream and the Menstrual Cycle," *Journal of Nervous and Mental Disease* 145, no. 5 (1968): 358–63.

p. 202 *ascertained in waking life*   E. Nyborg, "Drømte mig en drøm" (I dreamed a dream), *Hug* 9, no. 45 (1986): 23.

p. 203 *safety-valve function*   Charles Brenner, *An Elementary Textbook of Psychoanalysis* (New York: International University Press, 1974), 156, 168.

p. 203 *dealt with psychic problems*   Sigmund Freud, *A Metapsychological Supplement to the Theory of Dreams*, Standard Edition, vol. XIV (London: Hogarth Press, 1957), 219–37; Ole Olsen and Simo Køppe, "Psykoanalytisk psykologi og psykopatologi" (Psychoanalytical psychology and psychopathology), in J. Welner's *Psykiatri en tekstbog* (Psychiatry: A textbook) (Copenhagen: SADL–forlag, 1985), 69.

p. 203 *organic diseases on the basis of dreams*   Marie-Louise von Franz, "The Psychological Experience of Time," in *Eranos Yearbook* 47, eds. Adolf Portmann and Rudolf Ritsema (Frankfurt: Insel Verlag, 1981), 210.

p. 203 *periventricular epilepsy*   Jes Bertelsen, *Drømme, chakrasymboler og meditation* (Dreams, chakra symbols and meditation) (Copenhagen: Borgen, 1985), 25.

p. 204 *soon confirmed*   Jung, *Collected Works* 16, par. 344–48.

p. 204   *acute inflammation of the bladder*   Medard Boss, *The Analysis of Dreams* (New York: Philosophical Library, 1975), 160.

p. 204   *eagerness to pacify her*   Emil Gutheil, "Dreams and the Clinic," in *The Handbook of Dream Analysis* (New York: Liveright, 1951), 310.

p. 205   *"keeping her tied to her apron strings"*   Ibid., 318.

p. 205   *poor physical bearing, etc.*   Vedfelt, *Det kvindelige i manden*, 144–45.

p. 205   *somatic symptoms and dreams*   Arnold Mindell, *Working with the Dreaming Body* (London: Routledge and Kegan Paul, 1985), 13.

p. 206   *"the soul is expressing . . . through the sickness"*   Ibid., 8.

p. 206   *his therapeutic method*   Ibid., 6.

p. 206   *broke into tears*   Perls, *Gestalt Therapy Verbatim*.

p. 206   *like a bomb*   Mindell, *Dreaming Body*, 7.

p. 207   *her tumor disappeared*   Ibid., 12.

p. 207   *prolonged illness*   Røine, *Psykodrama*, 148.

p. 208   *dream interpretation*   Mindell, *Dreaming Body*, 88–89.

p. 208   *serious physical illness*   Ibid., 3.

p. 208   *I agree with Mindell*   Ibid., 8.

p. 208   *Jes Bertelsen*   Bertelsen, *Drømme, chakrasymboler og meditation*, 25.

p. 209   *". . . innocent and childish"*   Alexander Lowen, *Fornægtelsen af kroppen* (The betrayal of the body) (Copenhagen: Gyldendal, 1983), 38.

p. 210   *finally shouted for help*   Barbara Lerner, "Dream Function Reconsidered," in *Abnormal Psychology* 72, no. 2 (1967): 94.

p. 210   *somnambulation*   Ibid., 93.

p. 210   *compensated for in waking life*   Ibid., 88–89.

p. 211   *active in dreams*   Gutheil, "Dreams and the Clinic," 320.

p. 211   *". . . kinesthetic sense and the body image"*   Lerner, "Dream Function Reconsidered," 90.

p. 211   *the need for REM sleep*   G. Vogel and D. Giesler, "Exercise as a Substitute for REM–sleep," *Psychophysiology* 7 (1977): 300–301.

p. 211   *between dream and body language*   Patricia Garfield, *Creative Dreaming* (New York: Ballantine Books, 1976), 175; Cartwright, *Dreamlife*, 34.

p. 215   *unless the body is involved*   Mindell, *Dreaming Body*, 3.

p. 215   *physical and psychic effects*   Swami Devi Satyarthi, *Kroppens veje* (The body's ways) II (Copenhagen: Borgen, 1972), 187–88.

p. 216   *experiences and activities to come*   Karl Krackhauer, "Rolfing the Dreambody," in *Bulletin of Structural Integration* 7, no. 2 (1981): 14.

p. 217   *block of wood*   Ibid., 18–19.

p. 218   *genie just out of a bottle*   Ibid., 19–20.

p. 218   *often by meditation*   Arnold Mindell, *Dreambody* (London: Routledge and Kegan Paul, 1984), 56.

8. DREAMS AND PARAPSYCHOLOGY

p. 223   *Lincoln was assassinated*   Stanley Krippner, "Dreams and Other Altered Conscious States," *Journal of Communication* 21, no. 1 (1975): 173–82.

p. 223   *"a black, billowing mass"*   J. C. Barker, "Premonitions of the Aberfan Disaster," *Journal of the Society for Psychical Research* 44 (1967): 169–81.

p. 223   *crushed or buried alive*   Ibid., 173.

p. 224   *attitude toward occult phenomena*   Freud, "Drøm og okkultisme"; Jung, *Memories, Dreams, Reflections*, 173–74.

p. 224   *odds of 1:400,224*   C. G. Jung, "Synchronicity: An Acausal Connecting Principle," in *Collected Works* 8, 975–77.

p. 224   *ESP phenomena*   Ibid., 912.

p. 224   *parapsychological phenomena*   Montague Ullman, "Telepathy and Dreams," *Experimental Medicine and Surgery* 27 (1969): 20.

p. 225   *negative conception of parapsychological phenomena*   Jung, *Memories, Dreams, Reflections*, 173–74.

p. 225   *". . . verifiability notwithstanding"*   Freud, "Drøm og okkultisme," 48.

p. 225   *question of actual experiences*   Dean Sheils, "A Cross Cultural Study of Beliefs in Out-of-the-Body Experiences," *Journal of the Society for Psychical Research* 49 (1978): 697–741.

p. 225   *dreams they considered precognitive*   Abstract, *Human Behaviour* 5, no. 8 (1976): 34.

p. 225   *a jacket that was too small*   D. Scott Rogo, "Dreaming the Future," in *Psychic* 6, no. 4 (1975), 26–29.

p. 226   *closest to the dream*   Ullman, "Telepathy and Dreams," 26.

p. 226   *Christmas season*   Ibid., 26–28.

p. 227   *Krippner in collaboration with Ullman*   Montague Ullman, "The Role of Imagery," *Journal of Communication* 25, no. 1 (1975): 162–72; M. Ullman and S. Krippner, *Dream Studies and Telepathy* (Parapsychology Foundation Inc., 1970).

p. 227   *agitated masses*   Freud, "Drøm og okkultisme," 48.

p. 227   *external causal relation*   Jung, "Synchronicity," 984.

p. 227 *he showed it to the woman* Ibid., 982.

p. 227 *common meaning* C. T. Frey–Wehrlin, "Reflections on C. G. Jung's Concept of Synchronicity," *Journal of Analytical Psychology* 21, no. 1: 37–44.

p. 227 *Swedenborg's vision* Jung, "Synchronicity," 983–84.

p. 228 *archetypes in the collective unconscious* von Franz, *Jung, His Myth*, 247.

p. 228 *"higher consciousness"* Jes Bertelsen, *Højere bevidsthed* (Higher consciousness) (Copenhagen: Borgen 1983).

p. 228 *expectations, hope, and fear* Jung, "Synchronicity," 912.

p. 229 *travel in time, and so on* Stanislav Grof, *Beyond the Brain* (Albany: State University of New York Press, 1985).

p. 229 *stabilizing of the ego* René Spitz, *Die Entstehung der ersten Objektbeziehungen* (The creation of the first objective contact) (Stuttgart, 1973).

p. 229 *ego-stabilizing analysis* Marie-Louise von Franz, "Religiöse oder magische Einstellung zum Unbewussten" (Religious or magical ideation of the unconscious), in *Studien aus dem C. G. Jung–Institut* 17 (Zurich: Rascher Verlag, 1964).

p. 229 *game is to be found* von Franz, *Alchemy.*

p. 229 *vigilance function* Ullman, "Telepathy and Dreams," 25.

p. 229 *psychic boundary transgressions* Mental Health Abstracts Data Base. Key word: dream, parapsychol; ESP or Extra (Sensor?) and telepath; reincarna; rebirth; occult.

p. 229 *surmount any barrier* Ullman, "Telepathy and Dreams," 19–38.

p. 230 *know his secrets* Ibid., 24.

p. 230 *phenomena in psychoses* Jules Eisenbud, "The Use of the Telepathy Hypothesis . . . ," in *Specialized Techniques in Psychotherapy* 41–63.

p. 230 *as well as in psychotic states* Emilio Servadio, "Psychoanalysis and Telepathy," in G. Devereux (New York: International University Press, 1970), 210–20.

p. 231 *". . . crushed just like an egg"* Louisa Rhine, "The Subject Matter of Psi–Experiments," *Journal of Parapsychology* 40, no. 1 (1976): 53.

p. 231 *kind of "dreamwork"* Freud, "Drøm og okkultisme."

p. 231 *messages to the dreamer* D. Scott Rogo, "Dreaming the Future," in *Psychic* 6, no. 4 (1975): 26–29.

p. 232 *integrated in the dream interpretation* Freud, "Drøm og okkultisme," 33–34.

p. 232 *unrequited love* Eisenbud, "Telepathy Hypothesis," 51–53.

p. 233   *curing a client*   Frey–Wehrlin, "Jung's Concept of Synchronicity," 37–44.

p. 233   *as ESP or as telepathy*   Hans Dieckmann, "Die Konstellierung der Gegenübertragung" (Constellating the Countertransference), *Zeitschrift für analytisches Psychologie* 3, I (1971): 11–28.

p. 234   *sexual impulses were suppressed*   Ibid., 16–17.

p. 234   *unconscious processes in order*   Ibid., 11–28.

p. 235   *place the dream had indicated*   Rogo, "Dreaming the Future," 26–29.

p. 235   *fleeing with his family*   H. E. de Zoete, "Warning Dreams," *Mental Health Abstracts Data Base*, 0105484 HIS1973–07780.

p. 235   *this time he lost money*   Robert van de Castle, "Precognitive Dreaming," *Sundance Community Dream Journal*, vol. 2, no. 2 (1978): 185–86.

p. 236   *against a dream was successful*   Rogo, "Dreaming the Future," 26–29.

p. 238   *childish tendencies*   Jung, *Memories, Dreams, Reflections*, 173–74.

p. 240   *will often not be favorable*   David Foulkes, "Long Distance 'Sensory Bombardment': ESP in Dreams—A Failure to Replicate," *Perceptual and Motor Skills* 35, no. 3 (1972): 731–34.

p. 241   *besides the parapsychological*   Ullman, "Telepathy and Dreams," 25.

9. ESOTERIC DREAM UNDERSTANDING

p. 242   *double consciousness*   G. Raman, *Patanjalis Yoga Sutras* (Patanjali's yoga sutras) (Copenhagen: Strubes Forlag, 1968); Jes Bertelsen, *Højere bevidsthed* (Higher consciousness) (Copenhagen: Borgen, 1983), 81.

p. 243   *two stages from each other*   J.–P. Banquet et al., "Quantified EEG Spectral Analysis of Sleep and T.M.," in *Scientific Research on the Transcendental Meditation Program, Collected Papers* I (1977): 182–86, and diverse other articles, 151–82; Jan K. Olsen, *Mellem søvn og vågen* (Between sleep and waking) (Copenhagen: Bindu no. 13, 1975), 10–12.

p. 243   *verify the results*   R. R. Pagano, "Sleep During T.M.," *Science* 191 (1976): 308–10.

p. 243   *nonmeditators*   Faber et al., *Meditation*.

p. 244   *dreams on the other*   Jung, *Collected Works* 16, 546–64.

p. 244   *symbolism in tantric yoga*   Sir John Woodroffe (aka Arthur Avalon), *The Serpent Power* (New York: Dover Books, 1974).

p. 244   *energy vortexes called chakras*   Mindell, *Dreambody*, 51–54.

p. 244   *formerly five chakras*   Ibid., 37.

p. 244   *up to eighty-eight thousand*   Francis King, *Tantra for Westerners* (Wellingborough, Northamptonshire: The Aquarian Press, 1986), 37.

p. 244   *levels of development*   Bertelsen, *Drømme, chakrasymboler og meditation*, 52.

p. 245   *sources of whom Jung, Bob Moore*   C. G. Jung, *Yoga und der Westen* (Yoga and the West), in *Collected Works* 11, par. 859–76; Jung, *Memories, Dreams, Reflections*, 320–21; Robert S. Moore, "Physiology and Growth" I–VI, notes (Ringkjøbing, 1986–88); Robert S. Moore, "Couples Courses" I–V, notes (Ringkjøbing, 1986–88).

p. 245   *Mircea Eliade*   Mircea Eliade, *Yoga, Immortality and Freedom* (Princeton: Princeton University Press, 1969).

p. 245   *in relation to physical illnesses*   Mindell, *Dreambody*, 38–45.

p. 246   *upper and lower parts of the body*   Bertelsen, *Drømme, chakrasymboler og meditation*, 49–51.

p. 246   *chakra symbols*   Jung, *Collected Works* 16, 546–64.

p. 247   *kidney ailments and arthritis*   Mindell, *Dreambody*, 38–45.

p. 247   *encounter with the unconscious*   C. G. Jung, "Psychological Commentary on Kundalini Yoga," *Lecture* I–II (Zurich: Spring Publications, 1974), 1–30.

p. 247   *"a state of unconsciousness"*   Swami Janakananda, *Oplev Yoga Nidra* (Experience yoga nidra), guided deep relaxation (Copenhagen: Bindu, 1986).

p. 247   *experience of the hara chakra*   Bertelsen, *Drømme, chakrasymboler og meditation*, 73.

p. 247   *"by baptism with water"*   Jung, "Psychological Commentary on Kundalini Yoga," *Lecture* II–IV, 6.

p. 247   *root chakra's red color*   Heinrich Zimmer, "The Chakras of Kundalini Yoga," supplement to Jung's *Lecture* III–IV (Zurich: Spring Publications, 1974), 33–34.

p. 248   *venture to do this*   Jung, "Psychological Commentary on Kundalini Yoga," *Lecture* II–IV, 16.

p. 248   *transformation in the solar plexus*   Bertelsen, *Drømme, chakrasymboler og meditation*, 74.

p. 249   *"under the breastbone"*   Mindell, *Dreambody*, 38–45.

p. 249   *for the breath and the spiritual*   C. G. Jung, "The Phenomenology of the Spirit in Fairy Tales," in *Collected Works* 9I, 207–55.

p. 250   *twelve petals*   Zimmer, "Chakras of Kundalini Yoga," 33–34.

p. 000   *touches the disciple*   H. Coward, "Jung and Kundalini," *Journal of Analytical Psychology* 30 (1985): 389.

p. 252   *out-of-body experiences*   Bertelsen, *Drømme, chakrasymboler og meditation*, 64.

p. 252   *ought to attain*   Jung, "Commentary on Kundalini Yoga," *Lecture* II–IV, 6.

p. 252   *"the completely purified"*   Zimmer, "Chakras of Kundalini Yoga," 33–34.

p. 252   *"the music of the spheres"*   Bertelsen, *Drømme, chakrasymboler og meditation*, 52.

p. 252   *projections are pulled back*   Jung, "Commentary on Kundalini Yoga," *Lecture* II–IV, 16.

p. 253   *headcloth is blue*   Bertelsen, *Drømme, chakrasymboler og meditation*, 120.

p. 253   *throat infections*   Mindell, *Dreambody*, 38–45.

p. 253   *experience of unity*   Bertelsen, *Drømme, chakrasymboler og meditation*, 122.

p. 253   *experienced as more real*   Coward, "Jung and Kundalini," 391.

p. 254   *". . . living through all this"*   Swami Janakananda, *Oplev Yoga Nidra*.

p. 254   *penetrate into the conscious*   Mindell, *Dreambody*, 44.

p. 254   *gold and indigo*   Zimmer, "Chakras of Kundalini Yoga," 33–34.

p. 254   *eternity and temporality*   Bertelsen, *Drømme, chakrasymboler og meditation*, 123.

p. 254   *pure light and disappear*   von Franz, *On Dreams and Death*, 184.

p. 254   *"an indescribable radiance . . . hurts the eyes"*   Moody, *Life After Life*, 57.

p. 254   *annihilation of the ego*   Coward, "Jung and Kundalini," 390.

p. 255   *changes in their lives*   C. G. Jung, commentary to Richard Wilhelm's *The Secret of the Golden Flower* (London: Routledge and Kegan Paul, 1979), 106–7.

p. 255   *light-filled consciousness*   Bertelsen, *Drømme, chakrasymboler og meditation*, 67.

p. 255   *the lower chakras*   Ibid., 122.

p. 255   *came close to dying*   Ibid., 128.

p. 255   *visual disturbances*   Ibid., 125.

p. 256   *diamond body*   Ibid., 68, 129–30.

p. 256   *bright glow*   Jung, *Memories, Dreams, Reflections*, 320–21.

p. 257 *". . . my emotions"* Oliver Fox, *Astral Projection* (New York: University Books Inc., 1962), 32–33.

p. 257 *Saint-Denys . . . Ouspensky . . . Cayce . . . Castenada* Celia Green, *Lucid Dreams* (London: Hamish Hamilton, 1968), 33–35; P. D. Ouspensky, "On the Study of Dreams and Hypnotism," in *A New Model of the Universe* (New York: Vintage Books, 1913); E. Cayce, *Edgar Cayce on Dreams* (New York: Warner Books, 1969); C. Castaneda, *Journey to Ixtlan* (New York: Simon and Schuster, 1971), 126.

p. 257 *program of spiritual training* W. Y. Evans-Wentz, *Tibetan Yoga* (London: Oxford University Press, 1967).

p. 257 *taken up the subject* Mary Arnold-Forster, *Studies in Dreams* (New York: Macmillan Publishing Co. Inc., 1928); van Eeden, "A Study of Dreams," *Proceedings for the Society for Psychical Research* XXVI (1913).

p. 258 *you are dreaming* Green, *Lucid Dreams*, 33–35.

p. 259 *thinks she is awake* Patricia Garfield, *Creative Dreaming* (New York: Ballantine Books, 1974), 130–33.

p. 259 *in the usual manner* Ibid., 121.

p. 259 *in the dream* Castaneda, *Journey to Ixtlan*, 126.

p. 259 *last dream of the night* Garfield, *Creative Dreaming*, 130–33.

p. 259 *describe the room in detail* Fox, *Astral Projection*, 58–59.

p. 260 *"projections in the dreamer's own self"* George S. Sparrow, *Lucid Dreaming* (Virginia: A.R.E. Press, 1982), 2.

p. 260 *lucid dreams and meditation* Ibid., 50–52.

p. 261 *Jolande Jacoby* von Franz, *On Divination*; Jolande Jacoby, in C. G. Jung et al.'s *Man and His Symbols* (London: Aldus Books, 1964), 290.

p. 262 *lucidity, light, and accuracy* Bertelsen, *Højere bevidsthed*, 75.

p. 262 *than Jung did* Bertelsen, *Drømme, chakrasymboler og meditation*, 65.

p. 262 *self-aggrandizement and inflation* Coward, "Jung and Kundalini," 379.

p. 262 *imbalances or one-sidedness* Bertelsen, *Drømme, chakrasymboler og meditation*, 51.

p. 262 *lower level of consciousness* Jes Bertelsen, *Dybdepsykologi* (Depth psychology) III, *Den vestlige meditations psykologi* (The psychology of Western meditation) (Copenhagen: Borgen, 1980), 41–42.

p. 262 *messages to the dreamer* Jes Bertelsen, *Dybdepsykologi* (Depth Psychology) I (Copenhagen: Borgen, 1978), 121.

p. 262   *doing this is meditation*   Bertelsen, *Drømme, chakrasymboler og meditation*, 136, 150.

p. 262   *specific desired development*   Bertelsen, *Dybdepsykologi* III, 41–42.

p. 262   *". . . you yourself are constituted?"*   Jung, *Yoga und der Westen*, par. 859-76.

p. 264   *". . . aspect of one's personality"*   Moore, "Physiology and Growth" I–VI.

p. 265   *corresponding to the root chakra*   Philip Rawson, *Tantra: The Indian Cult of Ecstasy* (New York: Thames and Hudson, 1979), 18–19.

p. 267   *". . . Westerners could digest"*   Coward, "Jung and Kundalini," 379.

p. 267   *openness and resistance*   Bertelsen, *Kvantespring* (Quantum leap) (Copenhagen: Borgen, 1986), 18.

10. DREAM AND BIRTH EXPERIENCE

p. 269   *". . . reborn through the treatment"*   Freud, *Interpretation of Dreams*, 400.

p. 270   *had this dream repeatedly*   Gutheil, *Handbook of Dream Analysis*, 240–41.

p. 270   *fetal state and birth*   Hall, *Individual and His Dreams*.

p. 270   *symbolism to a personal experience*   Erich Neumann, *The Great Mother* (Princeton: Princeton University Press, 1963), 66–67.

p. 271   *psychological aspects*   C. G. Jung, "Concerning Rebirth" in *Collected Works* 9–1, par. 199–258.

p. 271   *baptism as spiritual rebirth*   Jung, *Symbols of Transformation* II, "Symbols of Mother and Rebirth," par. 300–418.

p. 271   *respiration, defecation, etc.*   Otto Rank, *The Trauma of Birth* (London: Kegan Paul, 1929).

p. 271   *strain at birth itself*   Grof, *Realms of the Human Unconscious* I–IV.

p. 271   *adversity, rejection, and so on*   Eve Jones, "Rebirthing," in R. J. Corsini's *Handbook of Innovative Psychotherapies*, 747–60.

p. 272   *transcendental experiences*   Ibid.

p. 272   *Greek mythology*   Jung, *Symbols of Transformation* II. "The Battle for Deliverance from the Mother," par. 419–63; Martin P. Nilsson, *Olympen* (The olympic) (Copenhagen: Haase & Søn, 1966).

p. 274   *important for him to learn*   Jones, "Rebirthing," 747–60.

11. DREAM AND CONSCIOUSNESS-EXPANDING TECHNIQUES

p. 275   *Indians peyote*   Furst, *Hallucinogens and Culture* (San Francisco: Chandler and Sharp, 1976); M. J. Harner (ed.), *Hallucinogens and Shamanism* (London: Oxford University Press, 1973).

p. 275   *opium to obtain inspiration*   Kramer, *Influence of Drugs on Dreams*, 305.

p. 275   *general anesthesia*   L. Grinspeer and Bakula, *Psychedelic Drugs Reconsidered* (New York, Basic Books); Jastov, "Anesthesia Dreams," 531–35.

p. 275   *the anesthetic Ketalar*   Gustav Hansen, "Ketamins psykotrope effect" (The psychotropic effect of Ketalar), *Bibliotek for læger* (Sept. 1966): 252–62.

p. 276   *biological birth*   Stanislav Grof, *Realms of the Human Unconscious* I, *Observations from LSD Research* (New York: Viking Press, 1975), 101–24.

p. 276   *individual's personality*   Grof, *Realms of the Human Unconscious* III, *LSD Psychotherapy* (Pomona, CA: Hunter House, 1980).

p. 276   *ordinary ego boundaries*   Grof, *LSD Research*, 33.

p. 276   *hallucinations can also be obtained*   Ibid., 34ff.

p. 276   *ordinary psychotherapy*   Ibid., 44.

p. 277   *like a newborn infant*   Ibid., 95–98.

p. 277   *mystical experiences*   Ibid., 154–58.

p. 277   *phases of psychic transformation*   Jung, *Ego and the Unconscious*, 55.

p. 277   *part of psychedelic therapy*   Grof, *LSD Psychotherapy*, 223–24.

p. 277   *their violent intensity*   Ibid.

p. 277   *". . . oceanic states"*   Ibid.

p. 277   *". . . no-exit situations"*   Ibid.

p. 278   *blood, mucus, urine, and feces*   Grof, *LSD Research*, 124.

p. 278   *". . . out-of-body travels"*   Grof, *LSD Psychotherapy*, 223–24.

p. 278   *you were actually there*   Personal communication from Grof.

p. 278   *dream and LSD*   Grof, *LSD Psychotherapy*, 223–24.

p. 282   *". . . connection to the birth process"*   Ibid.

p. 283   *hit the ocean*   Ibid.

p. 283   *". . . cataclysmic explosion"*   Ibid.

p. 283   *he was discharged*   Grof, *LSD Research*, 220.

p. 284   *dynamics play an important role*   Grof, *Realms of the Human Unconscious* IV, *Beyond the Brain* (Albany: State University of New York, 1985), 385.

p. 284   *dimensions in the psyche*   Grof, *Beyond the Brain*, 186.

p. 284   *psychotherapies for being intellectual*   Ibid., 176–77.

p. 284   *archetypal and transpersonal phenomena*   Ibid., 386.

p. 284   *matrices and transpersonal phenomena*   Ibid., 191.

p. 284   *"profound firsthand experiences"*   Ibid., 154, 179, 265, 353.

p. 284   *powerful techniques*   Grof, *LSD Research*, 99–100.

p. 285   *". . . LSD sessions of the individual"*   Ibid., 154.

p. 286   *impose on a client*   Grof, *LSD Psychotherapy*, 230.

p. 286   *scientific society*   Thomas Kuhn, *The Structure of Scientific Revolutions* (Chicago: University of Chicago Press, 1962).

p. 286   *material stuff it was made of*   Grof, *Beyond the Brain*, 419.

12. DREAM AND PSYCHOSES

p. 287   *affective psychoses . . . and paranoia*   J. Welner, *Psykiatri en tekstbog* (Psychiatry: A textbook) (Copenhagen: SADL, 1985).

p. 287   *overlap each other*   O. Olsen and Simo Køppe, "Psykoanalytisk psykologi og psykopatologi" (Psychoanalytic psychology and psychopathology), in *Psykiatri en tekstbog*, 86.

p. 288   *one could see in them*   C. G. Jung, "The Content of the Psychoses," in *Collected Works* 3.

p. 288   *impending psychosis*   Dieckmann, *Sprache der Seele*, 90.

p. 288   *symbolism of psychosis*   Jung, *Memories, Dreams, Reflections*, 150.

p. 289   *bloodthirsty and destructive*   Medard Boss, "Psychopathologie des Träumes bei schizophrenen und organischen Psychosen" (Psychopathology of the dreams of schizophrenics and organic psychoses), *Zeitschrift f. d. ges. Neurologie und Psychiatrie* 162 (1938): 467.

p. 289   *Swedenborg's dream book*   Ibid., 468.

p. 290   *integrating the archetypal contents*   Jung, *Ego and the Unconscious*, par. 250–52.

p. 290   *tips the scales*   Boss, "Träumes bei schizophrenen," 470.

p. 291   *pinning down actual reality*   Ibid., 476–77.

p. 291   *waking consciousness*   Ibid., 479.

p. 291   *macabre and brutal detail*   Ibid., 485.

p. 291   *erotic recollections and wishes*   Ibid., 483.

p. 292   *during the session*   von Franz, *Redemption Motifs in Fairy Tales*, 34.

p. 292   *emotionally indifferent toward them*   Boss, "Träumes bei schizophrenen," 485.

p. 292   *contact with the surrounding reality*   Ibid., 477–78.

p. 292   *narcissistic contents in the dreams*   Ibid., 470.

p. 292   *with dreams and with schizophrenics*   C. Brooks Brenneis, "Factors

Affecting Diagnostic Judgements of Manifest Dream Content in Schizophrenia," *Psychological Reports* (Yale University) 29, no. 3 (1971): 811–18.

p. 293 *ravages of an acute psychosis* R. Cartwright, "Sleep Fantasy in Normal and Schizophrenic Persons," *Journal of Abnormal Psychology* 80, no. 3 (1972): 275–79.

p. 293 *more resources . . . in the dreams* P. Carrington, "Dreams and Schizophrenia," *Archives of General Psychiatry* 26, no. 4 (1972): 343–50.

p. 293 *normal control groups* G. D. Astrachan, "The Structure of Dreams in Schizophrenia," in *Mental Health Abstracts*, Database Dialog File 86, key words: dream and schizo; borderline; psychot; mania; depressi; or psychopatho; Yuzuru Sunami, "A Psychophysiological Study on Dreams of Schizophrenics," in *Mental Health Abstracts*, *Psychiatria et Neurologia Japonica*.

p. 293 *prevailing mood* Boss, "Träumes bei schizophrenen," 459–94; Lotte Sussmann, "Beitrag zum Problem der Träume von Schizofrenen" (Contribution to the problem of dreams of schizophrenics), *Nervenarzt* 9 (1936): 453–66.

p. 293 *showing evidence of conflict* Jean B. Miller, "Dreams During Varying Stages of Depression," *Archives of General Psychiatry* 20 (May 1969): 560.

p. 294 *a control group* Peter Hauri, "Dreams in Patients Remitted from Reactive Depressions," *Journal of Abnormal Psychology* 85, no. 1 (1976): 1–10.

p. 294 *all kinds of projects* Olsen and Køppe, "Psykoanalytisk psykologi," 87.

p. 294 *surprised at my actions* Boss, *I Dreamt Last Night*, 122.

p. 295 *all of the city's sewers* Boss, "Träumes bei schizophrenen," 488.

p. 295 *abnormal dreams as before* Ibid., 470.

p. 295 *personality organization patients* Kernberg, *Borderline Conditions*.

p. 295 *ability to repress* Ibid.

p. 296 *opposite-sexed dream figures* Dieckmann, "Integration of the Ego Complex," 61.

p. 297 *a distinguished physician* H. G. Baynes, *Mythology of the Soul* (London: Methuen & Co.), 53–54.

p. 298 *no compensatory function* Alfred Ribi, "Forelæsninger om Hieronymus Boschs billeder" (Lectures on Hieronymus Bosch's pictures), at C.G. Jung Institute, Copenhagen, 1986.

p. 298 *meaningful* Jung, *Memories, Dreams, Reflections*, 151.

p. 299   *couldn't go back to the moon*   Jung, *Memories, Dreams, Reflections*, 151.

p. 299   *patriarchal worldview*   Pia Skogemann and Niels Reisby, *Carolines bog* (Caroline's book) (Copenhagen: Rosinante, 1985), 50.

p. 300   *bathed in sweat*   Boss, *I Dreamt Last Night*, 124–26.

p. 300   *". . . the case of a mere neurotic"*   Ibid.

p. 300   *nonaggressive life in society*   Harry A. Wilmer, "Dream Seminar for Chronic Schizophrenic Patients," *Psychiatry* 45, no. 4 (1982): 359.

p. 301   *sometimes having a narrative quality*   Ibid., 351.

p. 301   *couldn't reach my head*   Harry A. Wilmer, "Vietnam and Madness in Dreams of Schizophrenic Veterans," *Journal of American Psychoanalysis* 10, no. 1 (1982): 55.

p. 301   *never crying*   Ibid., 60.

p. 302   *duration of REM sleep*   Milton Kramer, et al., "The Influence of Drugs on Dreams," in *Symposium on Drugs and Sensory Functions* (Boston: Little Brown, 1968), 317–26; Milton Kramer, "Drugs and Dreams III: The Effects of Mipramine on the Dreams of Depressed Patients," *American Journal of Psychiatry* 124, no. 10 (1968): 1385–92.

p. 302   *reduce dream recall*   Kramer et al., "Influence of Drugs on Dreams," 305.

p. 302   *more often than those who did not*   Ibid., 308–9.

p. 302   *content and psychopharmaca*   David Foulkes, "Drug Research and the Meaning of Dreams," *Experimental Medicine and Surgery* 27 (1969): 39–52; Hauri, "Dreams in Patients," 2.

p. 303   *appeared in psychological tests*   Cartwright, "Sleep Fantasy," 275–79.

13. DREAM AND SOCIETY

p. 305   *events in the dreamer's life*   O'Nell, *Dreams, Culture, and the Individual*, 32–35.

p. 305   *dreams originated in the body*   C. G. Jung, *General Aspects of Dream Psychology*, in *Collected Works* 8, par. 457, 473.

p. 305   *vital social data*   Artemidorus, *The Interpretation of Dreams.*, ed. Robert White (Noyes Press, 1975).

p. 305   *reprinted twenty-four times*   Julia and Derek Parker, *Drømme, tolkning og symboler* (Copenhagen: Politikens Forlag, 1987), 15.

p. 305   *aid to avoiding dreams*   O'Nell, *Dreams, Culture, and the Individual*, 32–35.

p. 305   *prescribed a cure for the illness*   C. A. Meyer, *Antike Inkubation und moderne Psychotherapie* (Ancient incubation and modern psychotherapy) (Evanston, 1967).

p. 306   *skeptical of dreams*   O'Nell, *Dreams, Culture, and the Individual*, 32–35.

p. 306   *manifested in Jung and Freud*   Ellenberger, *Discovery of the Unconscious.*p. 306   *important work in this area*   O'Nell, *Dreams, Culture, and the Individual*, 77–80.

p. 306   *higher and truer reality*   Ibid., 26f.

p. 306   *elevated to permanent prestige*   A. Wallace, "Dreams and the Wishes of the Soul: A Type of Psychoanalytic Theory Among the Seventeenth Century Iroquois," *American Anthropologist* 60 (1958): 234–48.

p. 306   *who is inside the dream*   M. I. Meggitt, "Mae Enga Dreams," *South Western Journal of Anthropology* 18 (1962): 216–29.

p. 307   *takes place in young children*   J. Piaget, *Play, Dreams and Imitation in Childhood.*

p. 307   *Chuang Tse*   Pia Skogemann, "Chuang Tzu and the Butterfly Dream," *Journal of Analytical Psychology* 31 (1986): 75–90.

p. 307   *in terms of waking reality*   Meggitt, "Mae Enga Dreams," 216–29.

p. 307   *social importance*   O'Nell, *Dreams, Culture, and the Individual*, 28–30.

p. 308   *induced with special techniques*   Roy D'Andrade, "Anthropological Studies of Dreams," in *Psychological Anthropology* (Dorsey Press, 1961).

p. 308   *who is also a psychoanalyst*   Richard Noone, *In Search of the Dream People* (New York: Morrow, 1972); Kilton Stewart, "Dream Theory in Malay," in C. Tart's *Altered States of Consciousnesss* (John Wiley and Sons, 1969), 159–67.

p. 308   tohats   *Stewart, "Dream Theory in Malay," 160.*

p. 309   *beauty and knowledge to the group*   Ibid., 161–63.

p. 309   *friends will help you in them*   Ibid., 165.

p. 309   *unknown among the Senoi*   Ibid., 159–60.

p. 310   *some exotic culture or other*   Henri Baudet, *Paradise on Earth* (U.S.A.: Greenwood Press, 1976).

p. 310   *"creative dreaming"*   Garfield, *Creative Dreaming.*

p. 310   *entities that cannot be influenced*   von Franz, *On Dreams and Death.*

p. 310   *inspired by Senoi dreamwork*   Strephon Williams, *Jungian Senoi Dream Work Manual* (Berkeley: Journey Press, 1983).

p. 310   *claimed to be dream interpreters*   Barbara Tedlock et al., "Quiche Maya Dream Interpretation," *Ethos* 9, no. 4 (1981): 313–30.

p. 311   *more magical and projective*   A. Krohn and D. Gutmann, "Changes in Mastery Style with Age," *Psychiatry* 34 (1971): 289.

p. 311   *older men had fifteen*   Ibid., 292–93.

p. 312   *than the younger men*   Ibid., 295.

p. 312   *Bantu people in Africa*   Kenneth Colby, "Sex Differences in a Primitive Tribe," *American Anthropologist* 65 (1963): 116–22.

p. 312   *husband, mother, clothes, female person*   Ibid.

p. 313   *20 percent of the men*   M. Griffith, "The Universality of Typical Dreams," *American Anthropologist* 6 (1958): 1173–79.

p. 313   *"universal"*   Ibid.; O'Nell, *Dreams, Culture, and the Individual*, 6.

p. 314   *yearning attitude of the Chinese*   Wolfram Eberhard, "Social Interaction and Social Values in Chinese Dreams," *Journal of Sociology* 5 (1969): 61106.

p. 314   *character, thoughts, and outlook*   George Foster, "Dreams, Character and Cognitive Orientation in Tzintzuntzan," *Ethos* 1, no. 1 (1973): 106–21.

p. 314   *". . . hostile warfare between the sexes"*   Z. Giora et al., "Dreams in Cross–Cultural Research," *Comprehensive Psychiatry* 13, no. 2 (March 1972): 105–14.

p. 315   *a homosexual role*   Ronald Farrel, "Social Psychological Factors Associated with the Dream Content of Homosexuals," *International Journal of Social Psychiatry* 29, no. 3 (1983): 183–89.

p. 315   *worked outside the home*   Monique Lortie-Lussier et al., "Working Mothers Versus Homemakers," *Sex Roles* 12, nos. 9–10 (1985): 1009–21.

p. 315   *most were not in psychotherapy*   Charlotte Beradt, *The Third Reich of Dreams* (Wellingborough, Northamptonshire: The Aquarian Press, 1985), 12ff.

p. 315   *his back—his backbone—breaks*   Ibid., 5–8.

p. 316   *". . . Abolition of Walls"*   Ibid., 22.

p. 316   *dangerous rumors*   Ibid., 45–46.

p. 316   *understand myself*   Ibid., 52–53.

p. 316   *repetition on a fluttering banner*   Ibid., 40.

p. 316   *his personal archer*   Ibid., 117.

p. 317   *It read*   Ibid., 133–35.

p. 317   *opposition was impossible*   Bruno Bettelheim, "An Essay," in Beradt's *Third Reich*, 151.

p. 317   *"dreams of escape or revenge"*   Ibid., 156–58.

p. 318   *". . . by suppressing one's will"*   Ibid., 160.

p. 318   *". . . threw Goebbels out of the factory"*   Ibid., 161.

p. 318   *". . . more positive were his dreams"*   Beradt, *Third Reich of Dreams*, 98–100.

p. 318   *I plunged into the abyss*   Ibid.

p. 318   *"extremely agitated by it"*   Bettelheim, "An Essay," 167.

p. 319   *fantasy helped one to survive*   Ibid., 160.

p. 319   *"strongly coherent dream with many resources"*   Carrington, "Dreams and Schizophrenia."

p. 319   *specific to the Hitler regime*   Beradt, *Third Reich of Dreams*, 13.

p. 319   *propaganda as the Nazis*   Kenneth Johnson, "Modernity and Dream Content: A Ugandan Example," *Ethos* 6, no. 4 (1978): 212–20.

p. 319   *more collected inner attitude?*   P. Robbins and R. Tanck, "Community Violence and Aggressions in Dreams," *Perceptual and Motor Skills* 29, no. 1 (1968): 41–42.

p. 320   *less real than waking consciousness*   O'Nell, *Dreams, Culture, and the Individual*, 24.

p. 320   *universally widespread*   Kluger, "Archetypal Dreams," 9–10.

p. 320   *more of animals than of adults*   Krohn and Gutmann, "Mastery Style," 291.

p. 321   *function for the society*   Jung, *Visions Seminars* I, 5.

p. 321   *"murdering sleep"*   Bettelheim, "An Essay," 150–70.

p. 321   *find new resources*   Cartwright, *Night Life*.

p. 322   *severe sexual laws*   Jung, *General Aspects of Dream Psychology*, in *Collected Works* 8, par. 457, 473.

p. 322   *crude desires*   Freud, *Interpretation of Dreams*, 397.

p. 323   *anthropological facts*   K. Achte and T. Shakir, "Dreams in Different Cultures," *Psychiatria Fennica* (1981): 25–39.

p. 323   *". . . received support"*   Krohn and Gutmann, "Mastery Style," 290.

14. OTHER DIRECTIONS AND METHODS

p. 325   *developed in recent decades*   Corsini, *Handbook of Current Psychotherapies*.

p. 325   *Ernesto Rossi and Roberto Assagioli*   Ernesto Rossi, *Dreams and the Growth of Personality* (New York: Pergamon Press, 1972); Roberto Assagioli, *Psychosynthesis* (Turnstone Press, 1965).

p. 326   *child's behavior and experience*   Hall, *Clinical Uses of Dreams*, 40.

p. 326   *predilection for forming symbols*   Piaget, *Plays, Dreams and Imitation in Childhood*, 198.

p. 326   *untranslatable to normal language*   Samuels, *Jung and the Post-Jungians*, 240.

p. 326   *a former Freudian*   C. Rycroft, *The Innocence of Dreams* (London: Hogarth Press, 1979).

p. 326   *"the essentially unknown"*   von Franz, *Träume*.

p. 326   *what science regards as being true*   Schultz, *Drømmeforståelse*, 9–12; Madsen, *Sammenlignende videnskabsteori . . .* , 68–70.

p. 328   *dreams in the subsequent session*   David Zimmermann, "Dreams in Group-Analytic Psychotherapy," *International Journal of Group Psychotherapy* 17, no. 4 (1967): 526–27.

p. 328   *the individual in the group*   Ibid., 525.

p. 328   *less terrifying than in individual therapy*   Eva Klein-Lipschutz, "Dreams in Individual and Group Psychotherapy." *International Journal of Group Psychotherapy* 3 (1953): 143–49.

p. 328   *deeply personal material*   Amman, *Aktive Imagination*.

p. 328   *"more irrational" group process*   Edward C. Whitmont, "Recent Influences on Jungian Analysis," in Murray Stein's *Jungian Analysis* (London: Shambhala, 1984), 361–62.

p. 328   *include in a session*   Vivian Gold, "Dreams in Group Psychotherapy," *International Journal of Group Psychotherapy* 23, no. 4 (1973): 394–407; Montague Ullman, "The Experiential Dream Group," in *A Handbook of Dreams*, New York: Van Nostrand, 1979, 409.

p. 328   *eliminating such themes*   B. Fielding, "Dreams in Group Psychotherapy," *Psychotherapy: Theory . . .* 4, no. 2 (1967): 74–77.

p. 329   *interpretation that counts*   Ullman, *Forstå dine drømme*, 190–97.

p. 329   *". . . expert in others' dreams"*   Ibid., 15, 185, 186.

p. 329   *". . . the message it contains"*   Ullman, "Experiential Dream Group," 409.

p. 331   *overinterpretations*   Whitmont, "Recent Influences," 361–62.

p. 332   *paint their dreams*   Corsini, *Handbook of Current Psychotherapies*.

p. 332   *extremely useful tools*   Jacoby, *C. G. Jungs Psykologi*.

p. 332   *Aniela Jaffé*   Jaffé, *Symbolism in the Visual Arts*.

p. 332   *severely mentally ill*   S. Bach, *Spontanes Malen schwerkranker Patienten* (Spontaneous paintings of severely ill patients) (Wellingborough, Northamptonshire: The Aquarian Press, 1966.).

p. 332   *psychosocial development stages*   Hanne Hostrup Larsen, *Tegneterapi i neurosebehandling* (Drawing therapy in the treatment of neuroses) (Copenhagen: Dansk Psykologisk Forlag, 1979).

15. MULTIDIMENSIONAL DREAM INTERPRETATION

p. 335   *hermeneutics*   Gerard Radnitzky, *Contemporary Schools of Meta-science, Vol. 1* (Stockholm: Scandinavian University Books, 1970), 25-29.

p. 342   *multidimensional dream theory*   David Bohm, *Wholeness and the Implicate Order* (London and New York: Ark Paperbacks, 1980).

p. 342   *"dreams have the effect that . . ."*   Madsen, *Sammenlignende videnskabsteori . . .* , 97.

p. 342   *"reason why we should dream"*   Freud, *Interpretation of Dreams* I, 76.

p. 345   *". . . what is happening with him"*   Esben Hougård, *Psykoterapi som non-specifik behandling* (Psychotherapy as nonspecific treatment) (Århus: Psykologisk Skriftserie Århus Universitet, 1983), 45.

p. 352   *existing knowledge*   Ellenberger, *Discovery of the Unconscious.*

p. 353   *mutually conflicting theories*   Freud, *Interpretation of Dreams* I, 76; 10: Ole Vedfelt, *Drømmenes væsen* (The nature of dreams), *Psyke og Logos nr.* 1 (English summary), (Copenhagen, 1991): 21–42.

p. 353   *leading astrophysicists of our time*   S. W. Hawking, *A Brief History of Time* (New York: Bantam Books Inc., 1988).

BIBLIOGRAPHY

Abramson, Harold A. "The use of LSD as an Adjuvant to Psychotherapy." In *LSD A Total Study*. Westbury, New York: PJD Publications, 1975.

Achen, Sven Tito. *Symboler omkring os* (Symbols around us). Copenhagen: Gad, 1975.

Achte, K., and Shakir, T. "Dreams in Different Cultures." *Psychiatria Fennica* (1981): 25–39.

Adler, Alfred. "Dreams Reveal the Life Style." In *The New World of Dreams*. Edited by Ralph Woods and Herbert Greenhouse. New York: Macmillan Publishing Co. Inc., 1974.

———. *Individual Psychology*. London: Routledge and Kegan Paul, 1929.

———. "On the Interpretation of Dreams." *International Journal of Individual Psychology* 2 (1936): 13–16, 225.

———. *Social Interest: Challenge to Mankind*. London: Faber and Faber, 1938.

Adler, Gerhard. *The Living Symbol*. New York: Pantheon Books, 1961.

Allison, Truett, and Van Twyver, Henry. "The Sleep and Dreams of Animals." In *The New World of Dreams*. Edited by Ralph Woods and Herbert Greenhouse. New York: Macmillan Publishing Co. Inc., 1974.

Alveson, Mats. "Narcissisme i socialpsykologisk belysning" (Narcissism in the light of social psychology). *Nordisk Psykologi* 35, no. 2 (1983): 100–124.

Amman, A. N. *Aktive Imagination* (Active imagination). Olten: Walter Verlag, 1978.

Arkin, A., Hastey, J., and Reiser M. "Post-Hypnotically Stimulated Sleeptalking." *Journal of Nervous and Mental Disease* 142 (1953): 273.

Arlow, S. A., and Brenner, C. *Psychoanalytic Concepts and the Structural Theory*. New York: International University Press, 1964.

Arnold-Forster, Mary. *Studies in Dreams*. New York: Macmillan Publishing Co. Inc., 1928.

Arons, B. "First Reported Dreams in Psychoanalytic Group Psychotherapy." *American Journal of Psychotherapy* 32, no. 4 (1978): 544–51.

Artemidorus. *The Interpretation of Dreams*. Edited by Robert White. Noyes Press, 1975.

Assagioli, Roberto. *Psychosynthesis*. Turnstone Press, 1965.

Astrachan, G. D. "The Structure of Dreams in Schizophrenia." In *Mental Health Abstracts—Database Dialog File 86*.

Bach, S. *Spontanes Malen schwerkranker Patienten* (Spontaneous paintings of severely ill patients). Wellingborough, Northamptonshire: The Aquarian Press.

Bandler and Grinder. *Reframing*. Moab, Utah: Real People Press, 1982.

Banquet, J. P. et al. "Quantified EEG Spectral Analysis of Sleep and T.M." In *Scientific Research on the Transcendental Meditation Program. Collected Papers* I (1977): 182–86; and diverse other articles, 151–82.

Barker, J. C. "Premonitions of the Aberfan Disaster." *Journal of the Society for Psychical Research* 44 (1967): 169–81.

Barz, Ellinor. *Psykodrama* (Psychodrama). Diploma diss., C. G. Jung Institute, Zurich, 1985.

Baudet, Henri. *Paradise on Earth*. Greenwood Press, 1976.

Baynes, H. G. *Mythology of the Soul*. London: Methuen & Co.

Beradt, Charlotte. *The Third Reich of Dreams*. Wellingborough, Northamptonshire: The Aquarian Press, 1985.

Berger, Milton. *Gestalt Therapy Integrated*. New York: Vintage Books, 1974.

Bertelsen, Jes. *Drømme, chakrasymboler og meditation* (Dreams, chakra symbols and meditation). Copenhagen: Borgen, 1982.

———. *Dybdepsykologi* (Depth psychology) I. Copenhagen: Borgen, 1978.

———. *Dybdepsykologi* (Depth psychology) III. *Den vestlige meditations psykologi* (The psychology of Western meditation). Copenhagen: Borgen, 1980.

———. *Genfødslens psykologi* (The psychology of rebirth). Copenhagen: Borgen, 1979.

———. *Højere bevidsthed* (Higher consciousness). Copenhagen: Borgen, 1983.

———. *Kvantespring* (Quantum leap). Copenhagen: Borgen, 1986.

Bettelheim, Bruno. "An Essay." In C. Beradt's *Third Reich . . .* , 150–70.

The Bible: 6 Isaiah.

Blomeyer. "Die Konstellierung der Gegenübertragung" (Constellating the countertransference). *Zeitschrift für analytisches Psychologie* 3, I (1971): 28–39.

Bohm, David. *Wholeness and the Implicate Order*. London and New York: Ark Paperbacks, 1980.

Boss, Medard. *The Analysis of Dreams*. New York: Philosophical Library, 1975.

———. "The Dreamer Lives in a Real World." In *The New World of Dreams*. Edited by Ralph Woods and Herbert Greenhouse. New York: Macmillan Publishing Co. Inc.

———. "Dreaming and the Dreamed in the Daseinsanalytic Way of Seeing." In *On Dreaming*. Edited by Charles E. Scott. Chico: Scholar Press, 1977.

———. *I Dreamt Last Night*. New York: Gardner Press Inc., 1977.

———. "Psychopathologie des Träumes bei schizophrenen und organischen Psychosen" (Psychopathology of the dreams of schizophrenics and organic psychoses). *Zeitschrift f. d. ges. Neurologie und Psychiatrie* 162 (1938): 459–94.

Boysen, Birgit. Drømme, bevidsthed, selvudvikling (Dreams, consciousness, self-development). Copenhagen: Strubes Forlag, 1987.

Brandrup, E., and Vanggaard, T. "LSD—Treatment in a Severe Case of Compulsive Neurosis." *Acta Psychiatrica Scandinavia* 55 (1977): 127–41.

Breger, Louis. "Function of Dreams." *Journal of Abnormal Psychology* 72, no. 5 (1967): 1.

Brenneis, Brooks. "Male and Female Ego Modalities in Manifest Dream Content." *Journal of Abnormal Psychology* 76, no. 3 (1970): 434–42.

———. "Factors Affecting Diagnostic Judgements of Manifest Dream Content in Schizophrenia." *Psychological Reports* (Yale University) 29, no. 3 (1971): 811–18.

———, and Roll, S. "Manifest Dreams of Male and Female Chicanos." In *Psychiatry* 38 (1975): 172–85.

Brenner, Charles. *An Elementary Textbook of Psychoanalysis*. New York: Doubleday, 1974.

Brinton-Perera, Sylvia. *Descent to the Goddess*. Toronto: Inner City Books, 1981.

Brunak, Søren, and Lautrop, Benny. "Drømmesøvn. Naturvidenskabeligt set" (Dream sleep—In the light of science). *Hug* 45 (1986): 54–61.

Caligor, Leopold, and May, Rollo. *Dreams and Symbols*. New York: Basic Books, 1968.

Carrington, P. "Dreams and Schizophrenia." In *Archives of General Psychiatry* 26, no. 4 (1972): 343–50.

Cartwright, Rosalind. *Night Life*. Englewood Cliffs, NJ: Prentice-Hall Inc., 1977.

————. "Sleep Fantasy in Normal and Schizophrenic Persons." *Journal of Abnormal Psychology* 80, no. 3 (1972): 275–79.

Casement, Patrick. *On Learning from the Patient.* London: Tavistock, 1987.

Castaneda, Carlos. *Journey to Ixtlan.* New York: Simon and Schuster, 1971.

Cayce, Edgar. *Edgar Cayce on Dreams.* New York: Warner Books, 1969.

Chetwynd, Tom. *Dictionary of Symbols.* London: Granada Publishing Co., 1982.

Cirlot, J. E.. *A Dictionary of Symbols.* London: Routledge and Kegan Paul, 1967.

Colby, Kenneth. "Sex Differences in a Primitive Tribe." *American Anthropologist* 65 (1963): 116–22.

Corsini, R. J. *Handbook of Current Psychotherapies.*

Coward, H. "Jung and Kundalini." *Journal of Analytical Psychology* 30 (1985): 379–92.

Crick, Francis, and Michison, Graeme. "The Function of Dream Sleep." *Nature* 304 (1983): 111–14.

Dallet, Jane. *Active Imagination in Practice.* In *Jungian Analysis.* Edited by Stein and Murray. London: Shambhala, 1984.

————. "Theories of Dream Function." *Psychological Bulletin* 79, no. 6 (1973): 408–16.

D'Andrade, Roy. "Anthropological Studies of Dreams." In *Psychological Anthropology.* Dorsey Press, 1961.

Delage, Yves. Described by Celia Green in *Lucid Dreams.* London: Hamish Hamilton, 1968.

Dement, W. "The Effect of Dream Deprivation." *Science* 131 (1960): 1705–7.

————, and Wolpert, E. "The Relation of Eye Movements, Body Mortality, and External Stimuli to Dream Content." *Journal of Experimental Psychology* 55 (1958): 543.

Devereux, George. "Mohave Dreams and Rituals." In *American Anthropologist* 59 (1957): 1036–45.

de Vries, Ad. *Dictionary of Symbols and Imagery.* London: North Holland Publishing Co., 1974.

de Zoete, H. E. "Warning Dreams." *Mental Health Abstracts Data Base.* 0105484 HIS1973–07780.

Dieckmann, Hans. "Die Konstellierung der Gegenübertragung" (Constellating the countertransference). *Zeitschrift für analytisches Psychologie* 3, I (1971): 11–28.

——. "Integration Process of the Ego Complex in Dreams." *Journal of Analytical Psychology*, vol. 10, nr.1 (1962): 41–65.

——. "On the Methodology of Dream Interpretation." In *Methods of Treatment in Analytical Psychology*. Stuttgart: Bonz, 1980.

——. "Transference and Countertransference." In *The Journal of Analytical Psychology* 21 (1976): 25–36.

——. *Träume als Sprache der Seele* (Dreams as the language of the soul). Stuttgart: Bonz, 1984.

——. "Über einige Beziehungen zwischen Traumserie und Verhaltungsanderungen" (On some connections between dream series and behavioral changes). *Zeitschrift für Psychosomatisches Medizin* 8 (1962): 273–80.

Domhoff, Bill. "Home Dreams Versus Laboratory Dreams." In *Dream Psychology and the New Biology of Dreaming*. Edited by M. Kramer. Springfield, 1969.

Downing, Christine. "Poetically Dwells Man on This Earth." In *On Dreaming*. Edited by Charles E. Scott. Chico: Scholar Press, 1977.

Downing, Jack, and Marmorstein, Robert. *Dreams and Nightmares*. New York: Harper and Row. 1973.

Dreyfuss-Brisac. "The EEG of the Premature Infant and the Fall Term Newborn." In *Neurological and Electroencephalogic Correlative Studies of Infancy*. Edited by Kelloway and Petersen. New York: Grune and Stratton, 1969.

Eberhard, Wolfram. "Social Interaction and Social Values in Chinese Dreams." *Journal of Sociology* 5 (1969): 61106.

Edinger, E. *Ego and Archetype*. New York: Putnam, 1972.

Ehrenvald, Jan. "Psi Phenomena and the Existential Shift." *American Society for Psychical Research* 65, no. 2 (1978): 162–72.

——. *Telepathy and Medical Psychology*. New York: Norton, 1978.

Eisenbud, Jules. "The Use of the Telepathy Hypothesis . . ." In *Specialized Techniques in Psychotherapy* 41: 63.

Eisenstein, Victor W. "Dreams Following Intercourse." *Psychoanal. Quarterly* 18 (1949): 154–72.

Eliade, Mircea. *Shamanism*. Princeton: Princeton University Press, 1964.

——. *Yoga, Immortality and Freedom*. Princeton: Princeton University Press, 1969.

Ellenberger, Henri F. *The Discovery of the Unconscious*. New York: Basic Books, 1970.

Erikson, Erik H. *Barnet og samfundet* (The child and society). Copenhagen: Hans Reitzels Forlag, 1983.

———. "The Dream Specimen of Psychoanalysis." *Journal of the American Psychoanalytic Association* 2 (1954): 5–56.

Evans-Wentz, W. Y. *Tibetan Yoga*. London: Oxford University Press, 1967.

Faber, P. A., et al. "Induced Waking Fantasy—Its Effects Upon the Archetypal Content of Nocturnal Dreams." *International Analytical Psychology* (1983): 141–64.

———. "Meditation and Archetypal Content of Nocturnal Dreams." *Journal of Analytical Psychology* 23 (1978): 1–22.

Fairbairn W. R. D. *Psychoanalytic Studies of the Personality*. London: Tavistock, 1952.

Faraday, Ann. *Dream Power*. New York: Berkley Books, 1972.

Farrel, Ronald. "Social Psychological Factors Associated with the Dream Content of Homosexuals." *International Journal of Social Psychiatry* 29, no. 3 (1983): 183–89.

Fenichel, Otto. *The Psychoanalytical Theory of Neurosis*. London: Routledge and Kegan Paul, 1977.

Fielding, B. "Dreams in Group Psychotherapy." *Psychotherapy: Theory . . .* 4, no. 2 (1967): 74–77.

Fiss, Harry. "Current Dream Research—A Psychobiological Perspective." In *A Handbook of Dreams*. Edited by Benjamin B. Wolman. New York: Van Nostrand, 1979.

———. "The Need to Complete One's Dreams." In *The Meaning of Dreams*. Edited by J. Fisher and L. Breger. Los Angeles: California Mental Health Research Symposium 3, 1969.

Flammerion. *The Unknown*. London, 1900.

Fordham, M. *The Empirical Foundation of C. G. Jung's Work*. In LPA.

Foster, George. "Dreams, Character and Cognitive Orientation in Tzintzuntzan." *Ethos* 1, no. 1 (1973): 106–21.

Foulkes, David. *Children's Dreams: Longitudinal Studies*. New York: John Wiley and Sons, 1982.

———. "The Dreamlike Fantasy Scale." Sleep Study Abstracts. *Psychophysiology* 7: 335–36.

————. "Drug Research and the Meaning of Dreams." *Experimental Medicine and Surgery* 27 (1969): 39–52.

————. "How is the Dream Formed? Another look at Freud and Adler." In *The New World of Dreams*. Edited by Ralph Woods and Herbert Greenhouse. New York: Macmillan Publishing Co. Inc., 1974.

————. "Long Distance 'Sensory Bombardment'—ESP in Dreams: A Failure to Replicate." *Perceptual and Motor Skills* 35, no. 3 (1972): 731–34.

————. *The Psychology of Sleep*. New York: Charles Scribners Sons, 1966.

————. "You Think All Night Long." In *The New World of Dreams*. Edited by Ralph Woods and Herbert Greenhouse. New York: Macmillan Publishing Co. Inc., 1974.

————, and Fleischer, S. "Mental Activity in Relaxed Wakefulness." *Journal of Abnormal Psychology* 84: 66–77.

Fox, Oliver. *Astral Projection*. New York: University Books Inc., 1962.

French, Thomas, and Fromm, Erika. *Dream Interpretation: A New Approach*. New York, London: Basic Books, 1964.

Freud, Anna. *The Ego and the Mechanisms of Defense*. New York: International University Press, 1968.

Freud, Sigmund. *Beyond the Pleasure Principle*. 1922.

————. "Dreams and Occultism" in *New Introductory Lectures on Psychoanalysis*, vol. 22. London: Hogarth Press, 1933.

————. *The Ego and the Id*. Standard Edition. Vol. XIX. London: Hogarth Press, 1961.

————. *The Interpretation of Dreams*. London: Hogarth Press, 1981.

————. *A Metapsychological Supplement to the Theory of Dreams*. Standard Edition. Vol. XIV. London: Hogarth Press 1957.

————. "Revision af drømmelæren" (Revision of the theory of dreams). In *Nye forelæsninger til indføring i psykoanalysen* (New introductory lectures in psychoanalysis). Copenhagen: Hans Reitzel, 1973.

————. "Revision of the Theory of Dreams" in *New Introductory Lectures on Psychoanalysis*. Standard Edition. Vol. XXII. London: Hogarth Press, 1964.

————. *The Standard Edition of the Complete Psychological Works of Freud*. London: Hogarth Press, 1957. The following titles contain observations of significance for Freud's dream theory: 1901: *On Dreams*. Vol. 5; 1907: *Delusions and Dreams in Jensen's Gradiva*. Vol. 9; 1912–13: *Totem and Tabu*. Vol. 13; 1913: *An Evidential Dream*. Vol. 12;

1918: *From the History of an Infantile Neurosis.* Vol. 17; 1920: *A Case of Homosexuality in a Woman.* Vol. 18; 1923: *Two Encyclopedia Articles.* Vol. 18; 1923: *Remarks on the Theory and Practice of Dream Interpretation.* Vol. 19; 1925: *An Autobiographical Study.* Vol. 20; 1925: *Some Additional Notes upon Dream Interpretation as a Whole.* Vol. 19; 1938: *An Outline of Psychoanalysis.* Vol. 23.

Frey-Wehrlin, C. T. "Reflections on C. G. Jung's Concept of Synchronicity." *Journal of Analytical Psychology* 21, no.1: 37–44.

Freyh-Rohn, Liliane. *From Freud to Jung.* New York: Putnam, 1974.

Fromm, Erich. *Det glemte sprog* (The forgotten language, 1951). Copenhagen: Hans Reitzels Forlag, 1967.

Furst. *Hallucinogens and Culture.* San Francisco: Chandler and Sharp, 1976.

Garfield, Patricia. *Creative Dreaming.* New York: Ballantine Books, 1974.

————. *Your Child's Dreams.* New York: Ballantine Books, 1984.

Gedo, John E. *Portraits of the Artist.* New York: The Guilford Press, 1983.

Gendlin, Eugene. *Let Your Body Interpret Your Dreams.* Willmette, IL: Chiron Publications, 1986.

————. "Phenomenological Concept vs. Phenomenological Method." In *On Dreaming.* Edited by Charles E. Scott. Chico: Scholar Press, 1977.

"Gestalt Therapy Reading List." *Counseling Psychologist* 4, no. 4 (1974): 60–63.

Giora, Z. et al. "Dreams in Cross-Cultural Research." *Comprehensive Psychiatry* 13, no. 2 (March 1972): 105–14.

Gold, Leo. "Adler's Theory of Dreams." In *A Handbook of Dreams.* Edited by Benjamin B. Wolman. New York: Van Nostrand, 1979.

Gold, Vivian. "Dreams in Group Psychotherapy." *International Journal of Group Psychotherapy* 23, no. 4 (1973): 394–407.

Grant, John. *Dreamers.* London: Ashgrove Press, 1984.

Green, Celia. *Lucid Dreams.* London: Hamish Hamilton, 1968.

Greenberg, R., et al. "The Effect of REM-Deprivation on Adaption to Stress." *Psychosomatic Medicine* 34 (1972): 257–62.

Greenhouse, Herbert. "The Murder that Triggered World War I." In *The New World of Dreams.* Edited by Ralph Woods and Herbert Greenhouse. New York: Macmillan Publishing Co. Inc., 1974.

———. "Penile Erections During Dreams." In *The New World of Dreams*. Edited by Ralph Woods and Herbert Greenhouse. New York: Macmillan Publishing Co. Inc., 1974. 296–302.

Griffith, M. "The Universality of Typical Dreams." *American Anthropologist* 6 (1958): 1173–79.

Grinspeer, L., and Bakula. *Psychedelic Drugs Reconsidered*. New York: Basic Books.

Grof, Stanislav. *Beyond the Brain*. Albany: State University of New York Press, 1985.

———*LSD Psychotherapy*. Pomona, CA: Hunter House, 1980.

———*Observations from LSD Research*. New York: Viking Press, 1975.

———, and Halifax, Joan. *The Human Encounter with Death*. New York: E. P. Dutton, 1977.

Guntrip, Harry S. *Psychoanalytic Theory, Therapy, and the Self*. New York: Basic Books, 1971.

Gutheil, Emil. "Dreams and the Clinic." In *The Handbook of Dream Analysis*. New York: Liveright, 1951.

Gutmann, David. "Aging Among the Maya." *Journal of Personal and Social Psychology* 7 (1967): 28–35.

Hall, Calvin S. "A Cognitive Theory of Dream Symbolism." *The Journal of General Psychology* 48 (1953): 169–86.

———. "Diagnosing Personality by the Analysis of Dreams." *Journal of Abnormal and Social Psychology* 42 (1947): 68–79.

———. *The Meaning of Dreams*. New York: McGraw-Hill Book Co., 1966.

———. "A Modest Confirmation of Freud's Theory of the Distinction Between the Superego of Men and Women." *Journal of Abnormal and Social Psychology* 69, no. 4 (1969): 440–42.

———. *A Primer of Freud's Psychology*. New York: The New American Library, 1954.

———, and Domhoff, Bill. "Aggressions in Dreams." *International Journal of Psychiatry* 9 (1963): 259–67.

———. "The Difference Between Men and Women Dreamers." 1974.

———. "The Dreams of Freud and Jung." *Psychology Today* (June 1968).

———. "Friendliness in Dreams." *Journal of Social Psychology* 62 (1964): 309–14.

————. "A Ubiquitous Sex Difference in Dreams." *Journal of Abnormal Social Psychology* 62 (1963): 278–80.

Hall, Calvin, and Nordby, Vernon. *The Individual and His Dreams*. New York: New American Library, 1972.

————. *C. G. Jungs psykologi* (The psychology of C. G. Jung). Copenhagen: Hans Reitzels Forlag, 1976.

Hall, Calvin, and van de Castle, Robert. *The Content Analysis of Dreams*. New York: Appleton Century Crofts, 1966.

————. "An Empirical Investigation of the Castration Complex in Dreams." *Journal of Personality* 33 (1965): 20–29.

Hall, James A. *Clinical Uses of Dreams*. New York, London: Grune and Stratton, 1977.

————. *Jungian Dream Interpretation*. Toronto: Inner City Books, 1983.

Hannah, Barbara. *Encounters with the Soul*. Boston: Sigo Press, 1977.

————. *Regression und Erneuerung im Alter im Psychoterapeutische Probleme* (Regression and age restoration in psychotherapeutic problems). Zurich: Rascher, 1964.

Hansen, Gustav. "Ketamins psykotrope effect" (The psychotropic effect of Ketalar). *Bibliotek for læger* (Sept. 1966): 252–62.

Harner, M. J. (ed.). *Hallucinogens and Shamanism*. London: Oxford University Press, 1973.

Harris, T. D. "Dreams About the Analyst." *International Journal of Psychoanalysis* 43 (1961): 151–58.

Hartmann, Ernest. *The Functions of Sleep*. New Haven: Yale University Press, 1973.

————. "Longitudinal Studies of Sleep and Dream Patterns in Manic-Depressive Patients." *Archives of General Psychiatry* 19 (1968): 312–29.

————. "Psychological Differences Between Long and Short Sleepers." *Archives of General Psychiatry* 26 (1966): 463–68.

Hauer, Prof. "Tantra Yoga." Introduction in German to Jung, C. G. *Psychological Commentary on Kundalini Yoga*. Zurich: Psychologischer Club Zurich, 1933.

Hauri, Peter. "Dreams in Patients Remitted from Reactive Depressions." *Journal of Abnormal Psychology* 85, no.1 (1976): 1–10.

Hawkins, David R. "A Review of the Psychoanalytic Dream Theory in the Light of Recent Psycho-Physiological Studies of Sleep and Dreaming. *British Institute of Medical Psychology* 39 (1966): 85–103.

Hawking, S. W. *A Brief History of Time*. New York: Bantam Books, 1988.

Hillman, James. *The Dream and the Underworld*. New York: Harper and Row, 1979.

Hougård, Esben. "Psykoterapi som non-specifik behandling" (Psychotherapy as Non-Specific Treatment). *Psykologisk skriftserie Århus* 8, no. 6 (1983): 43.

Howells, Mary. In Jung, *Seminar on Dream Analysis*.

Huss, Paul D. "The Chosen People: A Psychological Study of the Biblical Experience of Election." Unpublished diploma diss., C.G. Jung Institute, Zurich, 1975.

Jacobsen, Erling. *Neuroserne og samfundet* (The neuroses and society). Copenhagen: Hans Reitzels Forlag, 1973.

Jacoby, Jolande. *Die Psychologie von C. G. Jung* (The psychology of C. G. Jung). Zurich: Rascher Verlag, 1959.

Jaffé, Aniela. "Symbolism in the Visual Arts." In *Man and His Symbols*. Edited by C. G. Jung, et al. London: Aldus Books, 1964.

Janakananda, Swami. *Oplev Yoga Nidra* (Experience yoga nidra). Guided deep relaxation. Copenhagen: Bindu, 1986.

Jastov, S. "Anesthesia Dreams." In *The New World of Dreams*. Edited by Ralph Woods and Herbert Greenhouse. New York: Macmillan Publishing Co. Inc., 1974.

Johnson, John R. "Vocation, Dreams and the Self." Diploma diss., C. G. Jung Institute, Zurich, 1977.

Johnson, Kenneth. "Modernity and Dream Content: A Ugandan Example." In *Ethos* 6, no.4 (1978): 212–20.

Jones, Ernest. *The Life and Works of Sigmund Freud*. New York: Basic Books, 1984.

Jones, Eve. "Rebirthing." In Corsini, R. J. *Handbook of Innovative Psychotherapies*. 747–60.

Jones, Richard M. *Egosynthesis in Dreams*. Cambridge, MA: Shenkman, 1962.

Jouvet, M. "The Function of Dreaming." In *Handbook of Psychobiology*. New York: Academic Press, 1975.

JUNG'S DISSERTATIONS AND SEMINARS PRIMARILY CONCERNED WITH DREAMS:

1928–30: *Seminar on Dream Analysis*. Edited by William McGuire. Princeton: Bollingen Series XCIX, 1984.
1930–32: *The Visions Seminars* I. Zurich: Spring Publications, 1976.

1932–34: *The Visions Seminars* II. Zurich: Spring Publications, 1976.

1934: *The Practical Use of Dream Analysis*. CW 16, par. 136–63.

1938–39: "Kinderträume" (Childhood dreams) I and II. Edited stenogram. Eidgenossische Hochschule, Zurich.

1948: *General Aspects of Dream Psychology*. CW 8, par. 237–80.

1948: *On the Nature of Dreams*. CW 8, par. 281–300.

1961: *Symbols and the Interpretation of Dreams*. CW 18, par. 185–266.

Jung, C. G. *Analytical Psychology, Its Theory and Practice*. New York: Pantheon Books, 1968.

———. Commentary to Richard Wilhelm. *The Secret of the Golden Flower*. London: Routledge and Kegan Paul, 1979.

———. *Collected Works*. The following titles contain observations of significance for Jung's dream theory:

"The Archetypes and the Collective Unconscious." CW 9, par. 54. "Concerning Rebirth." CW 9, par. 199–258.

"The Content of the Psychoses." CW 3; CW 16, par. 344–48, 546–64; CW 18, par. 135, footnote.

"General Aspects of Dream Psychology." CW 8, par. 457, 473.

"The Phenomenology of the Spirit in Fairy Tales." CW 9-I, par. 207–55.

"Psychological Types." CW 5, par. 163–65.

"Psychology and Alchemy." CW 12.

"Psychology and Religion." CW 2, par. 75–77.

"The Relations Between the Ego and the Unconscious." CW 7, par. 254.

"The Symbolic Life." CW 18, par. 274.

"Synchronicity: An Acausal Connecting Principle." CW 8, par. 417–532/

"Yoga und der Westen" (Yoga and the West). CW 11, par. 859–76.

———. *Memories, Dreams, Reflections*. London: Fontana Paperbacks, 1983.

———. *Modern Psychology* I–II. Zurich: Eidgenossische Technische Hochschule, 1959.

———. "Psychological Commentary on Kundalini Yoga." *Lecture* I–IV. Zurich: Spring Publications, 1974.

———. *Seminar on Dream Analysis*. Notes to the seminar given in 1928–30. Edited by William McGuire. Princeton: Princeton University Press, 1984.

———. *Symbols of Transformation* II: "Symbols of Mother and Rebirth," par. 300–418; "The Battle for Deliverance from the Mother," par. 419–63.

———, and Kerenyi, C. "The Psychology of the Child Archetype." In *Introduction to a Science of Mythology*. London: Routledge and Kegan Paul, 1951.

Kant, Otto. "Dreams of Schizophrenic Patients." *Journal of Nervous and Mental Disease* 95 (1952): 335–47.

Kernberg, Otto F. *Borderline Conditions and Pathological Narcissism*. New York. Jason Aronson Inc., 1981.

Khan, M. Masud R. "Dream Psychology and the Evolution of the Psychoanalytic Situation." *International Journal of Psychoanalysis* 43 (1962): 21–31.

King, Francis. *Tantra for Westerners*. Wellingborough, Northamptonshire: The Aquarian Press, 1986.

Klein-Lipschutz, Eva. "Dreams in Individual and Group Psychotherapy." *International Journal of Group Psychotherapy* 3 (1953): 143–49.

Kluger, Yehezkiel. "Archetypal Dreams and "Everyday" Dreams." *Israel's Annals of Psychiatry and Related Disciplines* 13 (1955): 6–47.

Knapp, Susan. "Dreaming: Horney, Kelmann and Shainberg" In *A Handbook of Dreams*. Edited by Benjamin B. Wolman. New York: Van Nostrand, 1979.

Kohut, Heinz. *The Analysis of the Self*. New York: International University Press, 1983.

Krackhauer, Karl. "Rolfing the Dreambody." In *Bulletin of Structural Integration* 7, no. 2 (1981): 14–24.

Kramer, Milton, et al. "Drugs and Dream Content." *Experimental Medicine and Surgery* 27 (1969): 210–23.

————. "Drugs and Dreams III: The Effects of Mipramine on the Dreams of Depressed Patients." *American Journal of Psychiatry* 124, no. 10 (1968): 1385–92.

————. "The Influence of Drugs on Dreams." In *Symposium on Drugs and Sensory Functions*. Boston: Little Brown, 1968.

————. "Manifest Dream Content in Normal and Psychopathological States." *Archives of General Psychiatry* 22 (Feb. 1970): 149–59.

————. "Patterns of Dreaming: The Interrelationship of the Dreams of a Night." *Journal of Nervous Mental Disease* 139 (1964): 426–39.

Kripke, D., and Sonnenschein, F. "A Biological Rhythm in Waking Fantasy." In *The Stream of Consciousness*. Edited by J. Pope and K. J. Singer. New York: Plenum Press, 1978.

Krippner, Stanley. "Dreams and Other Altered Conscious States." *Journal of Communication* 21, no. 1 (1975): 173–82.

Kris, Ernest. "On Preconscious Mental Processes." In *Psychoanalytic Explorations in Art*. International University Press, 1962.

Krohn, A., and Gutmann, D. "Changes in Mastery Style with Age." *Psychiatry* 34 (1971): 289–300.

Kübler-Ross, E. *Reif werden zum Tode* (Become ripe for death). Stuttgart: Kreuz, 1975.

Kuhn, Thomas. *The Structure of Scientific Revolutions*. Chicago: University of Chicago Press, 1962.

Laiblin, Wilhelm. *Märchenforschung und Tiefenpsychologie* (Folktale study and depth psychology). Darmstadt, 1969.

Laing, Ronald. *The Politics of Experience and the Bird of Paradise*. 1967

Lamberth, Kenneth. "A Critical Commentary to C. G. Jung's Seminar on Dream Analysis." *Journal of Analytical Psychology*.

Lamon, Ward Hill. "Abraham Lincoln's Dreams . . ." In *The New World of Dreams*. Edited by Ralph Woods and Herbert Greenhouse. New York: Macmillan Publishing Co. Inc., 1974.

Langs, Robert I. "Day Residues, Recall Residues, and the Dreams." *Journal of the American Psychoanalytic Association* 19 (1971): 499–523.

———. "Manifest Dreams from Three Clinical Groups." *Archive of General Psychiatry* 14 (1966): 634–43.

———. "Manifest Dreams in Adolescents: A Controlled Pilot Study." *The Journal of Nervous and Mental Disease* 145, no. 1 (1987): 43–52.

Larsen, Hanne Hostrup. *Tegneterapi i neurosebehandling* (Drawing therapy in the treatment of neuroses). Copenhagen: Dansk Psykologisk Forlag, 1979.

Lassen, Helle. "Symbolikken hos Chagall" (The symbolism in Chagall). *Louisiana Revue* 23, no. 2 (1983): 34–35.

Laursen, Ville. *Fritz Perls*. Copenhagen: Forum, 1980.

Leadbeater, C. W. *Chakraerne* (The chakras). Copenhagen: TS Forlag, 1986.

Lee, S. G. "Social Influences in Zulu Dreaming." *Journal of Social Psychology* 47 (1958): 265–83.

Lerner, Barbara. "Dream Function Reconsidered." In *Abnormal Psychology* 72, no. 2 (1967): 85–100.

Lipton, Samuel D. "Freud's Position on Problem Solving in Dreams." *British Institute of Medical Psychology* 40 (1967): 147–49.

Lortie-Lussier, Monique, et al. "Working Mothers Versus Homemakers." In *Sex Roles* 12, nos. 9–10 (1985): 1009–21.

Lowe, Walter James. "On Using Heidegger." In *On Dreaming*. Edited by Charles E. Scott. Chico: Scholar Press, 1977.

Lowen, Alexander: *Fornægtelsen af kroppen* (The betrayal of the body). Copenhagen: Gyldendal, 1983.

McCarley, Robert, and Hobson, Allan. "The Form of Dreams and the Biology of Sleep." In *A Handbook of Dreams*. Edited by Benjamin Wolman. New York: Van Nostrand, 1979.

MacKenzie, Norman. *Dreams and Dreaming*. London: Aldus Books, 1965.

Madsen, K. B. *Sammenlignende videnskabsteori for psykologer og pædagoger* (Comparative scientific theory for psychologists and educators). Copenhagen: Lærerforeningens materialeudvalg, 1980.

Maeder, A. "Über die Funktion des Träumes." *Jahrbuch für psychoanalytische und psychopatologische Forschungen* 5 (1913): 647–86.

Maslow, Abraham. *Motivation and Personality*. New York: Harper and Row, 1970.

Mattoon, Mary Ann. *Applied Dream Analysis*. London: John Wiley and Sons, 1978.

Meggitt, M. I. "Mae Enga Dreams." In *South Western Journal of Anthropology* 18 (1962): 216–29.

Menaker, Esther. *Otto Rank: A Rediscovered Legacy*. New York: Columbia University Press, 1982.

Mental Health Abstracts Database. Copenhagen: Det Kongelig Bibliotek, 1986.

Meyer, C. A. *Antike Inkubation und moderne Psycho-therapie* (Ancient incubation and modern psychotherapy). Evanston, IL: 1967.

———. *Die Bedeutung des Traumes* (The meaning of Dreams). Olten: Walter Verlag, 1972.

Miller, Jean B.. "Dreams During Varying Stages of Depression." *Archives of General Psychiatry* 20 (May 1969): 560–65.

Mindell, Arnold. *Dreambody*. London: Routledge and Kegan Paul, 1984.

———. *River's Way: The Process Science of the Dreambody*. London: Routledge and Kegan Paul, 1985.

———. *Working With the Dreaming Body*. London: Routledge and Kegan Paul, 1985.

Mittelmann, Bela. "Ego Functions and Dreams." *Psychological Quarterly* 18 (1949): 434–47.

Moody, Raymond. *Life After Life*. Georgia: Mockingbird Books, 1975.

Moon, Sheila. *Dreams of a Woman*. Boston: Sigo Press, 1983.

Moore, Robert S. "Couples Courses" I–V. Notes. Ringkjøbing 1986–88.

———. "Physiology and Growth" I–VI. Notes. Ringkjøbing 1986–88.

Mumford, John. *Ecstasy Through Tantra*. Llewelyn Publications, 1988.

Murray, Henry A. "Postscript." In *The Visions Seminars* (Jung).

Næss, Arne. *Filosofiens historie* (The history of philosophy) III. Copenhagen: Vintens Forlag, 1963.

———. *Moderne filosoffer* (Modern philosophers). Copenhagen: Vintens Forlag, 1965.

Nagera, Humberto. *Basic Psychoanalytic Concepts on the Theory of Dreams*. London: Marcsfield Reprints, 1981.

Neumann, Erich. *The Child*. New York: Putnam, 1973.

———. *The Great Mother*. Princeton: Princeton University Press, 1963.

———. "The Moon and Matriarchal Consciousness." In *Fathers and Mothers*. Zurich: Spring Publications, 1973.

———. "Zur Psychologie des Weiblichen" (On the psychology of the feminine). *Umkreisung der Mitte* II (1953): 9.

Nilsson, Martin P. *Olympen* (The olympic). Copenhagen: Haase & Søn, 1966.

N.N. "The Effect of LSD on Sleep Dream Cycles . . ." In *LSD: A Total Study*. Westbury, NY: PJD Publications, 1975.

Noone, Richard. *In Search of the Dream People*. New York: Morrow, 1972.

Nyborg, Eigil. *Drømmenes vej til selvet* (Dreams' way to the self). Copenhagen: Tiderne Skifter, 1986.

———. "Drømte mig en drøm" (I dreamed a dream). *Hug* 9, vol. 23, no. 45 (1986).

Olsen, Jan K. *Mellem søvn og vågen* (Between sleep and waking). Copenhagen: Bindu no. 13, 1975.

Olsen, Ole, and Køppe, Simo. *Psykoanalytisk psykologi og psykopatologi. Psykiatri, en tekstbog* (Psychoanalytical psychology and psychopathology: Psychiatry, a textbook). Copenhagen, 1988.

Olsen, Ole, et al. *Metapsykologi II. Indledning til Metapsykologisk supplement til drømmelæren* (Metapsychology I: Introduction to the metapsychological supplement to the theory of dreams). Copenhagen: Hans Reitzels Forlag, 1983.

O'Nell, Carl. *Dreams, Culture, and the Individual*. Los Angeles: Chandler and Sharp, 1976.

Ouspensky, P. D. "On the Study of Dreams and Hypnotism" In *A New Model of the Universe*. New York: Vintage Books, 1913.

Pagano, R. R. "Sleep During T. M." *Science* 191 (1976): 308–10.

Parker, Julia and Derek. *Drømme, tolkning og symboler*. Copenhagen: Politikens Forlag, 1987.

Pearlmann, Chester A. "The Adaptive Function of Dreaming." In *Sleep and Dreaming*. Edited by E. Hartmann. Boston: Little, Brown, 1970.

Perls, Fritz. *Gestalt Therapy Verbatim*. New York: Bantam Books, 1971.

———, Hefferline, Ralph, and Goodmann, Paul. *Gestalt Therapy* 1 & 2. New York: Julian Press, 1951.

Perry, J. W. *The Self in Psychotic Process*. Foreword by C. G. Jung. Los Angeles: University of California Press, 1953.

Piaget, Jean. *Play, Dreams and Imitation in Childhood*. New York: W. W. Norton, 1962.

Polster, Erving and Miriam. *Gestalt Therapy Integrated*. New York: Vintage Books, 1974.

Radnitzky, Gerard. *Contemporary Schools of Metascience, Vol. 1*. Stockholm: Scandinavian University Books, 1970.

Rafaelsen, Ole J. *Psykokemi i Psykiatri en tekstbog* (Psychochemistry in psychiatry: A text-book). Copenhagen, 1981.

Raman, G. *Patanjalis Yoga Sutras* (Patanjali's yoga sutras). Copenhagen: Strubes Forlag, 1968.

Rank, Otto. *The Trauma of Birth*. London: Kegan Paul, 1929.

Rawson, Philip. *Tantra: The Indian Cult of Ecstasy*. New York: Thames and Hudson, 1979.

Reding, G. R. "Systematic Transference Interpretations in the Sleep Laboratory." *The Journal of Nervous and Mental Disease* 149 (1969): 152–85.

The Research Libraries' Data Base. Decimal classification 13.6 (Depth psychology since 1979).

Rhine, Louisa. "The Subject Matter of Psi-Experiments." *Journal of Parapsychology* 40, no. 1 (1976): 53.

Ribi, Alfred. "Forelæsninger om Hieronymus Boschs billeder" (Lectures on Hieronymus Bosch's pictures). At C. G. Jung Institute, Copenhagen, 1986.

Richardson, A., and Moore, R. "On the Manifest Dreams in Schizophrenia." *Journal of the American Psychoanalytical Association* 11 (1963): 281–302.

Robbins, P., and Tanck, R. "Community Violence and Aggressions in Dreams." In *Perceptual and Motor Skills* 29, no. 1 (1968): 41–42.

Roffwarg, P. *Ontogenetic Development Science* 152 (1966): 604–19.

Rogo, D. Scott. "Dreaming the Future." In *Psychic* 6, no. 4 (1975) 26–29.

Røine, Eva. *Psykodrama* (Psychodrama). Oslo: Aschehoug, 1978.

Rolf, Ida. *Rolfing: The Integration of Human Structures*. Boulder, Colorado: The Rolf Institute, 1977.

Rossi, Ernesto. *Dreams and the Growth of Personality*. New York: Pergamon Press, 1972.

Rycroft, Charles. *A Critical Dictionary of Psychoanalysis*. New York: Penguin Books, 1979.

———. *The Innocence of Dreams*. London: Hogarth Press, 1979.

Salles, C. "Symbols of Transformation in a Dream." *Journal of Analytical Psychology* 30 (1985): 347–52.

Samuels, Andrew. "The Emergence of Schools in Analytical Psychology." *Journal of Analytical Psychology* 28 (1982).

———. *Jung and the Post-Jungians*. London: Routledge and Kegan Paul, 1985.

———, et al. *A Critical Dictionary of Jungian Analysis*. New York: Routledge and Kegan Paul, 1986.

Sankar, D. V. S. *LSD: A Total Study*. Westbury, NY: PJD Publications, 1975.

Saul, L. J. "Utilization of Early Current Dreams in Formulating Psychoanalytic Cases." *Psychoanal. Quarterly* 9 (1940): 453–69.

———, and Sheppard, Edith. "An Attempt to Quantify Emotional Forces Using Manifest Dreams." *Journal of the American Psychoanalytic Association* 4 (1956): 486–502.

———. "An Attempt to Quantify Emotional Forces." *Journal of the American Psychoanalytic Association* 4 (1956): 486–502.

Schultz, Erik. *Drømmeforståelse og drømmeteorier* (Dream understanding and dream theories). Ph.D. diss., University of Copenhagen, 1977.

Schultz, Hermann. *Zur diagnostischen und prognostischen Bedeutung des Initialtraumes in der Psychotherapie* (On the diagnostic and prognostic significance of initial dreams in psychotherapy). Ulm: Dissertation zur Universität Ulm, 1969.

Servadio, Emilio. "Psychoanalysis and Telepathy." In Devereux, G. New York: International University Press, 1970.

Shapiro, S.A. "A Classification Scheme for Out-of-Body Phenomena." *Journal of Altered States of Consciousness* 2, no. 3 (1976): 259–65.

Sheils, Dean. "A Cross Cultural Study of Beliefs in Out-of-the-Body Experiences." *Journal of the Society for Psychical Research* 49 (1978): 697–741.

Skogemann, Pia. *Arketyper* (Archetypes). Copenhagen: Lindhardt og Ringhof, 1986.

———. "Chuang Tzu and the Butterfly Dream." *Journal of Analytical Psychology* 31 (1986): 75–90.

———. *Kvindelighed i vækst* (Growing femininity). Copenhagen: Borgen, 1984.

———. *Religion og symbol* (Religion and symbol). Copenhagen: Borgen, 1988.

———, and Reisby, Niels. *Carolines bog* (Caroline's book). Copenhagen: Rosinante, 1985.

Sloane, Paul. *Psychoanalytic Understanding of Dreams*. New York, London: Jason Aronson, 1976.

Snyder, Frederich. "Towards an Evolutionary Theory of Dreaming." *American Journal of Psychiatry* 2 (1966): 121–42.

Sørensen, Villy. *Digtere og dæmoner* (Poets and demons). Copenhagen: Gyldendal, 1979.

Sparrow, George S. *Lucid Dreaming*. Virginia: A.R.E. Press, 1982.

Spitz, René. *Die Entstehung der ersten Objektbeziehungen* (The Creation of the first objective contact). Stuttgart, 1973.

Staff, V. S. *Remembered on Waking—Concerning Psychic and Spiritual Dreams*. Crowborough, Sussex: The Mysticism Committee of the Churches' Fellowship for Psychical and Spiritual Studies, 1975.

Stein, Leopold. *Analytical Psychology: A Modern Science*. In LPA.

Stern, Paul J. Foreword to Boss: *I Dreamt Last Night*. New York: Gardner Press Inc., 1977.

Stewart, Harold. "The Experiencing of the Dream and the Transference." *International Journal of Psychoanalysis* 54 (1973): 345–47.

Stewart, Kilton: "Dream Theory in Malay." In Tart, C. *Altered States of Consciousnesss*. John Wiley and Sons, 1969.

Sunami, Yuzuru. "A Psychophysiological Study on Dreams of Schizophrenics." In *Mental Health Abstracts*—Database Dialog File 86. *Psychiatria et Neurologia Japonica*.

Sussmann, Lotte. "Beitrag zum Problem der Träume von Schizofrenen" (Contribution to the problem of dreams of schizophrenics). *Nervenarzt* 9 (1936): 453–66.

Swami Devi Satyarthi. *Kroppens veje* (The body's ways) II. Copenhagen: Borgen, 1972.

Swanson, Ethel, and Foulkes, David. "Dream and the Menstrual Cycle. *Journal of Nervous and Mental Disease* 145, no. 5 (1968): 358–63.

Tart, Charles M. *Altered States of Consciousness*. New York: Doubleday, 1972.

Tedlock, Barbara, et al. "Quiche Maya Dream Interpretation." *Ethos* 9, no. 4 (1981): 313–30.

Teglbjerg, Stubbe. *Lev dine drømme*. Copenhagen: Klitrose, 1984.

Tolaas, J., and Ullman, M. "Extrasensory Communication and Dreams." In *A Handbook of Dreams*. Edited by Benjamin Wolman. New York: Van Nostrand, 1979.

Trillin, Calvin. "The Discovery of Rapid Eye Movements." In *The New World of Dreams*. Edited by Ralph Woods and Herbert Greenhouse. New York: Macmillan Publishing Co. Inc., 1974.

Ullman, Montague. "The Adaptive Significance of the Dream." *Journal of Nervous and Mental Disease* 129 (1959): 144–49.

———. "Dreaming Life Style and Physiology: A Comment on Adler's View of the Dream." *Journal of Individual Psychology* 18 (1962): 18–25.

———. "The Experiential Dream Group." In *A Handbook of Dreams*. Edited by Benjamin B. Wolman. New York: Van Nostrand, 1979.

———. *Forstå dine drømme* (Understand your dreams).

———. "The Role of Imagery." *Journal of Communication* 25, no. 1 (1975): 162–72.

———. "Telepathy and Dreams." *Experimental Medicine and Surgery* 27 (1969): 19–38.

Ullman, M., and Krippner, S. *Dream Studies and Telepathy*. Parapsychology Foundation Inc., 1970.

van de Castle, Robert. "Precognitive Dreaming." *Sundance Community Dream Journal* 2, no. 2 (1978): 174–90.

———. *The Psychology of Dreaming*. New York: General Learning Press, 1971.

Van Eeden. "A Study of Dreams." *Proceedings for the Society for Psychical Research* XXVI (1913).

Vanggaard, Thorkild. *Angst. En psykoanalyses forløb* (Angst: The course of a psychoanalysis). Copenhagen: Gyldendal, 1987.

Vedfelt, Ole. *Det kvindelige i manden*. Copenhagen: Gyldendal, 1985.

———. *Drømmenes væsen* (The nature of dreams). *Psyke og Logos nr. 1* (English summary). Copenhagen, 1991.

———. "Interview med Ole Vedfelt" (Interview with Ole Vedfelt) in *Hvad er psykoanalyse?* (What is Psychoanalysis?). Edited by Elna Bering. Copenhagen: Rosinante, 1988.

Verdone, P. "Temporal Reference of Manifest Dream Content." *Perceptual and Motor Skills* 20 (1965): 1253.

Vogel, G., et al. "Sleep Reduction Effects on Depressive Syndromes." *Archives of General Psychiatry* 18 (1968): 287.

Vogel, G., and Giesler, D. "Exercise as a Substitute for REM-sleep." *Psychophysiology* 7 (1977): 300–301.

von Franz, Marie-Louise. *Alchemy*. Toronto: Inner City Books. 1980.

———. *Creation Myth*. Zurich: Spring Publications, 1972.

———. *Jung, His Myth in Our Time*. Boston: Putnam, 1975.

———. *Jung's Typology*. Zurich: Spring Publications, 1979.

———. *On Active Imagination in Methods of Treatment in Analytical Psychology*. Edited by I. F. Baker. Zurich: Bonz, 1980.

———. *On Divination*. Toronto: Inner City Books, 1980.

———. *On Dreams and Death*. Boston and London: Shambhala, 1986.

———. *Problems of the Feminine in Fairy Tales*. Zurich: Spring Publications, 1972.

———. *The Process of Individuation*. In *Man and His Symbols*. Edited by Jung, et al. London: Aldus Books, 1964.

———. "The Psychological Experience of Time." In *Eranos Yearbook* 47. Edited by Adolf Portmann and Rudolf Ritsema. Frankfurt: Insel Verlag, 1981.

———. *Redemption Motifs in Fairy Tales*. Toronto: Inner City Books, 1980.

———. "Religiöse oder magische Einstellung zum Unbewussten" (Religious or magical ideation of the unconscious). In *Studien aus dem C.G. Jung-Institut*. Zurich: Rascher Verlag, 1964.

———. *Shadow and Evil in Fairy Tales*. Zurich: Spring Publications, 1974.

———. *Träume* (Dreams). Zurich: Daimon, 1985.

Waldhorn. *The Place of the Dream in Psychoanalysis*. New York: International University Press, 1967.

Wallace, A. "Dreams and the Wishes of the Soul: A type of Psychoanalytic Theory Among the Seventeenth Century Iroquois." *American Anthropologist* 60 (1958): 234–48.

Watson, Lyall. *Livstidevandet* (Life tide, 1979). Copenhagen: Gyldendals Bogklub, 1980.

Welner, J. "International Classification of Diseases" (8th edition). In *Psykiatri en tekstbog* (Psychiatry: A textbook). Copenhagen: SADL-forlag, 1985.

Wheelwright, Jane. *Death of a Woman*. New York: Putnam, 1981.

Whitman, R. M., et al. "Drugs and Dream Content." *Exp.Med.Surg* 27 (1969): 210–23.

Whitman, R. "Remembering and Forgetting Dreams in Psychoanalysis." *Journal of the American Psychiatric Association* 11 (1963): 752–74.

Whitmont, Edward H. "Recent Influences on the Practice of Jungian Analysis." In Stein, Murray. *Jungian Analysis*.

Williams, Strephon. *Jungian Senoi Dream Work Manual*. Berkeley: Journey Press, 1983.

Wilmer, Harry A. "Vietnam and Madness in Dreams of Schizophrenic Veterans." *Journal of American Psychoanalysis* 10, no. 1 (1982): 47–65.

———. "Dream Seminar for Chronic Schizophrenic Patients." *Psychiatry* 45, no. 4 (1982): 351–66.

Wolman, Benjamin. (ed.) *A Handbook of Dreams*. New York: Van Nostrand, 1979.

Woodroffe, Sir John (aka Avalon, Arthur). *The Serpent Power*. New York: Dover Books, 1974.

Woods, Ralph, and Greenhouse, Herbert. *The New World of Dreams*. New York: Macmillan Publishing Co., 1974.

Yalom, I. D. *The Theory and Practice of Group Psychotherapy*. New York: Basic Books, 1970.

Zimmer, Heinrich. "The Chakras of Kundalini Yoga." Supplement to Jung. *Lecture* III–IV, on Kundalini. Zurich: Spring Publications, 1974.

Zimmermann, David. "Dreams in Group-Analytic Psychotherapy." *International Journal of Group Psychotherapy* 17, no. 4 (1967): 524–35.

INDEX